The Art & Science of Coaching Series

COACHING OFFENSIVE LINEMEN

Dave Christensen
James A. Peterson

ISBN: 1-57167-208-7
Library of Congress Catalog Card Number: 98-85406

Cover Design: Joe J. Buck; Dody A. Bullerman
Interior Design: Michelle A. Summers
Illustrations: Dwaine Nugent
Developmental Editor: Jeff Walker

The information presented on pages 7-11 in this text is based in part on material from *Bill Walsh: Finding the Winning Edge* by Bill Walsh, Brian Billick, and James A. Peterson, pages 124-129; used by permission.

Coaches Choice Books is a division of: Sagamore Publishing, Inc.
P.O. Box 647
Champaign, IL 61824-0647
Web Site: http//www.sagamorepub.com

DEDICATION

I would like to dedicate this book to my wife, Susie, who has been my biggest fan and the best support system any coach could ever dream of having. She has provided unrelenting inspiration from the time we were starving GA's working on masters degrees to the point where we are today. To my children—Katie, D.J., and Emily—who provide me with their unconditional love whether dad wins or loses.

I would also like to dedicate this book to the two coaches who have had such a tremendous influence on my life and career. First, Tony Whitefield—my high school football coach. Tony gave me my initial lesson on how loyalty, hard work and being organized will give you a chance to not only succeed in football, but in life. Second, Don James, the renowned former head football coach at the University of Washington. Coach James has had the single most positive influence on my life. In ways too numerous to list, Coach James has made this non-scholarship walk-on feel as important as any All-American he ever coached.

ACKNOWLEDGMENTS

We must all recognize that great football teams and great coaches are a by-product of great players. Without the total dedication and resolute commitment of these extraordinary players, it is highly likely that no team or coach would ever receive the attention that might otherwise be due to them. It is because of those types of talented individuals that I was able to put this book together. In that regard, I would like to acknowledge each and every player that I have had the good fortune to come in contact with throughout my career.

In addition, I would like to specifically acknowledge two other individuals who have put me in positions to write this book. First, Gary Pinkel, the head football coach at the University of Toledo, for hiring me, for inspiring me to ever-higher levels of excellence, and for promoting me to the position I currently hold on his staff as the Rockets' offensive coordinator. I would also like to thank Dr. Jim Peterson for all his hard work, time, and effort spent working on this project. Without these two men believing in me, this book would not have become a reality.

CONTENTS

Dedication 3

Acknowledgments 4

Preface 7

Diagram Key 8

Chapter

1 Selecting the Offensive Linemen 9

2 Fundamental Concepts for Offensive Line Play 17

3 Presnap Fundamentals and the Exchange 31

4 One-Man Blocks 41

5 Two-Man Blocks 67

6 Pull Blocks 105

7 Run-Blocking Drills 125

8 Pass Blocking 147

9 Pass-Blocking Drills 173

10 Goal Line blocking 187

11 Offensive Linemen in the Kicking Game 195

12 Pass Protection Schemes 209

13 Run-Blocking Schemes 225

14 Adopting an Alignment Philosophy 239

About the Authors 248

PREFACE

Football is a game of fundamentals. Almost any week of September, a veteran football coach can be heard urging his players to consider the basic simplicity of the game as he exhorts his team to remember—"Football is blocking and tackling." Over one hundred years of football have proven this maxim to be true. The flow of the game, the success of the game plan, and the dominance of the struggle are all related to the fundamental simplicity of the sport.

To Walter Camp, the game was a matter of mastering the fundamentals of blocking and tackling. To Knute Rockne, the game was a matter of "hitting them hard and hitting them quick." To Vince Lombardi, the game was a matter of execution and toughness. To all of the past coaching legends, the contest was won in the trenches. For you and the future coaches of the modern game, the fundamentals of the game will not change. In order to be successful, your team must be better at blocking and tackling than your opponent.

The point to remember is that you win football games by out-coaching and out-playing the opposition in the trenches. Teaching your players to master the fundamentals and techniques of offensive line play can help guarantee that your team plays to the best of its abilities and talent level. More importantly, mastering the fundamentals and techniques of offensive line play can help enhance the likelihood that your players will experience many sweet memories of victory.

DIAGRAM KEY

Each of the gaps listed below is defined on page 21:

A; B; C; D

All of the following defensive line techniques (0 through 9) are defined on page 23:

0; 1; 2; 3; 4i; 4; 5; 7; 6; 9

B .... Backer (Linebacker)
N .... Nose Tackle
T .... Tackle
E .... End
CB .... Cornerback
FS .... Free Safety
M .... Mike (Middle Linebacker)
S .... Sam (Strongside Linebacker)
W .... Will (Weakside Linebacker)
SS .... Strong Safety
WS .... Weak Safety
LB .... Linebacker
DL .... Defensive Linemen
WT .... Weakside Offensive Tackle
WG .... Weakside Offensive Guard
C .... Center
SG .... Strongside Offensive Guard
ST .... Strongside Offensive Tackle
TB .... Tailback
FB .... Fullback
TE .... Tight End
QB .... Quarterback

CHAPTER 1

Selecting the Offensive Lineman

The first thing you should consider when building a championship-level offensive line is your criteria for personnel selection. In identifying who you want to be your offensive linemen, you should establish a process of selection that will result in the acquisition of at least five individuals who can practice, play, and win, as a team. The criteria for selecting an athlete to play on the offensive line can include several considerations, including the following traits and skills:

- One of the most important factors to consider when selecting an offensive lineman is hip flexibility. From a football standpoint, the most reliable measure of hip flexibility is the lineman's ability to squat to a position in which his thighs are parallel to the ground while keeping his heels flat on the ground. He should be able to squat to such a parallel position while holding hands behind his neck. Accordingly, offensive linemen must work daily to develop and maintain their hip and trunk posterior flexibility through stretching exercises and drills.

- Ideally, potential offensive linemen should possess exceptional upper- and lower-body strength. However, this trait is something that can be developed if the offensive line candidate demonstrates a good baseline level of flexibility, an appropriate measure of quickness, and a desire to do "whatever" is necessary in the weight room to maximize his strength.

- Offensive linemen should demonstrate exceptional quickness for their size. An offensive lineman should be able to demonstrate a high turnover rate within a three-yard distance. In addition, he should be able to use his hands in sharp, brisk movements.

- Offensive linemen should generally possess a relatively high level of pain threshold because they have to be physically and mentally tough on the field at all times. In turn, an offensive linemen must be able to maintain his self-confidence during times of adversity. Within the confines of the total football team, an offensive lineman should feel that he is a member of an elite corps.

- Ideally, offensive linemen should possess large frames. With regard to the previously mentioned requisite traits and skills for an offensive lineman, the size of an offensive lineman can be either the least important or the most important factor for selection. As a general rule, the weight given to the consideration of size as a factor in selecting offensive lineman generally increases with the

ascending level of competitive play. All factors considered, the higher the level of competition, the more important size as a factor becomes to the selection criteria. Conversely, the lower the level of play, the less important the size factor typically is to the coach who is selecting offensive lineman personnel. Credence to this conclusion is provided by the simple truth which every high school coach knows—*"The most important muscle of the body is the heart."* Certainly, no coach can state that he hasn't heard at least one high school line coach fondly reminisce with his "war" stories about the 155-pound guard who wouldn't back down. Certainly, most coaches who have worked with the offensive line have a personal anecdote about a pint-sized, relatively scrawny kid who could get off the ball and drive block almost every defensive lineman that he faced—whatever the size of the defender.

- The productive offensive lineman is an over-achiever with many positive qualities. He is an athlete who is continually developing his skills. Since blocking is an unnatural act, the athlete must possess a burning desire to learn the mechanics of blocking. Blocking, unlike running a 4.5 forty, can be mastered by anyone who is exposed to a good teacher.

- The successful offensive lineman will have exceptional body balance and hip response. To a point, balance can be developed through training, but hip response is more indicative of an athlete's natural ability to punch through an opponent with a low-to-high delivery. Hip response is the term used to describe to the action of the player's hips and pelvis snapping forward upon contacting the opponent. Whatever the precise definition, a relatively high level of hip response is a trait generally possessed by both effective blockers and skilled tacklers.

- An offensive lineman should have the personality makeup and the psychological training that allows him to play unselfishly. He should be an athlete who takes accountability for his performance and understands that relatively little opportunity exists for praise from the media and fans. The point to remember is that an effective offensive lineman doesn't react to a setback: he responds. Furthermore a good offensive lineman knows that no substitute exists for toughness, competitiveness, inner strength, and team unity.

Most of the other primary considerations that can affect your decisions regarding more basic factors, such as the offensive line involve more basic factors, such as the level of play, your team's offensive scheme, the ability of your team to match-up with your opponents, and the fundamental demands of each position. As a rule, these considerations address the following points:

- *The level of play.* The level of play should be a significant influence on your personnel selections for the offensive line. You should strongly consider your district competitors' personnel and style of play when identifying what criteria you should employ to select athletes to play on your offensive line.

- *Your team's style of offense.* Various offenses place particularly task-specific demands on the offense line. For example, an I-formation offense requires a different standard for offensive line selection than a Wing-T offensive scheme. The I-formation offense is characterized by a need for large-bodied, "wheel and turn"-type blockers—blockers who can knock the defensive lineman off the ball and maintain contact. On the other hand, a Wing-T scheme requires offensive linemen who can run—linemen who sweep pull and trap pull. Although Wing-T linemen benefit from a predominance of "angle" blocking assignments within the scheme, they must possess exceptional quickness. Accordingly, before establishing a precise list of selection criteria for the offensive line, you must have a firm idea of what offensive scheme you plan to have your team employ.

- *The prevalent style of defense used by your common opponents.* A common opponent is an opponent whom your team typically plays on a year-to-year basis. Without question, "the road to success" goes through your opponents. As such, the style of defensive play that is prevalent among your common opponents should be considered when making decisions on offensive line personnel. For example, if seven of your ten common opponents use an even defensive front, you should consider placing your two most physical and dominating players at the offensive guard positions. On the other hand, if seven of your ten common opponents use an odd defensive front, you should consider placing your two most physical and dominating players at the offensive tackle positions. While this factor can easily be overlooked or overemphasized, "street-wise" coaches who have been charged with rebuilding struggling programs know they have to structure their offensive and defensive schemes in a manner that best enables them to beat those teams who must be beaten—year in and year out.

- *The position demands.* Just as the demands of your team's offensive system may affect some of the personnel decisions within your offensive line, the generic differences between the various offensive line positions may influence the personnel selection process. As a general rule, the four different offensive line positions (three different *interior* line positions) involve the following unique considerations:

  - **Center.** The offensive center has an essential role in a team's offensive system. Not only must he start every play with a flawless executed snap, he is typically the key man in making line calls. These calls are vital, and there is no way a team can do without them. For example, with the constant defensive changes that occur during a game, the offensive line must react to those changes if an adjustment in the blocking scheme is required. Because he is literally at the "center" of the action (i.e., in the middle of things), the center is the obvious member of the offensive line to identify and communicate to the other offensive linemen what blocking adjustments must be made. As a result, the center must have a thorough command of the offensive line blocking system, the game plan, and individual defensive players his team is facing. In a few isolated instances, some teams use an offensive guard to make line calls because the guard is either more experienced or more adept at making them.

As a general rule, the center doesn't have to be an exceptional blocker. The center usually doesn't have to block the nose tackle one-on-one, although if he can, it provides a considerable advantage to his team. The center who can isolate one-on-one with a nose tackle will take tremendous pressure off of the offensive line, particularly the guards. Most teams typically find a way to help the center with the nose tackle (e.g., slide a line). If the other team is in an alignment that doesn't have a nose tackle (e.g., the 4-3 defense) or has the nose tackle stunt away from the center, the center helps a teammate with his blocking responsibilities.

One additional factor related to the center that some teams address is his height. Although there have been successful centers at all competitive levels who were relatively tall, many teams feel that, all factors considered, a shorter (relative to the height of the other offensive linemen) center is better. Not only does a shorter center have a lower center of gravity (thereby facilitating body balance), he also tends to be more mobile—a trait that offers significant benefits to an individual who must operate in a relatively small area. Most teams prefer a center who is able to quickly move in between people. In most cases, a shorter center can do that better than a tall, rangy one. By the same token, the weight of the center can also be a factor in his selection. A large body can be a hindrance in a small area (somewhat analogous to the limitations imposed on a basketball player who is carrying too much weight).

– **Offensive Guards.** Similar to some of the offensive line positions, the requirements for playing guard depend to a great extent on the type of offensive system in which he plays. In this regard, two obvious options exist: either the offensive guard has to be selected based on his capacity to contribute to a team's existing system of offense or a team has to style its offense according to who its guards are. Typically, the latter option prevails. A team adapts its offensive style to the abilities of its guards. An example of how a team adapts its offensive system to its guards occurs when a particular offensive guard can or cannot do something to his right or left. If the left guard can pull and trap, then the team is more likely to run plays to the right with the left guard pulling (and vise versa). The guard positions are "personalized" according to what they can do. Typically, one of the offensive guards on a team is stronger or weaker in a particular technique or the ability to get the job done.

As a rule, great offensive guards possess several traits, including quickness, agility, explosiveness, the ability to pull and trap, and the ability to go inside-out on a linebacker. Offensive guards must also be able to pass block. Generally speaking, girth, stability and body balance are essential factors in this skill. Because the offensive guard can usually get help as a pass protector, he just has to have enough power to avoid being knocked back. Just the sheer number of people inside will help the guard pass block. As a result, the guard can have some limitations as a pass blocker as long as he has enough girth to keep the defensive tackle from picking him up and moving him.

All factors considered, the offensive guard position requires less technique for pass protecting than is essential for an offensive tackle. On the other hand, the offensive guard position requires more blocking and movement skills. For example, the guard is used on numerous blocking combinations where he must get from point "A" to point "B," pulling through a hole, trapping, pulling on sweeps, coming inside-out on a blitzing linebacker, etc. Collectively, this capability requires that the offensive guard has agility, mobility, and a refined level of techniques.

– **Offensive Tackles.** The one absolute essential trait for all offensive tackles is natural body girth. In addition to girth, offensive tackles must be very strong and have a high level of agility (body control). Accordingly, the position of offensive tackle is typically filled by the most athletic (particularly on the weakside) of the offensive line candidates.

  Because an offensive tackle tends to function most of the time in the game in a two-yard square area, the ability of this individual to move his feet quickly and purposefully within this area is absolutely critical. A substantial part of this ability can be developed and enhanced to a degree. On the other hand, if an offensive tackle has "slow feet," he may improve somewhat, but he will always be limited. An offensive tackle should also have strong, long arms to facilitate those blocking tasks involving leverage. From a blocking perspective, however, the timing of the block itself (i.e., the timing of the extension) is the critical factor. In addition, the offensive tackle must have an intuitive sense of feeling or knowing where to intersect defenders.

  At most competitive levels of football today, the offensive tackle must be able to anticipate and be ready to handle any one of three to four different situations that might occur. Historically, the offensive tackle only had to deal with one or two possible scenarios. Over the years, however, as defenses have become relatively more complex, the possible adjustments the offensive tackle must make have become more diverse. For example, the offensive tackle must be able to adapt to a situation where a linebacker blitzes from the outside and the defender he was expecting to block drops back into pass coverage. As a result, the offensive tackle must be sharp enough to quickly identify the scenario and be able to move and adjust to the circumstances as needed. He must also be extremely well-versed and prepared in the skills and the techniques required to handle a variety of situations.

The nature of the position of offensive tackle also requires that athletes who play this position possess a level of inner-confidence and natural self-control that enables them to deal with frustration (e.g., the defender head slaps him, the play is stopped for no gain, etc.) and, on some occasions in a football-sense, disaster (e.g., his man sacks the quarterback). Regardless of the circumstances, the offensive tackle must be able to regain his focus and function at a high level of performance within a relatively brief time. The point to keep in mind when selecting your offensive tackles is that some athletes appear to have a better disposition to deal with potentially disruptive elements of others.

– **Tight End.** The requirements for playing tight end depend primarily on the system a team deploys. Accordingly, each team must find the athlete who best fits the team's approach to offensive football. Some teams want a tight end who had girth, ballast and strength. For these teams, the tight end is one of the primary keys to their offensive system because he had the size and physical tools to secure the point of attack. If the tight end is able to block a defensive linemen who is positioned on the edge of the offense, then a team automatically has an increased likelihood of having a running game with just that single feature.

In many of the defensive alignments of the 1990s, defensive linemen are lining up adjacent to or across from the tight end, whereas years ago they weren't. If the tight end can block those defensive linemen, then the entire offense has a focal point from which to work. This type of tight end can be a dominating factor. He is bigger and stronger, though less quick and agile, than the other type of tight end. Teams tend to fashion their passing game with him in the vicinity of the linebackers. Accordingly, he must have both the ability to absorb a ball as he is being hit and soft hands. On virtually every pass thrown to him, he is going to be hit almost simultaneously with the catch. This type of tight end also does not need to possess great speed—a 5.0 time on the 40-yard dash will get the job done. The major shortcoming attendant to his lack of extraordinary speed is the fact that he is not going to be able to clear defenders on certain pass patterns to help other receivers. All in all, that limitation is not that significant compared to all the blocking capabilities he provides.

The other extreme would be a Mark Chmura-type tight end, who can be a major factor all over the field. This type of tight end has the ability and the foot speed to go anywhere on the field quickly—across the field, to the outside, down the field, etc.—and the ability to catch passes in traffic. In the process, he will be able to either bring defenders with him or find openings in the defenses. This kind of tight end needs the body control, the great hands and a lot of the skills of wide receiver, although more girth (size) than a wide receiver because many of the passes he catches will be in the vicinity of linebackers and even defensive linemen. The quicker and faster type of tight end will utilize an all-technique (rather than bulk) approach when blocking. It is essential that he learns and develops those blocking techniques that he can use with a reasonable level of effectiveness against defensive linemen and linebackers. Unlike the stronger, bigger type of tight end, he will not be able to use a mass-against-mass approach to blocking.

CHAPTER 2

Fundamental Concepts for Offensive Line Play

In any offensive line system, certain fundamental concepts must be established. Different systems may vary in the designation of these concepts, but every system must include the following elements: hole numbering; gap lettering; and defensive alignments.

HOLE NUMBERING

The term "hole numbering" refers to the identification of a particular area through where the ball carrier will run. Most offensive coaches number the holes for identification. The common method of numbering the holes assigns numerical values to the offensive line positions. In this method, the values of the numbers increase as you count outward from the center. The center's right leg is assigned the number 0, and his left leg is assigned the number 1. Counting outward from the center's right leg, the number 2 is assigned to the right hip of the guard, the number 4 is assigned to the right hip of the tackle, and the number 6 is assigned to the right hip of the end. The number 8 identifies the wide hole (i.e., the area between the imaginary fourth man on the line of scrimmage and the sideline). Counting outward from the center's left leg, the number 3 corresponds to the left hip of the guard, the number 5 corresponds to the left hip of the tackle, the number 7 corresponds to the left hip of the end, and the number 9 corresponds to the wide hole. Diagram 2-1 illustrates such a numbering system.

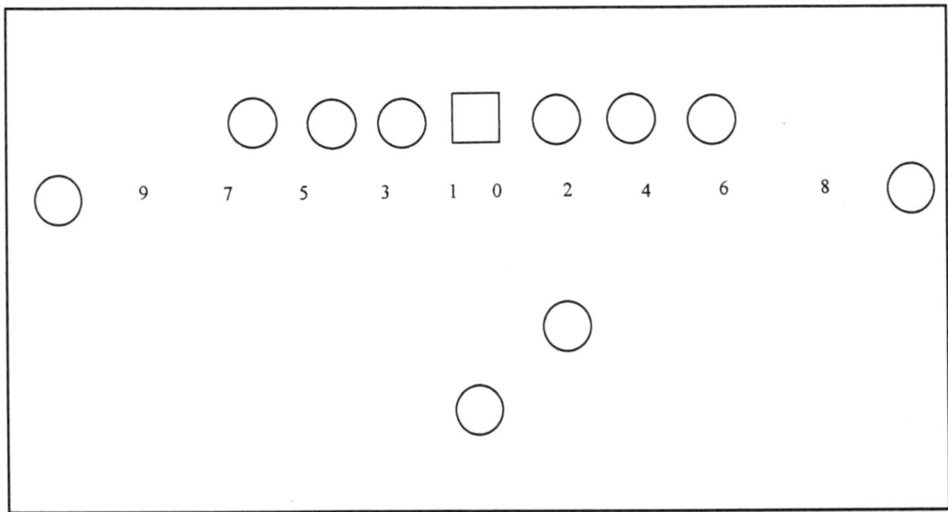

Diagram 2-1: The common numbering system.

Several different hole numbering philosophies are available to the offensive coach. A number of coaches number the holes in a reverse manner. These coaches use a system that counts inward, starting with the wide hole and stopping with the near leg of the center. In this numbering system, the number 8 is assigned to the right leg of the center; the number 9 is assigned to the left leg of the center. This system is believed to be useful when calling audibles. Since the most common numbering system assigns the lower values to the center, the reverse system prevents an audible from being deciphered by the defense. This type of numbering system is shown in Diagram 2-2.

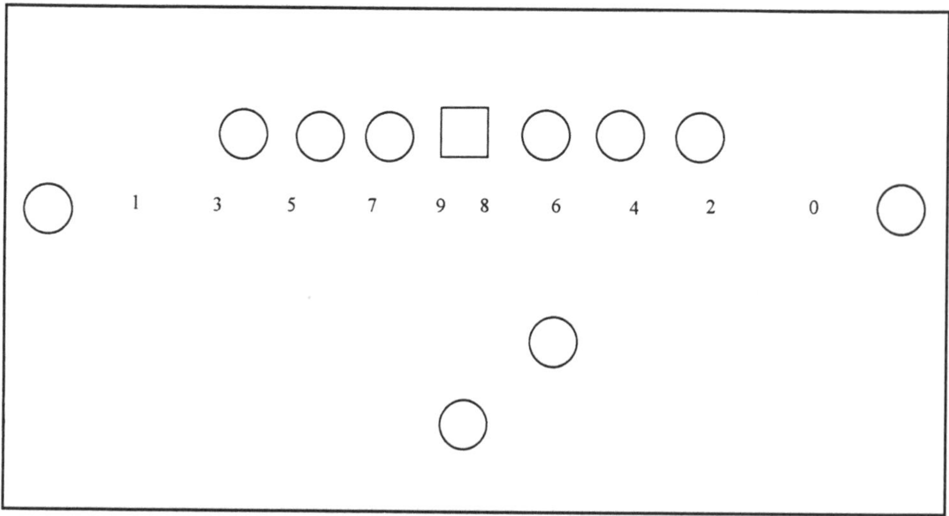

Diagram 2-2: The reverse numbering system.

A third numbering system is the right-to-left concept. The right-to-left numbering concept is a system in which the numbers increase in value from right to left. In this system, the wide hole on the right side of the ball is number 1. The number 2 corresponds to the outside hip of the right end, the number 3 corresponds to the outside hip of the right tackle, the number 4 corresponds to the outside hip of the right guard, the number 5 corresponds to the tailbone of the center, the number 6 corresponds to the outside hip of the left guard, the number 7 corresponds to the outside hip of the left tackle, the number 9 corresponds to the outside hip of the left end, and the number 0 corresponds to the wide hole on the left side of the ball. Numbering the holes consecutively from right to left is rarely used, even though it is probably the oldest numbering system in use. Since the right-to-left system is rarely used, it is also a good system to use if you are concerned about the security of your audibles. Diagram 2-3 shows the right-to-left system.

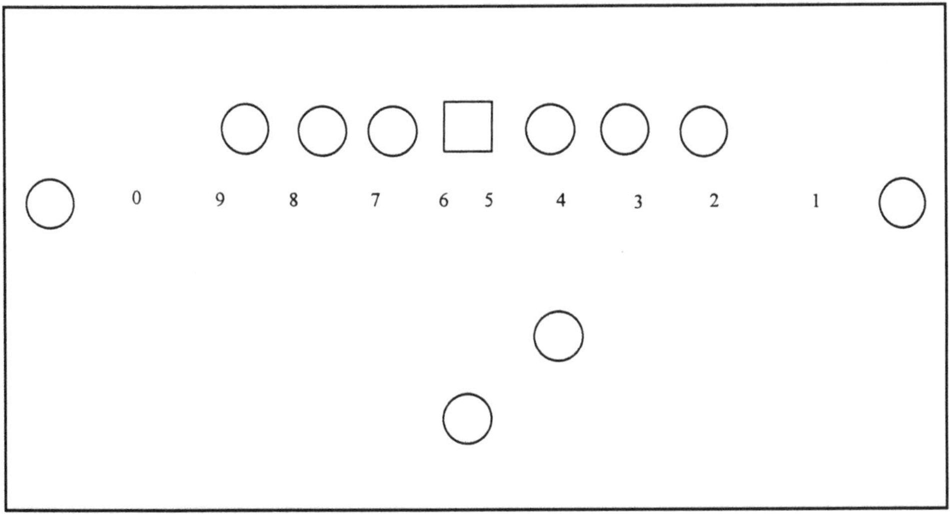

Diagram 2-3: The right-to-left numbering system.

The hole numbering philosophy is sometimes linked to the structural philosophy of the formation alignment. In the flip-flop system discussed in Chapter 14, the hole numbers can flip with the player, although all factors considered, I personally prefer that the numbers stay the same—right and left—regardless of whether a flip-flop system is employed. In a system where the hole numbers switch according to a formation strength call, a strong tackle will carry the number 4 hole with him when he flips from side to side. In other words, the even-numbered holes flip with the strong side lineman and the odd-numbered holes flip with the weak side lineman. Diagrams 2-4 and 2-5 illustrate the concept of the numbered holes flip-flopping with the offensive strength call.

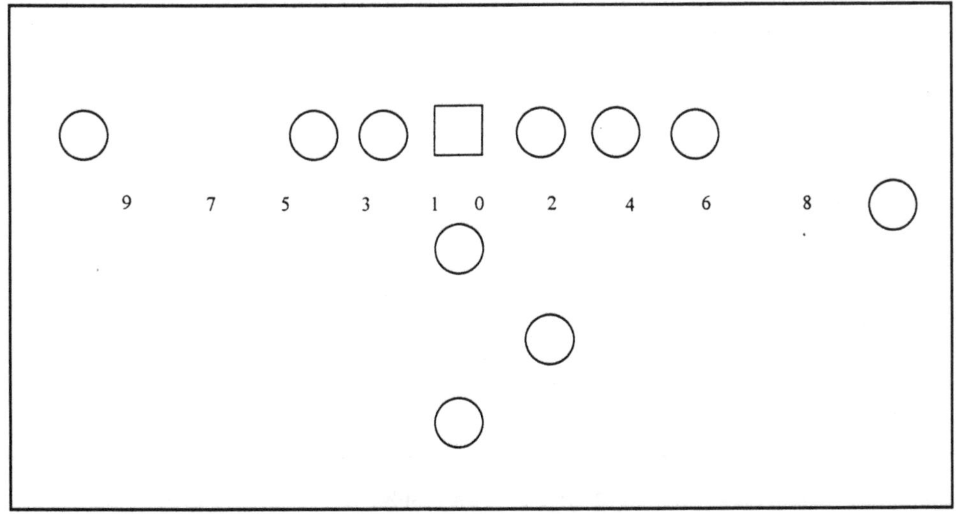

Diagram 2-4: In a flip-flop system, the even-numbered holes are to the right in a pro right formation.

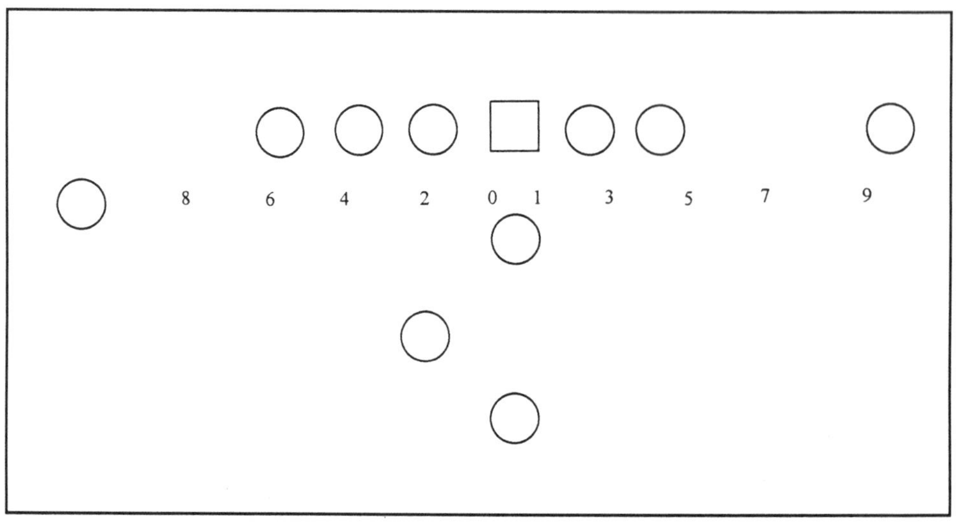

Diagram 2-5: In a flip-flop system, the even-numbered holes are to the left in a pro left formation.

The same-side philosophy of alignment keeps the numbered holes in static positions. The numbers remain in the same location in every formation. Diagrams 2-6 and 2-7 illustrate this concept.

A relatively small number of offensive coaches don't employ a hole numbering system. These coaches teach their plays without reference to a specific hole identification system, teaching landmarks that identify the aiming points with phrases such as "hip of the tackle," "leg of the guard," etc.

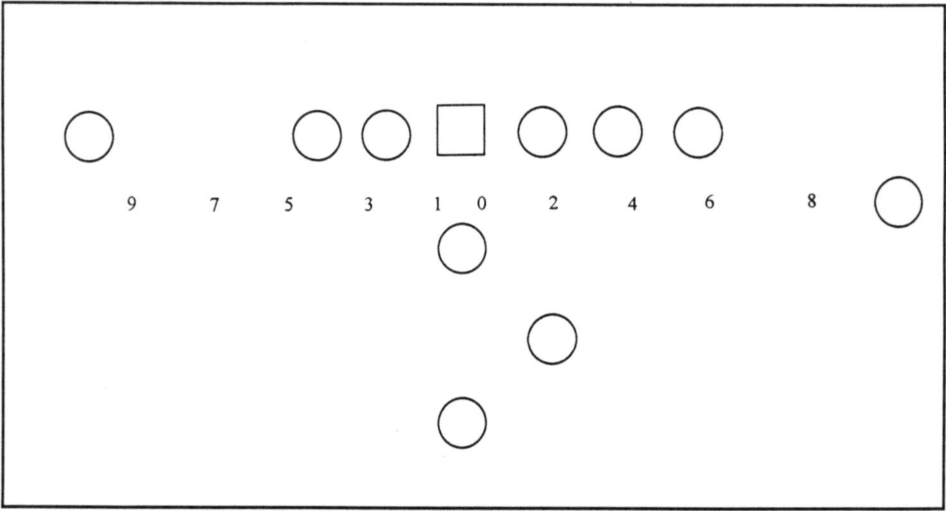

Diagram 2-6: In a same-side system, the even-numbered holes are to the right regardless whether a pro right formation is called.

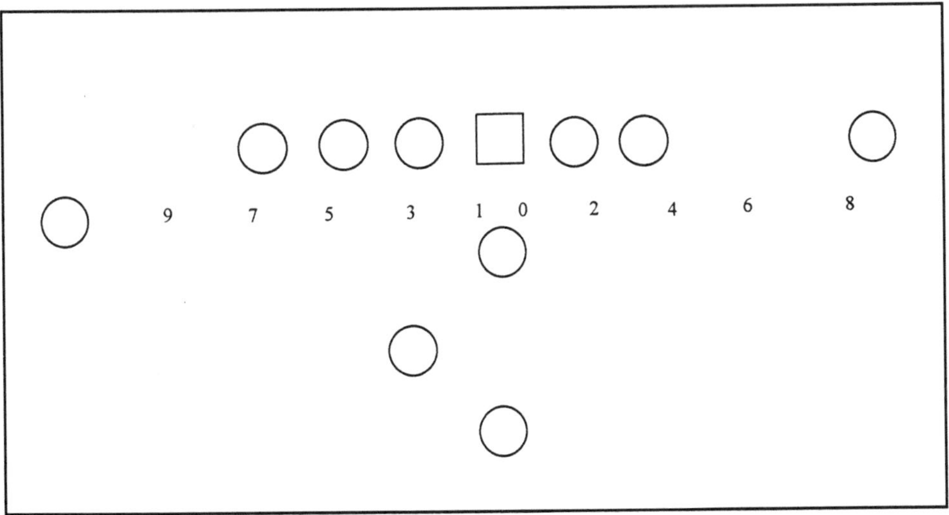

Diagram 2-7: In a same-side system, the even-numbered holes are to the right regardless whether a pro left formation is employed.

GAP LETTERING

Gaps refer to the area between adjacent offensive linemen. Generally, the gaps are labeled with letters. Each center-guard gap is called an "A" gap. Each guard-tackle gap is called a "B" gap. Each tackle-end gap is called a "C" gap. The area corresponding to the wide hole is called the "D" gap. A particular gap is identified by designating it an onside or offside gap. The prefix onside is attached to the letter of the gap when the ball is moving toward the side of that gap. For example, the right "A" gap is the "onside 'A' gap" when the play is designed to hit over the right side. On such a right-handed play, the left "A" gap is the "offside 'A' gap." Diagram 2-8 shows how gaps are assigned basic letters.

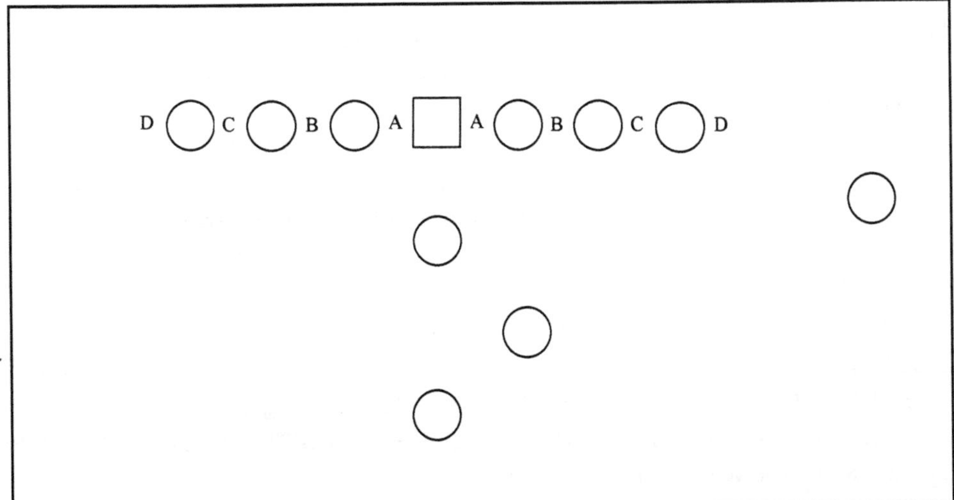

Diagram 2-8: Gap lettering.

IDENTIFYING DEFENSIVE ALIGNMENT TECHNIQUES

The alignments of the defensive front are identified by recognizing the individual alignment techniques of the defensive linemen. Several different concepts are used to designate the alignment of the defensive linemen throughout the many levels of play. One of the best concepts for identifying the defensive front alignments is shown in Diagram 2-9.

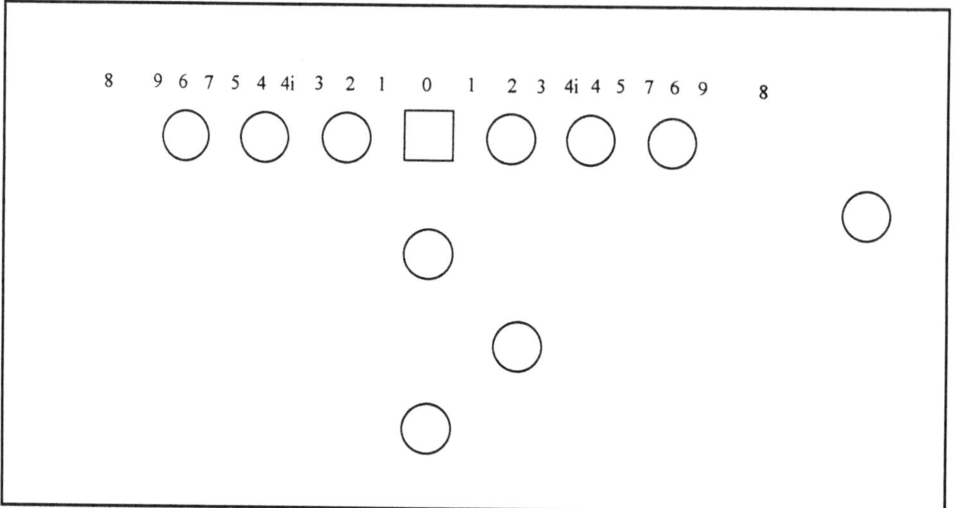

Diagram 2-9: Defensive line techniques.

Chart 2-1 details the parameters of each defensive line technique shown in Diagram 2-9. It is extremely important that your offensive linemen not only be able to recognize and verbally identify defensive technique alignments, but be able to explain the responsibility of that particular defensive technique .

In the defensive technique numbering model shown in Diagram 2-9, an even-numbered technique corresponds to a headup technique. Outside shades are odd-numbered techniques. The 7 technique is the one exception to the outside shade technique correlating to the odd-numbered technique. The 7 technique is the only inside shade technique identified by an odd number. The remaining inside shades are specified by even numbers. An even-numbered technique also corresponds to a headup technique.

The letter "i" is used to specify when the even-numbered technique is an inside shade and not a headup alignment. For example, the inside shade alignment on the offensive guard is called a "2i" technique. An inside shade alignment on the offensive tackle is called a "4i" technique. Another quirk of the classical numbering system is realized when you attempt to identify a gap technique.

Chart 2-1: Defensive line technique parameters.

TECHNIQUE	GAP ASSIGNMENT	LEVERAGE ARM (FREE ARM)
0	Playside "A" gaps	Playside arm
1	"A" gap	Inside arm
2	"A" gap	Inside arm
3	"B" gap	Outside arm
4	"B" gap	Inside arm
5	"C" gap	Outside arm
7	"C" gap	Inside arm
6	"C" gap	Inside*
9	"D" gap	Outside
8	"D" gap	Outside

* The leverage arm of the 6 technique may vary in response to the blocking scheme.

With one exception, no identifying number for a gap alignment exists in the classical system. In order to identify a defender as a gap alignment technique, you must add the word "gap" after the technique number. For example, when a defender aligns in the gap between the guard and tackle, he is said to align in a "4 gap." You could also accurately describe that particular gap alignment as a "3 gap." The designation of a defender aligned in the guard-tackle gap as either a "4 gap" or a "3 gap" is a matter of preference. A defender who aligns in the gap between the offensive tackle and the tight end may also be designated by one of two names. The defender aligned in tackle-tight end gap can be called a "5 gap" or a "7 gap." The choice of which name is best is one of personal preference. The classic numbering system calls the defender who is aligned in the center-guard gap a 1 technique.

IDENTIFYING DEFENSIVE FRONTS

Defensive fronts are classified as either seven-man or eight-man fronts. An alternate method of classifying fronts is according to their structure. Three different front structures include all of the standard defensive fronts—even structures; odd structures; and goal line structures. Five basic defensive fronts fall under the category of even-structured defense; the odd-structured defensive classification encompasses four basic defensive fronts; and six basic defensive fronts are included in the category of goal line structured defense. Chart 2-2 shows the basic defensive fronts and the category to which they belong. Diagrams 2-10 through 2-24 illustrate each front.

Chart 2-2: Defensive front structures.

EVEN STRUCTURES	ODD STRUCTURES	GOAL LINE STRUCTURES
20	30	20 Double Crash
40	30 Eagle Strong	53
43	30 Eagle Weak	62
61	30 Double Eagle	65
Slide		7-1
		Gap 8

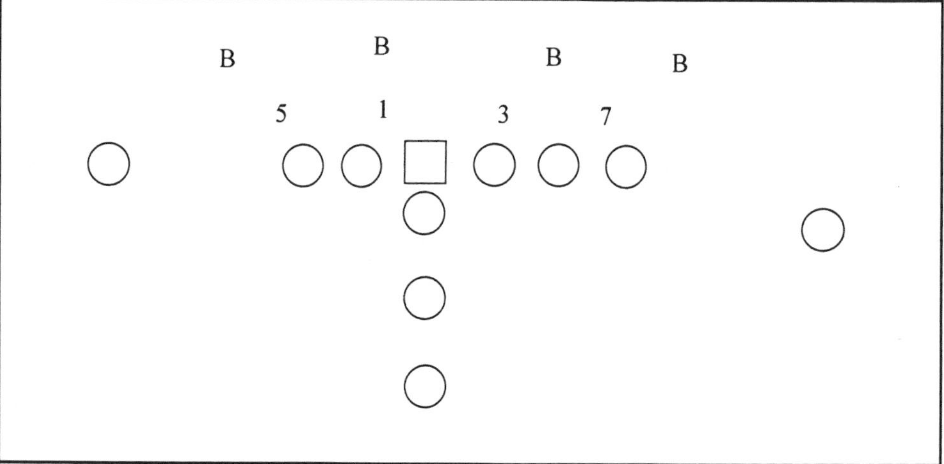

Diagram 2-10: 20.

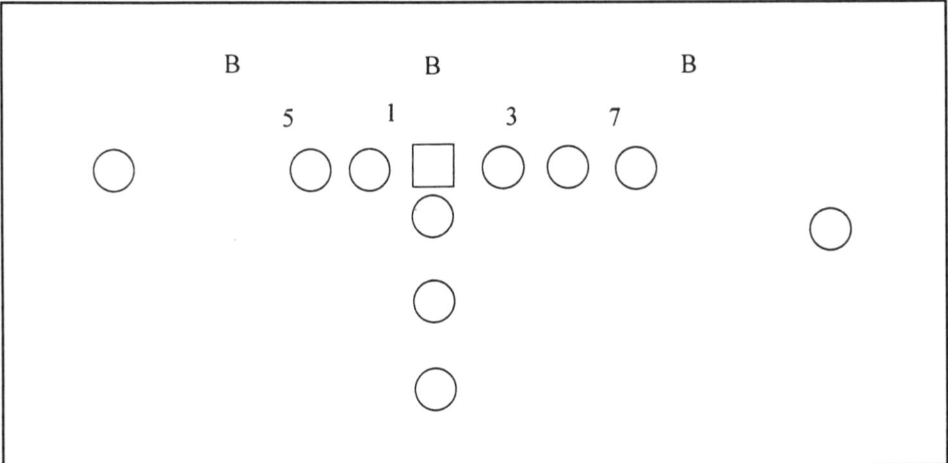

Diagram 2-11: 40.

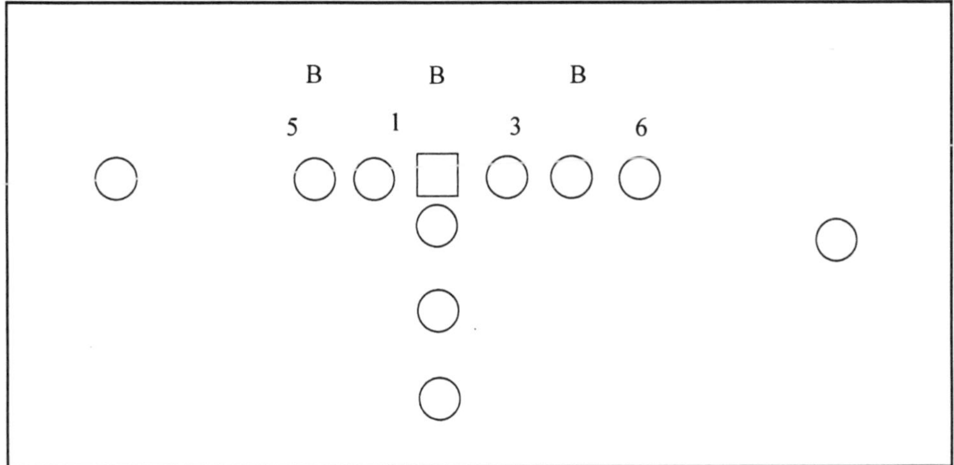

Diagram 2-12: 43.

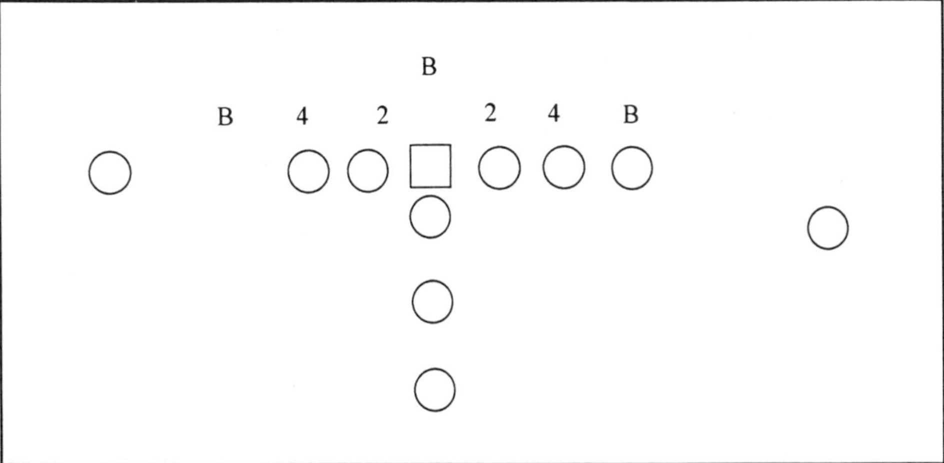

Diagram 2-13: 61.

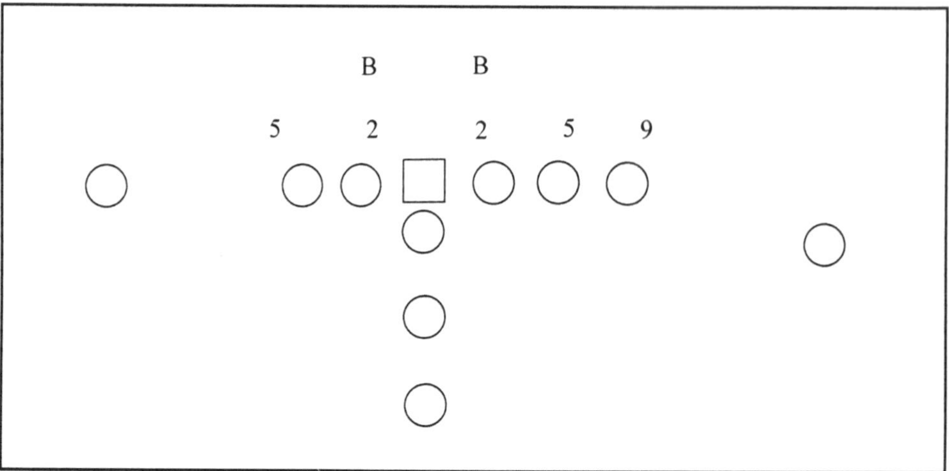

Diagram 2-14: Slide.

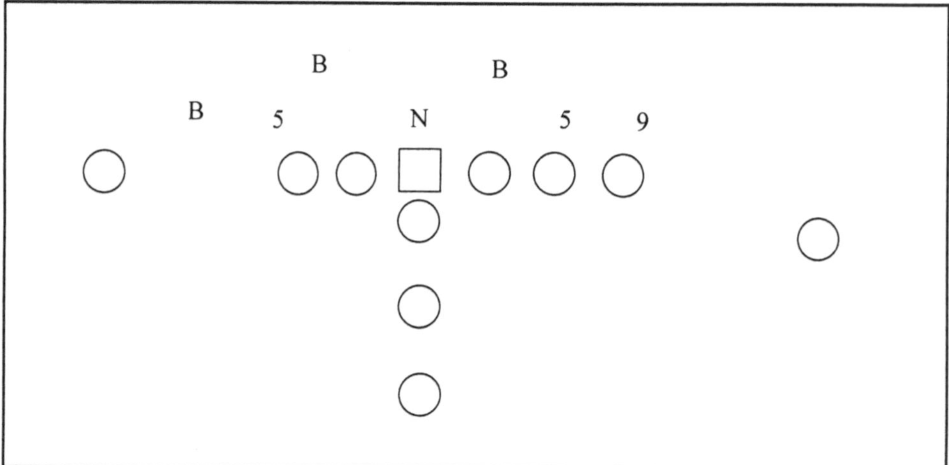

Diagram 2-15: 30.

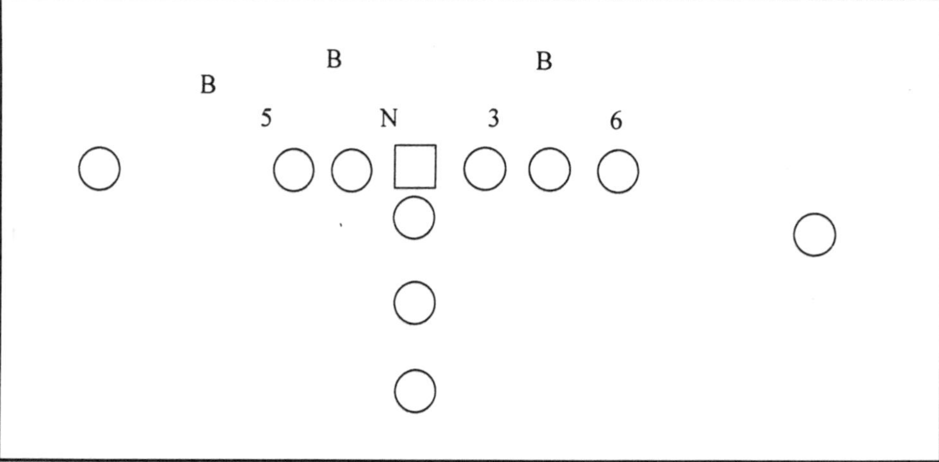

Diagram 2-16: 30 Eagle Strong.

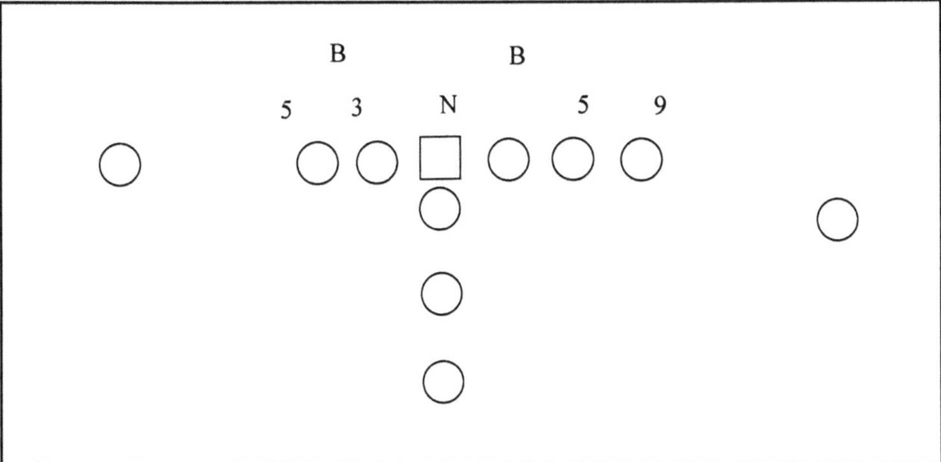

Diagram 2-17: 30 Eagle Weak.

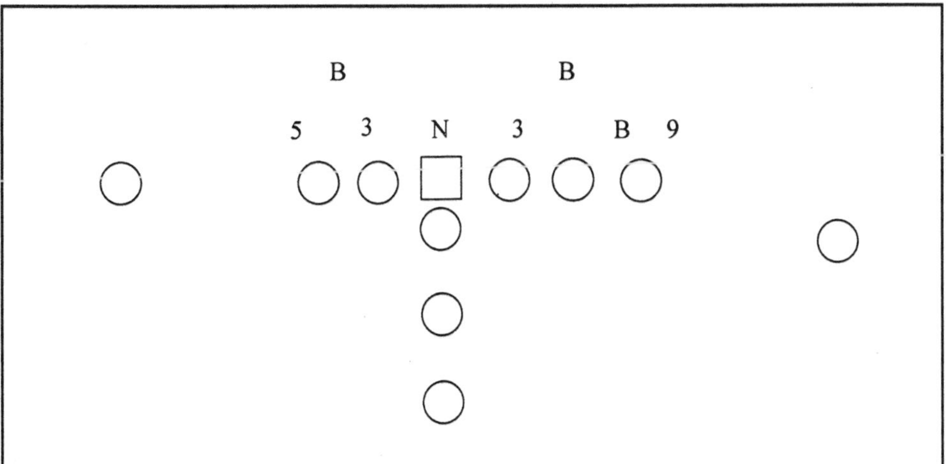

Diagram 2-18: 30 Double Eagle (46 look).

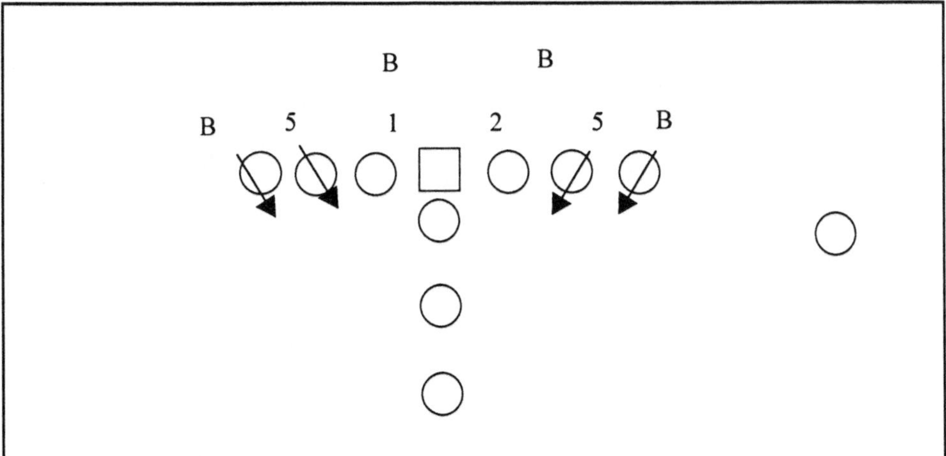

Diagram 2-19: 20 Double Crash.

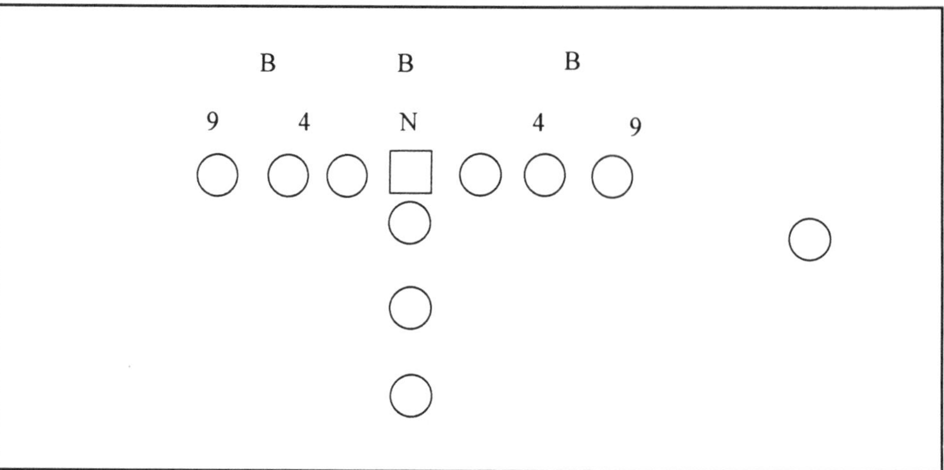

Diagram 2-20: 53.

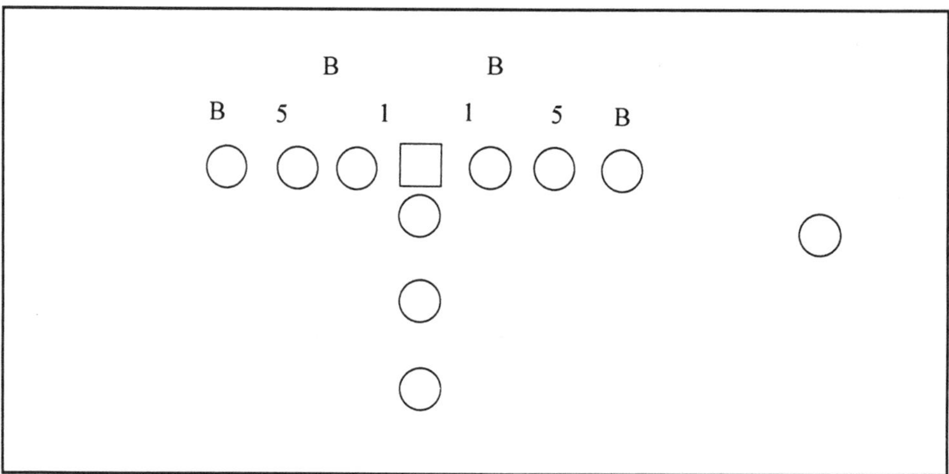

Diagram 2-21: 62.

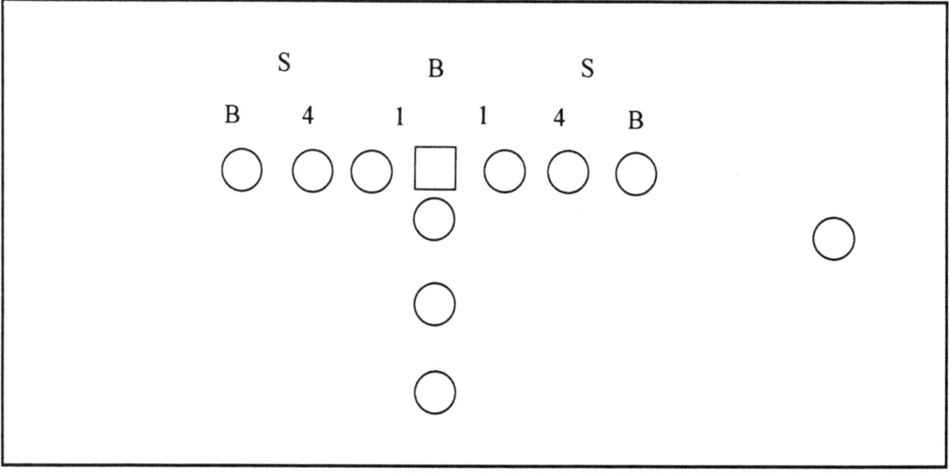

Diagram 2-22: 65.

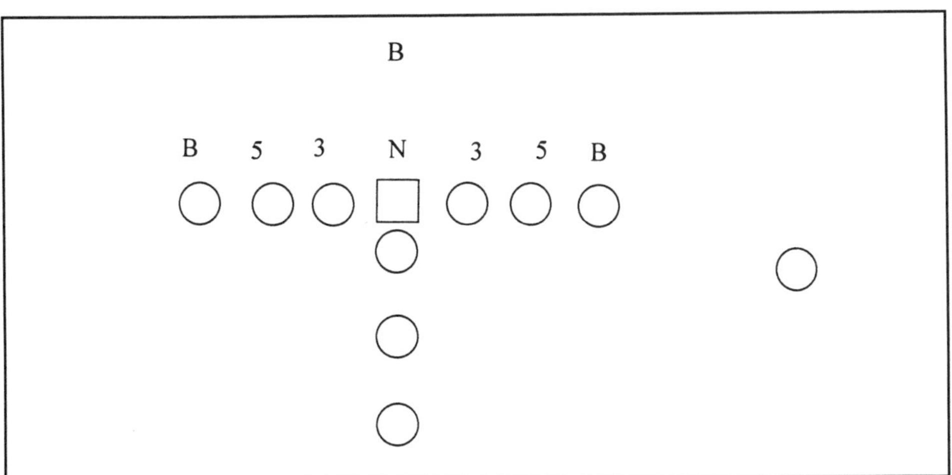

Diagram 2-23: 7-1.

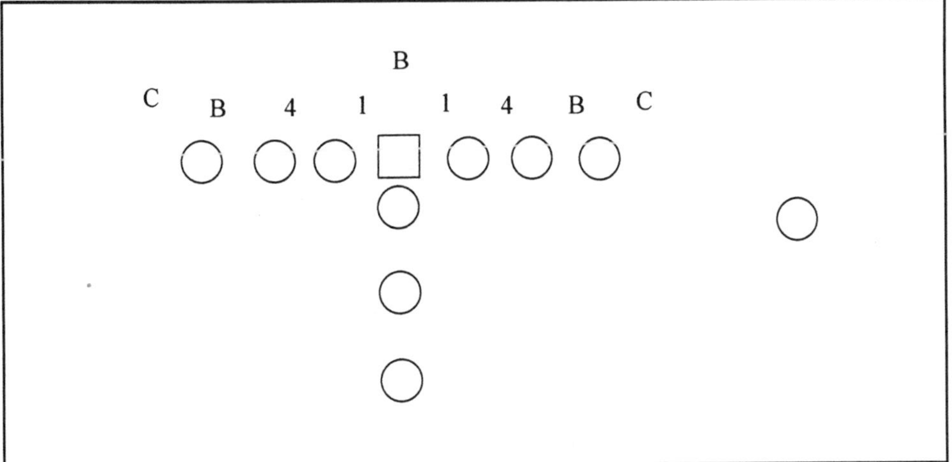

Diagram 2-24: Gap 8.

CHAPTER 3

Presnap Fundamentals and the Exchange

As a general rule, an offensive lineman should not change his stance from play to play. His stance should remain consistent on every snap, regardless of his assignment. The most common error committed by a young lineman occurs when he adjusts his stance to help himself accomplish his task. Young linemen often bend their elbows, or lean forward on their hands, so that they may fire off the ball more quickly and drive block their opponent. When assigned to pull on a play, inexperienced linemen tend to lean backward in their stance, barely touching the ground with their hands so that they may pull to lead interference for the ball carrier.

A lineman is more likely to feel the need to adjust his stance when he has not practiced the correct stance fundamentals on a daily basis. If a player leans backward to pull for interference, he hasn't received enough repetitions on pulling from a balanced stance. If a player leans forward on his fingers and tilts his body for a drive block, he hasn't received sufficient practice at drive blocking from a balanced stance. The only acceptable circumstances under which an offensive lineman can adjust his stance to gain an advantage are such situations as a definite passing down, a goal line short-yardage situation, or a time-related passing situation. The key point to keep in mind is that under normal circumstances, the offensive lineman should align in a balanced stance, no matter what his assignment.

As with any football position, the proper technique begins with the proper stance. Normally, the ideal stance serves both the run blocking and the pass blocking technique. A balanced stance gives the offensive lineman the ability to move in eight different directions without tipping off his assignment to the defense. The eight directions of movement from balanced stance are shown in Diagram 3-1.

The basic football stance that I recommend is a three-point balanced stance. A three-point stance gives the player an opportunity to maximize his leverage when performing all of the tasks of blocking. From drive blocking to pulling, the three-point stance is the best stance to initiate a proper run-blocking demeanor. A balanced three-point stance typically exhibits the following characteristics :

- *A good base:*
  - The feet should be positioned slightly wider than the width of the shoulders.
  - The feet should be placed close to a parallel position, not staggered.

- The toes should be pointed forward.
- The weight of the player should be centered on the inside of his feet.
- The base should be centered in his hips and buttocks.
- The player should be able to lift his down hand without affecting his balance.

• The proper power angle formed through the hips and shoulders:

- The ankles should be flexed.
- The heels should be on the ground (never raised).
- The knees should be ahead of the toes.
- The hips are flexed along with the bend of the knees and the flex of the ankles.

• The hands in a position to set the proper demeanor:

- The thumb of the down hand should be positioned inches forward of the shoulders.
- The weight should be slightly forward on the fingertips of the down hand.
- The off hand should be held open and placed on the side of the knee with the thumb pointing forward.
- The off-hand elbow should be tight to the body.
- The offensive linemen on the left side of the center should use a left-handed stance (i.e., left hand down).
- The offensive linemen on the right side of the center should use a right-handed stance (i.e., the right hand down).
- The center may use a one-handed (i.e., three-point) stance or a two-handed (i.e., four-point) stance.

• The shoulders forming an adequate blocking surface:

- The shoulders should be square to the line of scrimmage.
- The shoulders should be parallel to the ground.

• The head and eyes leading the block:

- The head should be positioned so that the upper screws which connect the facemask to the headgear are facing forward.
- The eyes should be focused straight ahead, as the blocker looks through the down defender.

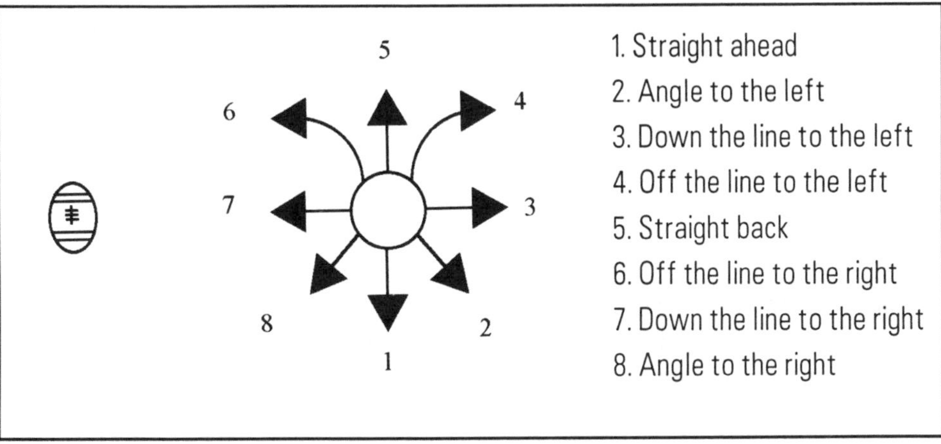

Diagram 3-1: The right directions in which the offensive linemen moves.

THE CENTER'S STANCE

The center is the most unique position on the offensive line. Unlike coaching the other four to six positions, coaching the center requires that you teach how the ball is to be gripped, monitor the mechanics of the snap to the quarterback, and explain the nuances of blocking while snapping the football.

The stance employed by the center is a balanced stance. The heels are slightly raised, and the neck is bowed. The hips are slightly higher than the flat of the back. The feet are evenly spaced with no stagger. The feet must be slightly wider than shoulder width, but only slightly wider. An exaggerated width of the stance is a detriment to blocking. The center can roll his heels slightly outward in his stance. The stance is opened by the heels rolling outward, thereby creating a power line and a torque in the hips. As a learning exercise for you as a coach, you should try assuming the center's stance and roll your heels slightly outward. In this instance, you should be able to feel the sensation of increased power in your hips.

To many coaches, a four-point center stance is a preferred stance for balance. The four-point stance for the center offers specific positive features. For example, it lowers the center's shoulders. The four-point stance also benefits the back-block technique of the center, giving him a push hand or point hand as he blocks back to fill for a backside pulling guard. The four-point stance gives the center a push hand that allows him to push off as he snaps the ball. This capability adds more initial force on the center's movement. When blocking back, the center may use his onside hand as a point hand. The point hand is the hand the center uses to point or open to the defender. As the center snaps the ball, the point hand snaps out to the target, providing a rubber-band effect on the body of the center.

The three-point stance does not provide the center with these advantages. The three-point stance places the hand of the center behind the shoulders of the body. In the three-point center stance, the center normally rests his forearm across his knee. This will cost the center momentum as he loses a push hand and a point hand. The three-point stance, however, can give the center an advantage in pass blocking—particularly against a nose tackle. His up hand is placed near his knee, thereby making it closer to the target area of the nose tackle's chest. His hand may be driven forward at the same moment of the ball moving backward on the snap. The up hand should be used to gain a feel and establish an inside leverage position to the defender's chest, given the fact that it should strike the nose tackle slightly ahead of the snapping hand.

For coaches who like a large bodied center, a three-point stance is preferred. An unduly large center will usually get top heavy in the four-point stance. On the other hand, a larger bodied center tends to have more power in the hips. Thus, he may get away with a slightly slower time to domination.

Time to domination is the term used to describe the actual time it takes to obtain the three-inch movement of the drive block. A blocker's time to domination is a product of his foot quickness and explosiveness off the ball. Great blockers get their first three steps down and obtain the desired three-inch movement in a minimum time to domination.

The center's grip on the football is an important coaching point. The fingers of the center's off hand should be spread. The center places the ball under the corresponding eye of his snapping hand—only an inch or so to the side of his nose. A right-handed center places the ball under his right eye, while a left-handed center places the ball under his left eye. Although the ball should be placed as close to the midline of the center's stance as possible; placing the ball under the eye allows the center to snap the ball in a straight line.

The center grasps the ball using a quarterback's grasp. However, his four fingers should not be on the laces. He places his thumb on the laces, however, with his hand over the forward third of the ball. Without covering the point, he wraps his hand around the forward third of the ball. His wrist is rolled outward. Rolling the wrist outward forces the ball to tilt slightly with the nose up. The wrist should be locked in this position throughout the snapping motion. Keeping the wrist locked causes a natural rotation of the ball on the snapping motion. As a result, the quarterback will receive the ball slightly turned. The nose of the ball will turn left with a right-handed center, while the nose will turn right with a left-handed center.

A right-handed quarterback should ideally have a right-handed center, while a left-handed quarterback should ideally have a left-handed center. Nevertheless, the center and the quarterback are cross-matched—the ball can still be delivered with the quarterback receiving the ball with the laces in the correct position. To get the perfect delivery with the cross-matched center and the quarterback, the quarterback need only move his grip a few inches toward the side of his weak hand. A right-handed quarterback should move his hands more to the left for a left-handed center, while a left-handed quarterback should move his hands more to the right for a right-handed quarterback.

Part of any center-quarterback exchange is the role of the quarterback. The quarterback should be included in many of the center's group drills, so that they develop a partnership under stressful conditions. One coach should be in charge of the center-quarterback exchange. All factors considered, his responsibility should not be shared by the quarterback coach and offensive line coach. The offensive line coach can be responsible for coaching the quarterback on the proper hand placement and the snap-taking mechanics. Much time is often wasted on arguing over who is at fault during a bad snap. The thing to look for in a center-quarterback exchange is consistency. Even a repetitious problem can be fixed, if the problem is of a consistent nature. However, an exchange problem in which the center and the quarterback continually experience multiple breakdowns is probably best addressed by finding a new center.

After only a few days of instruction, the center and quarterback should develop an appropriate level of consistency to their exchange. As with the offensive line coach, the most important thing for you to remember as the instructor of the center- quarterback exchange is: *Every center must practice daily with every quarterback. And—it is the responsibility of the quarterback to make the adjustment to the individual nuances of each center's particular snapping technique.*

You can prepare yourself for the inevitable "bugs" that may arise in the center-quarterback exchange by familiarizing yourself with the common problems experienced in the exchange. Your understanding of the cause of these problems and the respective cure for each position will go far in instilling confidence in your players. Among the factors that you should recognize with regard to a bad exchange are the following:

Problem	**Cause**	**Solution**
QB getting the point of ball	Center not cocking wrist	Correct the center's grip
Ball hitting the QB's bottom hand	Center not snapping ball up	Correct elbow from flying out
Bad snap; ball drops straight down	QB pulling out too soon	Make QB throw hands forward on snap
Bad snap; ball drops straight down	QB's bottom hand not pressing up	Make QB lock thumbs of each hand
Bad snap; ball rolls backward	Center is slinging the ball	Correct elbow from flying out
Bad snap; ball flies upward in air	Center is short-arming the snap	Make sure center gets work under stress

Center-quarterback exchange problems commonly occur in the red zone, close to the opponent's goal line. Red zone defenders usually align in the gaps in a goal-line stance. Situations in which the defensive overloads the middle (e.g., blitzes, 4th and short, etc.) require that the quarterback be especially conscious of receiving the snap before pulling out from the center. The center must be trained to expect surprise blitzes from the line of scrimmage and must not panic. The quarterback can often help the center by pausing his snap count if linebackers crowd the line of scrimmage over the center. The point to emphasize is that it is the quarterback's responsibility to never allow the blitzing defenders to get a timed running start through the "A" gap.

The center can be trained to take advantage of a defensive encroachment. He can snap the ball when he recognizes that a defender is in the neutral zone. You can train your center to quickly snap the ball if he sees an encroaching defender. However, the quarterback must also be trained to expect a quick snap. You should keep in mind that the officials may not necessarily make the correct call and flag the encroachment. The result of the officials missing the play is a wasted play at best. A missed encroachment call and a quick snap on a 4th down play results in a wasted play and a loss of possession. Teaching your center and quarterback to execute the quick snap can be a productive strategy. It would be erroneous, however, to believe that such a strategy has never been a pivotal factor in the loss of a big game. In fact, games have been lost on a quick snap when the officials didn't see the encroachment and didn't make the call.

SPLIT

The second important concept to master with regard to run blocking is the split. The term split refers to the distance between two adjacent lineman. The width of a split determines the size of the aforementioned gap. For instance, if a guard gets a large split from the center, the "A" gap is widened. If a tackle gets a large split from the guard, the "B" gap is widened. The player on the outside controls the split to his inside.

Splits across the line of scrimmage can be firmly set as standard widths. However, splits across the line of scrimmage can be individually set by the players on a snap-to-snap basis. The accordion-like movement of a player who changes his split to enhance his blocking technique from down-to-down is called split manipulation. Some offensive schemes incorporate split manipulation as part of the offensive system. Option offenses and Wing-T offenses often require their lineman to manipulate their splits according to the play called.

Generally speaking, line splits should ideally be kept at a standard distance from play-to-play. The split should be as wide as the distance that the outside player can control with an angle blocking technique. Quicker, stronger, more talented, offensive linemen can usually take larger splits than their slower, weaker, less talented, counterparts. The width of the split is also related to the talent levels and the techniques employed by the offensive linemen's opponent. The penetrating technique of a talented defensive lineman may require your offensive lineman to close (i.e., reduce) his split.

Diagram 3-2 shows the basic splits of a standard offensive attack. A list of the other factors that should be considered when setting your line splits include the following: the field conditions; the down-and-distance situation; the zone of operation (e.g., red zone, etc.); your predominant blocking scheme; and the blitzing patterns of the defense.

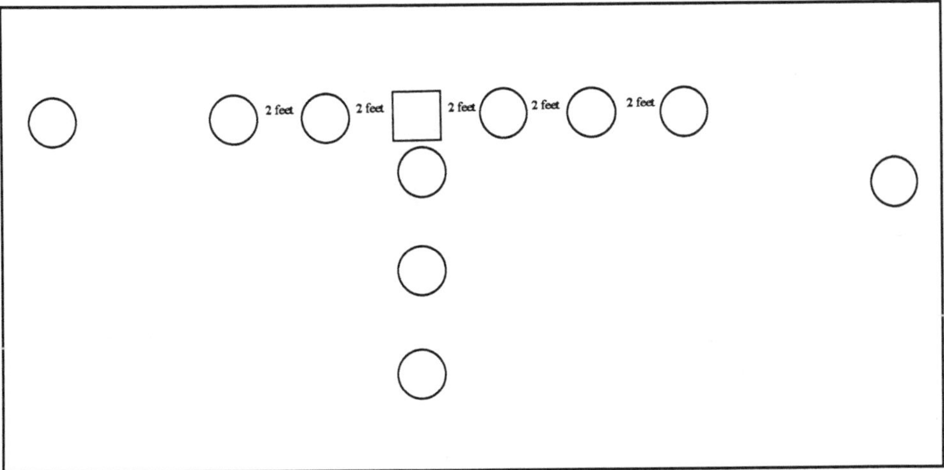

Diagram 3-2: Basic line splits of a standard offensive attack.

ALIGNMENT DEPTH

The depth of the offensive alignment is determined by your philosophy of blocking, as well as the style of your offensive attack and the talents of your offensive line personnel. The alignment of your interior line can have a critical impact on the speed of the initial line charge. The alignment is also vital to the timing for both the single point of attack blocks (i.e., one-man blocks) and the combination blocks (i.e., two-man blocks). By rule, no part of an offensive lineman's body can break the plane of the football before the snap of the ball. The only exception to this rule is the center position. Most centers, however, place the ball far enough in front of their body as to effectively comply with this rule.

The area between the defenders and the offensive line is called the neutral zone. If an offensive lineman aligns as tight to the ball as he legally can, he can reduce the size of the neutral zone. This type of tight alignment to the ball is usually preferred by offensive line coaches who have physically strong, dominating personnel. It is a favored alignment of the "wheel and turn" specialists in the I formation offensive attack. The primary objective of a tight alignment is for an offensive lineman to engage the defender as quickly as possible and use his superior size and strength to carry him backward.

Other styles of offensive attacks utilize a deeper alignment, thus creating a cushion in the neutral zone. In this type of style of attack, the blocking schemes are usually two-man schemes—particularly zone blocking schemes. Zone blockers can use the larger neutral zone to their advantage as they work together in reading the defensive reaction in a target area. As discussed in Chapter 5, a zone blocker will work together with an adjacent teammate to seal a pair of defenders from the pursuit. The dynamics of the zone block depends upon the reaction of the defenders.

Any type of blocking scheme that includes a read of the defender as an integral part of the scheme's execution is best facilitated by the offensive line aligning farther off the ball. As discussed in Chapter 6, most pass protection techniques are better served by an offensive lineman aligning as far off the ball as he is legally allowed. A pass protector wants to initially snap-up and create a cushion between him and the defender.

Younger, inexperienced, offensive linemen may have difficulty keeping their alignment uniform down the line of scrimmage. You should be aware of this potential problem during the preseason and conduct drills that are designed to help the linemen develop a sense of the appropriate individual alignment landmarks to ensure uniform, straight, alignment down the line of scrimmage.

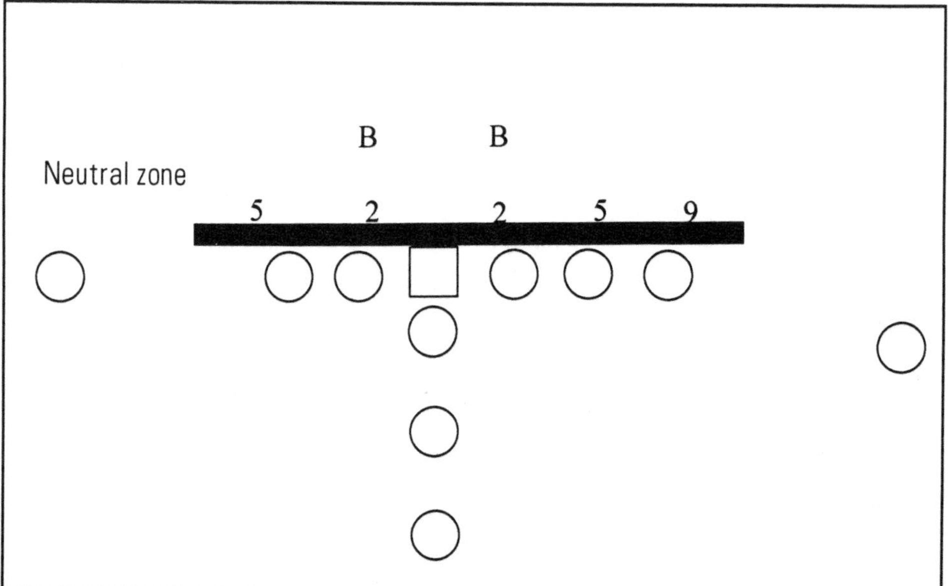

Diagram 3-3: The offensive linemen are aligned close to the ball, resulting in a narrow neutral zone.

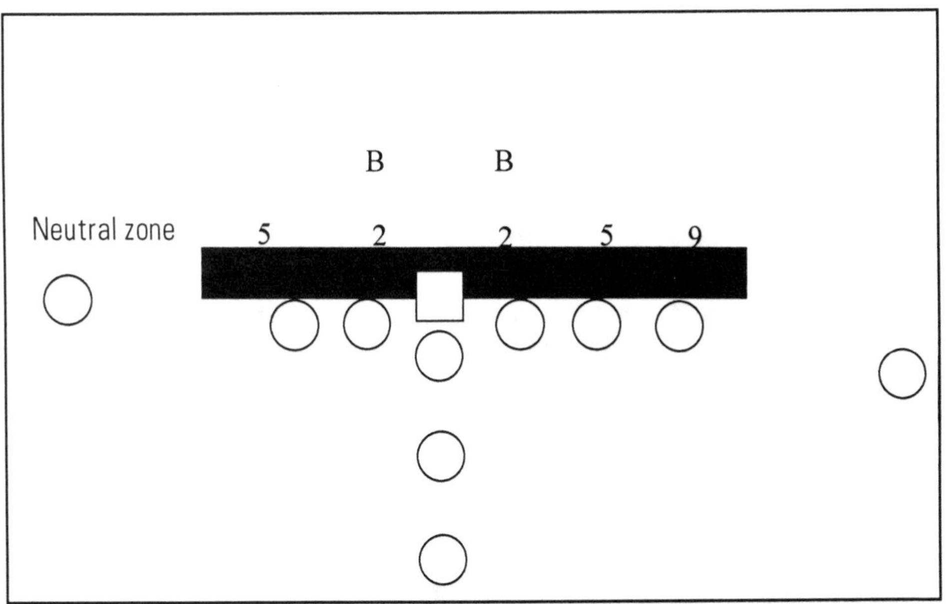

Diagram 3-4: The offensive linemen are aligned off the ball, resulting in a cushioned neutral zone.

Generally, two main methods of landmark instruction are effective. One method involves having the linemen set their alignment by using the foot of their inside teammate as a guideline. You can stand on the end of the formation and look down the offensive line to check their alignment. Once you have adjusted their alignments to get them aligned uniformly at the desired depth, instruct the players to take note of their inside foot's relationship to their teammate's foot. You should then tell them to make sure their inside foot is in that same relationship each time they address the line of scrimmage.

The second method of ensuring uniform alignment along the offensive line is to have the players use their teammates' inside hand as a landmark. When using the inside hand as a landmark, the guards put their hand down on a plane passing behind the football. The tackles then place their hand down on the same plane as the adjacent guard's hand. This method is best when used by offensive linemen who align in a four-point stance.

Whichever technique you use as a method of guaranteeing uniform alignment, make sure your offensive linemen are trained to remember that they cannot raise their hand once it touches the ground. This mistake is a common error by a younger lineman. More often than not he will realize that he didn't align properly after putting his hand down, then pick up his hand to move inside, or move forward. The result is an illegal procedure penalty.

An excellent instructional aid for alignment uniformity involves the use of a hose. During our team's preseason drills, you can place an old fire hose—or mark a chalk line—on the field. The offensive linemen can use this hose as a line marking the offensive edge of the neutral zone. They then can take note of their respective position to their inside teammate as they align as close to the hose as possible. To develop uniformity in a system that utilizes the deeper alignment, you can simply place the ball across the hose. The offensive linemen subsequently can use the hose as a guideline for their foot placement. This hose is marked with the standard spacing along the offensive line and can be used as a teaching tool during the entire season, not only for the offensive line, but for the running backs when they run their drills without offensive linemen.

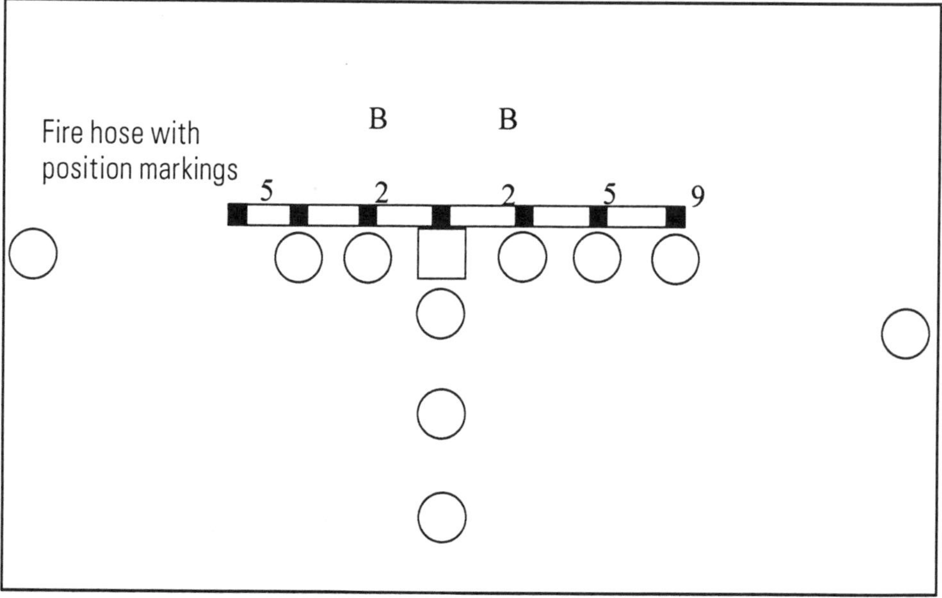

Diagram 3-5: The fire hose with position markings can be used to teach uniform alignment on the ball.

CHAPTER 4

One-Man Blocks

Run blocking is divided into three categories: man blocking techniques; two-man blocking techniques, and pull techniques*. Blocks categorized as man blocks are characterized as being techniques executed by only one lineman. The various types of man blocking include the following:

- Drive block
- Cut-off block
- Down block
- Influence block
- Level block
- Fan block
- Butt block
- Escape move
- Arc release
- Block release
- Alley block
- Reach block

When a blocker puts together the coaching points of an effective run block, he is said to be in the proper run-blocking demeanor. A key part of every run block, establishing a proper run-blocking demeanor figures heavily into the execution of one-man blocks.

THE RUN-BLOCKING DEMEANOR

The proper run-blocking demeanor is a combination of the correct body positioning and the blocker's movement during the "fit" stage of the block. A blocker fits with the defender at the moment of contact. A proper fit is a position that allows the blocker to maintain a sufficient blocking surface on the defender. The fit includes the stage of the block in which the offensive lineman maximizes his leverage. The proper run-blocking demeanor is an important aspect of the man blocks, particularly the drive block. A blocker exhibiting the correct blocking demeanor should demonstrate the following:

- Hips low
- Knees bent
- Ankles flexed
- Feet slightly wider than shoulder width
- Lower back arched (i.e., hyperextended)
- Toes pointing outward
- Shoulders slightly elevated
- Elbows tight to the body
- Hands open with thumbs up

**Two-man blocking is examined in Chapter 5, while pull blocks are discussed in depth in Chapter 6.*

Optimal use of the leverage angle or power angle from low to high.

- Feet flat—maximizing the opportunity for contact with the ground.
- Toes turned slightly outward.
- Knees turned slightly inward.
- Hands to target. Depending on the type of angle desired, a flipper or both hands should be punched into the chest of the opponent in a low-to-high lifting fashion.
- Elbows remain tucked inward while the thumbs point upward.
- Pad under pad. The shoulders of the blocker should be lower than the shoulders of the defender.
- The chin is kept level so that the head remains level while the neck is bowed.
- Head remains behind the plane of the chest with the screws of the headgear facing forward.

The mechanics of the correct blocking demeanor should be practiced on a year-round basis. Similar to a proper golf swing, the correct blocking demeanor has multiple components which must fall into place. You should continually drill the players in the development of the individual components of the blocking demeanor. Slow-speed drills with an emphasis on controlled movement help to keep the offensive lineman finely tuned on the mechanics of maintaining the proper demeanor.

DRIVE BLOCK

Of all the man blocks, the most basic is the drive block. Illustrated in Diagrams 3-2 and 3-3, the drive block is at the core of the man-on-man struggle in the trench. Mastering the techniques involved in the drive block is essential for an offensive lineman developing a complete repertoire of skills. As an offensive line coach, it should be your objective to develop at least five offensive linemen and two tight ends who can whip their opponent with a drive block. You should keep in mind that the outcome of most of the two-man blocking techniques usually depends on the movement created by a drive blocker.

The drive block consists of three main elements: the set to drive; the attack step; and the leverage step. The set to drive is the departure step of the offensive lineman (i.e., the first step of the blocker). This step is a four-inch jab step that serves as either a directional step or a settle step. The set to drive is a directional step when the offensive lineman is firing off the line to meet the stunting defender. When the defender is not a threat to stunt, the set to drive is a settle step.

Setting to drive entails the lead foot grazing the turf to quickly plant and enhance the power of the offensive lineman's demeanor. It is important for the offensive lineman to arch his lower back and flex his large muscle groups as he sets to drive. His eyes should focus on the target or the point-of-aim as he attacks the neutral zone.

The attack step is the offensive lineman's second step. When drive blocking a defensive lineman, the attack step is made just before contact is made with the defender. Ideally, the offensive blocker should make contact with the down defender after the third step; however, contact is usually made with the down defender after two and one-half steps. The attack step is also a tracking step. On the attack step, the blocker's inside foot steps toward the defender's inside foot, thereby putting the blocker on the track to strike the landmark with a full blocking surface. The attack step propels the blocker through the neutral zone as the blocker gains momentum to hit through the defender.

"Hit through them, not to them" is a good phrase to use when coaching inexperienced offensive linemen. Beginning offensive linemen tend to stop at the moment of contact. As an offensive line coach, you should note that while blocking is a fundamental part of football, it is one of the more unnatural physical acts in the world of sports.

Blocking should be taught in a manner that enables a blocker to overcome his fear of propelling his body into an opponent. One way of accomplishing this objective is to teach young kids to block through relatively soft dummies that are held with minimum resistance. In keeping with the concept of minimum resistance, you should refrain from standing on the blocking sled during repetitions. Indeed, many young players are not strong enough to explode through the heavier five-man and seven-man sleds. Standing on sleds only teaches the young offensive lineman to "hunker" on contact with the pad, the result being the development of major mechanical flaws and a negative psychological outlook on blocking.

The next step (i.e., the third step) after the attack step is the leverage step. Against an outside shaded defender such as a 3 technique, the leverage step is made with the outside foot. The leverage step allows the blocker to gain depth and initiate the finish of the block. It is on this step that the blocker gets the lift on the defender as the fit is secured. The blocker should fit snuggly with his pads under the defender's pads. "Pads under pads" is the commonly used phrase used to reinforce the concept of fitting with the defender on the third step. You should coach your linemen to attempt to get the third step down before contact is made. The three-step progression must be made with four-inch strides completed in rapid fire succession.

The net result of the rapid three-step departure to gain leverage with pad-under-pad contact should result in the proper run-blocking demeanor. As the blocker completes his third step and engages the defender he begins to attempt to gain lift on the defender. The blocker begins to apply his effort with regard to the "three-inch rule." I recommend using a three-inch rule in determining a blocker's production. The three-inch rule of offensive line blocking states that if the blocker can achieve a vertical dominance on the defender in a manner to knock him back off the line approximately three inches, the blocker will be successful in his block. In other words, after a blocker engages a defender, it is a matter of whether the blocker can achieve only three inches of movement. My years of experience have led me to believe that in the first fraction of a second the success of a block is determined. Almost without fail, a blocker who achieves three inches of movement and maintains a proper fit with the opponent will dominate the defender.

Lift is achieved primarily from the violent punch and thrust of the hands through the opponent's chest. Shooting the hands from the knee and ground causes the blocker's hips to snap forward on contact. As the hips snap forward, the feet must accelerate to chase the hips, thus providing even more momentum to the blocker's forward thrust. By forcing the defender to elevate his head and pads, the blocker is able to finish the block. Once the defender elevates and the blocker begins to chase his hips by accelerating his feet, the defender becomes off balance and vulnerable to being pancaked.

By simply running through the defender and not to him, the blocker can shoot the hands, elevate the defender, and pile drive him into the turf after he topples. Multiple pancakes during a ball game invariably swing the psychological pendulum in favor of the offensive lineman. Few things are more mentally devastating to a defender than being pancaked on multiple occasions during the early part of a game.

Another way for a lineman to finish the block is to maintain contact until the whistle blows. If your lineman forces his opponent to take an extra step to get to the ball carrier, your lineman has achieved a degree of success. The question to answer is a question of accountability. Did the blocker inhibit or prevent the defender from getting to the ball carrier? If the answer is yes, the blocker measured up to his level of accountability in executing the drive block. Diagrams 4-1 to 4-3 illustrate three types of different drive blocks (an inside shade, an outside shade, and a man over you).

CUT-OFF BLOCK

A cut-off block is commonly called a scramble block. A cut-off block is a backside blocking technique. This factor means that the ball carrier is moving away from a cut-off blocker. The objective of a cut-off block is to stop the penetration and pursuit of the defender. When the ball is moving toward the far end of the offensive line, the cut-off block is a useful technique against the inside shade alignments of down defenders. Most productive when the ball is being run wide, a cut-off block is especially effective against inside slanting technique defenders.

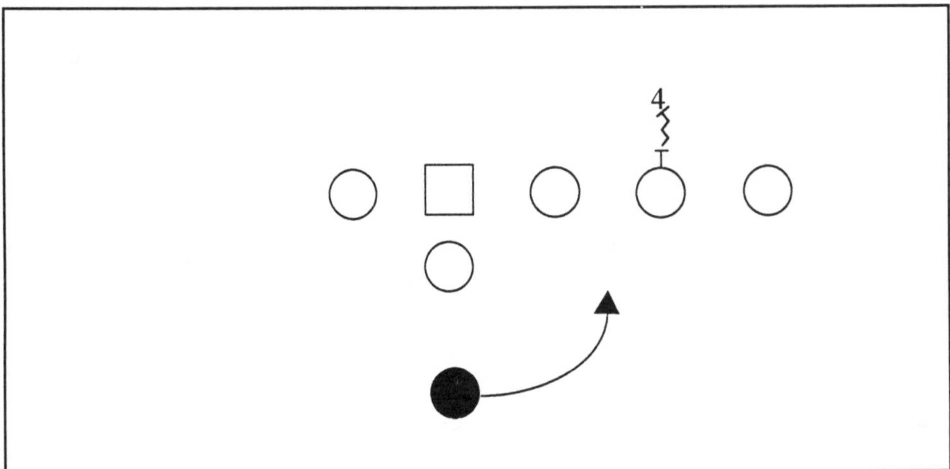

Diagram 4-1: The drive block.

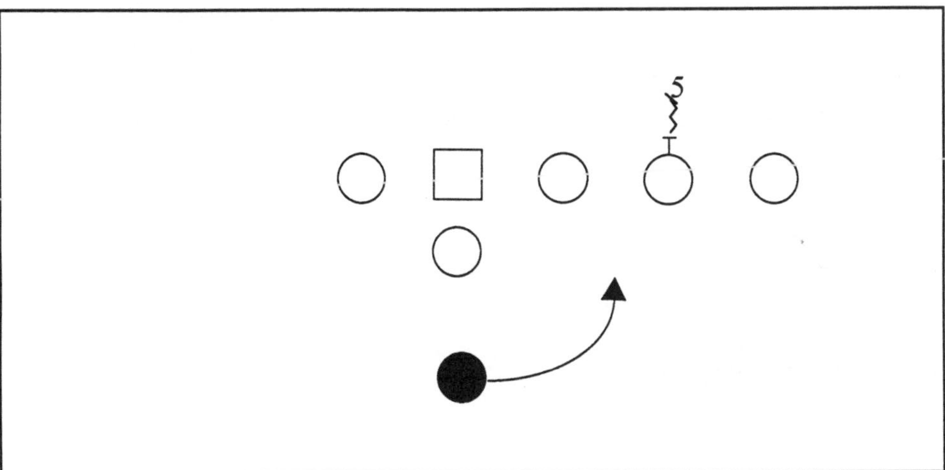

Diagram 4-2: The drive block.

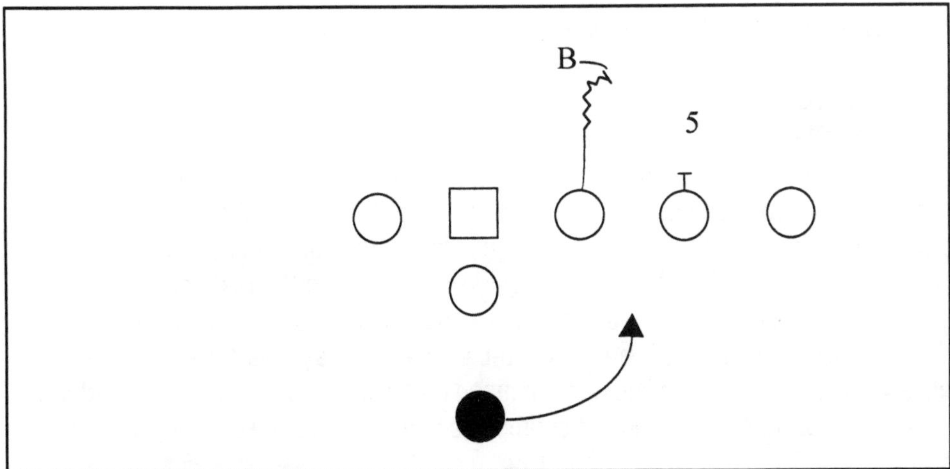

Diagram 4-3: The drive block.

When executing a cut-off block, the blocker pushes off his outside foot and steps with the inside foot to gain playside leverage on the down defender. On the second step, the blocker throws his backside arm and leg through the crotch of the defensive lineman. Since the defender will be moving inside as a result of his response to either the lead step of the blocker or a predetermined slant called in the defensive huddle, the blocker should throw his backside fist to the inside of the defender's playside knee. Throwing the backside fist to the inside of the defender's playside knee will result in the backside arm hooking the defender between his crotch and playside knee. Furthermore, throwing the backside arm in this manner will keep the blocker's backside shoulder low and level. Punching through the crotch with the backside arm also keeps the blocker's playside shoulder free. Keeping the playside shoulder free guarantees that the blocker will obtain inside leverage on the defender—a key coaching point for the cut-off block.

Once inside leverage has been obtained, the blocker will bear crawl for several feet upfield. His shoulders should remain square as he quickly bear crawls to the second level. Once the blocker has cleared the first level, he should snap to his feet and sprint to the alley. The cut-off is a quick, sharply executed block. The blocker should not be concerned with the reaction of the defender. He must quickly scramble inside and get upfield to sprint to the alley.

If the defender makes contact with the cut-off blocker and a wreck occurs, the blocker should fight to his feet and sprint to the third level. Components of a successful cutoff block include the following:

- Pushing strongly off the outside foot.
- Setting to reach with the lead foot to gain inside leverage upfield.
- Throwing the backside arm through the crotch of the defender.
- Squaring the shoulders and bear crawling upfield to the second level.
- Getting to his feet on the run and sprinting to the alley.

DOWN BLOCK

A down block is an angle block toward the inside (i.e., toward the center). The down blocker will choose one of two landmarks to attack. The scouting report may dictate the choice of the landmark. Another factor to consider is the defender's technique during the last few scrimmage downs, or during the last scrimmage of a similar down-and-distance situation. Two landmarks are possible because a down defender will demonstrate one of two techniques. He may be a penetrator (i.e., a defender who attacks the line of scrimmage on the snap), or he may be a reader (i.e., a defender who sits on the line of scrimmage and reacts to the blocking scheme).

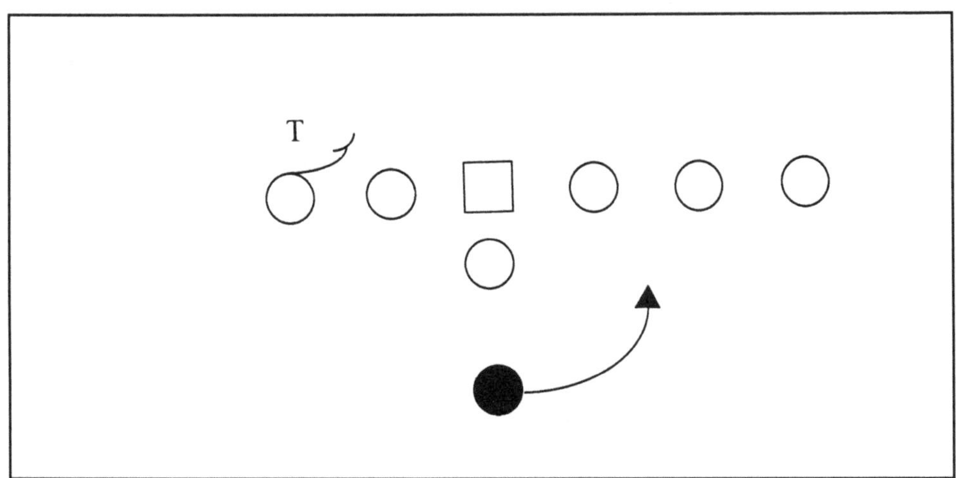

Diagram 4-4: The cut-off block.

A penetrator has little regard for the particular blocking scheme. His role is to charge the line of scrimmage. By charging the line, the penetrating defender hopes to force your offensive linemen to tighten their splits.

In order to block a penetrator, the offensive lineman should aim for the opposite shoulder of the defender. The blocker should drive his outside arm and pad through the near shoulder of the defender as his facemask fits into the neck of the defender. He must keep his hips down and his lower back arched as he punches through the defender. The blocker should punch his inside hand to the chest of the defender while he drives his outside hand under the armpit of the penetrating defender. Driving the fist up through the near armpit of the defender forces the defender's near shoulder to elevate, thus increasing the likelihood of a pancake block. When punching through the near armpit of the penetrating defender, the blocker's outside hand should be kept open so that he may wedge the armpit between his thumb and index finger. Positioning the outside hand to wedge the armpit gives the blocker an excellent feel of the defender's escape move. The hand locks in the defender, cements the fit, and prevents his escape.

A read technique defender will attempt to anchor the gap and fight the pressure of the blocker. He will attempt to cross the face of the blocker and fight outside on a lateral plane. The read technique down lineman is usually exceptionally strong in his upper body. Using his outside shoulder, this type of defensive lineman will dip and rip his inside shoulder across the face of the blocker to pursue toward the outside.

Since the read technique defensive lineman doesn't move forward to any significant depth, the proper aiming point for the blocker is on a sharper angle from the blocker. The blocker doesn't fire out on a flat angle to block down on the reading defender. The aiming point against the reading defender is the defender's hip, not his shoulder.

Because the inside reading defender will usually get an outside pull read by the inside blocker, the defender will be on the move toward the outside at the moment of the down blocker's contact.

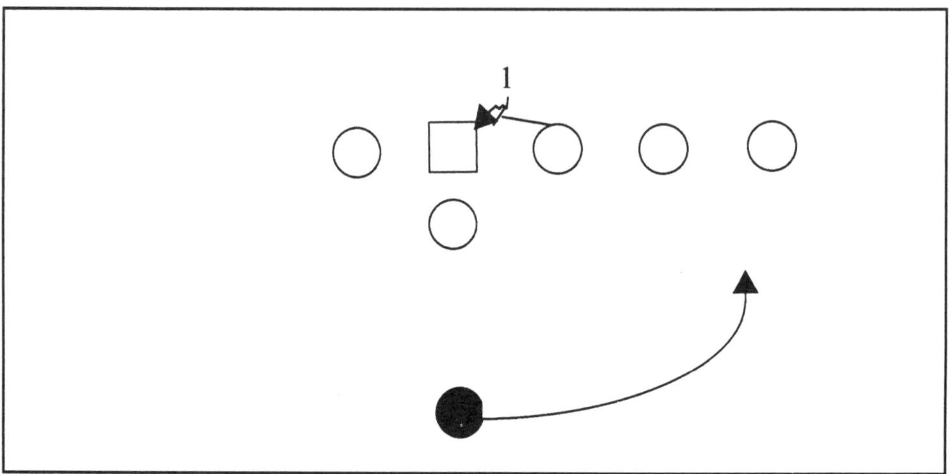

Diagram 4-5: The down block versus a penetrating defender.

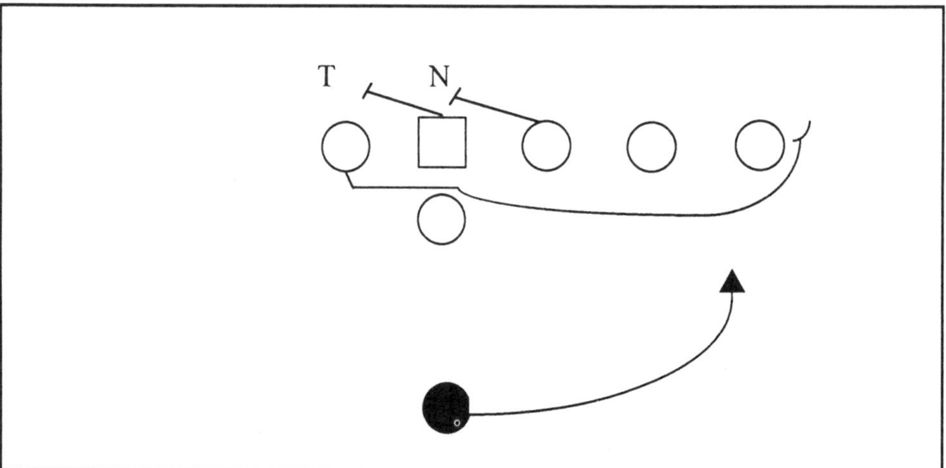

Diagram 4-6: When the center executes a down block, it is called a back block.

If the down blocker were to aim for the defender's shoulder, the read technique defender would gain several inches of clearance across the blocker's face. By aiming to the hip of the defensive reader, the down blocker can meet the defender with a secure fit as the defender reacts to the outside pull read. The finish technique is the same finish technique that is used against the penetrator. The outside hand, arm, and shoulder provide a violent thrust and lift into the outside half of the defender's body. The well-coached defender will keep his shoulders nearly parallel to the line of scrimmage as he reacts to the outside pull. (If the defender commits the technique error of "facing up" to the blocker, he will be hit head on and easily pancaked by the down blocker's momentum.) The blocker should use his inside hand to punch across the defender's chest and grab cloth. His outside hand cements the fit and prevents the defender's escape.

If the landmark is correctly secured and the fit is cemented, the down blocker can easily dominate the inside defender. By the same token, the size of the split should be directly related to the capabilities of the down blocker (i.e., the more skilled the blocker, the greater the split). For example, if a blocker is ineffective when down blocking, you should first consider cutting his split. For young players it is particularly important that you build from success, instead of correct from failure. This means that you should develop the down blocking technique of young linemen from smaller splits. Developing the inexperienced lineman's down blocking technique from a tighter split gives him the opportunity to experience the feel of success. A smaller distance between the defender and the blocker allows the blocker to concentrate on his departure, demeanor, and finish of the block. Working from inflexible, fixed splits is a waste of time if your linemen aren't physically capable of controlling the split. You should concentrate on teaching the technique of the down block first, then gradually widen the splits as your linemen become more skilled at down blocking.

Some coaches install a system of splits without taking into account the undeveloped down blocking skills of younger linemen. They are eventually forced to tighten the splits so that the blockers can achieve their goal. Achieving the goal is then complicated further by the blocker's fear of failure and lack of confidence caused by his previous inability to control the larger split. It is much better to start with tighter splits and progress to down blocking with wider splits. The point to keep in mind is that it is easier to build from success than from failure.

Successful down blocking is a matter of the linemen adhering to several coaching points, including:

- Keeping the eyes and hands on target.
- Keeping the hips down.
- Keeping a proper run-blocking demeanor.
- Being able to redirect to prevent the defender's escape.

The most common error of a down blocker relates to his blocking angle. Down blocking on too sharp an angle allows the penetrating defender to easily drive through the head of the blocker. Down blocking on too flat an angle allows the reading defender to easily rip his inside arm across the face of the blocker in an uppercut fashion. The reading defender can also easily spin-out against the down blocker who targets the landmark on too flat an angle.

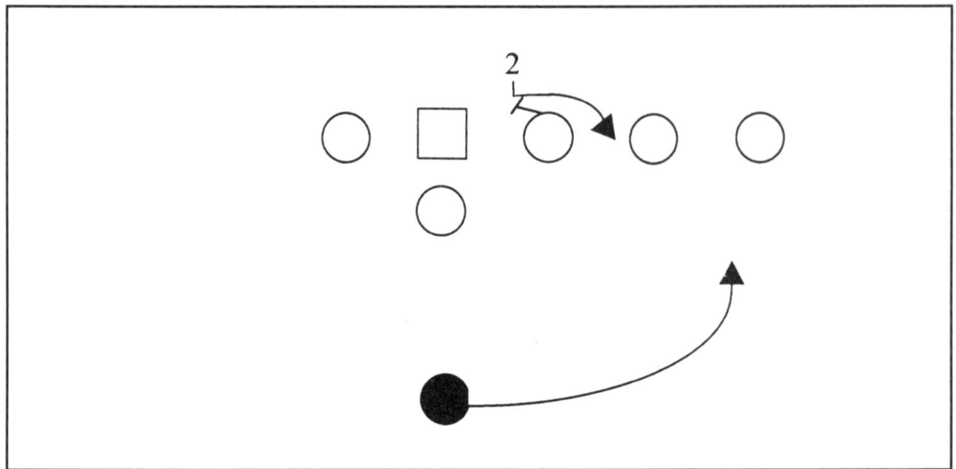

Diagram 4-7: The guard blocks too flat versus the penetrating defender; the defender ricochets though the B gap.

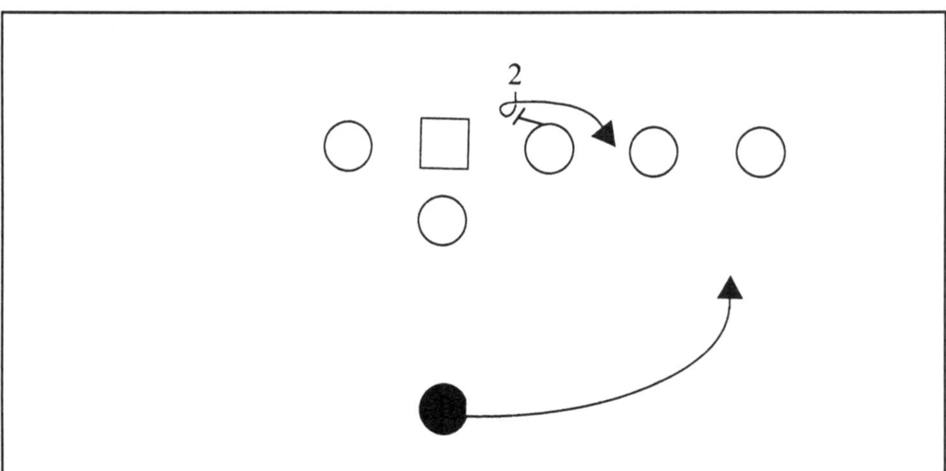

Diagram 4-8: The guard blocks too flat versus the reading defender.

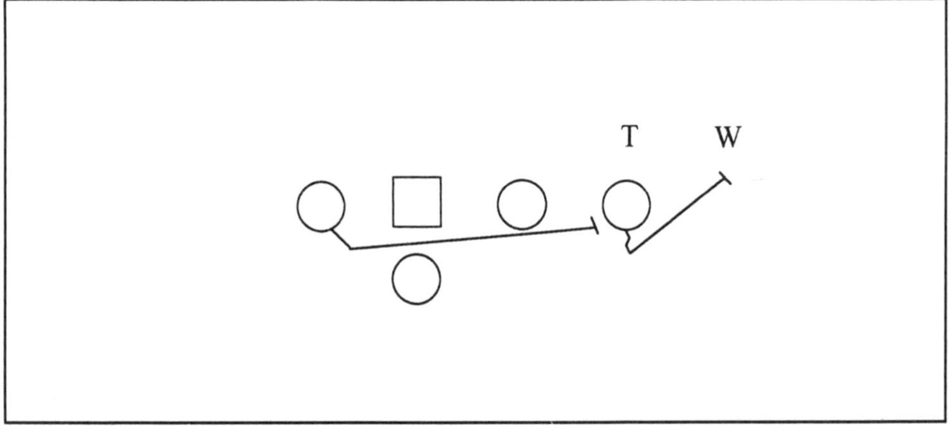

Diagram 4-9: The tackle influence block.

INFLUENCE BLOCK

Two types of influence blocks exist. Each of the types of influence blocks is a block that combines the technique of two different blocks. The influence block is part of a trapping scheme.

A trap scheme is a blocking scheme in which a lineman pulls on a trap angle from the offside. The trap scheme is one of the oldest blocking schemes in football. Some football coaches of the premodern era felt that the block should be outlawed due to its inherent trickery. It was deemed by many to be unsportsmanlike—and, as such, was given the slightly ill-suited name of "mouse-trap." The name was eventually shortened into the currently used expression "trap"—a less colorful moniker but a more football-like term.

One type of influence block—the pass influence block—is a baiting mechanism to draw the defensive lineman upfield to open a crease inside and make the defender a relatively easy target for the trapper. The pass influence block is a combination of a modified pass set and a trap pull. This block requires the blocker to pop his head and hands up to give the defensive lineman a "high-hat" read. This pass set tricks the defender into charging upfield to pass rush. The timing of the second phase of the pass influence block is such that just as the defender has his momentum going forward to rush the passer, the blocker pushes hard off his inside foot and takes a sharp inside-out trapping angle toward the nearest outside defender. In essence, two traps occur—the kick-out of the nearest outside defender by the influence blocker and the trap of the baited defender.

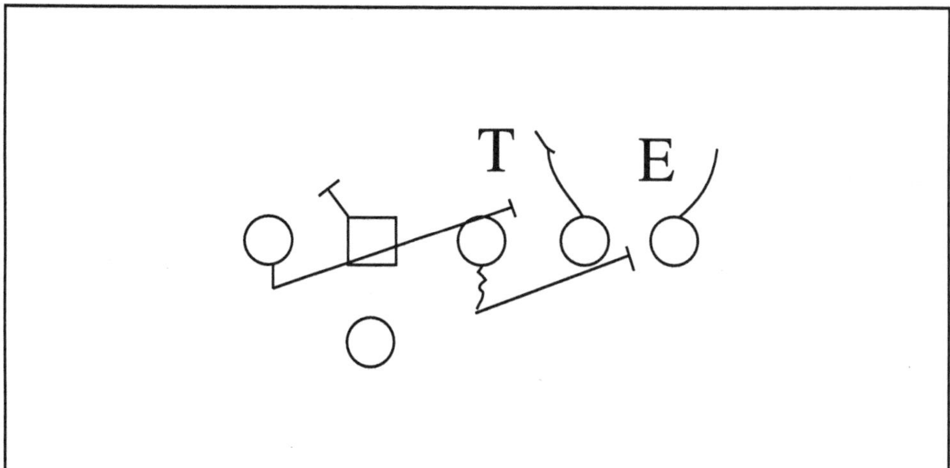

Diagram 4-10: An influence pass set by the right guard.

The second type of influence block—the pull influence block—is a baiting mechanism to draw the defender outward with an outside pull read. The pull influence is used in offenses that incorporate an extensive guard pulling game for sweeps and toss plays. If successful, it results in a wide gash opening inside of the defender, thereby giving the trapper an excellent trapping angle.

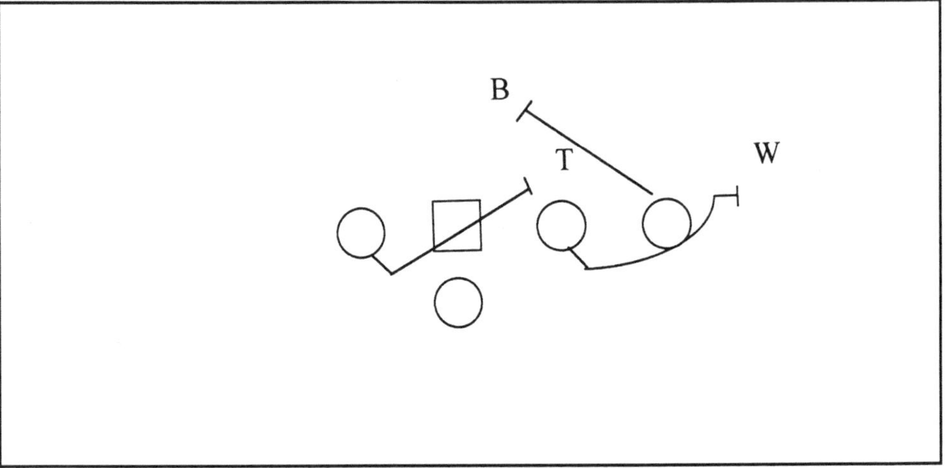

Diagram 4-11: An influence pull by the right guard.

A successful influence block includes the blocker adhering to the following coaching points:

- Selling the influence whether it is a pass influence or a pull influence.
- Pushing off the inside foot to dig into the line of scrimmage and kick-out the nearest outside defender.
- Sway up into a good pass pro demeanor.

LEVEL BLOCK

A level block is a backside blocking technique used exclusively by the tackle. The level block is normally used by the backside tackle when he happens to be aligned on the split side of the formation. When scenario occurs the defense will normally employ a stack alignment behind a weakside 4 and 5 technique tackle if there is no weakside tight end. The stack alignment may be a loose stack alignment or a vertical stack alignment.

The level blocking technique results in the offensive tackle moving on an upfield plane through the first two levels. The level blocking tackle's assignment is to cut-off the pursuit of any defender who attempts to cross his face. It is important that the tackle step to a point between the set-to-reach landmark and the set-to-drive landmark so that he can use only the outside half of his body to block the defender in his path. Ideally, the tackle wants to use his outside shoulder and flipper to slam the inside portion of the down defender before proceeding into the second level. The tackle's objective is to disrupt the pursuit of the defensive tackle and force him to go behind the block. Keeping the shoulders square as he moves upfield, the offensive tackle should immediately begin to search for the outside backer. The outside backer will likely hang for a moment before he begins to shuffle inside to check cutback. This momentary hang and shuffle action gives the level blocking tackle an opportunity to rip up through the defensive tackle's inside shoulder and move up through the second level to cut-off the pursuit of the linebacker.

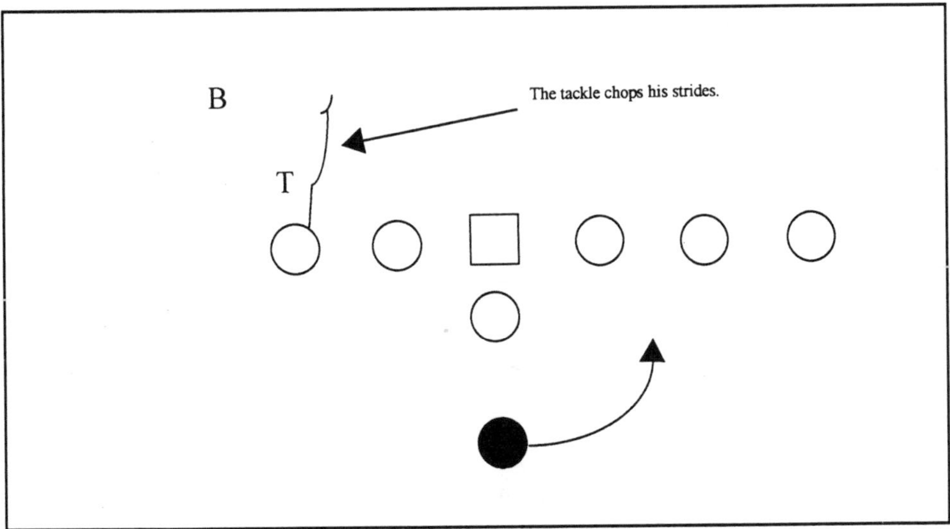

Diagram 4-12: The level block versus the loose stack.

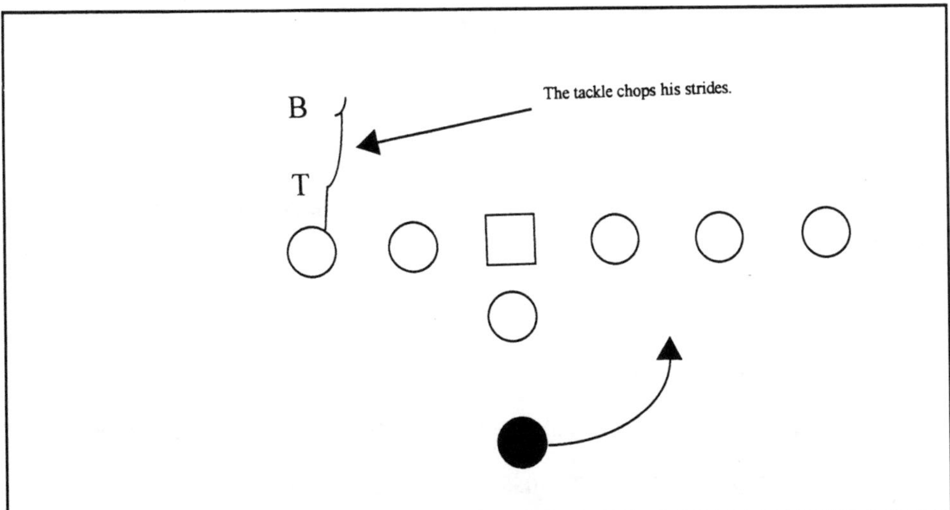

Diagram 4-13: The level block versus the vertical stack.

The level block is usually a fun block for the offensive tackle. If he executes the technique properly, he can be credited with blocking two defenders on one play. The level block is a particularly effective block on cutback plays. By moving up to the second level to wall out the outside linebacker, the offensive tackle can provide the touchdown breaking block on an inside cutback. It is the outside linebacker who normally is responsible for stopping the cutback.

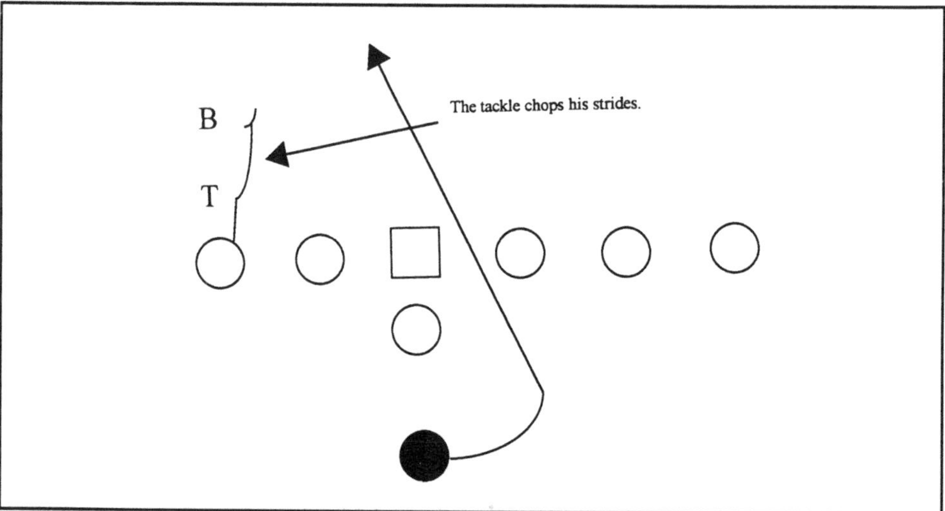

Diagram 4-14: The level block can break the cutback lane open.

One of the most important points of emphasis of the level block technique should be the necessity of the offensive tackle chopping his feet and widening his base as he enters the second level. By cutting his stride length and widening his feet, the blocker postures himself in the proper run-blocking demeanor to wall out the shuffling outside backer. The choppy footwork and the wide base also help to ensure the timing of the tackle's arrival at the junction point. Once the tackle reaches the junction point, he should execute a high "run through" block as he drives his outside shoulder pad into the chest of the outside linebacker.

An effective level blocking technique involves the following prescribed coaching points:

- Taking the appropriate set to level block.
- Keeping the shoulders square at all times.
- Chopping the feet and widening the base when moving into the second level.
- Preventing any defender from crossing the blocker's face.

FAN BLOCK

A fan block is an angle block toward the outside (i.e., away from the center). In this type of block, the blocker attacks the near hip of the defender. All factors considered, the fan block is one of the easier blocks to execute. This ease occurs because of the natural leverage angle created by the defender's alignment and the defender's relative position to the hole through which the ball carrier runs. When executing a fan block, the blocker must address the fact that a down defender will demonstrate one of two techniques. He may be either a penetrator—a defender who attacks the line of scrimmage on the snap or a reader—a defender who sits on the line of scrimmage and reacts to the blocking scheme.

In order to fan block a penetrator, the offensive lineman should pay close attention to his mechanics in maintaining the proper run-blocking demeanor. His feet should be slightly wider than his shoulders, and he should use his hands to punch, extend, and grab cloth on the chest of the defender. He must keep his shoulders on a lower plane than the defender's shoulders. His elbows should stay close to the body so that he may cement the fit into the defender. It is particularly important that the fan blocker keep his face up so that he doesn't become top-heavy in the block. Balance is one of the critical keys to executing an effective fan block.

On a fan block, the inside arm of the blocker is the dominant leverage arm. The fan blocker's inside arm fulfills the same role as the outside arm of the down blocker. Since both the fan block and the down block are angle blocks, the techniques are mirrored techniques. What the outside arm is for the down blocker is comparable to what the inside arm is for the fan blocker.

The fan blocker should drive his inside hand up through the near armpit of the defender. By punching to the armpit, the inside arm forces the inside pad of the defender to elevate. When one shoulder of a defender elevates, he becomes off balance and is easily toppled. Since the inside pad of the outside shade technique is his attack pad, driving the defender's inside shoulder upward removes his leverage.

The outside hand of the fan blocker punches to the inside number of the defender. The fan blocker should use his hand to grab cloth and control the defender. Extending the outside arm into the defender produces a lateral thrust. This thrust actually helps to facilitate the outward push of the blocker against the defender, thereby widening the hole. The outside arm also functions as a mechanism to allow the blocker to feel the pressure of the defender.

Feeling the pressure of the defender cues the blocker to redirect his momentum and maintain contact. The inside arm provides the lift and forces an imbalance of the defender's posture; the outside arm assists in knocking the defender outward and helps to cement the fit.

The wider the alignment of the defender, the flatter the attack angle the blocker should take. The placement of the set-to-drive step is dependent upon the defender's width and depth from the line of scrimmage. Staying on line to the defender's near hip is especially important for the success of the fan block. Firing out on too flat of an angle usually results in the defender easily ripping his outside shoulder across the face of the blocker. Firing out on too sharp of an angle usually results in the defender running behind the block to easily make the play. The fan block technique is particularly sensitive to the blocker making the proper set-to-drive and attack step.

The components of an effective fan block include the following factors:

- A proper set-to-drive step.
- A proper attack step.
- Keeping the eyes and hands on target.
- Maintaining a proper run-blocking demeanor.
- Fighting pressure so that the blocker can redirect and maintain the fit.

BUTT BLOCK

The butt block is a supplemental technique used with the set-to-reach step. Exclusively a backside blocking technique, the butt block may appear to be slightly unorthodox. It is, however, an effective technique to use against a backside

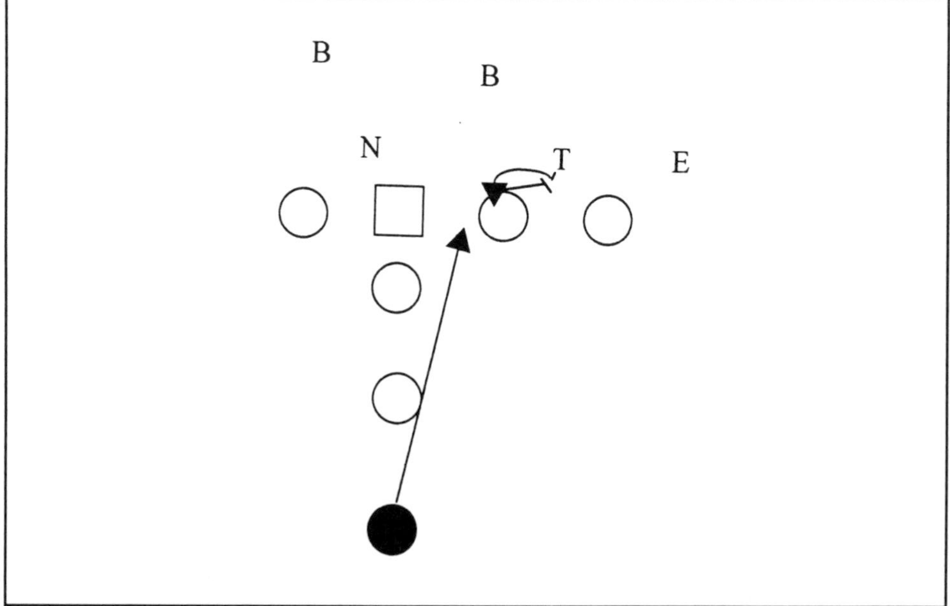

Diagram 4-15: The guard fires out too flat on his fan block, resulting in the defender crossing his face.

defender who attempts to "olay" behind the inside zone blocker. Similar to the level blocking technique, the butt block is only used by the offensive tackle against a 50 defensive front structure. The tackle should not use the butt block unless he is sure that a defensive lineman aligned on the backside guard is accounted for by a teammate. If the defensive lineman aligned on the guard is accounted for by rule, the backside tackle can freely use the butt block technique when he steps to reach playside.

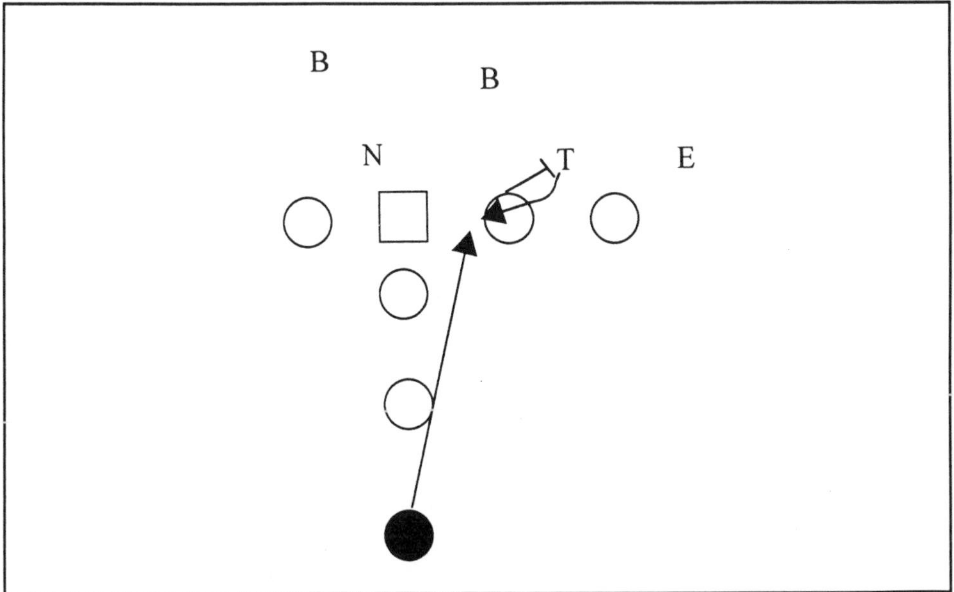

Diagram 4-16: The guard fires out too sharply on his fan block—the defender runs around and makes the play.

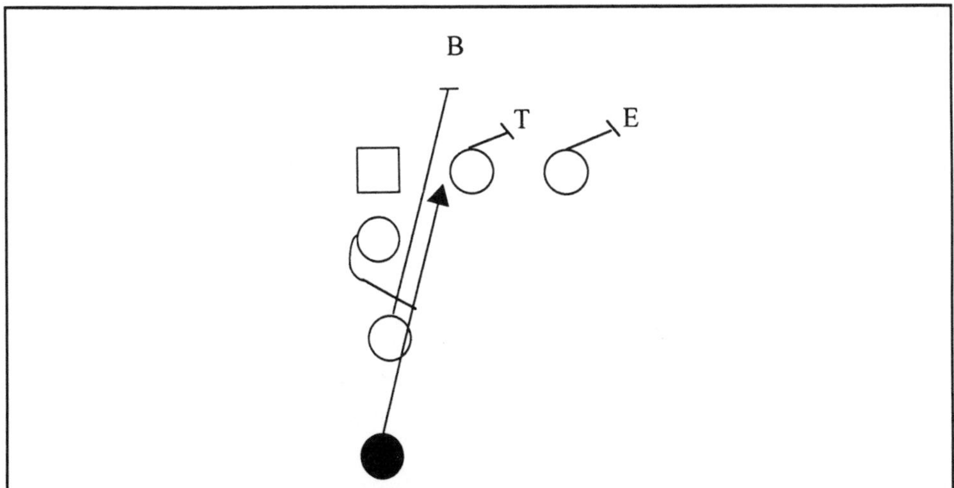

Diagram 4-17: An isolation play with effective fan blocking on the playside.

The butt blocking tackle uses his buttocks as the primary blocking surface. To use the butt blocking technique, the tackle sets to reach inside but plants and backs up into the playing defender. (The defender can be using an olay technique or simply attempting to run around the block as he dips behind the tackle's butt) When backing into the defender, the tackle will swing his backside arm as a large wing and hook the defender with his elbow. The finish position of the butt block involves a situation where the blocker is facing upfield and the defender is facing the backfield. They fit together closely at the hip—the tackle's outside hip to the defender's inside hip. To secure this hip-to-hip position, the tackle uses his outside arm to swing backward and pinch the defender between the back of his upper arm and his ribs. The tackle must then continue to shuffle his feet backward to maintain the fit which is secured by his outside arm.

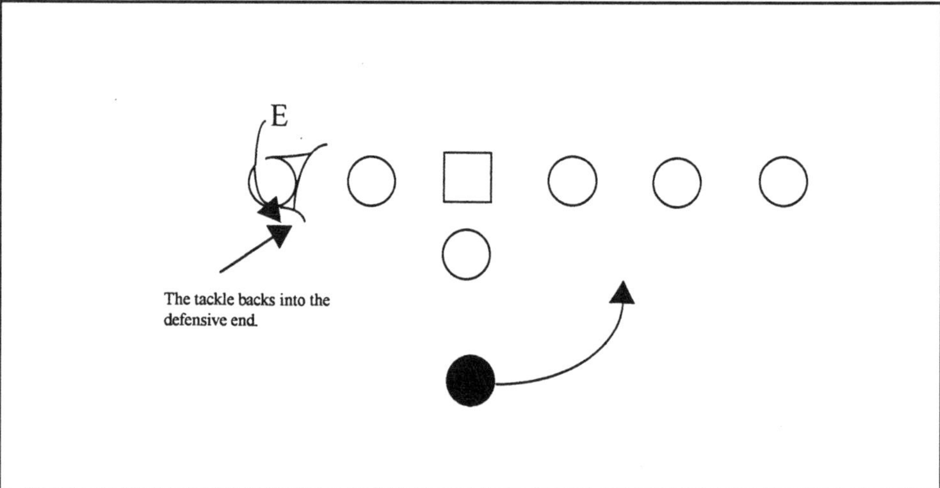

Diagram 4-18: The butt block.

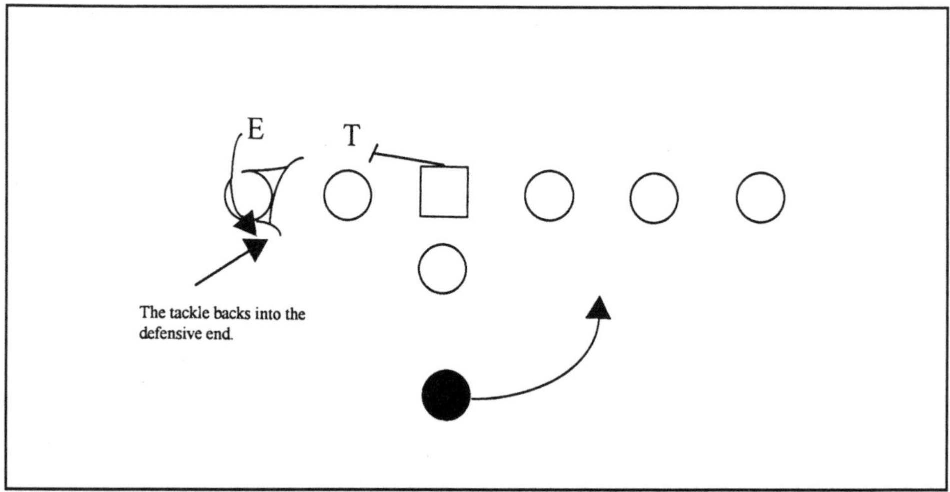

Diagram 4-19: The butt block is an option versus the even front when the center blocks back.

ESCAPE MOVES (OLAY AND RIP)

Two basic inside moves are used to clear a defender. These moves are closely linked to the influence block, since they are both escape mechanisms for a blocker to slip underneath a defensive lineman and thus create an inside crease for a trapper coming from the offside.

The first inside move to consider is the olay move. The term "olay" is a common term for a move used on both the offensive and defensive sides of the ball. It refers to a quick overhead swimming motion by the arm opposite the direction in which the player is going. On offense, the olay technique is normally used as an escape move to the inside. It is more commonly used by a tight end when escaping the clutches of the defensive end to release into a pass pattern. The tight end uses the olay technique to escape both to the outside and inside. For an offensive guard, the olay is an effective move to get to the inside and clear the trap bait.

To olay, the guard must quickly swim the outside hand over the head of the defender. The olay move is made easier by the guard setting to drive (or pass setting the defender) and immediately slapping the defender with the inside hand. The guard then drives the outside leg across the defender and swims the outside hand over the top. The outside hip must quickly follow the outside foot as the guard crosses the defender's face. The olay is extremely effective in creating a crease for the trapper to exploit.

The rip move is the more common escape move. As such, it offers its own unique advantage. First, the rip move is a slightly quicker escape move. The offensive lineman pushes hard off the outside foot and steps to a 45-degree angle inside with the inside foot. He rips his outside arm across the defender in an uppercut fashion as he dips his outside shoulder.

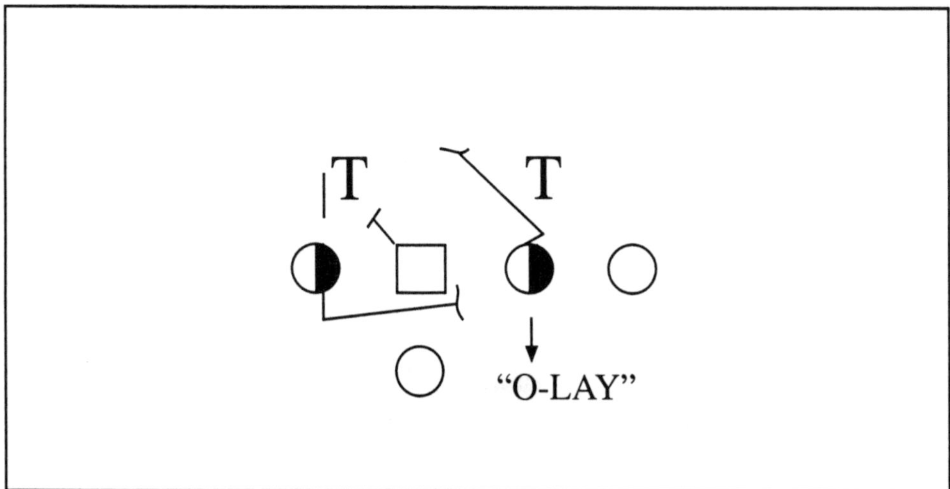

Diagram 4-20: The guard executes an olay move to the inside.

Dipping the outside shoulder decreases the available surface area that the defensive lineman can use as leverage. The defensive lineman is trained to shoot his hands inside to the chest of the blocker. When the blocker's outside shoulder dips and twists across the defender, the defender has no surface to strike with his outside hand. A defensive lineman—even a well-coached one—tends to respond to the blocker's lowered shoulder by placing his outside hand on the back of the blocker's shoulder. The act of the defender placing his hand on the back of the blocker's shoulder actually assists the ripping blocker in gaining clearance to the inside. The defender will normally push against the back of the blocker's shoulder, thereby aiding him in crossing the blocker's face. Defensive coaches often work hard on training the defensive linemen to keep their outside hand low—under the ripping blocker's outside shoulder.

The blocker uses his outside arm to drive across the defender's body and to break free to the inside. Once the second step is completed, the ripping blocker will work upfield with his shoulders square. According to his assignment, the escaping blocker will work up through the second level to seal a linebacker or combo-off a 3 technique.

When a defensive lineman is aligned on an inside teammate, the ripping offensive lineman should use a glide step in finishing his escape (the reader should refer to the section on glide stepping for more details). When no defensive lineman is positioned on the offensive lineman to the inside, the ripping lineman will take a more angular first step (i.e., flatter down the line of scrimmage). Stepping flatter into the line of scrimmage allows the ripping lineman to gain more clearance from the baited defensive lineman.

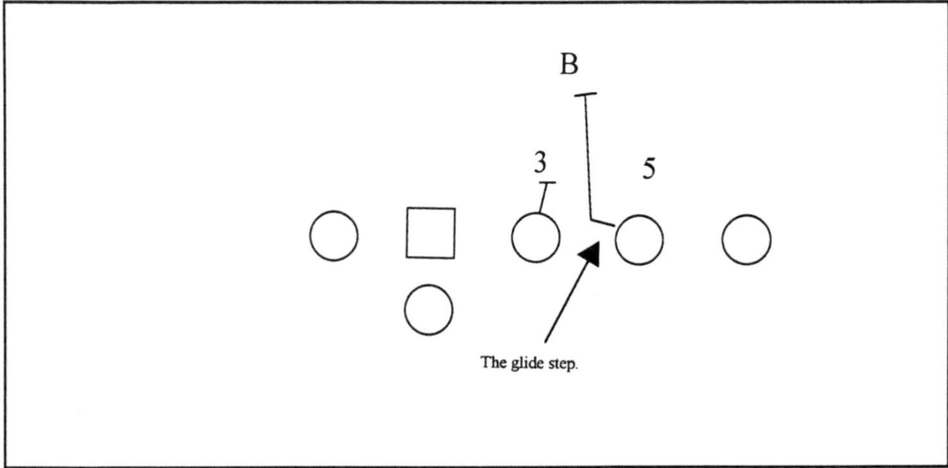

Diagram 4-21: The tackle rips inside with a glide step.

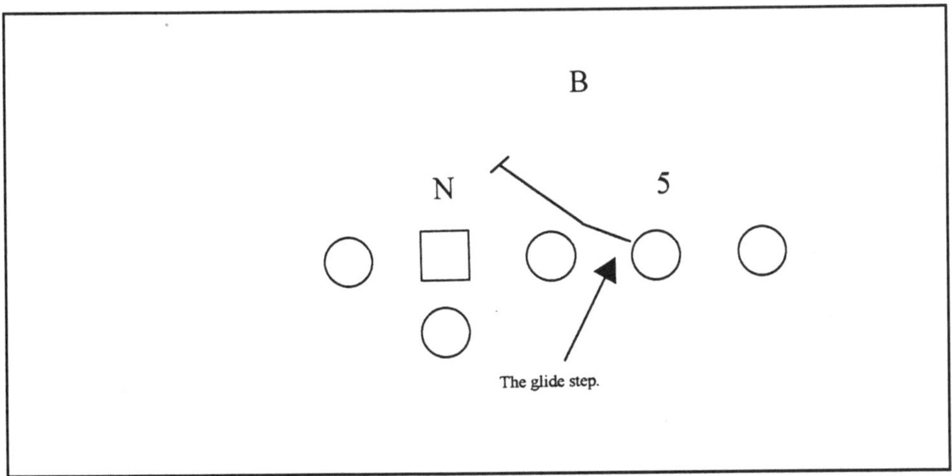

Diagram 4-22: The glide step can be flatter depending on the defensive alignment and the tackle's assignment.

A blocker who uses either an olay move or a rip move should focus on achieving the following objectives:

- Clearing the defender with the outside hip snapping across the defender.
- Taking the appropriate inside step to accomplish the secondary objective.
- Quickly swimming over or ripping under the outside arm.
- Taking a good split so that the defender can't jam him inside.
- Setting up the swim move with a set to drive and a slap to the inside shoulder of the defender.

ARC RELEASE

The arc release is a block used by the tight end to escape the defensive end and to release outside to block a second- or third-level defender. The arc release is also used by the tight end to get a wide release and to run a vertical pass route into the seam of the secondary.

To execute an arc release, the tight end executes a sweep pull technique to the outside. The bucket step of the outside foot creates distance from the line of scrimmage. Unlike the drop step type of bucket step by a loop blocker in the fold blocking combination, the arc-release bucket step includes a pivot and push off of the inside foot to gain width. The cushion created by the bucket step prevents the defensive end from getting his hands on the tight end. Adequate depth also allows the arc-releasing tight end to read the action of the secondary force. Once the depth is gained, the tight end squares his shoulders and looks upfield.

Used primarily with option attacks, the arc release gets the tight end to the defensive flank with a desirable degree of timing. As a blocker, the arc-releasing tight end's normal role is to work upfield to position himself so that he may hook the force defender. (The force defender is the secondary defender who is responsible for turning the ball carrier inside to the defensive pursuit.)

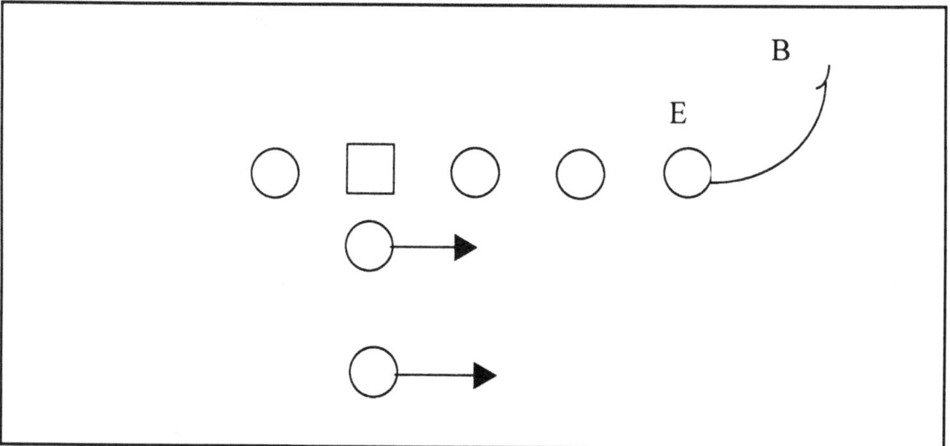

Diagram 4-23: The arc block by an arc-releasing tight end.

BLOCK RELEASE

An escape mechanism used exclusively by the tight end, the block release allows the tight end to attack the defensive end, then use his leverage to release cleanly into the pass pattern. The block releasing tight end slams his shoulder into the defender. The tight end's head is kept to the side of the desired release. For an outside block release, the end slams the defender with his inside shoulder. Once the blow is delivered, the end quickly disengages and releases into the pattern. A key coaching point of the block release is the tight end's leverage on the defender. The tight end must strike the blow from the hips and hit upward through the defender.

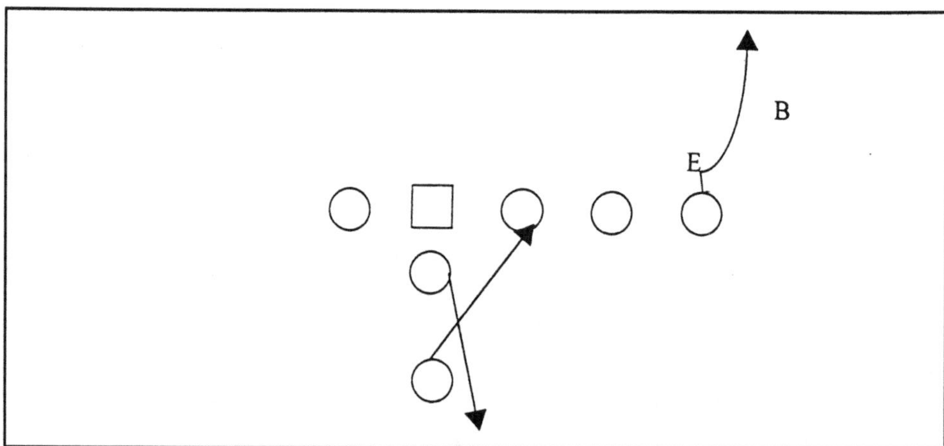

Diagram 4-24: The block release by the tight end.

ALLEY BLOCK

The alley block is a backside cut-off block that is carried up through the third level. Once a cut-off blocker has worked upfield to cut-off the pursuit of the first and second level defenders, the cut-off blocker turns to sprint to the sideline. The width to which he sprints is dependent upon the width of the play called. If the play is a wide play (such as a sweep), the alley blocker will sprint further across the field because the alley will be wider. When the alley is wide, the alley blocker should sprint across the field at a depth of approximately seven yards deep. He will intercept the alley just as the ball carrier hits the alley with his shoulders square. If the play is an off-tackle play, the alley will be tighter. When the alley is tight to the ball, the alley blocker will angle further upfield to enter the alley approximately 10 to 15 yards downfield.

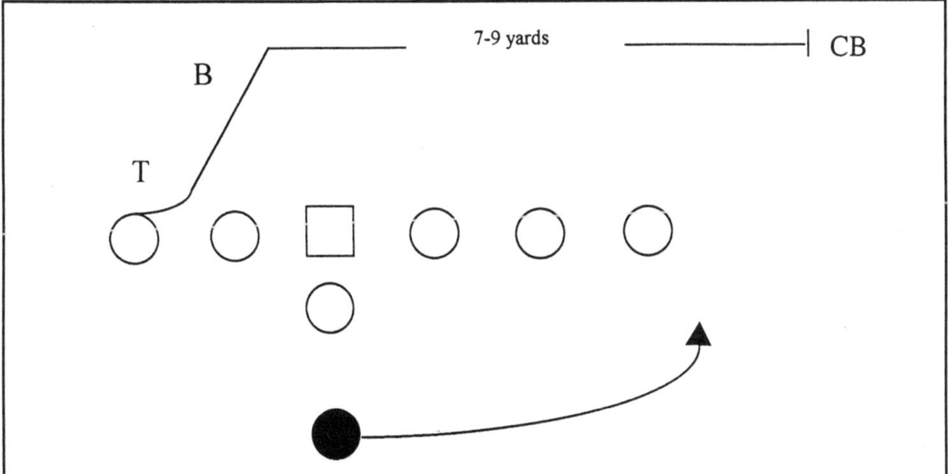

Diagram 4-25: The alley block for the wide play.

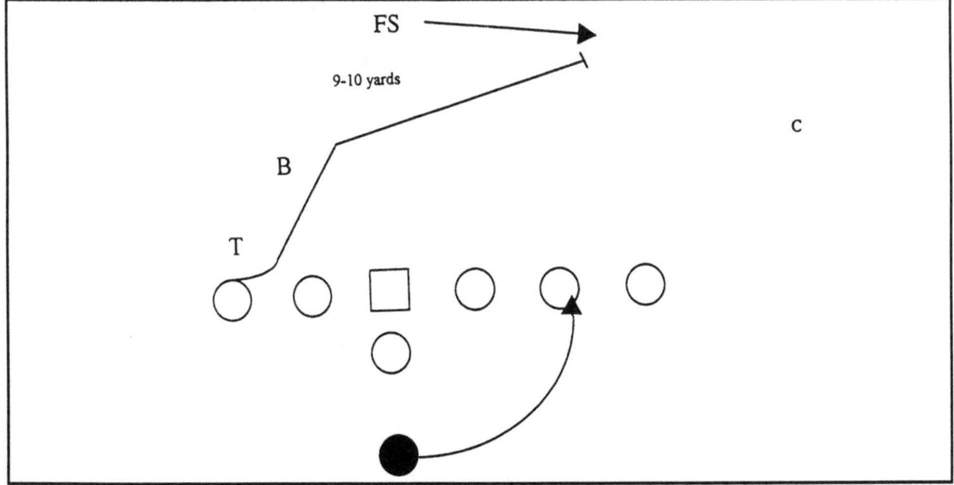

Diagram 4-26: The alley block for the off-tackle play.

The primary objective of the alley blocker is to enter the alley on a near-perpendicular path to the ball carrier and blindside a third-level tackler. The most common recipient of an alley block is the free safety. A free safety usually attempts to fill the alley and make the hit on the ball carrier. In filling the alley, the free safety intently focuses on the ball carrier. The alley blocker will get a blindside shot on the free safety as he attacks from the inside. The alley blocker should make sure that the momentum of his block is delivered from a position that is forward of the free safety, thereby avoiding the possibility of a illegal block in the back. Backside linemen who hustle and master the alley blocking technique will often help facilitate a situation where a long rushing play is broken into a touchdown rushing play.

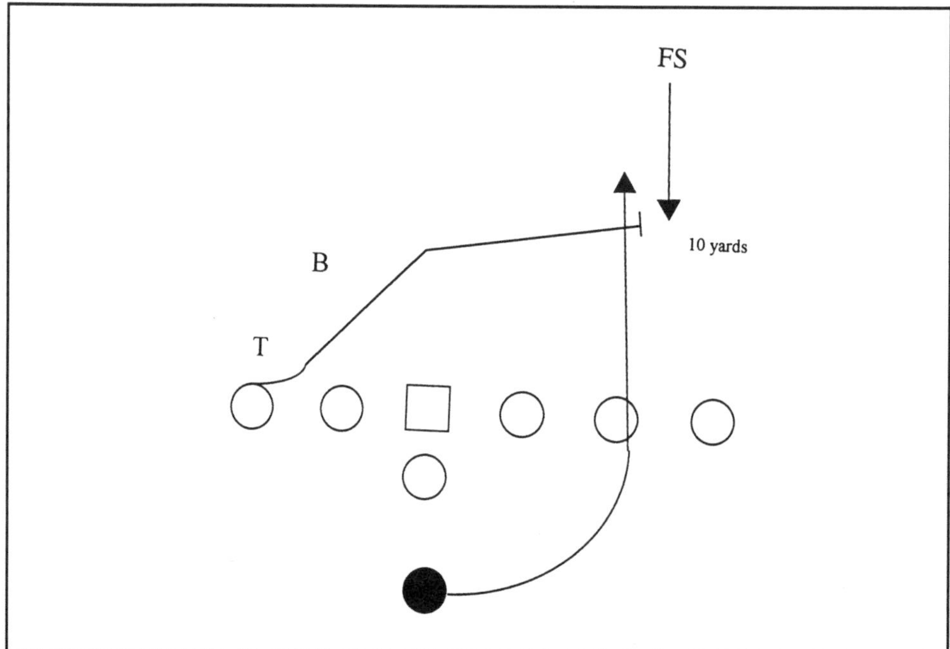

Diagram 4-27: The alley block blindsides the free safety in the alley.

The free safety is often unaccounted for by the blocking scheme. By utilizing your offensive linemen in this manner, you can provide a means of accounting for the free safety. The alley block can be performed by any backside blocking technique who eventually works his way through the second level. The alley block can be performed off of the inside zone or the fold block.

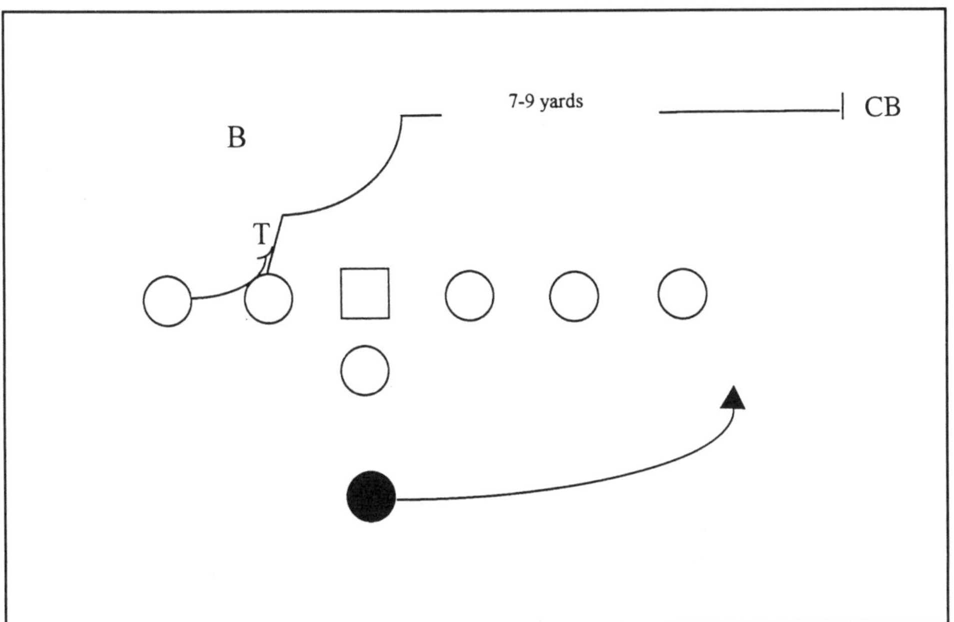

Diagram 4-28: The alley block for the wide play off an inside zone block.

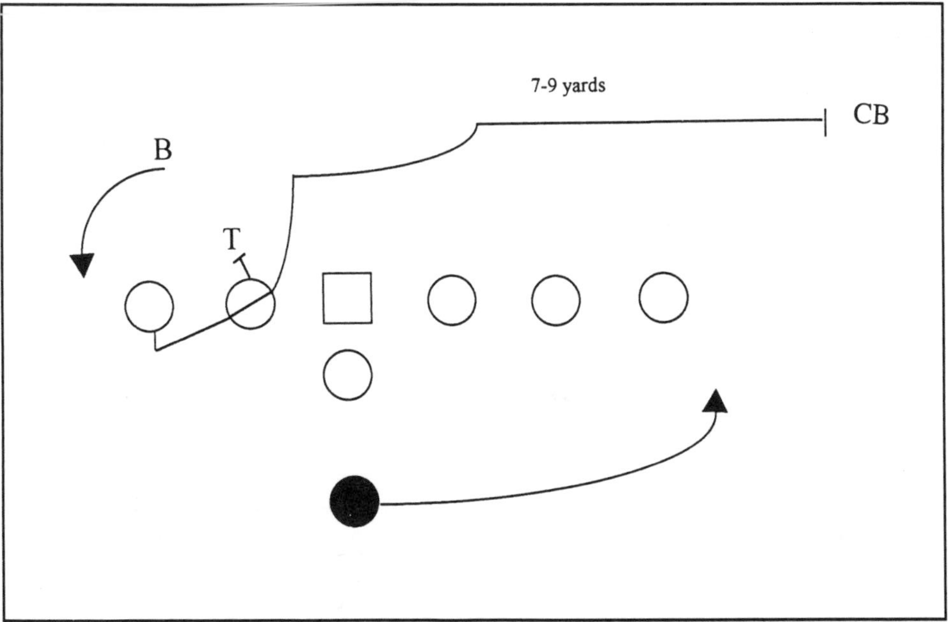

Diagram 4-29: The alley block for the wide play off a tag block.

REACH (HOOK) BLOCK

The reach block (i.e., hook block) is by definition an onside blocking technique. It is technically the outside portion of the outside zone block described in Chapter 5. To perform a reach block, the onside offensive lineman should set to reach. Setting to reach involves the blocker pushing off his inside foot and taking a set-to-reach step with his outside foot. The second step is made through the crotch of the defender as the blocker rips his inside arm across the defender's chest. The blocker can use his inside arm to rip with the flipper and secure the fit against the defender. The reach blocker's objective is to initially overtake the defender in width. The reach blocker can then ride the outside shoulder of the defender as he works up to the next level.

The reach blocker should use his flipper to push against the defender and prevent the defender from grabbing the blocker and pulling him to the ground. Lateral movement with outside leverage is integral to a successful reach block.

The reach block is the mirrored blocking technique of the inside zone blocking combination "zone" call. Both blocks are J blocks that are characterized by the blocker flattening his path to junction the defender's pursuit.

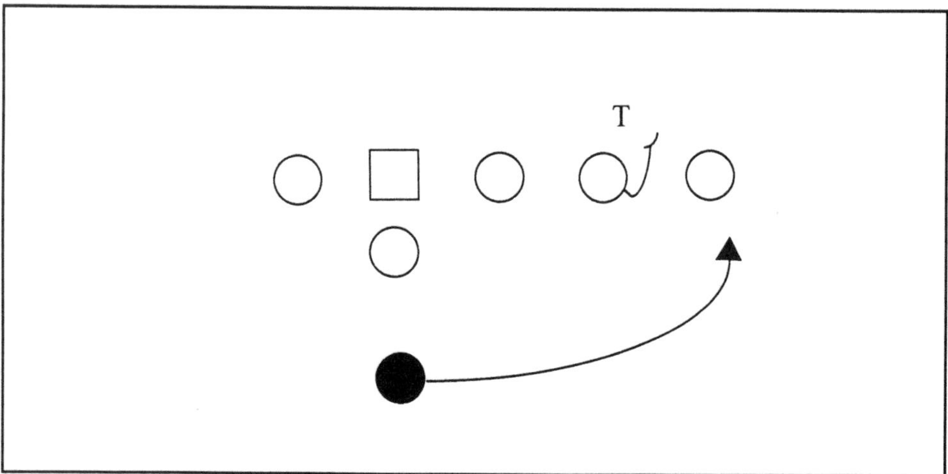

Diagram 4-30: The reach block.

CHAPTER 5

Two-Man Blocks

The second major category of offensive line run blocks is the two-man block. Two-man blocks involve blocking techniques executed by two linemen working together as a tandem unit. Among the various types of two-man blocks are the following:

- Combo block
- Cross block
- Deuce block
- Double team
- Fold block
- Inside zone block
- Outside zone block

COMBO BLOCK

Also known as the bump block, the combo block is an excellent scheme to counter defensive stack alignments. The combo is nearly identical to the double-team block in that it consists of a post block and a seal block executed by two adjacent offensive linemen.

The primary objective of a combo block is two-fold—vertical movement of the down defender accomplished with an outside seal of the linebacker. The inside man (the post blocker) of the combo block drives his man backward, thereby winning the three-inch battle.

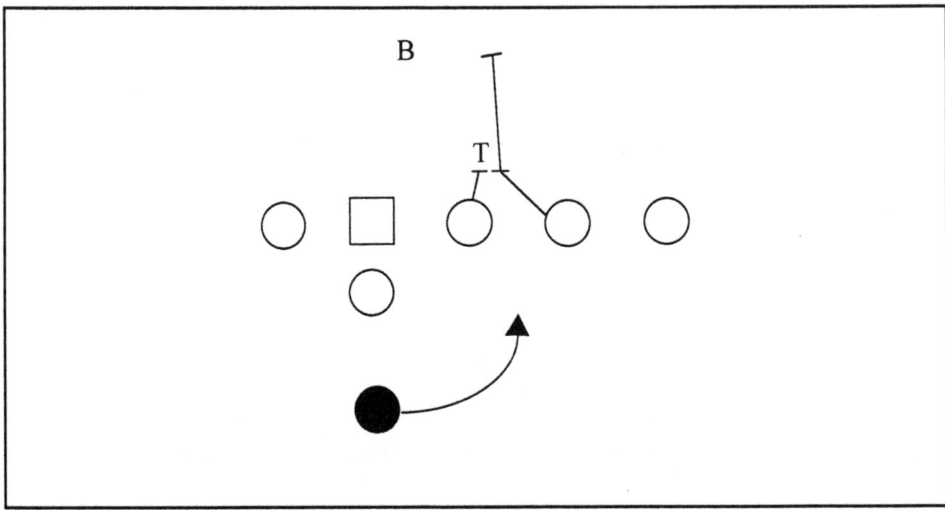

Diagram 5-1: A guard-tackle combo with the guard as the post blocker and the tackle as the seal blocker.

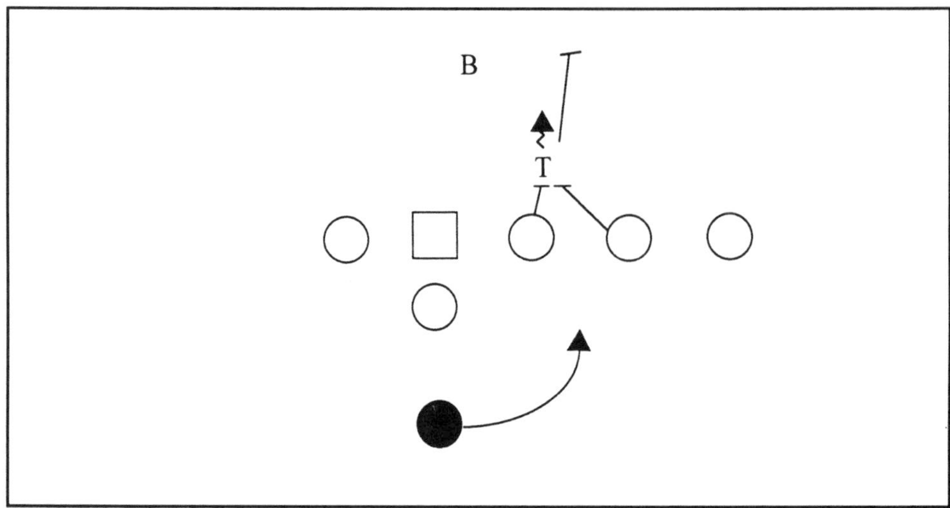

Diagram 5-2: Vertical movement of the defensive lineman is the primary objective of the combo block.

The outside man (seal blocker) glide steps inside and strikes the defensive lineman with the flat surface of his inside shoulder pad. The seal blocker's primary objective is to lift and turn the outside shoulder of the defender. This action opens the shoulders of the defensive lineman so that the post blocker can swing his hips to the outside and gain outside leverage as he drives the defender upfield. When the defender's outside shoulder is elevated and twisted backward, the blocking surface is increased for the post blocker. The post blocker then needs only to slide his head and hips to the outside edge of the defensive lineman to gain outside leverage as he drives him upfield.

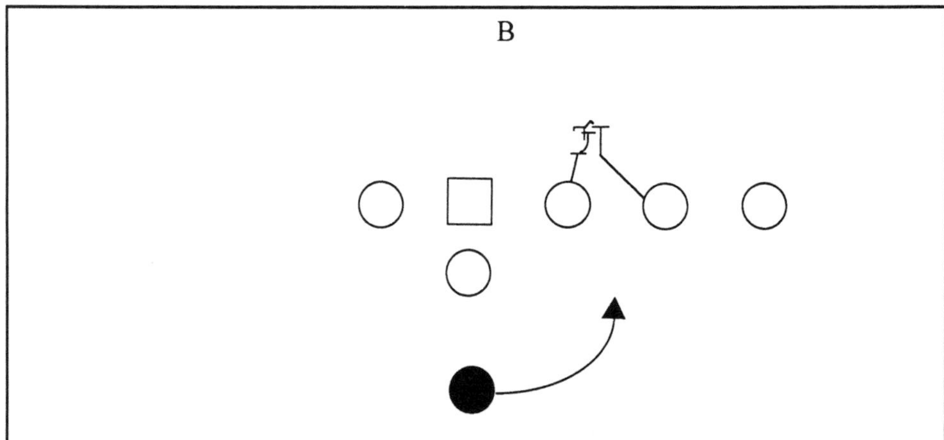

Diagram 5-3: Seal blocker knocks the defender's outside shoulder backward.

After driving through the outside shoulder of the defensive lineman, the seal blocker ricochets off the block and cuts the outside thigh pad of the linebacker. This portion of the combo block is sometimes referred to as the "bump-seal."

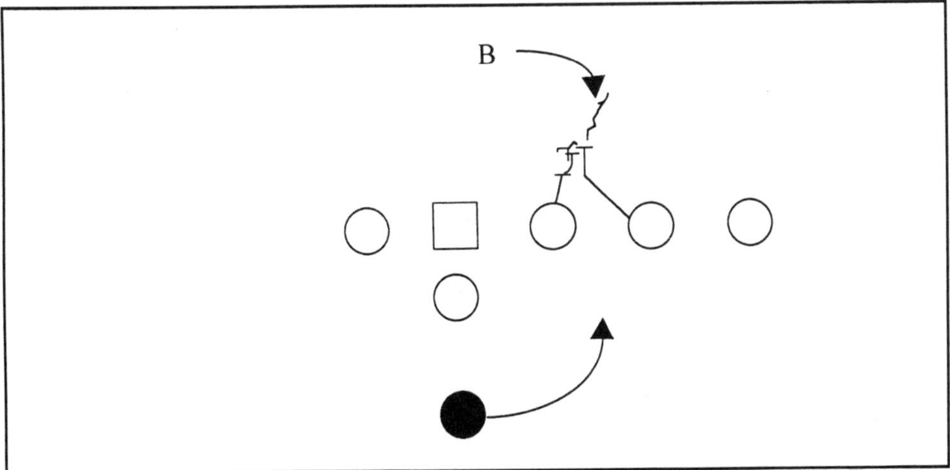

Diagram 5-4: The seal blocker knocks the defender's outside shoulder backward and then seals the linebacker.

The dynamics of the combo block allow it to account for any action of the stacked defenders. This feature of accountability versus the stack games (stunts) begins with the set to drive step by the post blocker. The post blocker will set to drive with either his outside foot or his inside foot, depending upon the anticipated action of the down defender. If the defender is aligned in a position from which he could stunt inside, the post blocker sets to drive with his inside foot. If the defender is aligned in a definite outside shade, the post blocker sets to drive with his outside foot because the defender is not a threat to successfully stunt inside. It should be kept in mind that the set-to-drive step—if properly executed—is only a four-inch step. The post blocker keeps his pads square at all times. Over-striding on the set-to-drive step inside will create a gap between the hips of the post blocker and the seal blocker.

The second feature of the combo block that provides accountability for the stack games is the hip-to-hip coaching point. Although the post blocker has some responsibility in maintaining hip-to-hip contact with the seal blocker; it is primarily the responsibility of the seal blocker to establish the hip-to-hip relationship. Once their hips make contact, the seal blocker must work to maintain this hip-to-hip relationship with the post blocker. Maintaining hip-to-hip contact between the seal blocker and the post blocker guarantees the seal between the two blockers and denies the down defender the opportunity to split the blockers.

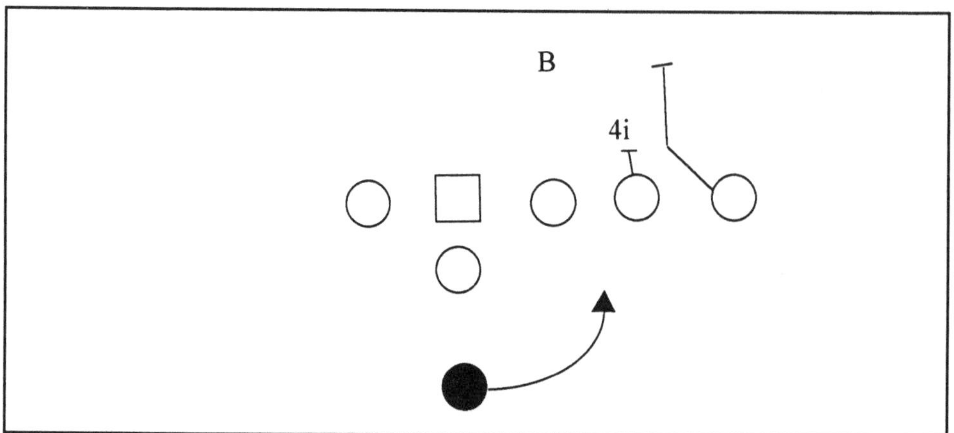

Diagram 5-5: Versus a defender shaded inside, the post blocker sets to drive his inside foot.

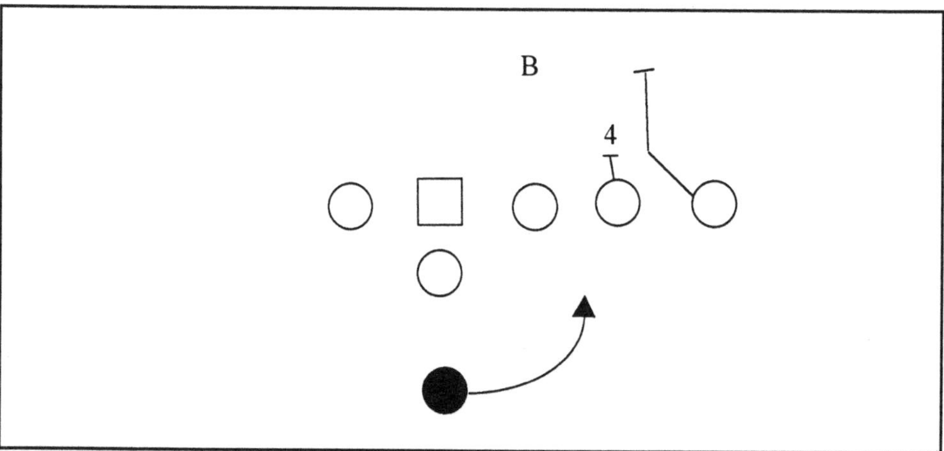

Diagram 5-6: Versus a defender aligned head up, the post blocker sets to drive with his inside foot.

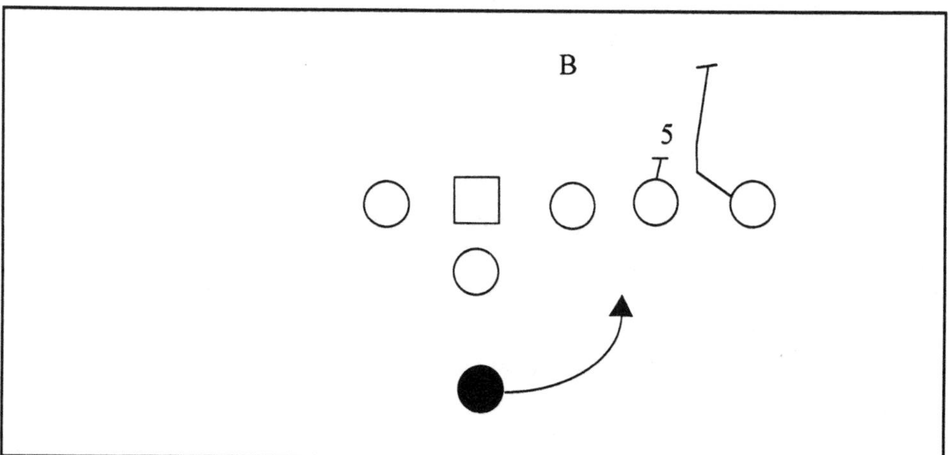

Diagram 5-7: Versus a defender shaded outside, the post blocker sets to drive with his outside foot.

If the down defender splits the blocker's hips, he can keep outside leverage on the post blocker and break the seal of the combo. It should be remembered that sealing the defenders inside is the second element of the two-fold objective of the combo block.

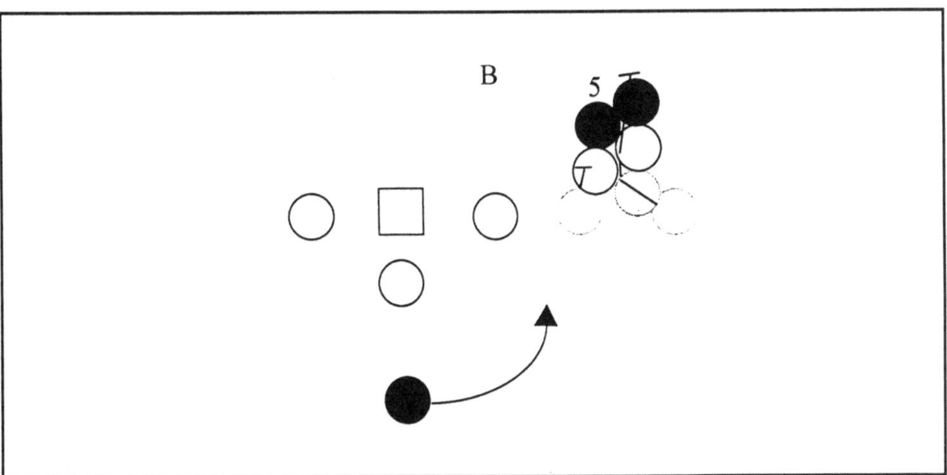

Diagram 5-8: The seal blocker is responsible for maintaining hip-to-hip contact with the post blocker.

Achieving lift on the defender is one of the primary goals of the two blockers. Lift is accomplished by both blockers punching upward in an uppercut manner to the defensive lineman's breast plates. Some defenders—particularly outside shaded defenders—will attempt to drop to the ground when they recognize the seal blocker glide stepping inside. This defensive technique can break down the integrity of the hip-to-hip seal if the blockers are not hitting on the rise through the defender.

To hit on the rise, both blockers should use their near arm as a hook. The seal blocker uses his inside arm as a hook, while the post blocker uses his outside arm as a hook. If the blockers keep their shoulders square, the hooking technique with the near arms can catch the defender before he drops to the ground.

An important coaching point to emphasize is that: *You should coach your seal blocker to stay engaged on a down defender until he feels vertical movement on the defender—or until he feels the defender stunt inside across the face of the post blocker.* The uppercut hooking technique by both blockers is discussed in greater detail in this chapter's section on the double-team block.

For the seal blocker to contact the outside shoulder flush with his inside shoulder pad, the blocker has to glide step. The glide step is a sideways step inside to the post blocker. A good glide step is made slightly upfield with the toes pointing forward. The step is enhanced by the blocker pushing forcefully off his outside foot.

A proper glide step keeps the shoulders square as the seal blocker engages the defender and allows the blocker to use his inside arm in the hooking manner described previously. The glide step is also the first step of an escape move used by a playside blocker on the trap. Escape moves are discussed in greater detail in Chapter 4.

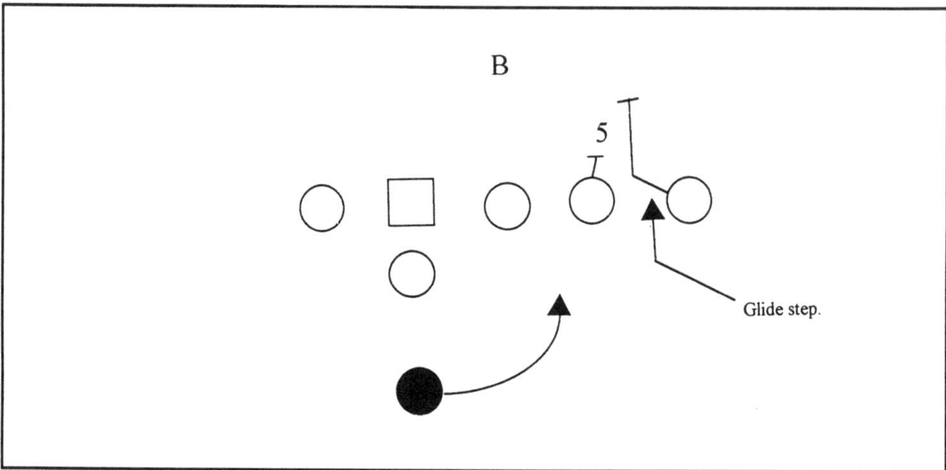

Diagram 5-9: The seal blocker takes a glide step.

As previously stated, a successful combo block achieves two primary objectives—the down defender is knocked off the ball and sealed inside and the scraping linebacker is cut down by the seal blocker. To cut down the linebacker, the glide-stepping seal blocker must rip his inside arm and pad through the outside pad of the down defender. As he clears the defender, the seal blocker must look inside to pick up the angle of the linebacker's scrape. He should then adjust his path and chop his stride to junction the linebacker from a snug outside-in blocking demeanor.

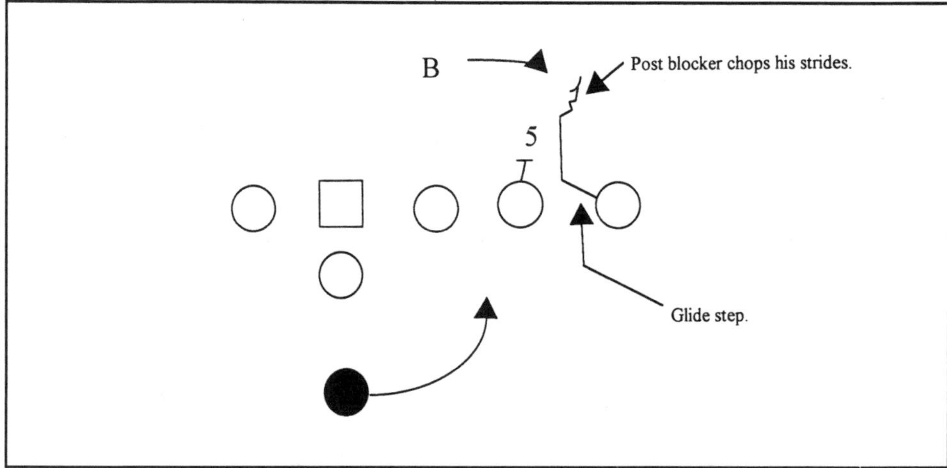

Diagram 5-10: The seal blocker chops his strides off the down defender.

Two finishing techniques are available to the seal blocker. The seal blocker may either finish the combo block by driving his inside shoulder pad through the outside hip and thigh pad of the linebacker or finish the combo block by drive blocking the linebacker with a good fit and run-blocking demeanor. If the seal blocker attempts to cut the linebacker, he should make sure he snaps his head up as he delivers the blow to the outside hip of the linebacker.

Many offensive linemen tend to drop their head down when they execute a cut block. This action is a major blocking flaw which prevents the blocker from hitting through the defender. When the head is down, the force of the blow is delivered toward the turf. The point to emphasize is that the blocker should always strike the opponent with a low-to-high blow delivery.

A few additional factors should be considered concerning the seal block combination. The coaching points for the post blocker and the seal blocker account for all possible defensive stunts. If the down defender stunts outside as shown in Diagram 5-11, the combo block turns into a double team. When gliding inside, the seal blocker should keep his eyes on the near foot and hip of the down defender. If the defender's outside foot steps outward, the seal blocker can recognize the defender stunting outside. Once the seal blocker recognizes the outside stunt, he converts the combo block into a solid double team block.

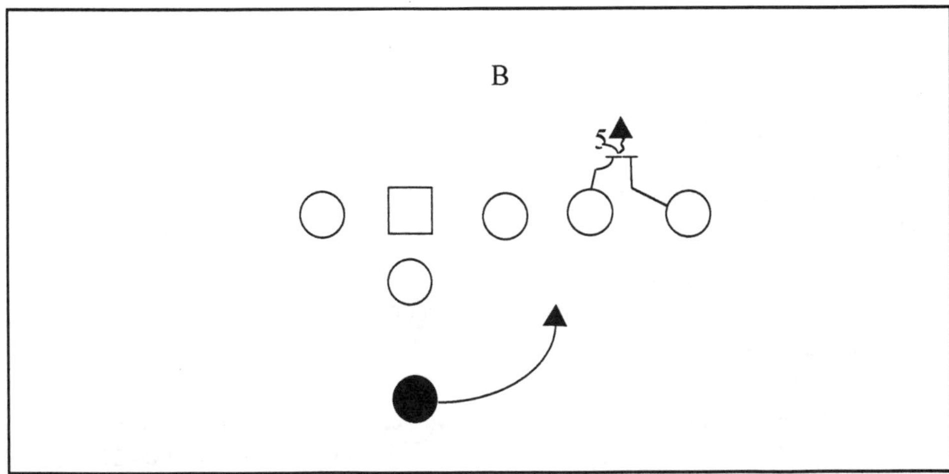

Diagram 5-11: The seal blocker sticks on the defender stunting outside.

If the down defender stunts inside, the seal blocker can read the near foot and hip of the defender disappearing inside. The seal blocker can then immediately find the linebacker. Searching out the linebacker allows the seal blocker to immediately move to junction the linebacker's path. When the down defender stunts inside, the seal blocker should use the drive blocking technique against the linebacker. Such a defensive game characteristically has a tight scraping linebacker. In such a situation

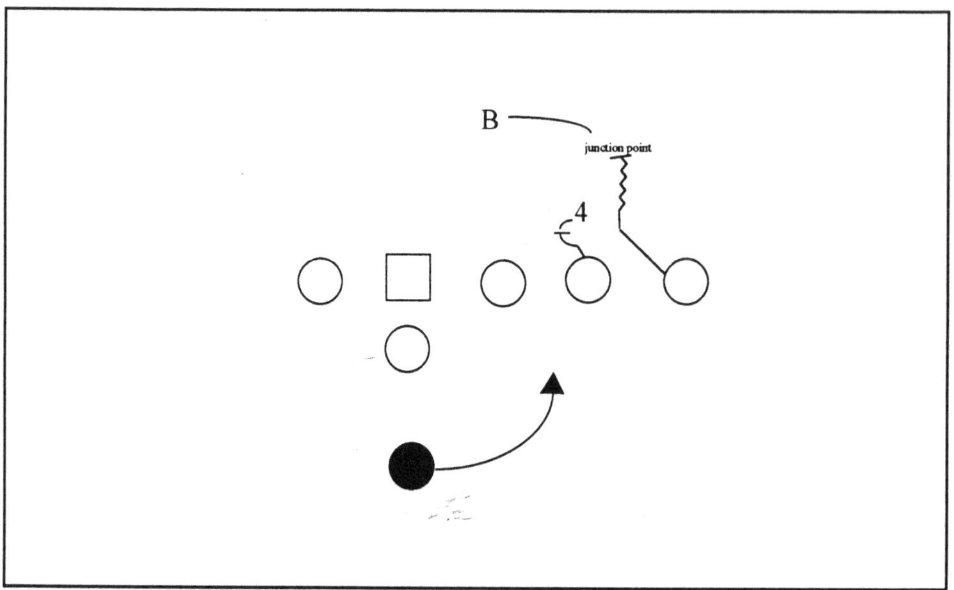

Diagram 5-12: The seal blocker moves up to the second level to junction the linebacker when the down defender stunts inside.

the face-up drive blocking technique with a good fit and run-blocking demeanor is the better technique against a tight scraping linebacker.

CROSS BLOCK

The cross block is similar to the fold block in that two blockers cross paths to create a seam. However, that similarity is the only common ground between these two types of two-man blocks. Performed by two adjacent offensive linemen, the cross block is a blocking scheme in which two blockers perform angle blocks on two down defenders.

The blocker positioned on the outside of the tandem goes first as he executes a down block. The inside blocker takes a position step with his outside foot, opening his shoulders so that his outside teammate has clearance for his down block. The inside blocker should jerk his outside elbow backward to open his hips as he position steps. His initial step is very similar to the first step of a G-block pull. The trap pull section on the G block in Chapter 6 provides a detailed discussion of the G-block technique.

As the down blocker clears underneath the set of the inside blocker, the inside blocker takes his second step. As the inside blocker steps with his inside foot on the second step, he should reach to grab the outside cheek of the down blocker's buttocks. Using his inside hand, the inside blocker should pull himself forward on a tight angle off the tail of the down blocker. This reach-and-pull technique with the inside hand ensures a tight fit off the tail of the down blocker and a good inside-out path to the defender.

To finish the hybrid fan block-trap pull, the inside blocker aims for the near hip of the defender. Against a reading defender, the fit of the inside blocker's technique must be that of a proper fan block—not too flat and not too sharp. The one-man fan block section in Chapter 4 provides an overview discussion of the proper landmark of the fan block. Against a penetrating defender who is ignoring the down block of the outside blocker, the fan block becomes a short trap pull. The inside blocker must kick out the penetrating defender with the trap pull technique, using his outside shoulder to drive the defender outward.

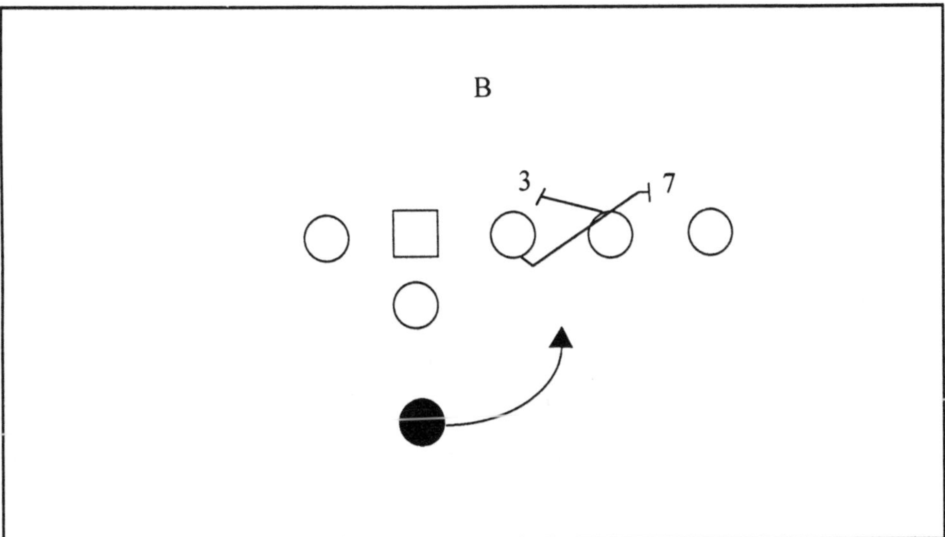

Diagram 5-13: The cross block.

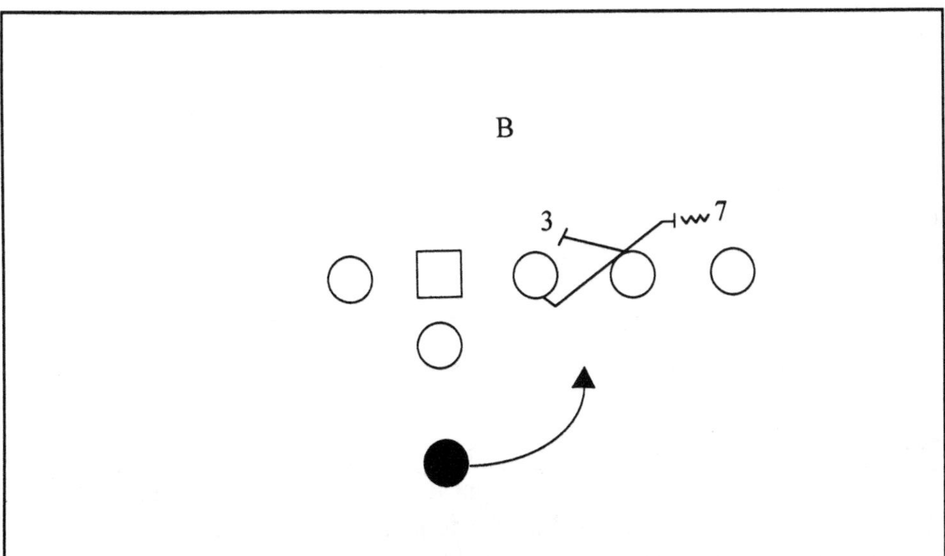

Diagram 5-14: The cross block versus a reading defender.

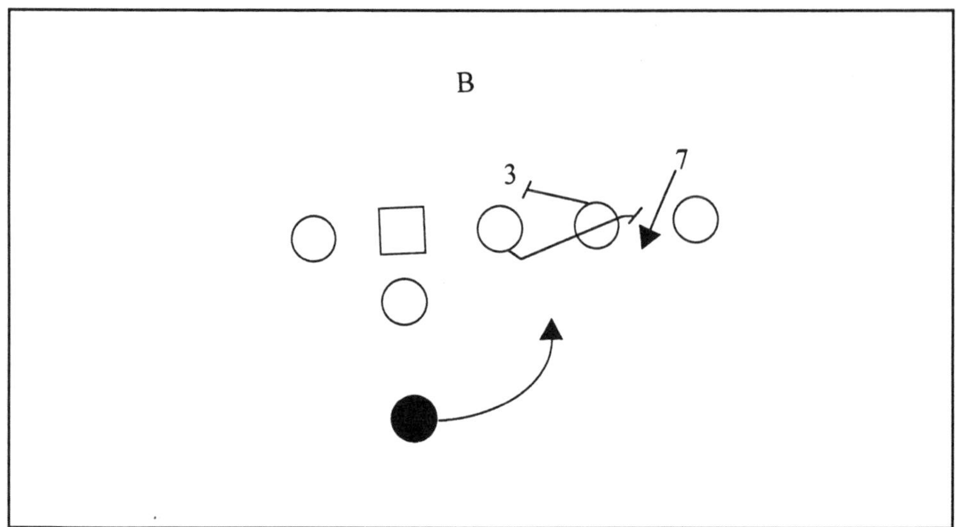

Diagram 5-15: The cross block versus a penetrating defender.

The cross block is an excellent isolation scheme against an 4-4 even front. When facing a playside 3 technique tackle with a playside 7 technique end, the cross block scheme is the favored scheme for splitting the "B" gap on the isolation play.

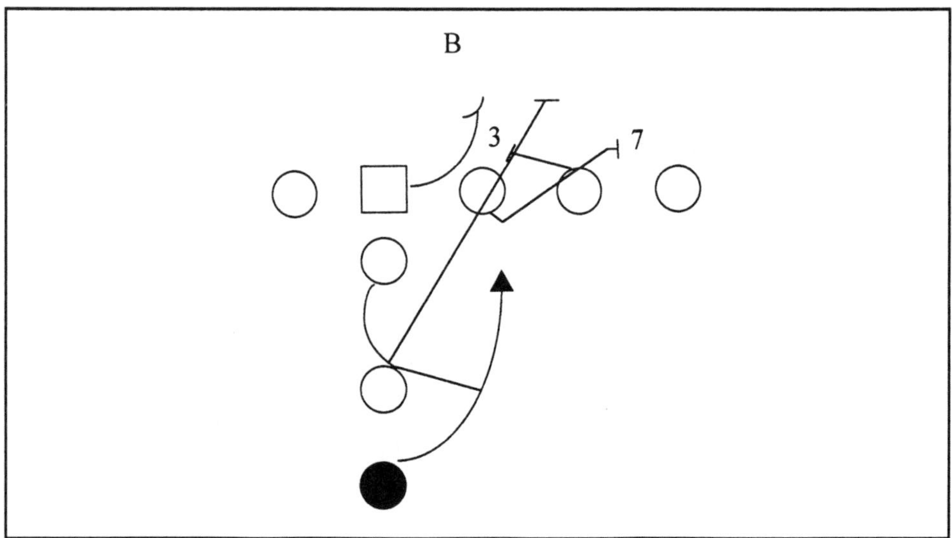

Diagram 5-16: The isolation play with a cross block.

The cross block is also a great way to split the weakside of the defense from the one-back set when the defensive front removes a linebacker to cover a running back who is aligned as a wide receiver. The trips formation can provide you with an excellent opportunity to use the cross block against the weak side of the defensive front.

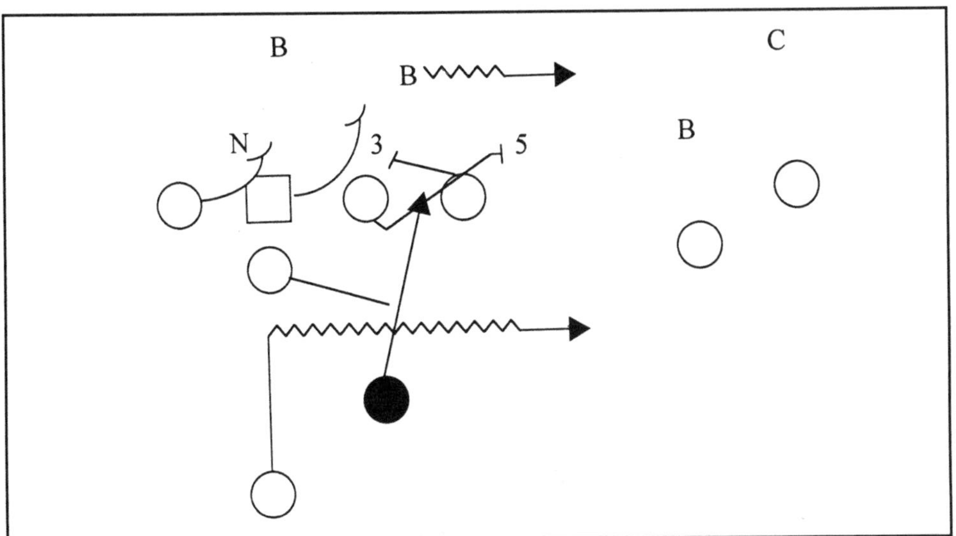

Diagram 5-17: The dive play with a cross block off motion to the trips formation.

An important coaching point with regard to the cross block is that it is basically a line call. This point refers to the fact that the block is called at the line by one of the two blockers. Since the block is usually executed by the playside guard and the tackle, the block is normally called by the guard when he and the tackle are each facing a defensive lineman. The cross block should only be called when the inside blocker is facing an outside shade. If the inside blocker is facing an inside shade, the cross block scheme is an inappropriate scheme.

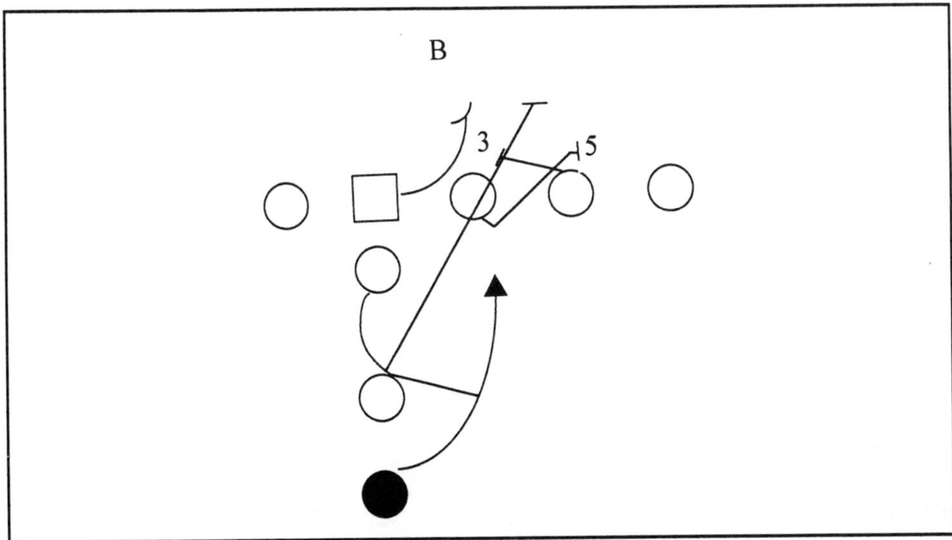

Diagram 5-18: The isolation play with a cross block against a 3 technique and a 5 technique.

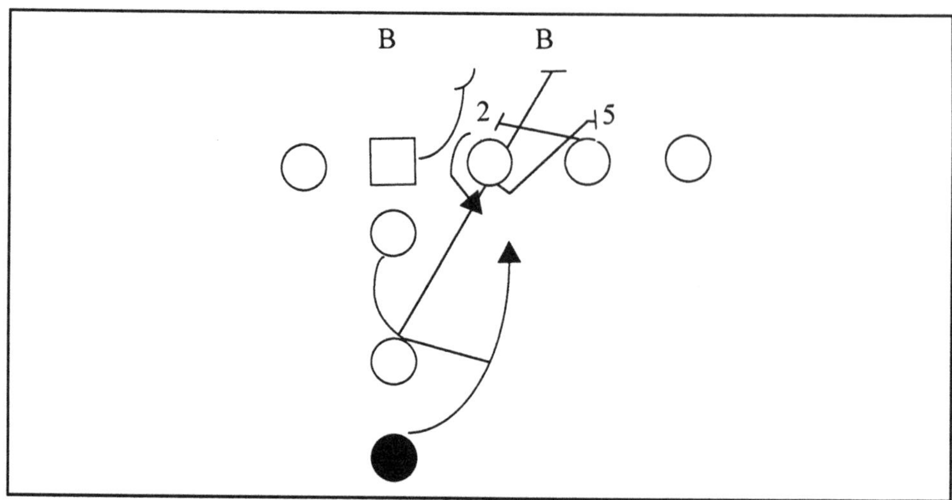

Diagram 5-19: The isolation play with a cross block against a 2 technique.

When calling a cross block, the offensive guard must understand the relationship of the linebacker to the formation. For example, if a guard calls a cross block when the play is a base dive from a one-back set, he must understand that the near linebacker must be removed to a position outside of the offensive tackle box.

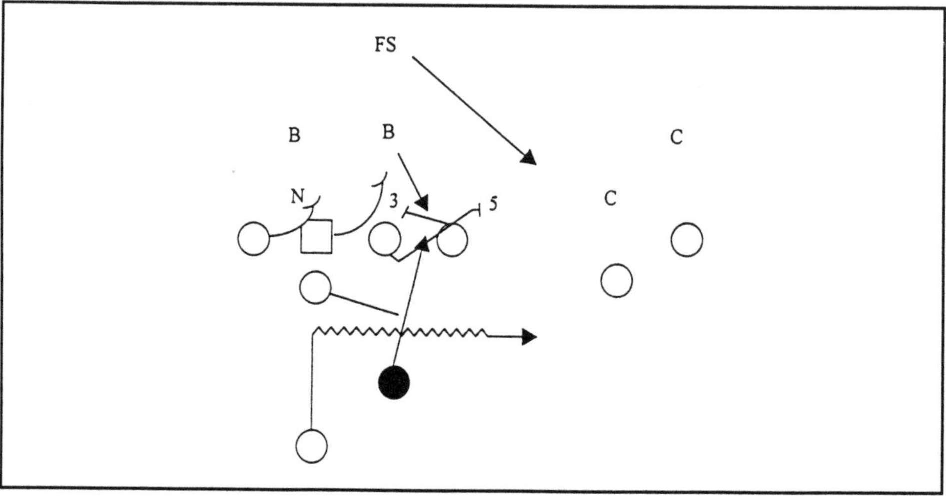

Diagram 5-20: The dive play with a cross block off motion to the trips formation, where the linebacker doesn't bump out.

DEUCE BLOCK

Appropriately described as an inside-out combo block, the deuce block is a two-man scheme that is used on the playside of the counter trey play. The deuce block technique is also similar to the inside zone block in that the inside blocker executes a "hanging" technique as he drives the defensive lineman backward.

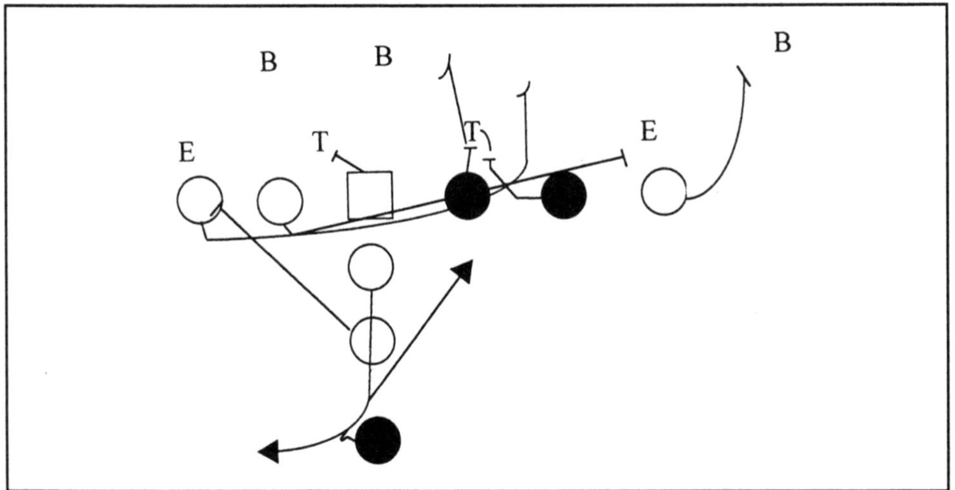

Diagram 5-21: The deuce block by the right guard and right tackle on the counter trey play.

When properly executed, the deuce combination seals the down defender inside while it carries him upfield. The deuce block begins a double team as the primary blocker sets to drive with his outside foot. The outside blocker initially blocks down on the defensive lineman but quickly adjusts his technique to that of a backside blocker in an inside-zone combination.

Like an inside zone technique and the combo block, the premium is on getting vertical movement of the defensive lineman. The inside blocker is the primary blocker as he initially uses a drive blocking technique to engage the inside half of the defender's body. It is his responsibility to hang on to the defensive lineman until the outside blocker works his tail around to gain a face-up position on the defender.

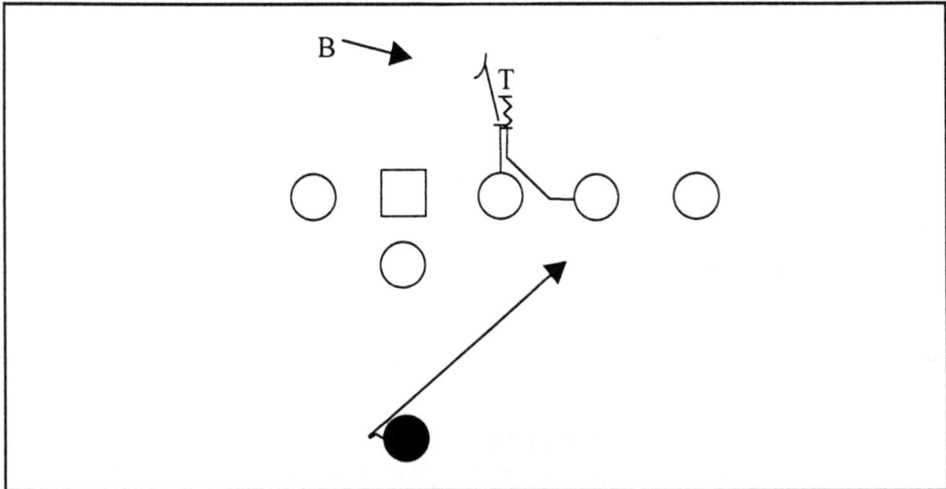

Diagram 5-22: The tackle knocks the guard off to the inside as he takes over on the deuce block.

The timing of the block is such that the outside blocker normally takes over the defender between the third and fourth step of the inside blocker's hanging post block. The inside blocker can release off the hanging technique when he feels the outside blocker mesh with him and take over the vertical movement of the defender. In essence, the outside blocker bumps the inside blocker off to the inside and takes over control of the defender.

Once the outside blocker bumps the primary blocker to the inside, the primary blocker looks to seal the inside linebacker. The timing of the release of the primary blocker off the double team normally puts him in a position to capture a linebacker who has diagnosed the counter trey and is redirecting his flow back to the playside. One important coaching point to the primary blocker's technique that should be emphasized is: *If the primary blocker recognizes that a linebacker has prematurely recognized the counter flow and is scraping underneath the deuce block, the primary blocker must immediately disengage the vertical movement and come off on the scraping linebacker.* The most dangerous defender in a pair of defenders is always the defender to the inside. Therefore, even though the inside blocker functions as the primary force of vertical movement against the defensive lineman, his ultimate responsibility is the linebacker. Some coaches refer to the technique of the inside blocker as a "peek" technique. The inside blocker can afford to hang on the down defender as long as he peeks inside for the linebacker and sees no threat.

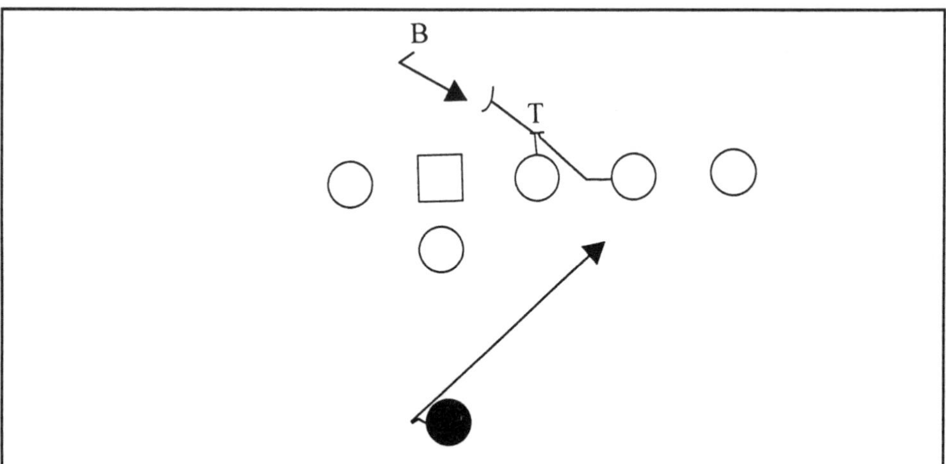

Diagram 5-23: The guard sees the linebacker getting a quick read and slipping underneath.

If the primary blocker feels that the inside linebacker is not a presnap threat, he alerts the outside blocker that he is hanging. If the primary blocker feels that the inside linebacker is a threat because of his presnap alignment, the primary blocker can alert the outside blocker with a "gap" call. When the inside blocker calls "gap," the outside blocker changes his technique from an inside zone technique to a down block.

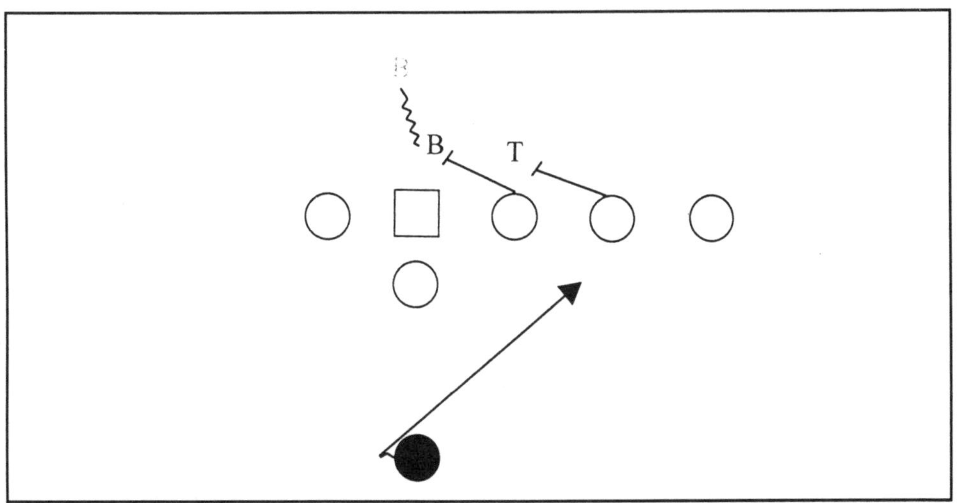

Diagram 5-24: The linebacker cheats into the "A" gap. The guard makes a "gap" call.

The gap call results in both blockers blocking inside with a down block technique. The down block technique allows the blockers to stop defensive penetration and caves the defensive line down to the inside.

DOUBLE TEAM BLOCK

Without question, the oldest two-man blocking scheme in football is the double team. The standard double team involves both blockers getting the point of their shoulders together to form one large blocking surface. They work hip-to-hip as they sweep the defensive lineman upfield. The double team is ideally finished with the blockers flipping the defensive lineman over and pinning him on his back approximately five to seven yards past the line of scrimmage.

Double teams are commonly thought of as outside-in blocks as shown in Diagrams 5-25 through 5-27. The inside blocker normally provides the post (i.e., lift and movement) to the combination, while the outside blocker secures the outside leverage and assists in the lift and movement. Inside-out double teams are also effective schemes against the inside shaded defender—particularly when the defense offsets the nose tackle away from the shade as shown in Diagram 5-28.

On an inside-out double team, the outside blocker is the post blocker while the inside blocker is the seal blocker who seals the defender out of the running lane. The outside blocker provides the lift and movement, while the inside blocker secures the inside leverage and assists in the lift and movement of the inside shaded defender.

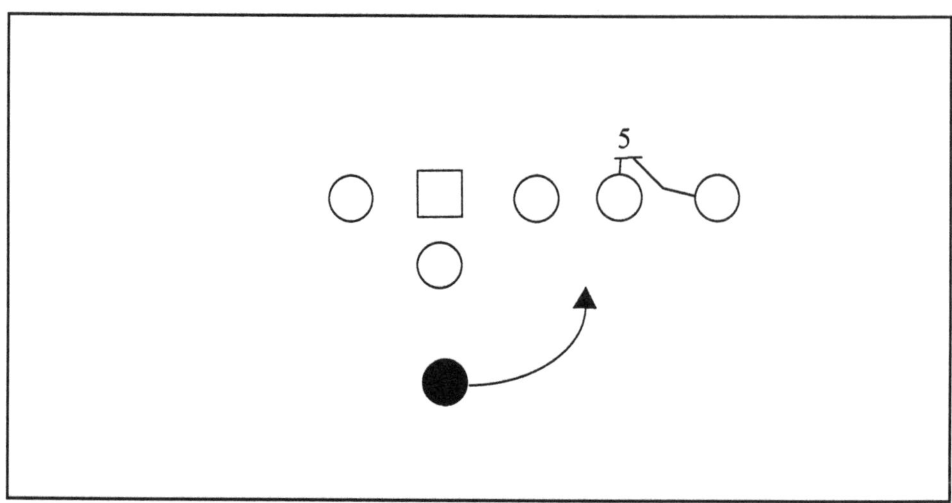

Diagram 5-25: The double team by the tackle and tight end.

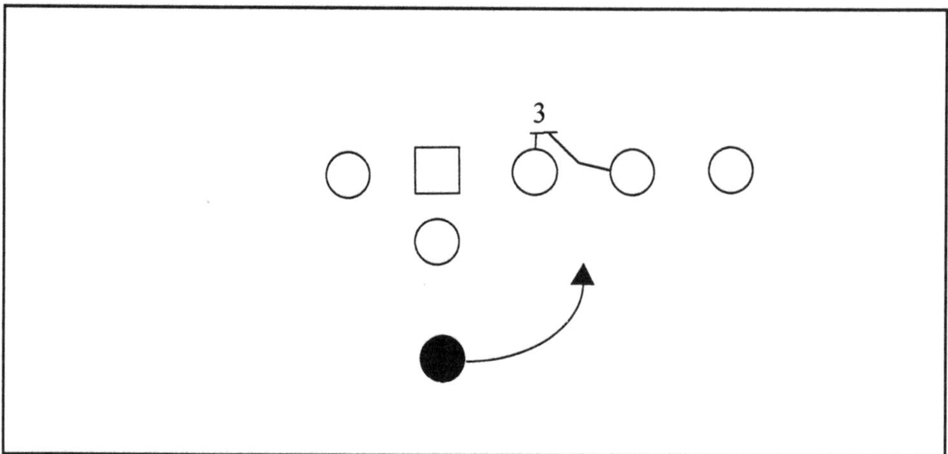

Diagram 5-26: The double team by the guard and the tackle.

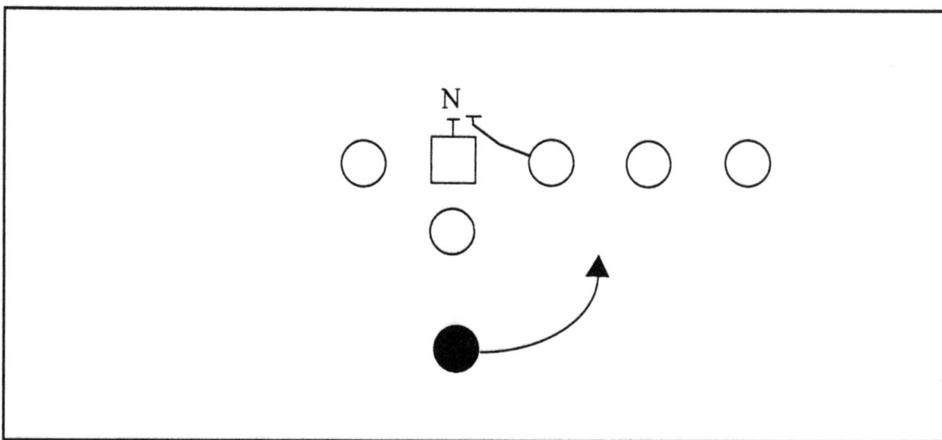

Diagram 5-27: The double team by the center and the guard.

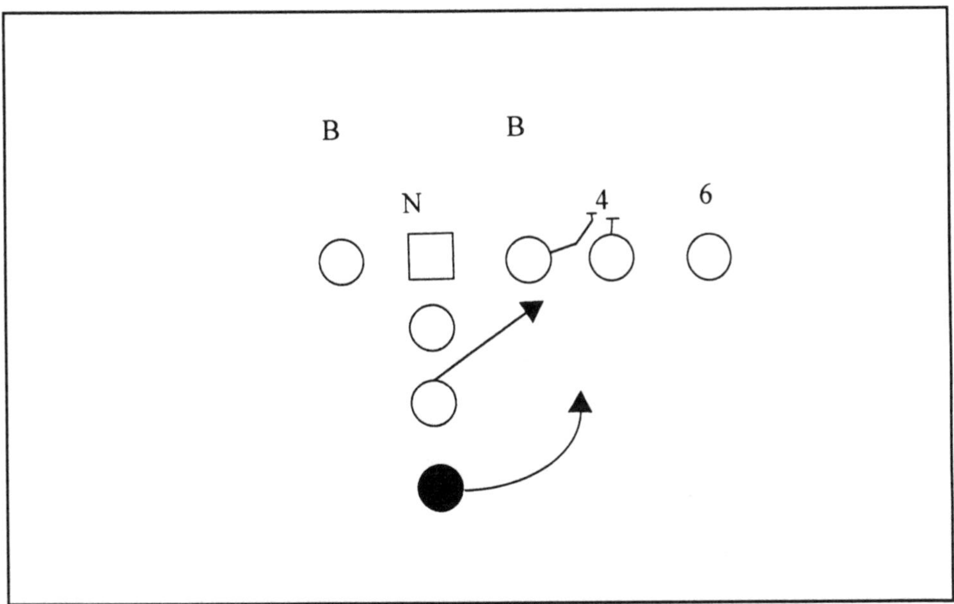

Diagram 5-28: The inside-out double team by the guard and the tackle.

Two basic coaching philosophies predominate the teaching of the double team block. One philosophy strictly requires both blockers to sell out on the defender, sticking on him regardless of his action. The more liberal philosophy of coaching the double team calls for the double team to convert to a combo block if the defender stunts away from the hole—across the face of the post blocker.

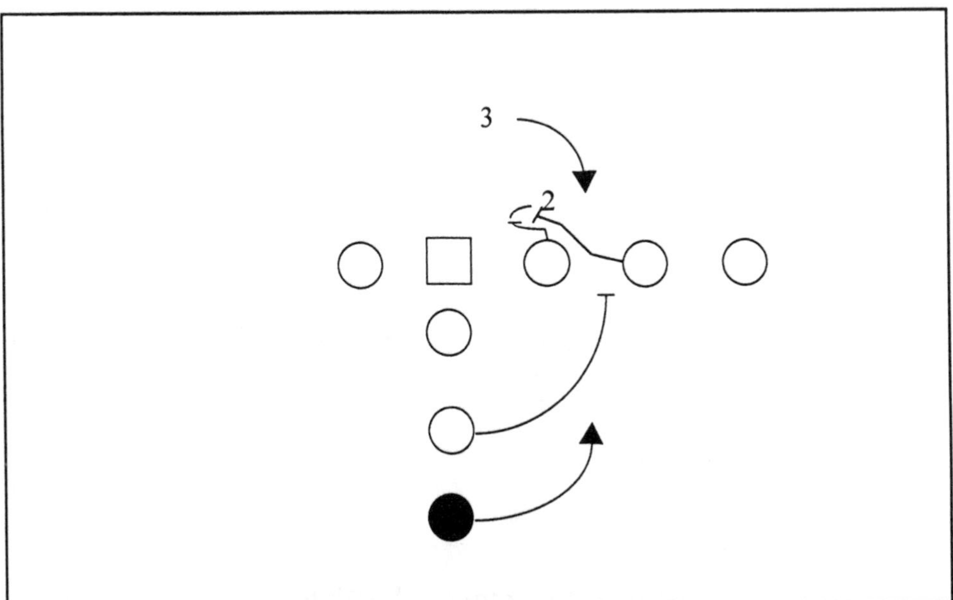

Diagram 5-29: A strict interpretation of the double team concept calls for the seal blocker to stick on the defensive linemen, even if he stunts inside.

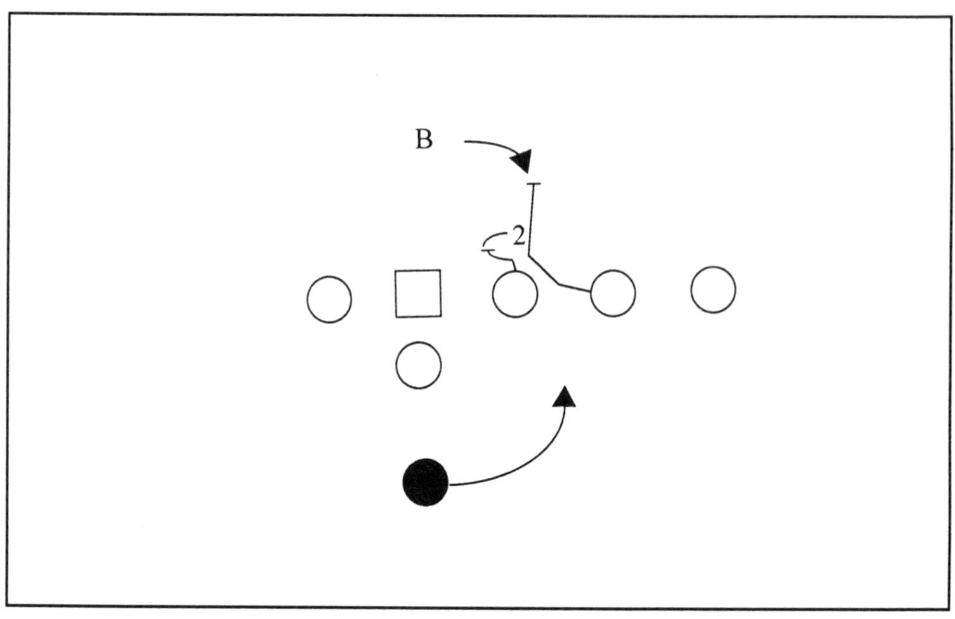

Diagram 5-30: The more liberal interpretation of the double team concept allows the seal blocker to go up on the linebacker if the defensive linemen stunts across the face of the post blocker.

I believe that a strict interpretation of the double team is a waste of a blocker. If a defensive lineman stunts across the face of a post blocker, the seal blocker will stay on his vertical path and go up on the linebacker. I feel that an appropriate emphasis on the proper footwork and proper run-blocking demeanor can provide any team with a legitimate opportunity to successfully pick up any defensive game man-on-man.

With the exception of the single-minded focus on obtaining maximum vertical movement of the defender, the double-team blockers execute their technique in exactly the same manner as the combo blockers. Among the shared coaching points of the double team and combo block are the following:

- Post block
    - Executed with drive block coaching points.
    - Emphasis on vertical movement.
    - Both hands uppercut punch through the defender to lift defender's shoulders.
    - Win the three-inch battle.
    - Stick on the defender and work to gain playside leverage.

- Seal block
  - Executed with a glide step (toes forward, over and up into the defender).
  - Post-side arm rips upward in the manner of an uppercut to lift defender's near shoulder.
  - Eyes read the near foot, knee and hip of the defender.
  - Foot goes inside and the knee and the hip disappear (i.e., the defender crosses the face of the blocker's teammate); seal blocker goes up on the linebacker.
  - Foot goes outside; seal blocker sinks his hips and sticks on the defender.
  - The defender's near shoulder is driven backward to open his shoulders and to maximize the blocking surface for the post blocker.

For more information on the dynamics of the double team, the reader should refer to the previous section in this chapter on the combo block.

FOLD BLOCK

The fold block may be an inside fold block or an outside fold block. Most offensive coaches give the two-fold block techniques different names. Even more coaches identify each individual fold blocking combination with a specific name. An example of a terminology system that assigns individual names to each of the fold blocking combination is shown in Chart 5-1.

Chart 5-1: A sample terminology system for various fold blocking combinations.

- *Fold.* A center-guard fold block; the center down blocks backside and the guard loops around the center's tail.
- *Gut.* An inside guard-tackle fold block; the guard fan blocks outward and the tackle loops around the guard's tail.
- *Tag.* An outside guard-tackle fold block; the tackle blocks down and the guard loops around the tackle's tail.
- *Tom.* An inside tackle/tight end fold block; the tackle fan blocks outward and the tight end loops around the tackle's tail.
- *E.T.* An outside tackle/tight end fold block; the tight end blocks down and the tackle loops around the tight end's tail.

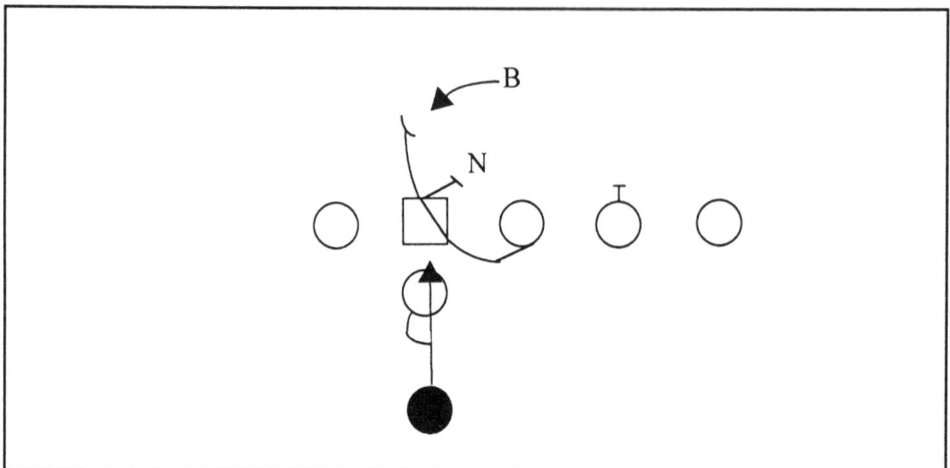

Diagram 5-31: The fold block.

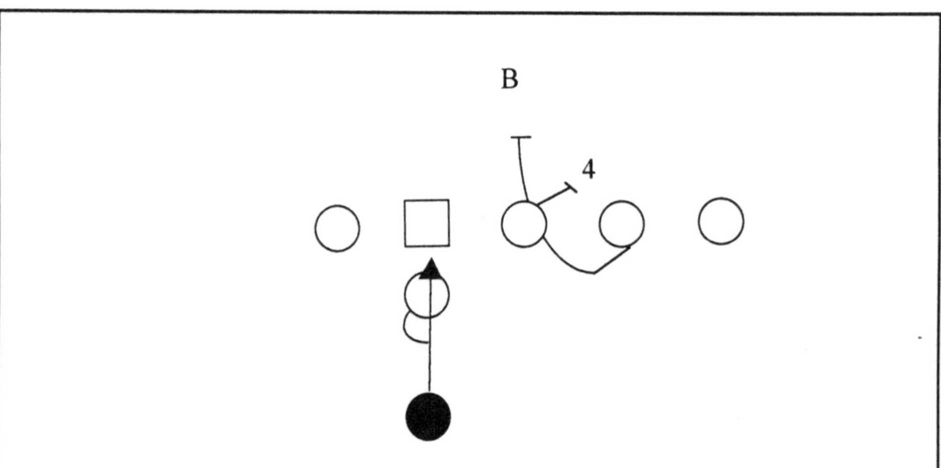

Diagram 5-32: The gut block.

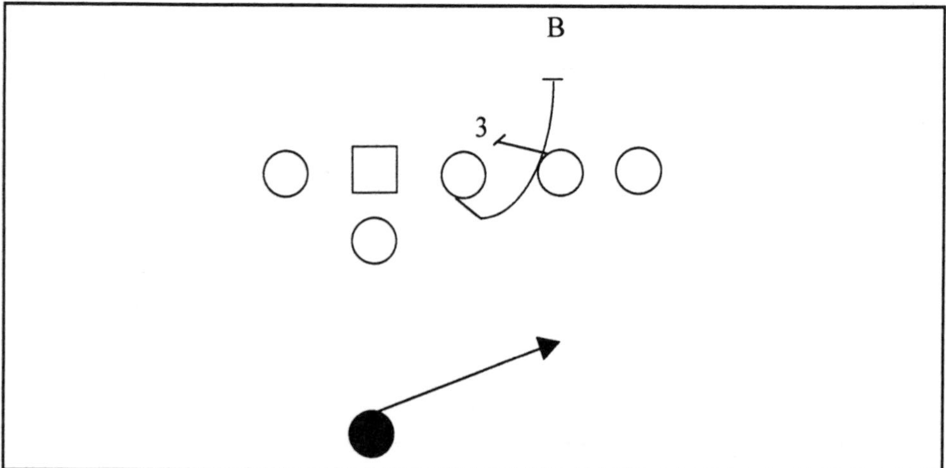

Diagram 5-33: The tag block.

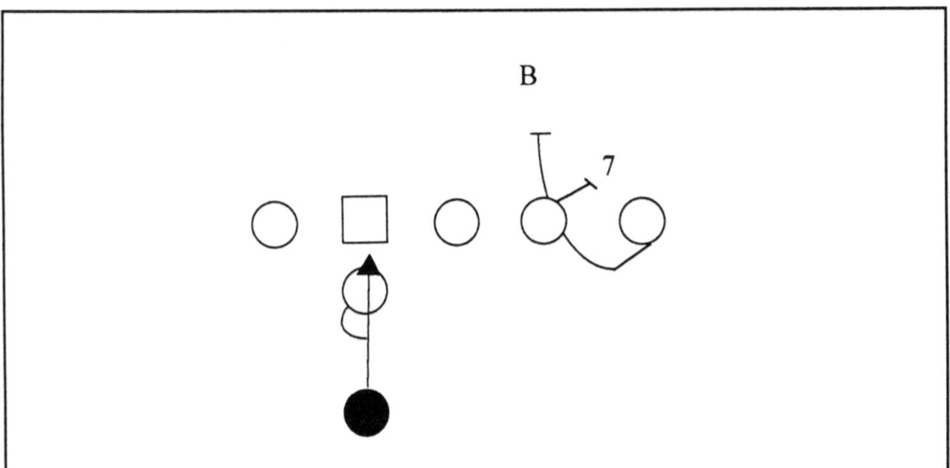

Diagram 5-34: The Tom block.

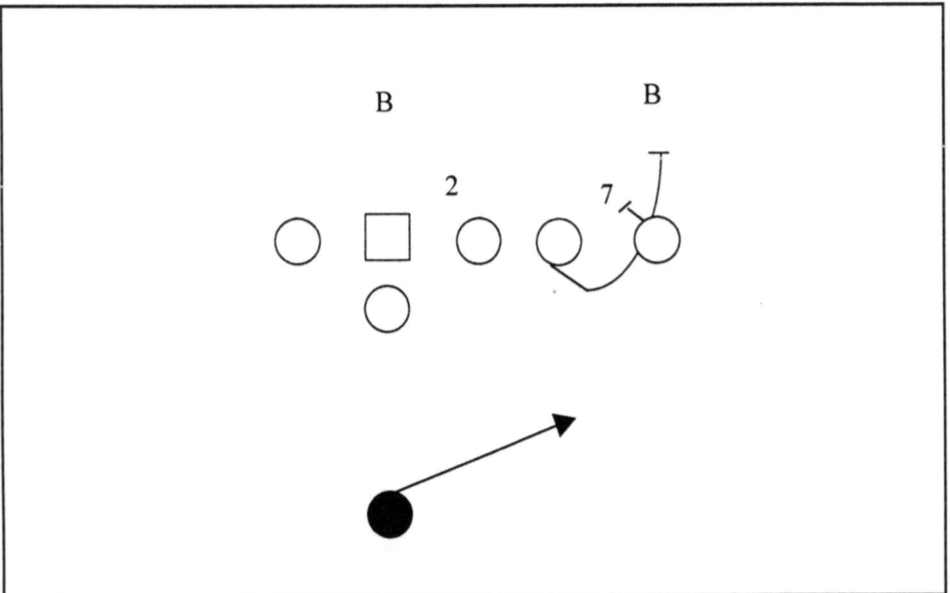

Diagram 5-35: The E.T. block.

The fold block involves two adjacent linemen executing separate techniques with regard to a couple of factors—whether the fold block is an outside fold or an inside fold and whether the particular player is positioned on the inside or the outside of the tandem. The inside fold block is characterized by a fan block outward by the inside player. On the inside fold block, the outside blocker is responsible for looping around behind the inside blocker to get into position to drive block the linebacker. Keeping the shoulders square is an important coaching point for the loop blocker. Proper footwork allows the loop blocker to keep his shoulders square as he "rounds the horn" underneath on the linebacker.

On an inside fold block, the proper footwork for a loop blocker involves him taking a drop step with his outside foot. The drop step is made to the inside as the blocker momentarily crosses his feet. He immediately follows with his inside foot stepping back to regain a good base. After the second step, the loop blocker is facing the line of scrimmage with his shoulders square. At that point, he is positioned two big steps behind the line of scrimmage. The loop blocker is then able to read both the outward movement of the fan blocker and the filling action of the linebacker. Upon stepping backward with his inside foot, the loop blocker immediately drives off his outside foot to drive block the linebacker with a proper run-blocking demeanor. The loop blocker should attempt to fit closely off the tail of the fan blocker to junction the linebacker. The junction point of the linebacker's path is usually closely related to the backfield flow of the play. You should take care to include a simulation of the linebacker's expected flow when practicing the fold block. Inside fold blocks are normally used with dive plays which exhibit some form of counter action.

On an outside fold block, the proper footwork for a loop blocker involves him taking a drop step with his inside foot. The drop step is made to the outside as the blocker momentarily crosses his feet. He immediately follows with his outside foot stepping back to regain a good base. After the second step, the loop blocker is facing the line of scrimmage with his shoulders square at a depth of two big steps behind the line of scrimmage. The loop blocker is then able to read both the down block and the filling action of the linebacker. Upon stepping backward with his inside foot, the loop blocker immediately drives off his inside foot to drive block the linebacker with a good run-blocking demeanor. He should attempt to fit closely to the tail of the down blocker as he rounds the horn to junction the linebacker. The junction point of the linebacker's path is usually closely related to the backfield flow of the play. You should take care to include a simulation of the linebacker's expected flow when practicing the fold block. Outside fold blocks are normally used with stretch plays designed to hit off tackle or outside the end.

INSIDE ZONE BLOCK

The inside zone blocking combination is an area blocking scheme which seals off the backside pursuit. It involves two adjacent lineman blocking an area in tandem—one blocker acting as a frontside blocker and one blocker acting as a backside blocker.

The frontside blocker of an inside zone combination sets to drive with the foot nearest the defender. His primary objective is to maintain playside leverage on the down defender as he fits tightly with his backside flipper in contact with the defender. He should avoid being caught up with the defender, yet maintain pressure against the defender as he works up to the next level.

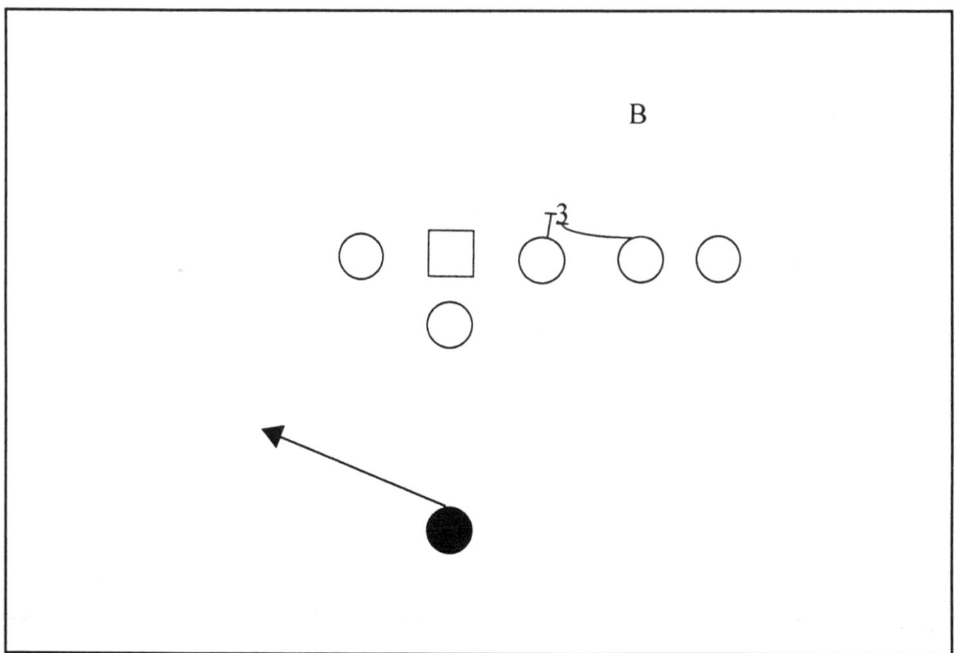

Diagram 5-36: The inside-zone zone block by the backside guard and the backside tackle versus a 3 technique.

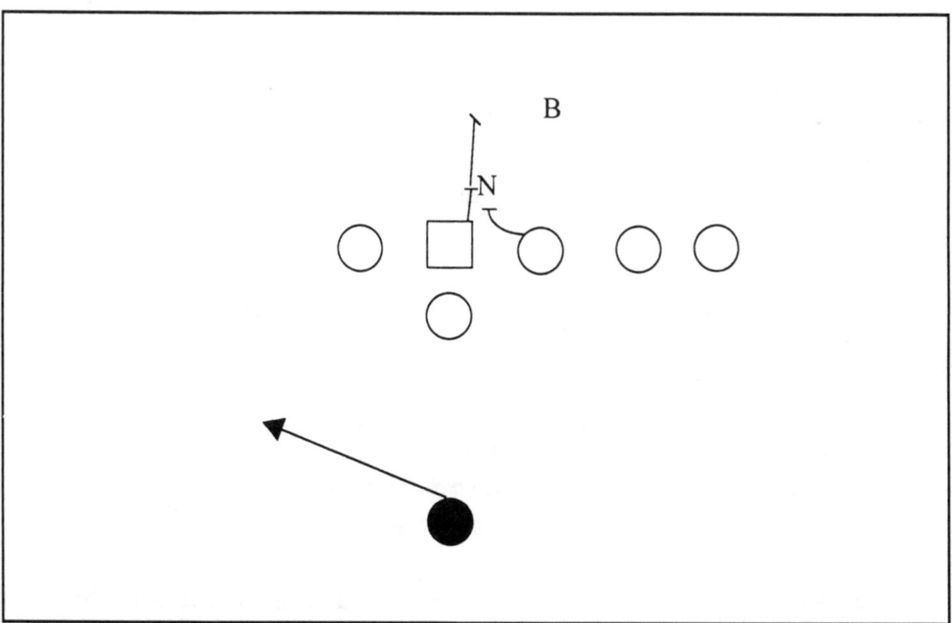

Diagram 5-37: The inside-zone zone block by the center and the backside guard versus an offset nose tackle.

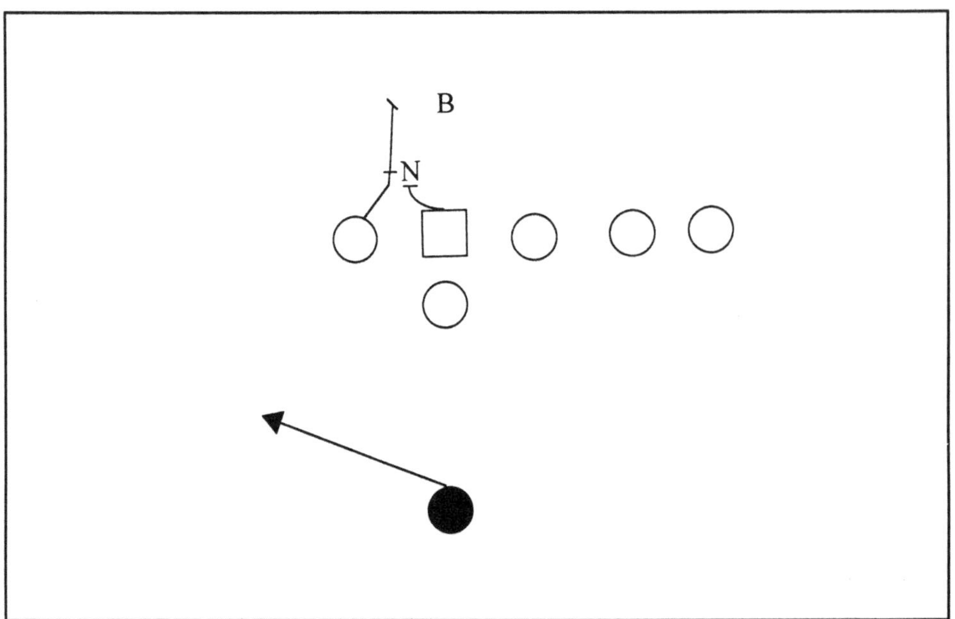

Diagram 5-38: The inside-zone zone block by the frontside guard and the center versus an onset nose technique.

Maintaining pressure on the defender with the backside flipper is called "hanging" on the defender. The hanging technique is the basic technique of the frontside blocker of the inside zone. The backside blocker can be alerted to the frontside blocker's use of the hanging technique by the "I'm hanging" call of the frontside blocker. The frontside guard makes an "I'm hanging" call when the linebacker is aligned away from the playside. The linebacker may be stacked or offset away from the call as shown in Diagrams 5-39 and 5-40.

If the linebacker is aligned over the frontside blocker, the frontside blocker will make a "zone" call to backside blocker. The zone call tells the backside blocker that he has the defensive lineman without any help. The point to remember is that the frontside blocker cannot afford to hang on the down defender if the linebacker is aligned on the playside of the down defender. The zone call results in both blockers setting to reach the playside shoulder of the defenders. Instead of the emphasis being on the vertical movement of the down defender as with the "I'm hanging" call, the emphasis is placed on cutting off the defender's pursuit.

The inside zone block technique results in a moving wall which mows down the backside pursuit. It is an excellent combination scheme to create a cutback running lane between the tackles. With the exception of the "zone" call, vertically moving (i.e., knock him off the ball) the down defender is the primary objective of the inside zone combination. Key coaching points for the inside zone blocking combination include the following:

- The frontside blocker taking a solid set-to-drive step into the down defender when hanging.
- The frontside blocker keeping his playside arm free.
- The frontside blocker using the flipper technique to hang into the defender when appropriate.
- The frontside blocker communicating the "I'm hanging" or "zone" call to the backside blocker.
- The frontside blocker keeping his eyes open for the linebacker attempting to scrape over the top.
- The backside blocker obtaining a good fit to the defender.
- The backside blocker sweeping his backside shoulder upfield to get square on the down defender and gain playside leverage.
- Both blockers pushing the defender upfield until the backside blocker takes over.
- Both blockers gaining playside leverage on the linebacker and down defender.

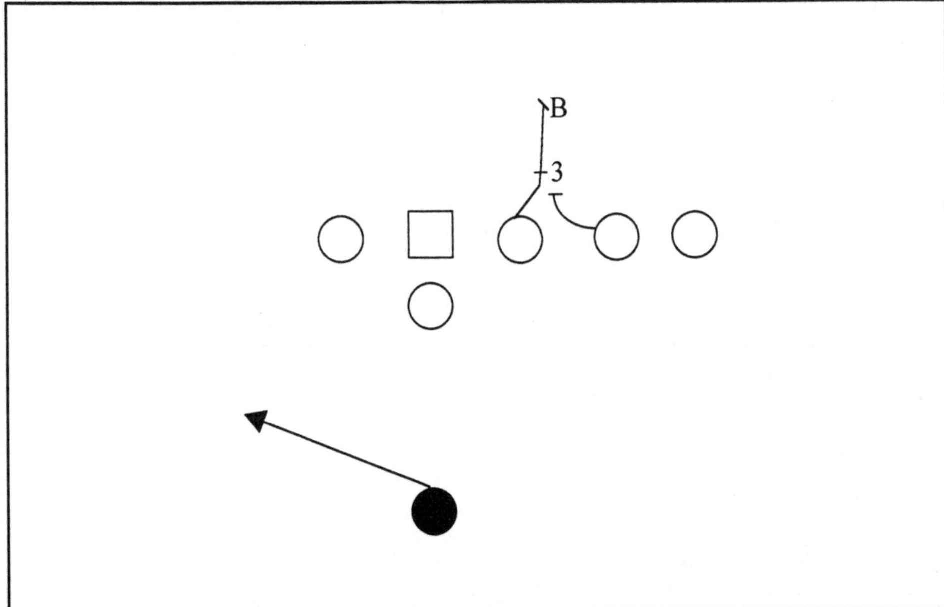

Diagram 5-39: The linebacker stacked behind the down technique results in an "I'm hanging" call.

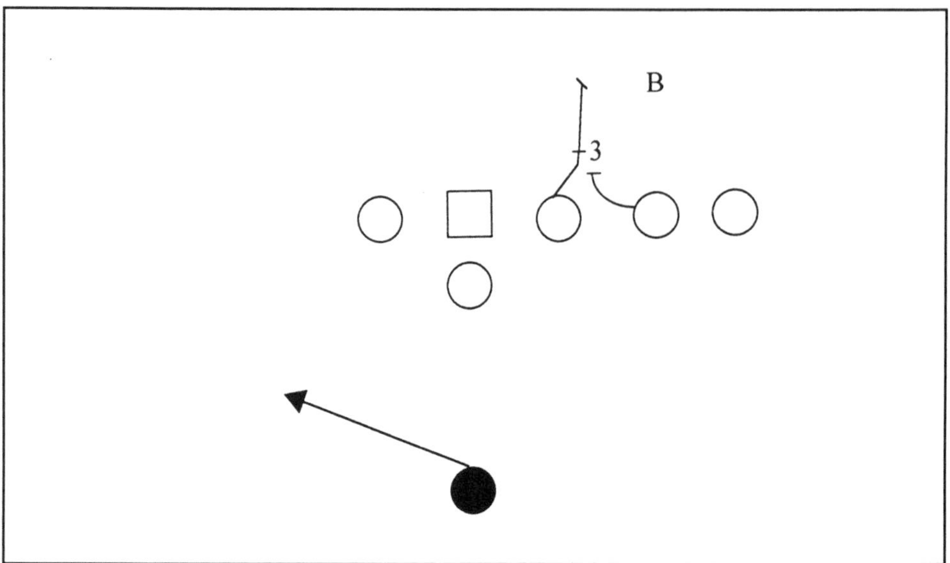

Diagram 5-40: The linebacker offset away from the play results in an "I'm hanging" call.

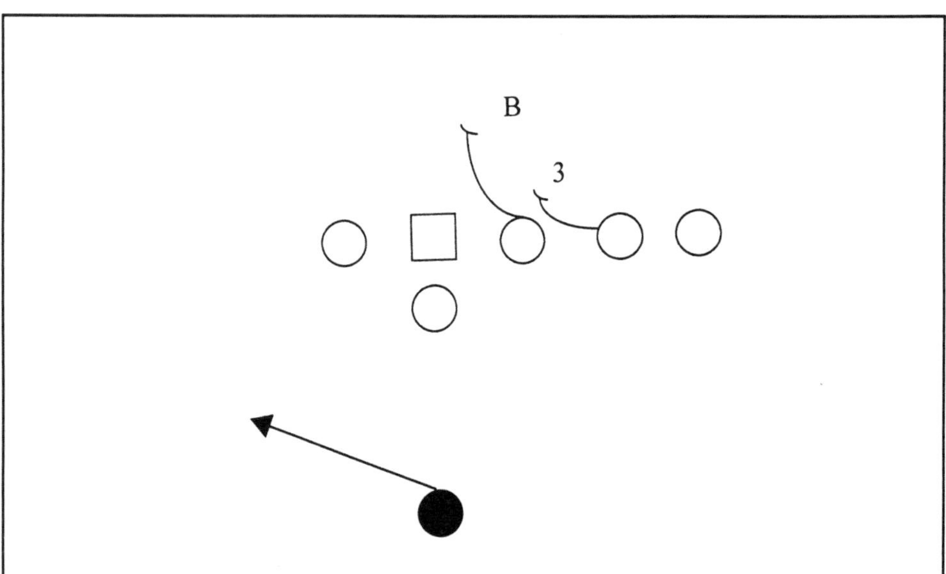

Diagram 5-41: The linebacker aligned over the frontside blocker results in a "zone" call.

OUTSIDE ZONE BLOCK

An outside zone block is a two-man reach block characterized by a frontside blocker and a backside blocker. The outside zone block is by definition an onside blocking technique that has two independent parts—an outside blocker (i.e., frontside blocker) and an inside blocker (i.e., backside blocker). Actually, the outside zone block is a five-man block, because when one offensive lineman has an outside zone block as his rule, all the other offensive linemen typically have the zone block as their playside rule. An excellent blocking technique for quick-hitting flank plays (e.g., toss sweeps, stretch, etc.), the outside zone block is normally used at the point of attack along with a massive backside moving wall sweeping over and up to the side of the play.

To perform an outside zone block, the onside offensive lineman should set to reach. Setting to reach involves the blocker pushing off his inside foot and taking a set to reach step with his outside foot. The second step is made through the crotch of the defender as the blocker rips his inside arm across the defender's chest. He can use his inside arm to rip with the flipper and secure the fit against the defender. The outside zone blocker's objective is to initially overtake the defender in width. The outside zone blocker can then ride the outside shoulder of the defender as he works up to the next level. The blocker should use his inside arm and hand to prevent the defender from grabbing the blocker and pulling him to the ground.

The technique of the block usually depends upon the defensive front structure. For example; when the right guard recognizes a 30 defense, he faces a man *over* him. The guard also recognizes that the 30 defensive structure places a man *on* the adjacent tackle. (Note: "Over" identifies a defender as a linebacker; "On" identifies the defender as a lineman.)

To execute the outside zone against the 30 defensive front structure, the right guard should set to reach and read the defensive tackle's reaction. If the outside play is called at the most opportune time, the 4 technique defensive tackle will be

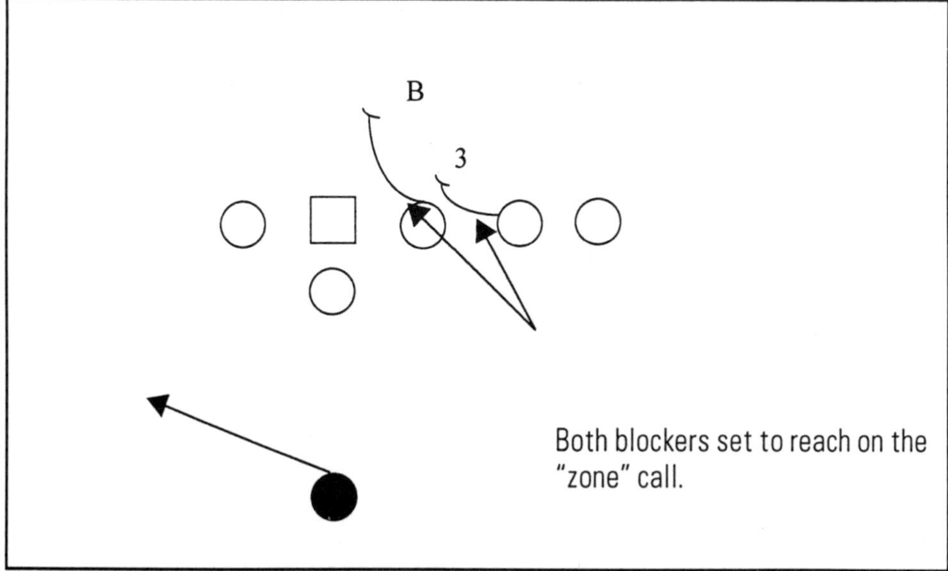

Diagram 5-42: The linebacker aligned over the frontside blocker results in a "zone" call.

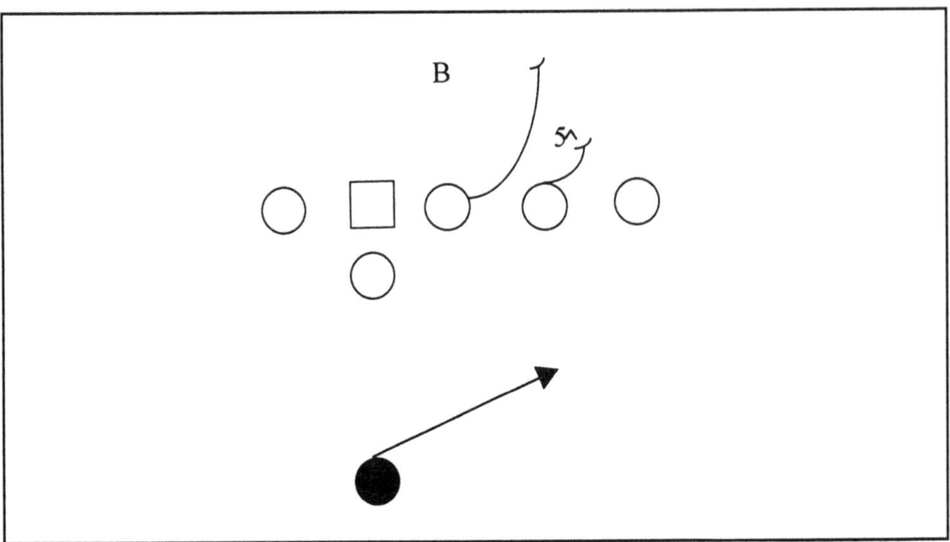

Diagram 5-43: The blockers set to reach on the outside zone block.

running an angle stunt inside or sparking inside. An angle-stunting 4 technique attacks on a direct line to the outside eye of the guard; whereas a sparking 4 technique attacks with an over-and-up move, with the defender keeping his shoulders square as he slides upward through the "B" gap.

The offensive guard's first step should be made to one of two landmarks. When expecting an angle charge by the defensive tackle, the guard should step to the tighter landmark (i.e., the tackle's near foot). When expecting a sparking tackle or a reading tackle, the guard should step to the outside foot of the tackle. In summary, the wider the defensive tackle's alignment, the wider the landmark should be. The

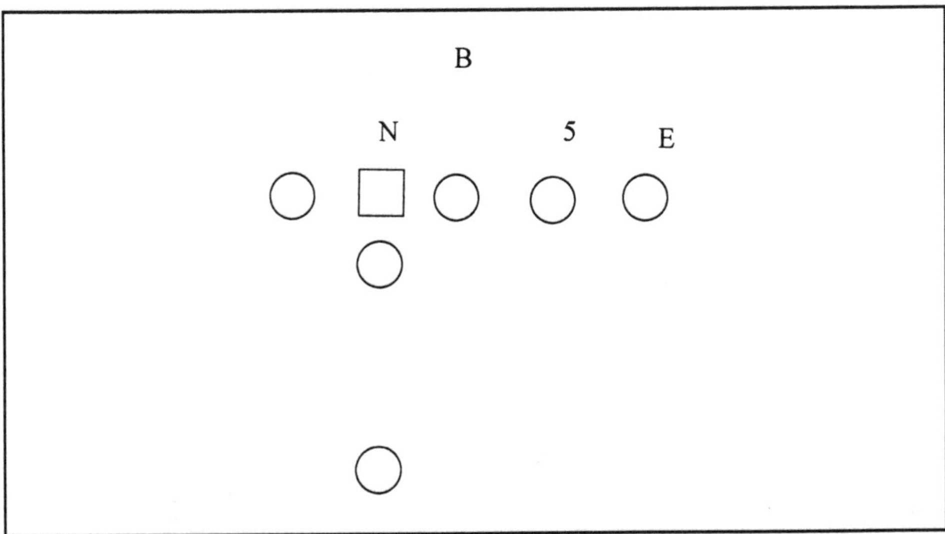

Diagram 5-44: In a standard odd front such as the "30," the linebacker is *over,* while the 5 technique is *on.*

key to the first step is tied to the backside zone blocker's head placement. When performing the outside zone block from an inside position of a blocking tandem, the blocker should attempt to get his outside earhole to the inside hip of the teammate. For example, the guard should attempt to get his outside earhole to the tackle's inside hip.

Once the offensive guard takes off to this landmark, he may adjust his angle upfield to gain leverage on an inside stunting defender. Putting his near ear to the near hip of the outside teammate guarantees that the backside blocker can achieve outside leverage against the man aligned *on* the outside man.

The second step of the backside blocker is critical to achieving success against the inside stunting defensive lineman. Against an inside stunting defender, the backside portion of the zone should angle off his second step. Angling off the inside step entails the blocker adjusting the angle of his inside step to secure the proper fit and establish the correct run-blocking demeanor. If the defender sparks inside, the guard takes a flatter second step as he slides outside with his shoulders parallel to the line of scrimmage. Working to keep the shoulders parallel and securing outside leverage are the keys to successfully outside zone blocking the sparking defender.

If the defender is angling inside on a direct path to the backside blocker's original alignment, the blocker's second step should strike more upfield. If the play is run to the wide hole, the backside blocker can simply run through the outside shoulder of the angling defender. To run through the angle-stunting defender, the backside blocker drives his inside shoulder through the outside shoulder of the stunting defender. Generally, the backside blocker's back foot should always step on or near a 45-degree angle toward the defender aligned *on* the outside teammate.

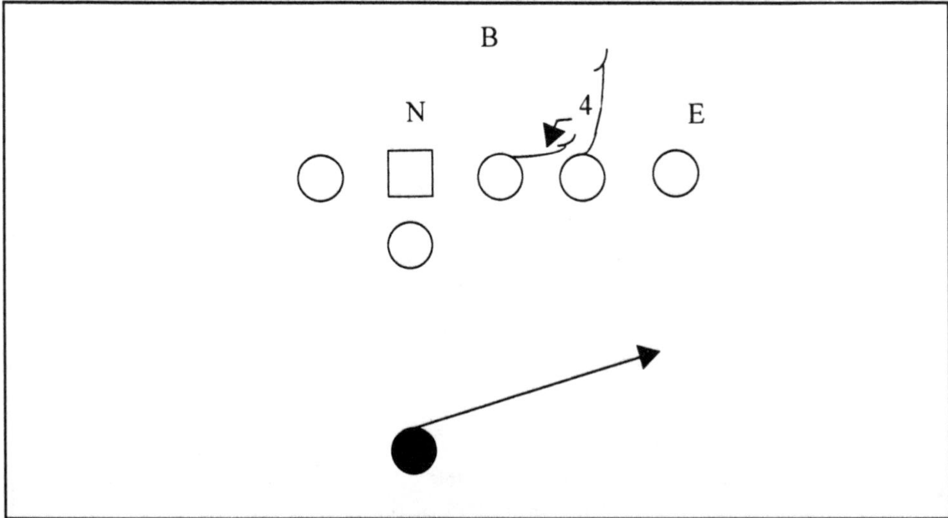

Diagram 5-45: The backside blocker drives his backside shoulder through the playside shoulder of the sparking defender.

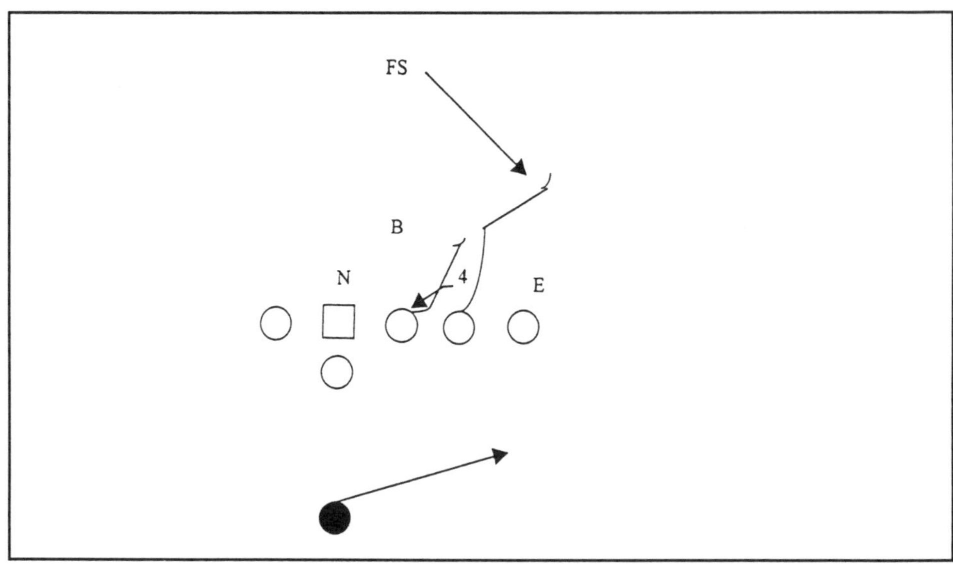

Diagram 5-46: The backside blocker drives his backside shoulder through the playside shoulder of the slanting defender and continues to the next level.

If an offensive guard is to properly read a 4 technique's reaction to the outside zone combination, he must focus on the near foot of the 4 technique. If the foot points toward the blocker, the blocker knows that the defensive tackle is stunting inside. A veteran offensive guard can read the point of the foot. If the defensive tackle steps to the inside, but keeps his toe pointed forward, he is running a spark. If the defensive tackle steps to the inside and points his toe on angle toward the guard, the defensive tackle is running an angle stunt inside. If the defender is playing a read technique, his near foot will step away from the guard, and his toe will point to the outside.

Upon reading the defender's toe pointing to the outside, the backside blocker can continue on his hook-shaped path upfield. The backside blocker's outside shoulder should rub against the frontside blocker's inside shoulder as the two work outside and upfield as a tandem. Once the tandem is formed, the backside blocker can immediately feel the defensive tackle's reaction to the frontside blocker's set to reach. If the defensive tackle fights hard to the outside, the defender's near hip will disappear across the face of the frontside blocker. In this case, the backside blocker will have no blocking surface to secure on the defender. The backside blocker will then continue upfield on his hook-shaped path to angle off and cut down the second level defender—the linebacker.

If the defender's near hip doesn't disappear, the backside blocker will feel an available blocking surface as the defender hangs on the frontside blocker. When the defensive tackle hangs on the frontside blocker, the backside blocker should push the frontside blocker off the tandem zone block and secure the fit to the outside hip and shoulder of the defensive tackle.

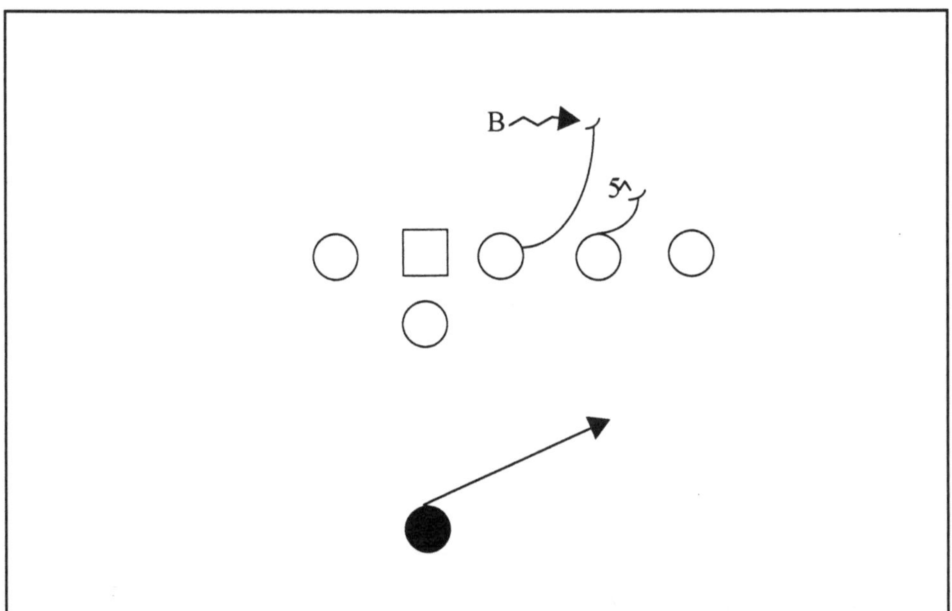

Diagram 5-47: The backside blocker turns up on the second-level defender when the defender fights across the face of the frontside blocker.

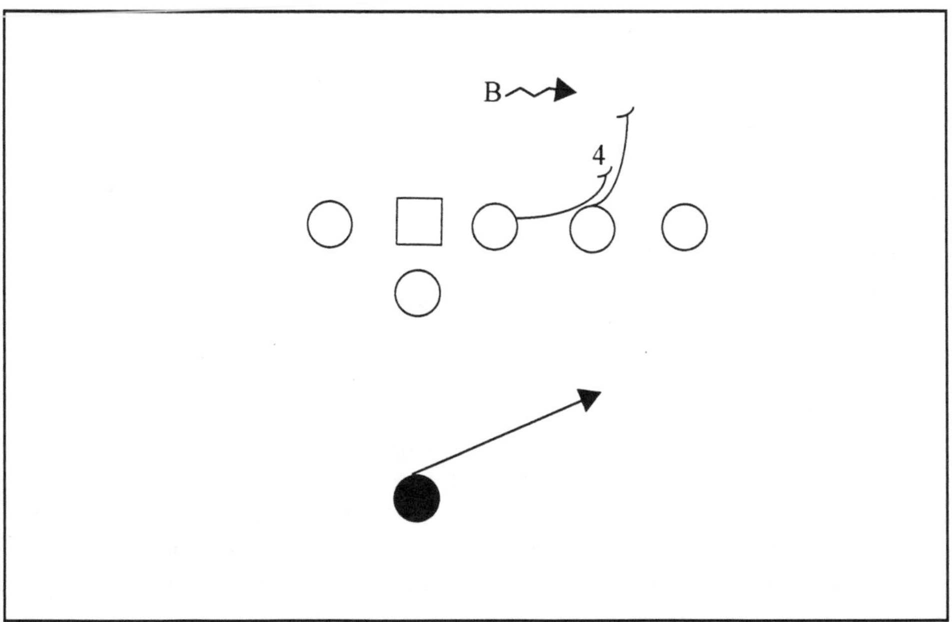

Diagram 5-48: The backside blocker bumps the frontside blocker off the hanging defender.

The backside blocker secures the fit to the defender's outside by using his inside hand to grab the defender's chest and to pinch the defender into a secure fit between the blocker's head and backside shoulder. In this manner, the outside zone block evolves from various one-man blocks along the line of scrimmage to a true two-man blocking scheme.

For an inside blocker who is reach blocking a man on his teammate, the components of an effective outside zone block include the backside blocker's responsibility to accomplish the following tasks:

- Set to reach.
- Throw the inside arm through the defender's crotch.
- Dip the inside shoulder to get the pad under the defender's pad.
- Read the near foot of the defender to determine if he is penetrating.
- Get the ear to the near hip of the outside teammate.
- Work upfield as part of an inside tandem against a floating defensive lineman.
- Keep the outside shoulder free and the inside shoulder fitted to the playside hip of the defender.

On the outside zone, the frontside blocker who faces a defender playing *on* him will step to reach according to the width of the defender's alignment. If the defender is an inside shade, the blocker will set to reach with a vertical step (i.e., up the field). Versus an inside shaded defender, the frontside blocker will step his outside foot to a point just outside of the defender's outside foot. He will keep the toes of his outside foot pointing upfield as he steps to reach the inside shade. The blocker will then drive his inside shoulder through the outside armpit of the defender. His inside arm should be ripped upward in the manner of an uppercut punch.

The frontside blocker should get his inside arm's bicep under the outside armpit of the defender. Getting the bicep to this position lifts the outside shoulder of the defender. This punch knocks the defender's outside shoulder backward while simultaneously tilting both of the defender's shoulders. The tilt of the shoulders is caused by the upward thrust of the uppercut punch and the resulting lift of the outside shoulder. The shoulder tilt and the backward push of the outside shoulder result in the defender's chest opening. By opening the defender's chest, the frontside blocker gives the backside blocker an improved blocking surface—a surface conducive to the proper fit of the backside blocker's head as he attempts to get around for outside leverage. This component of opening the defender's shoulders is crucial to the two-man dimension of zone blocking the inside shaded defender.

A common error of the frontside blocker in the two-man zone tandem block is overstriding the set to reach. If the frontside blocker steps too wide versus the inside shaded defensive lineman, the backside blocker cannot properly punch through the defender's armpit. An excessively wide set to reach by the frontside blocker creates an unwanted spacing between the backside blocker and frontside blocker. Any type of gap or space between the two blockers will give the defender a crease through which he may split the two-man zone. The set to reach against the inside shaded defensive lineman must be a tight vertical step, only inches outside of the defender's outside foot.

Once the frontside blocker punches through the armpit of the inside shaded defender, he throws his eyes to the second level to find the scraping linebacker. Every sound defensive scheme that uses an inside shade defensive lineman will support the inside shade with a fast scraping linebacker. Therefore, the lead blocker of the outside zone tandem must be on the lookout for a fast scraping linebacker as he rips through the outside pad of the defensive lineman.

The frontside blocker should flatten his path to the outside as he rips through the inside shade. Flattening the path gives the blocker an opportunity to junction the scraping linebacker's outside knee, hip, and shoulder. Once the frontside blocker junctions the linebacker's path, the blocker should explode with his inside shoulder pad driving through the backer's thigh and hip. The key to obtaining the proper fit at the junction point is for the blocker to regain control of his body. When a frontside blocker rips through an inside shade, he tends to become prone to overextend his power angle and to be slightly forward in his demeanor. He must chop his feet on his fourth step—much as he does when he blocks the levels on the backside. (Additional information on level blocking is presented in Chapter 4).

Chopping his fourth and fifth steps allows the blocker to reset his demeanor to gain a proper fit at the junction point. Since the junction point usually occurs between the sixth and seventh step, the frontside blocker can easily reset his demeanor before reaching the junction point.

The frontside blocker's failure to chop his strides after clearing the inside shade will result in the blocker losing the proper relationship in his path to the junction point. Unless he chops his stride, the frontside blocker will either overrun the linebacker and allow him to cut underneath or lose outside leverage on the linebacker as he scrapes across his face.

If the man *on* the frontside blocker is an outside shade, the set to reach is wider—slightly outside the playside shoulder of the lineman. The toe should remain pointed straight ahead as the blocker sets to reach. On his second step, the blocker should punch his inside arm through the chest/armpit of the lineman. The inside arm will uppercut through the chest/armpit of the defender as the frontside blocker plants his attack step (i.e., second step). The third step should secure outside leverage as the frontside blocker works to gain width and depth. The outside shaded defender will likely attempt to fight to the outside in an attempt to keep his outside arm and leg free. The blocker should use his inside hand to grab cloth and pull himself to obtain the proper fit. If the defender continues to fight across the frontside blocker's face, the blocker should maintain contact on the defender while working up through the first level to the second level.

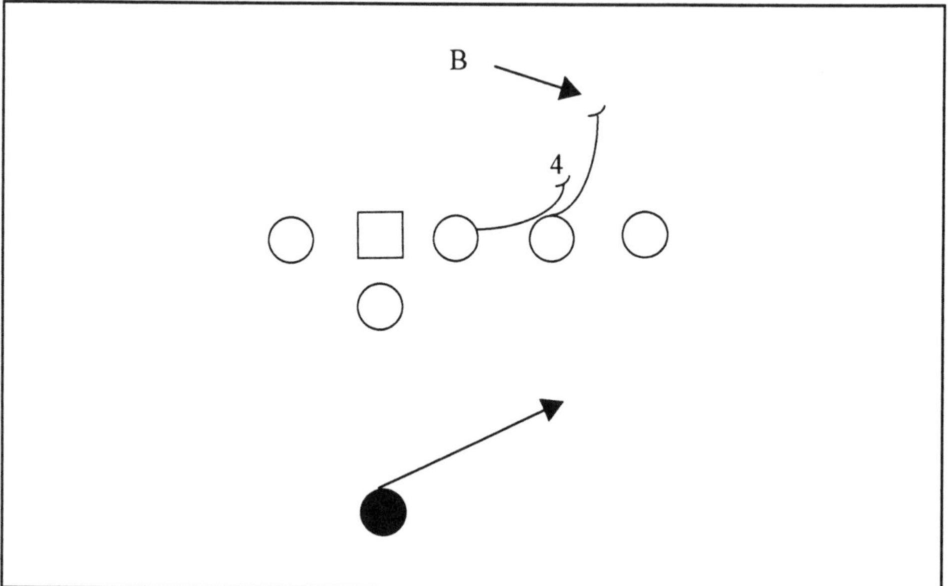

Diagram 5-49: The frontside blocker is shown working to the proper junction point.

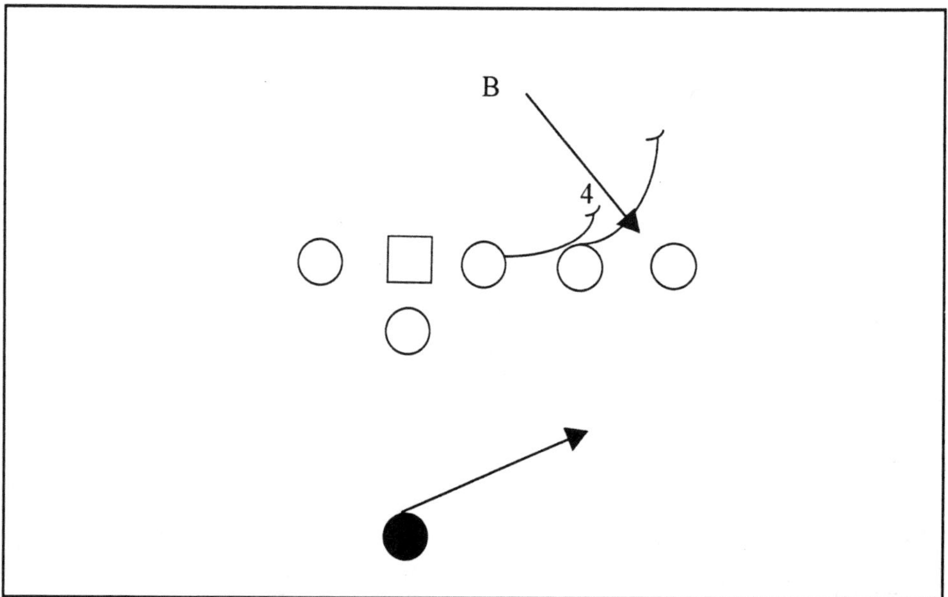

Diagram 5-50: The frontside blocker is shown overrunning the junction point.

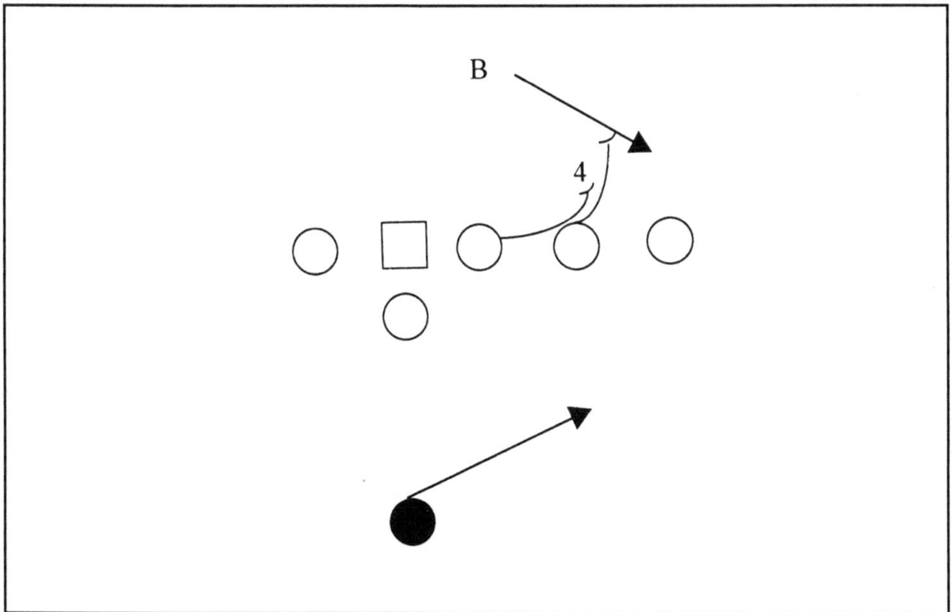

Diagram 5-51: The frontside blocker is shown letting the linebacker cross his face.

Once the blocker enters the second level, he can push off the defensive lineman to flatten his path. Flattening his path gives the frontside blocker an opportunity to make a second block on a shuffling linebacker. If a linebacker doesn't show, the blocker should continue flattening his path so that he can junction the path of a third-level defender such as a free safety.

Riding the defensive lineman's outside shoulder through level one and flattening his path to cut a second- or third-level defender are ideal objectives for the frontside zone blocker. It is more important, however, that the frontside zone blocker never allow the outside shaded defender to fight outside to regain the outside leverage. If a frontside zone blocker can overtake the outside shade defender and maintain outside leverage, the likelihood of offensive success is relatively high. If you give credit to the opponent's defensive coaching staff, this outcome is probably the best outcome you can hope for as an offensive line coach.

For the frontside blocker of the outside zone blocking tandem, the components of an effective outside zone block include the blocker's responsibility to accomplish the following tasks:

- Set to reach.
- Uppercut punch the inside arm through the chest/armpit of the defender.
- Gain ground with the attack step through the chest/armpit.
- Accomplish the objective of the three-inch rule and obtain a vertical push on the defender.

- Continue to work outside and upfield as the blocker moves through the second level.
- Release and flatten to junction a second level defender as he enters the second level.
- Chop his feet and widen his base as he enters the second level to regain the proper run-blocking demeanor and cut the linebacker.
- Continue flattening to the outside to junction a third level if the second level defender doesn't show.

For the frontside blocker who is performing an outside zone block against a man *over* him (i.e., linebacker), the blocker must set to reach just as he would set to reach against a wider down technique defender. A linebacker naturally has a greater opportunity to flow on the snap prior to the frontside blocker reaching him. Therefore, the blocker must take the proper path after setting to reach. The proper path against a linebacker is a path that allows the frontside blocker to progressively close toward the linebacker while maintaining a tight outside leverage fit to the movement of the linebacker. Maintaining a tight fit to the linebacker's movement prevents the blocker from overextending his angle, thereby allowing the linebacker to plant and slip underneath the block.

The blocker's path to the junction point starts with a movement that is sometimes referred to as a J-step. The J-step terminology has its roots in the letter's resemblance to the desired path of outside zone blocker as it is drawn on a chalkboard.

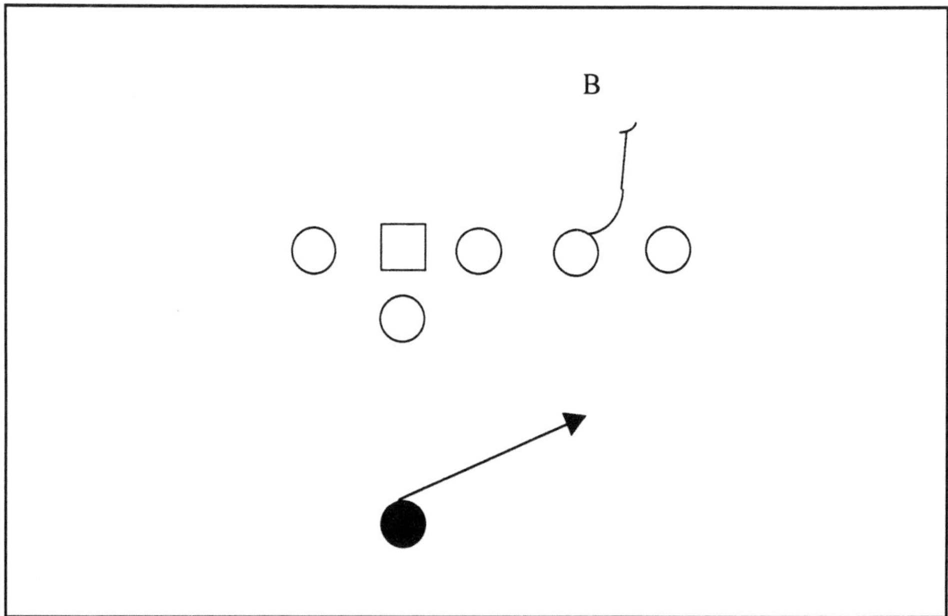

Diagram 5-52: The outside zone block resembles the letter J.

The set to reach is a lateral step that provides some upfield momentum into the neutral zone. After the set to reach, the blocker should move in a near vertical angle as he proceeds to the junction point. It is imperative that the frontside blocker keep his eyes on the linebacker at all times as he moves toward the junction point. If the linebacker bucket-steps, the threat of the linebacker slipping underneath the J-step is eliminated. As a result, the blocker may angle off his path slightly to intercept the bucket-stepping linebacker. If the linebacker steps sharply into the line of scrimmage as he reads the play, the frontside blocker should keep his shoulders square and work up the field on a vertical path, thus preventing the linebacker from attempting to slip underneath.

Once the frontside blocker reaches the junction point, he should deliver a sharp blow through the linebacker's playside thigh and hip. As described previously, the blocker should drive his inside pad through the linebacker's outside leg and hip. The blocker must take care to chop his steps and widen his base as he approaches the junction point. It is also important that the blocker snap his head upward as he delivers the blow through the linebacker's hip. Novice offensive linemen often neglect to snap their heads upward as they attempt to block a moving linebacker. In reality, it is natural for a blocker to attempt to look at the ground as he attempts to cut a linebacker. When a blocker looks at the ground, he usually fails to deliver a low-to-high blow, striking downward instead. Snapping the head up also helps the blocker to keep his back flat as he cuts the linebacker. Snapping the head up, keeping a flat back, and a delivering a low-to-high shoulder blow are crucial elements of being able to effectively blocking a linebacker who is on the move.

CHAPTER 6

Pull Blocks

The third primary category of offensive line run blocks is the pull block. Pull blocks are characterized as techniques executed by a lineman pulling to either side. A list of the various types of pull blocks includes the following:

- Sweep hammer pull
- Sweep wall pull
- Trap pull
- Bootleg/waggle pull
- Horn pull
- Quick screen pull
- Spin pull

SWEEP HAMMER PULL

The sweep pull may be a short or a long pull. Short sweep pulls are pulls from the onside of the ball out toward the defensive flank. Long sweep pulls are pulls from the offside of the ball across the center to the playside. Sweep pulls are called "log blocks" or "wall blocks" when the pulling guard or tackle uses his inside shoulder to seal the defensive end inside. Sweep pulls are called "kick-out blocks" or "hammer blocks" when the pulling guard or tackle attacks the defender from an inside-out position. The hammer block—a specialized type of kick-out block used with the Wing-T—was developed for single wing football and is still an effective method of creating the alley crease on the buck sweep series.

Sweep pulls differ from trap pulls in several ways. The biggest difference between a sweep pull and a trap pull is the angle of attack. The sweep pulling lineman gains depth on his pull, while the trap pulling lineman attacks on a flatter path into the line of scrimmage. The sweep pull can be either a log block or a kick-out block, whereas a trap pull is designed solely to be a kick-out block. The sweep pull is made off of a deeper pivot and a bucket step, while the trap pull is normally made of a sharp push flat down the line of scrimmage. Finally, the sweep pull is characterized by the blocker snapping his playside elbow around so that the hand can slap his buttocks while the trap pull is characterized by the pivot and handshake move of the blocker's lead hand.

The initial movements for both the short sweep log and kick-out blocks are identical. Only the finishing movements are different. The short sweep pulling guard begins with a hard push off the inside foot as he simultaneously rotates the toes inward. Rotating the toes of the push foot inward allows the hips to open to 90 degrees or more. When pulling right, the left foot is the push foot. The right foot is yanked backward as the right elbow is jerked backward and to the left.

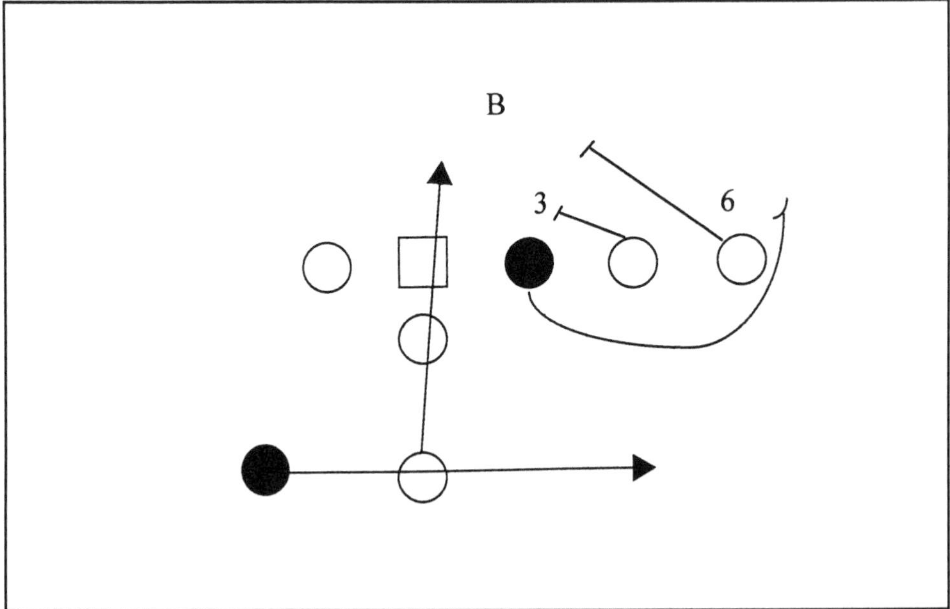

Diagram 6-1: A short sweep log by the right guard.

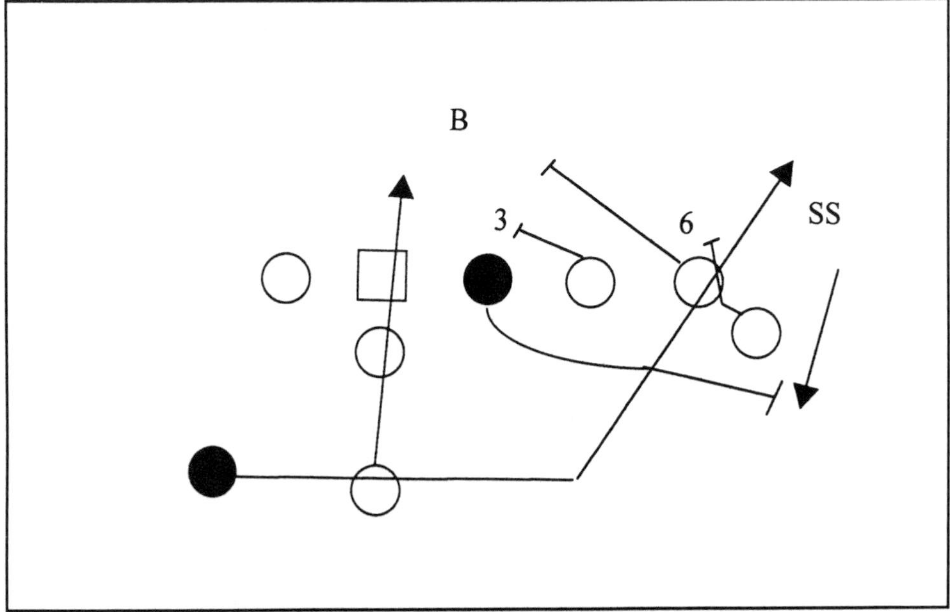

Diagram 6-2: A short sweep kick-out by the right guard.

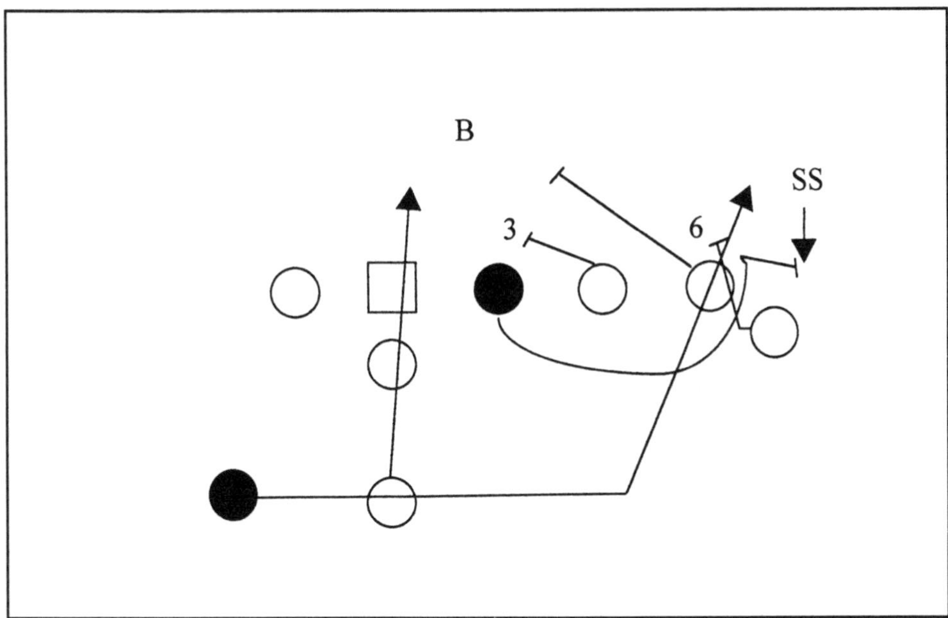

Diagram 6-3: A short sweep hammer block by the right guard.

Young linemen can be trained to open deeply by having them to attempt to slap their left buttock with their right hand. This movement snaps their shoulders around and forces the hip to open. The right foot is also forced to bucket step, a key coaching point to sweep pulling. The bucket step forces the guard to pivot approximately 110 degrees so that he is heading backward to some degree. The second step crosses over to a point where the heel is directly in front of the toes of the bucket foot. The inside shoulder dips and the guard gets his eyes to the target area as the bucket foot makes the third step and regains a normal base. On the fourth step, made with the inside foot, the guard gets his shoulders back to parallel with the line of scrimmage. At the point of the fourth step, the hammer pulling guard and the log pulling guard should be approximately two and one-half yards behind the line of scrimmage. The sweep blockers gain depth for two reasons: first, they want to clear any wreckage which may be caused by a penetrating defender through an outside gap; second, they want to gain depth so that they can hit the line of scrimmage with their shoulders parallel to the line of scrimmage while they read the edges of the alley.

It is on the fifth step that the short sweep pulling guard's technique begins to take the identifying characteristic of being either a wall or a kick-out block. The log blocker will tighten his path into the neutral zone to fit tightly to the outside hip of the seal blocker.

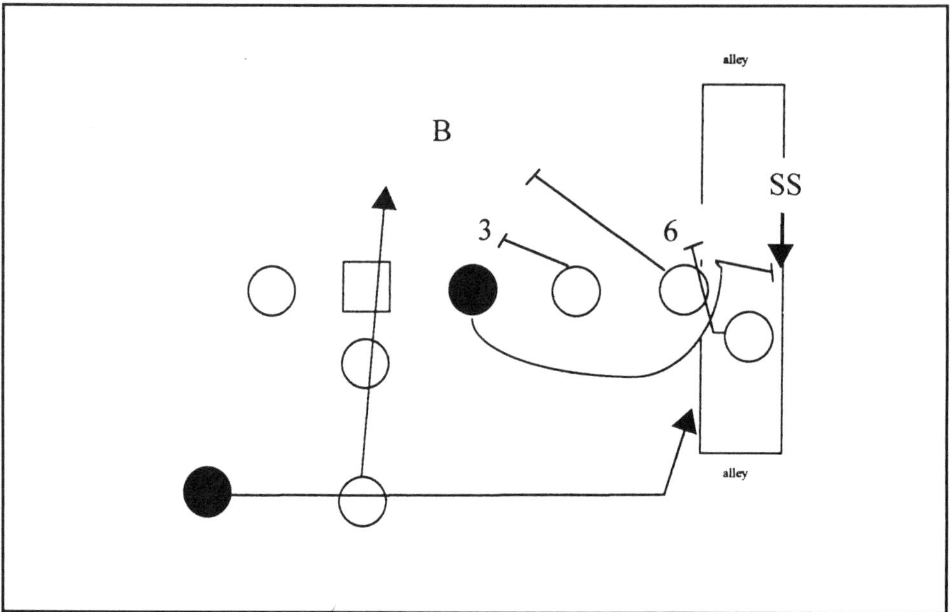

Diagram 6-4: A short sweep hammer block by the right guard—kicking out the force out of the alley.

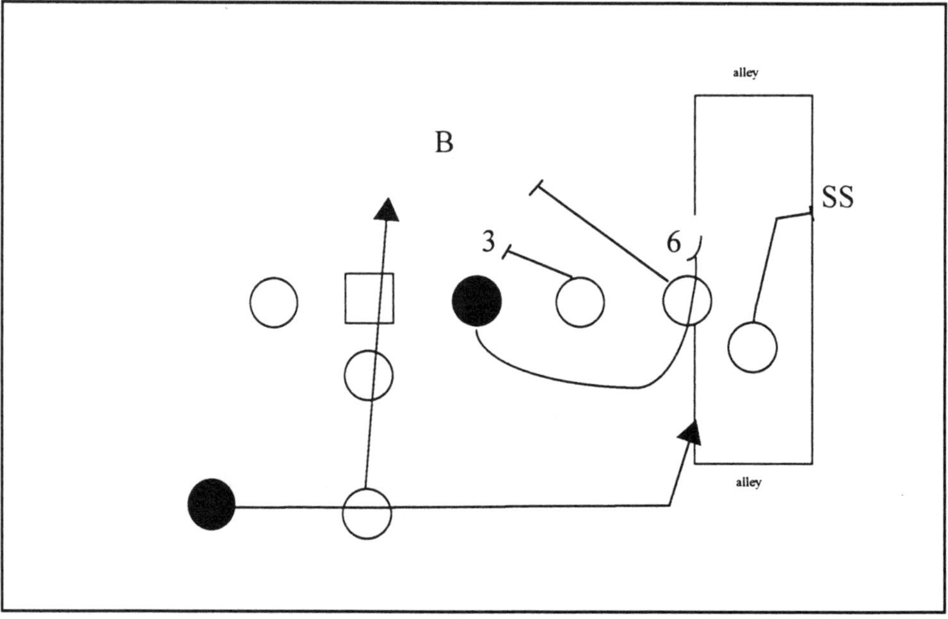

Diagram 6-5: A short sweep wall (i.e., log) block by the right guard—sealing the contain man inside of the alley.

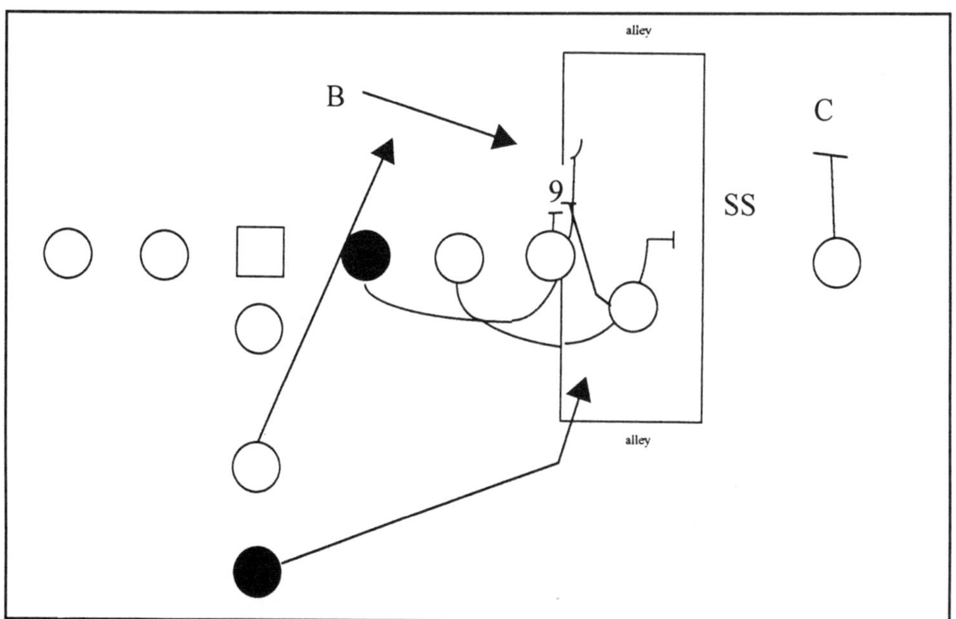

Diagram 6-6: A short sweep wall (i.e., log) block by the right guard—fitting to the outside hip of the seal blocker.

It is between the fourth and fifth step that the hammer blocker analyzes the action of the force. The fifth step is made straight ahead as the guard reads the relative positioning of the force. If the force is coming hard, the offensive guard plants the inside foot at a 45-degree step, thereby keeping the toe forward. The sixth step is a 45-degree plant step called the hammer step. The seventh step is made with the outside foot off of the 45-degree hammer step. The outside foot is a 90-degree step to a point where the guard may meet the upfield shoulder of the force defender. The inside foot then follows, and the guard moves along a plane which is parallel to the line of scrimmage.

He then moves outward and widens his base to contact the force with what had been his outside shoulder. A hammer block on the right side is made with the right shoulder. The head of the guard should ideally be positioned slightly behind the force defender. This head positioning makes the defender run around the hammer block to make the play. By the time he is able to run around the block, the ball carrier has hit the crease of the alley.

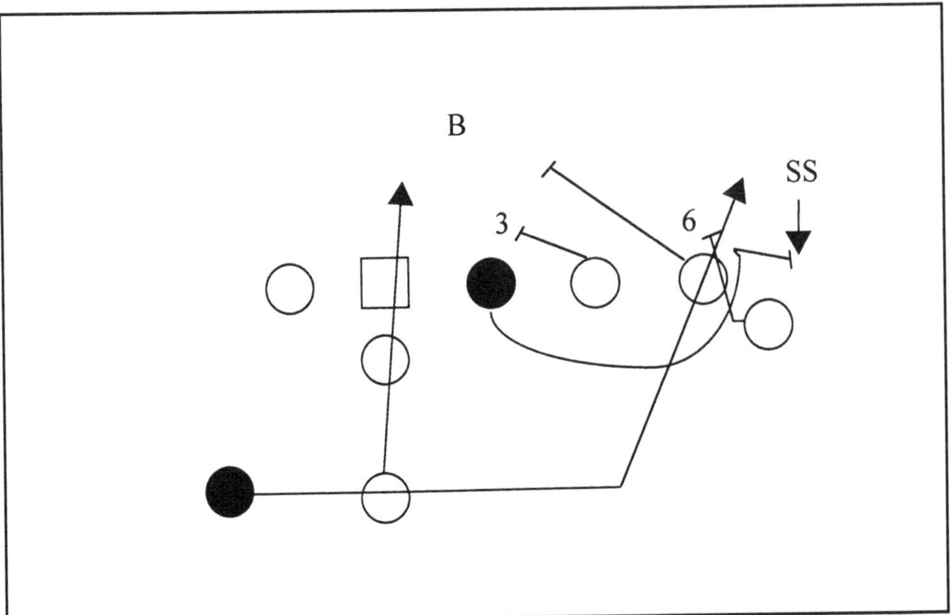

Diagram 6-7: A short sweep hammer block by the right guard.

The kick-out block technique off of the short pull is very different from the hammer pull. As described in the previous paragraph, for the first four to five steps, the hammer blocking guard pulls on the same track as the wall blocking guard. The kick-out technique pulling guard departs from this path on his second step. Obtaining depth and tracking on a vertical charge toward the line of scrimmage are key coaching points of the wall and the hammer blocks.

The kick-out blocker doesn't gain significant depth off the line of scrimmage when pulling. His angle is near that of a long trapper. He keeps his shoulders facing the sideline as he moves to kick-out the hard charging force. On contact with the force defender, the kick-out sweep pulling technique is identical to that of the trap pulling contact. If the kick-out blocker is sweep pulling to the right, he should contact the force defender with his right shoulder. If the kick-out blocker is sweep pulling to the left, he should contact the force defender with his left shoulder.

The long sweep pull starts out like a long trap. It normally is used as a wall blocking technique. The initial step is a flat step off of a push with the outside foot. The guard's shoulders face a plane parallel to the line of scrimmage as he passes between the quarterback and the center. The split of the guard should be wide enough to allow him to clear the center as he makes his third step.

A tight split alters the timing of the pull, as well as presents a potential threat for causing a fumble. Guards who take too tight a split may hit the ball on the handshake opening of the long trap technique. They sometimes cause a fumble as they hit the ball before the quarterback can properly seat the ball. Once the guard clears the center on his third step, he crosses over and gains depth. The crossover is sometimes called the "Heisman pull" because the movement resembles the Heisman trophy pose. Depth is gained to approximately two yards behind the line of scrimmage.

The backside wall pulling blocker will then attack the outside hip of the blocker assigned to seal the edge of the defense. The landmark of the backside wall pulling is the outside hip of the seal blocker. The backside guard should keep his eyes inside as he looks for leakage between the tackles. Once he hits the landmark with his shoulders square, he uses his inside shoulder pad to drive through any defender's outside shoulder. With proper technique, the backside guard may seal one, two, or even three defenders as he continues on the proper path.

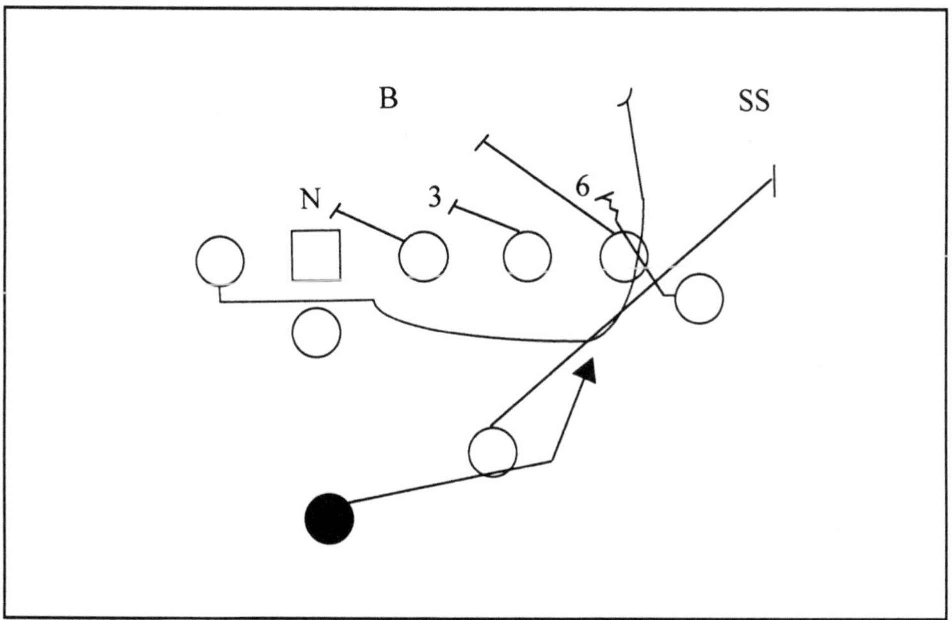

Diagram 6-8: A long sweep wall block by the backside guard.

Similar to the onside short sweep pull, the long sweep pull from the backside is also used as a play pass protection in the bootleg/waggle scheme. Some run and waggle blocking schemes require both the onside and the backside pulling guards to read the defensive flow on the perimeter. In this case, the long pulling wall guard from the backside could transform into the hammer blocker if the frontside short pulling guard chooses to wall off the edge. Additional details on the reading sweep pulling technique are provided in the discussion of the bootleg/waggle scheme later in this chapter.

Previously, the sweep pulls were discussed solely with regard to the guards pulling. In reality, however, tackles and even centers can sweep pull. These positions pull sometimes as an alternative scheme when one or both of the guards are facing a defensive linemen. While an uncommon tactic, the backside tackle has been known to provide an effective wall block as a backside waggle/bootleg blocker. Likewise, some offensive schemes have made effective use of pulling the uncovered center as a wall blocker on the sweep. In addition, the playside tackle is an extremely effective lead blocker when using either the hammer or the kick-out short pulling technique on quick toss plays.

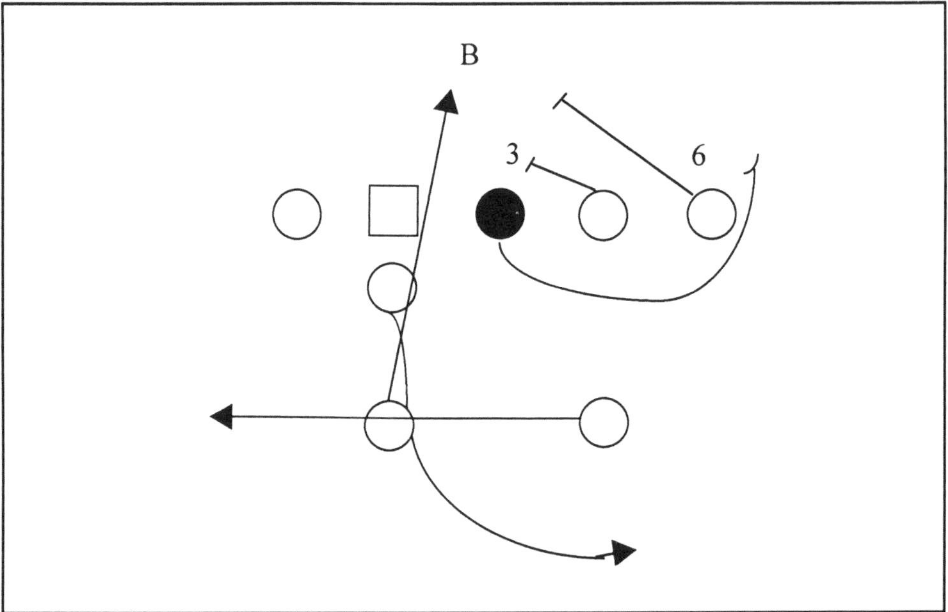

Diagram 6-9: A short sweep wall by the frontside guard on the bootleg.

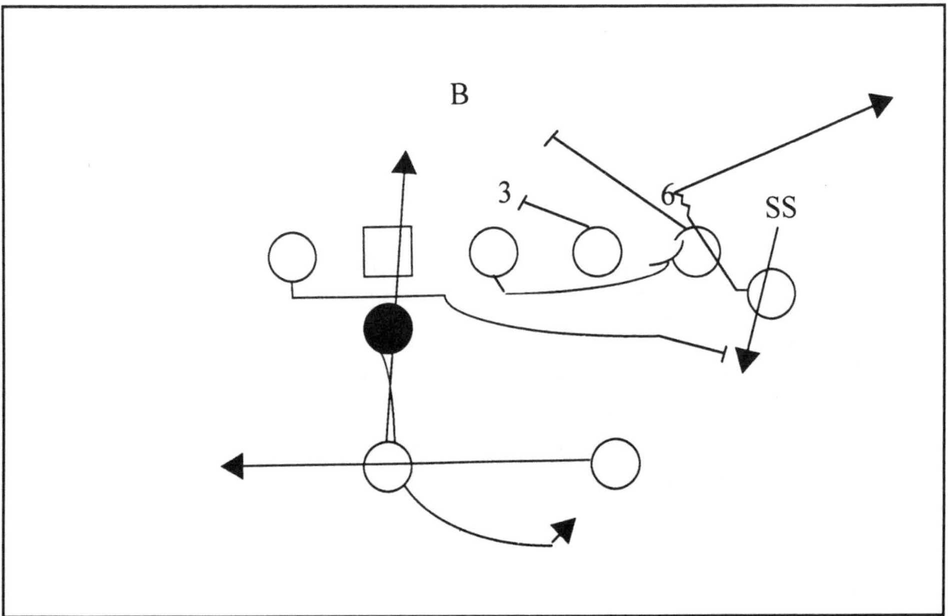

Diagram 6-10: A long sweep kick-out block by the backside guard on the bootleg.

TRAP PULL

The trap pull is one of two basic types of pulling techniques. The other type is the sweep pull. The term "trap pull" is normally used to describe a trap pull from the offside to the onside. However, a trap pull technique is also used as an onside trap pull known as a G-block.

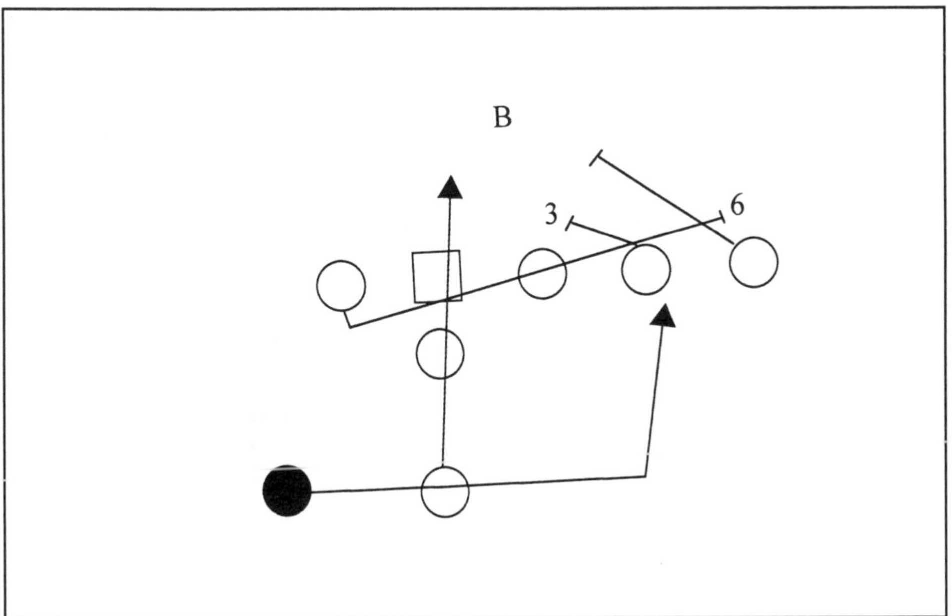

Diagram 6-11: A trap pull from the offside to the onside by the left guard.

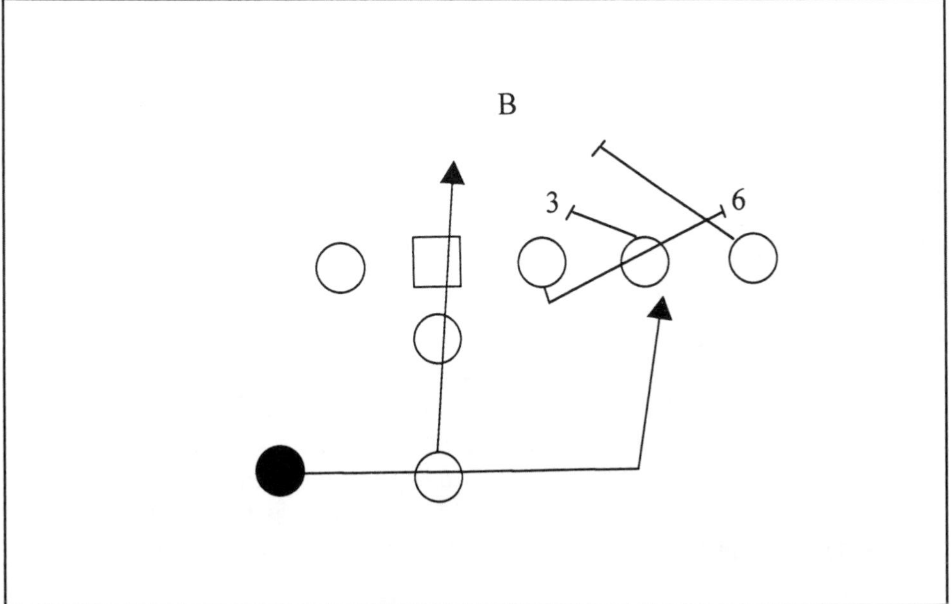

Diagram 6-12: A trap pull G block by the onside guard.

A trap pulling lineman pushes off hard on his push foot. When pulling to trap across the ball, the offensive lineman can use his down hand to help push with his outside foot. This pushing action forces the trapper's hips to open in what is called the pivot stage of the trap pull. During the pivot, the trapper should jerk his inside elbow backward so that his lead hand opens to the path he is about to take.

The opening of the hand to the trapping path is called the handshake move, because the finish of the move results in the lead hand being in the position of a handshake being offered. The length of the trap influences the depth to which the lead shoulder should be opened. For a longer trap, the inside elbow should snap backward in a manner closer to a sweep pull technique. Snapping the elbow further back opens the shoulder to a greater degree, thereby resulting in the trapper being in a position to better track flat down the line of scrimmage. To track sharper into the line of scrimmage on a short trap, the lineman should offer a sharper handshake (i.e., pointing his fingers into the line of scrimmage).

The track of the inside foot off of the initial pivot-push starting sequence should be on the same angle as the point of the handshake. The footwork of any trap is the pivot-push footwork. The blocker uses the handshake to facilitate the opening of the hips and the pivot. The inside foot plants near the desired track as the outside foot pivots to turn the backside knee inside. The outside foot then pushes hard against the turf to propel the trapper on the track. The outside foot pivots, then pushes to track the blocker on his trapping angle.

While offensive guards most commonly function as trappers, tight ends and tackles also trap. Guards run long and short traps. Tackles run only long traps. Tight ends normally trap off of a formation shift and motion across the center—an action that makes them primarily a short trapper. The length of a trap is significant because it determines the angle of the trapper's track to the defender. Short trappers run short angles off a sharp handshake move. Long trappers run a flatter angle. In fact, long trappers should run their track on a parallel plane to the line of scrimmage. A long trapper should run on his flat track until he clears the center. As he passes the playside leg of the center, the trapper should immediately begin angling inward to kick-out the defender.

The two-fold cardinal rule of trap pulling is: "pull left—hit left; pull right—hit right." While several extended coaching points can be included in coaching the trapper, the cardinal rule explains trapping in a clear and concise way to players of all levels. The rule has a straightforward meaning to offensive linemen. *When pulling to the right, the trap pulling lineman must contact the targeted defender with his right shoulder. When pulling to the left, the trap pulling lineman must contact the targeted defender with his left shoulder.* If a lineman adheres to the trap rule when he pulls, he is guaranteed to be on the correct trapping path. He will always be on the kick-out angle.

Unfortunately many coaches "over-coach" the trapper. These coaches often require the trapper to read the action of the defender. If the defender closes down the line of scrimmage to stuff the trapper, the pulling lineman can simply convert his trap technique to a log technique and seal the defender inside. The ball carrier is trained to read the log and skip off the butt of the log blocking lineman. The term "over-coach" is not necessarily a derogative reference with regard to this coaching technique. It simply refers to the degree of extended teaching that can be attempted in coaching the trap. Many offensive schemes require "over-coaching" the trap as an integral part of the scheme. For an offensive system such as the Wing-T, the trap must be a series that cannot be stopped. Accordingly, the Wing-T offensive line coach is well-advised to spend as much time as possible coaching the various elements of the trap pull.

On the other hand, some offensive line coaches feel that the over-coaching of the trap leads to poor trap angles by the blocker. In this situation, the blocker becomes tentative and gets caught between the sharp trap angle and the rounded finish of the log block. These coaches feel that you can eliminate the problem of a defensive lineman closing down and spilling the trap if you call the trap at the proper time, thereby setting the defense up during its most vulnerable alignment and game situation.

You should remember that the trap is an opportunistic type of play. It is most successful when run on passing downs—when the defense least expects it. Traps can keep the dominant defensive lineman honest as you take advantage of his aggressiveness. Traps can hurt the penetrating front that is supported by linebackers from a deep alignment. G-blocks are highly effective against defensive ends who are outside conscious. Positioning a wingback near a defensive end enhances the G-block's effectiveness, because the defensive end becomes extremely alert to the threat of the wingback blocking down on him.

The G-block is simply an outside trap by the playside guard. The trapping guard doesn't cross the center, as on other traps. The G-blocking technique is a true mirror technique of the normal trapping guard's technique: the blocker's pivot is to the outside; his outside hand makes the handshake move; and he pushes off the inside foot to track inside out to the defensive end. The G-blocking guard always kicks out the first man on or outside the tight end. The defensive end may be set up by a rip move of the tight end to the inside, or a combination of a rip move to the inside by the tight end and a down block influence by the wingback.

Offensive linemen don't use a down block influence move. It is a move used exclusively by a wingback. On a down block influence, the wingback baits the defensive end by driving toward his outside shoulder—faking a down block—and then planting off the inside foot to angle outside to kick-out the strong safety.

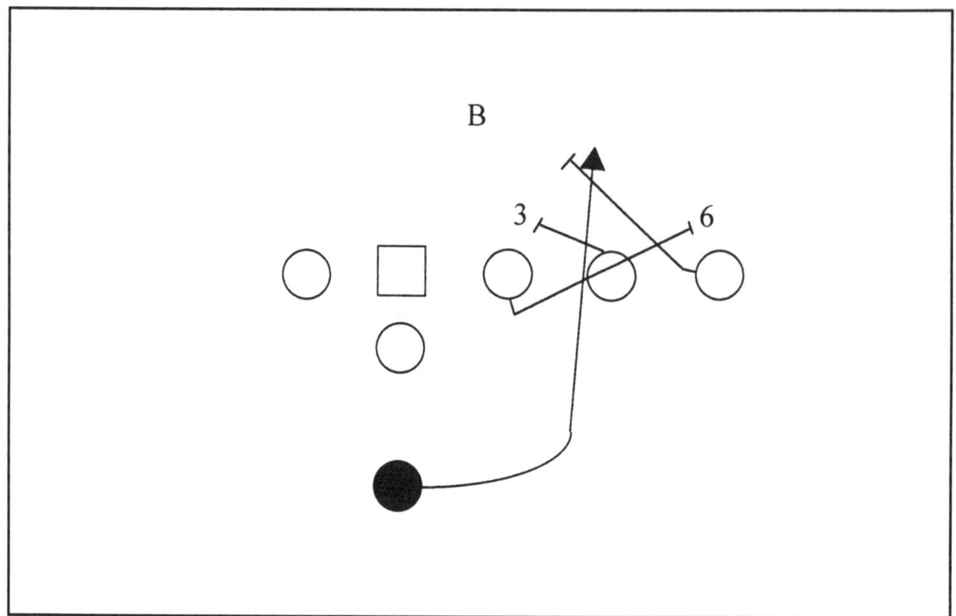

Diagram 6-13: A trap pull G block by the onside guard as the tight end rips underneath.

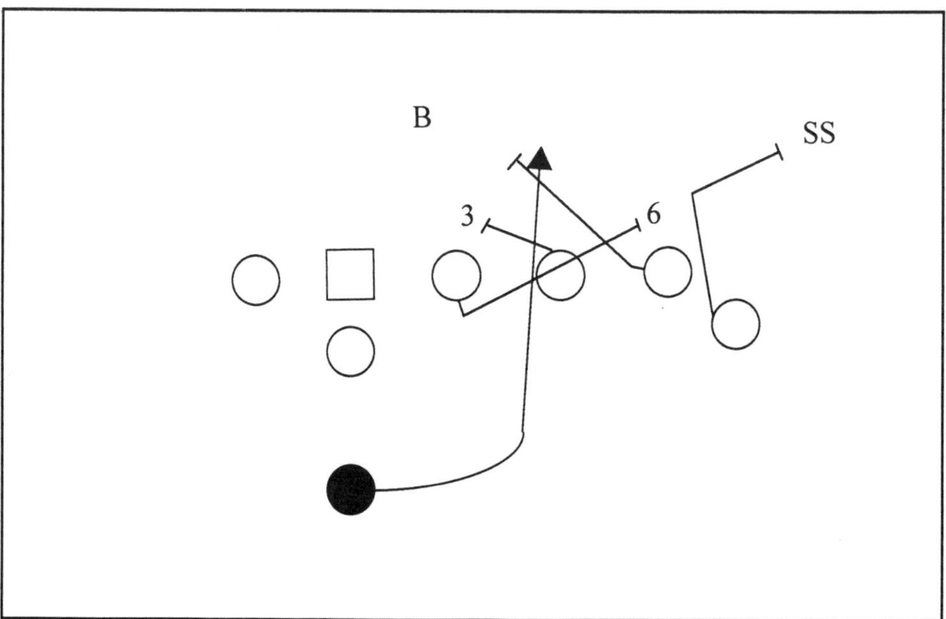

Diagram 6-14: A trap pull G block by the onside guard with an influence block by the wingback.

WAGGLE/BOOTLEG PULL

The terms waggle and bootleg are essentially synonymous terms for a type of play pass (i.e., pass executed off the fake of a run). The waggle/bootleg involves one or two linemen pulling opposite the flow of the backfield.

A play pass action, the waggle/bootleg is an excellent play and important part of any offensive attack, from the full house T formation to the one-back spread scheme. On the waggle/bootleg action, the playside is the side opposite the side to where the running backs flow. On the waggle/bootleg, the playside guard will short sweep pull to gain two to three yards depth and will immediately focus his line of sight on a triangular area slicing through the outside hip of the near tackle (refer to Diagram 6-15). By throwing his eyes to the tackle's hip, the guard can immediately recognize the action of the man on the tackle. The quick recognition of the defender's reaction enables the guard to take the proper path to log block the defender.

The backside guard pulls flat past the center and gains depth on his third step. The backside guard also looks through the triangle. If he recognizes an upfield charge by the defensive end, the guard will flatten out and trap block the defensive end. On a trap block, the pulling lineman blocks with the shoulder corresponding to the direction of his pull. When pulling to the left, the right guard will trap block using his left shoulder to make contact with the defender. This block drives the defender outward and allows the quarterback to duck under in the seam between the log of the playside guard and the trap of the backside guard (refer to Diagram 6-16).

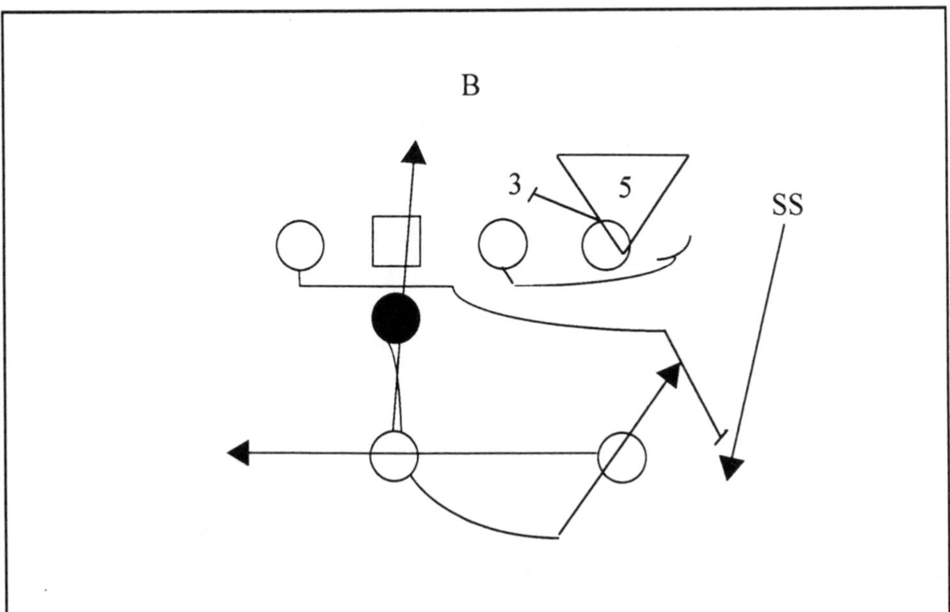

Diagram 6-15: The lead guard immediately sights the triangular area off the tackle's hip.

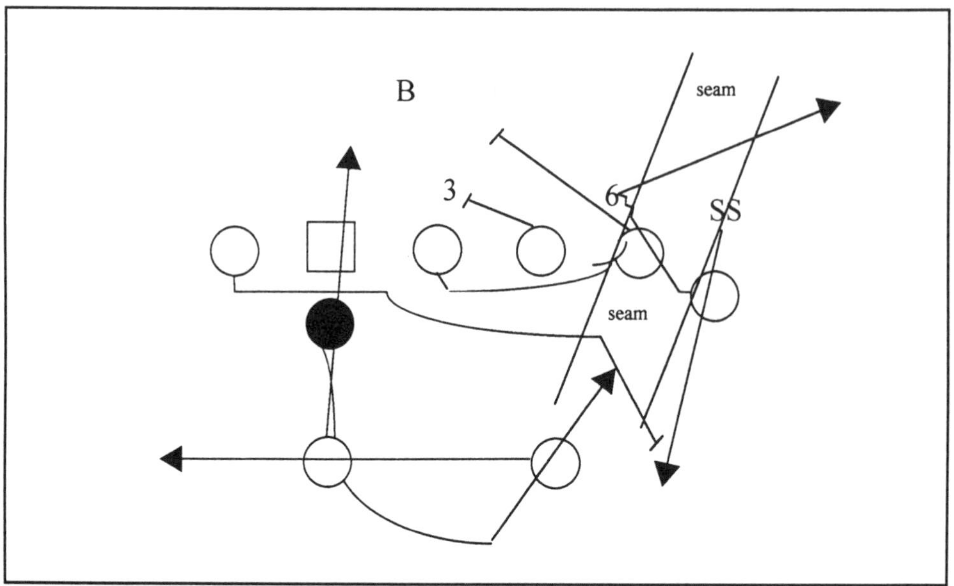

Diagram 6-16: The backside guard reads the strong safety blitz and kicks-out the strong safety, thereby creating a seam for the quarterback to suck under the blitz.

PULL CHECK

The backside tackle executes a "pull-check" on the waggle. This term refers to the fact that the tackle will pull into the space vacated by the backside pulling guard. If no defender is on the guard, the tackle will pull into the space and check the linebacker. If the linebacker does not attack the space, then the tackle may peel back to the backside to pick up a corner blitz (refer to Diagram 6-17).

If a defender is aligned on the guard, then the backside tackle will pull hard into the space. The tackle will attempt to place his outside shoulder on the inside knee of the defender. The technique involves the tackle pushing off his outside foot and taking a slight bucket step with his inside foot. This action puts him on an arcing path to the inside knee of the defender. If the defender slants inside to the center, the tackle should not over commit to the defender. The tackle blocks an area, not a man. Once the defender slants to the center, the tackle squares his pads and checks for a linebacker. If no linebacker shows, then he may peel back for a corner blitz. See Diagram 6-18.

HORN PULL

An alternative to a drive block against the inside-shaded defensive tackle is the guard horn block. The horn block should be used with off-tackle plays in which the guard is drive blocking the linebacker in the 30 front. Normally, this block is a read block since the guard makes a presnap read of whether he should pull around the horn instead of drive blocking the linebacker.

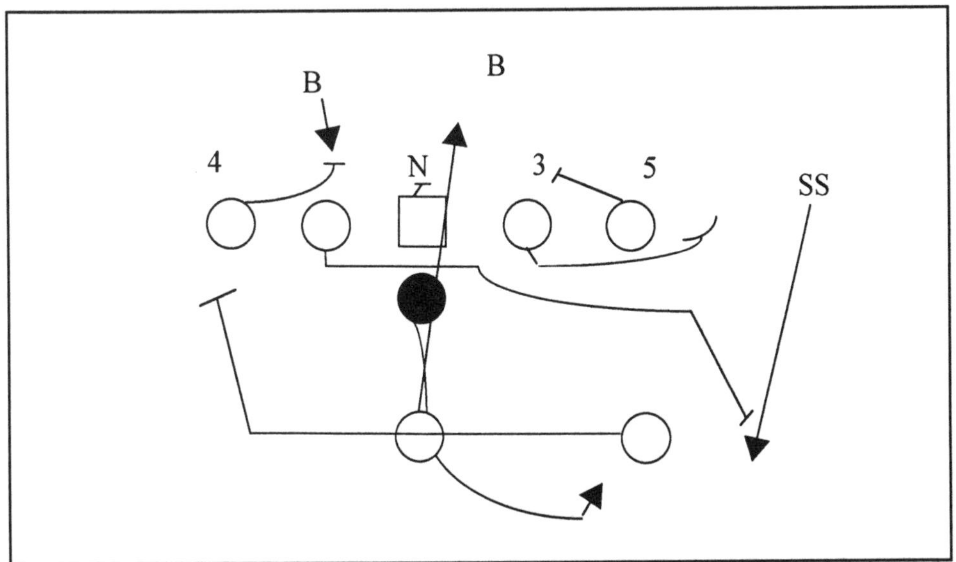

Diagram 6-17: The backside tackle pull checks to pick up the blitzing linebacker backside on the waggle.

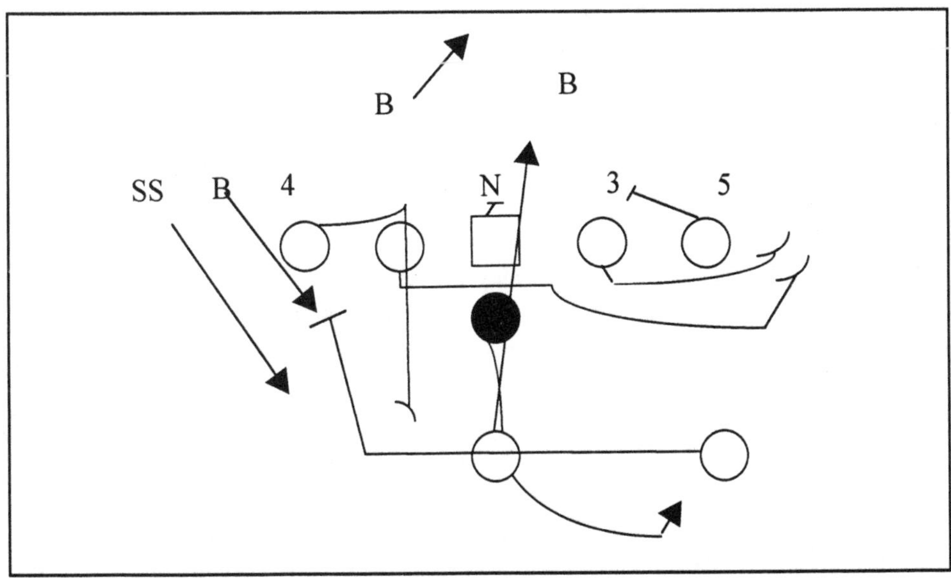

Diagram 6-18: The backside tackle pull checks and bails out to pick up the outside blitz if the inside linebacker doesn't blitz.

The basis for converting the drive block into a horn pull is the presence of a 4i technique defensive tackle. A 4i defensive tackle—particularly a gap 4i technique tackle—blocks the guard's path to the playside number of the linebacker. When he reads an off tackle play, the linebacker can easily scrape over the top as the defensive tackle occupies two blockers—the guard and tackle. Diagram 6-19a shows the 4i technique blocking the offensive guard from getting on the proper track to engage the linebacker's playside number.

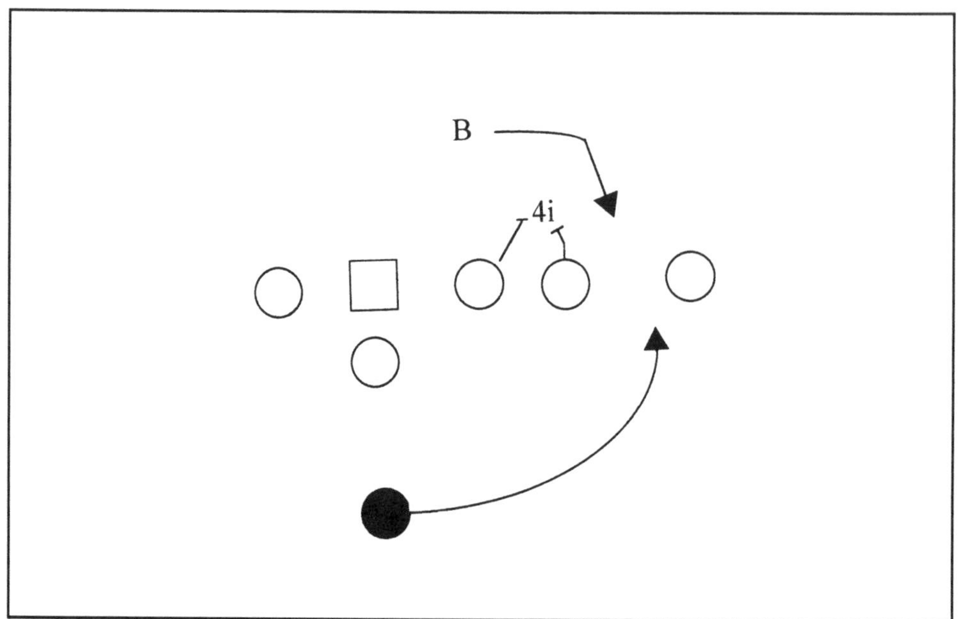

Diagram 19a: The 4i technique obstructs the guard's drive blocking angle to the linebacker on the off-tackle play.

Some coaches feel that the outside zone block combination is a better scheme for dealing with the 4i technique in a 30 front. However, a combination block—such as the outside zone—involves precise execution by two players working as one. The horn pull—while a combination in theory—involves only the tackle caving down the 4i technique, while the guard simply uses his tag technique to step around the horn and seal the linebacker. The drive block by the tackle and the horn pull by the guard is a much simpler and easier-to-execute scheme than the outside zone. Additional comparative information on the outside zone block (versus a horn pull) is presented in Chapter 5.

An important coaching point for the guard to remember when horn blocking is to keep his shoulders parallel as he steps back to read the flow of the linebacker. He can use the tag block technique of stepping back with his inside foot, then driving off the tackle's hip. Additional information on the guard's first step in the tag block technique is presented in Chapter 5 in the section on the fold block combination.

The guard may also execute the horn block by simply stepping laterally off the line with his outside foot and reading the linebacker's flow. With either technique, the most important coaching point for the guard is to keep his eyes on the linebacker.

If the defensive scheme puts the tackle in a 4 technique and plays games—sometimes sparking him inside and other times sparking him outside, the horn pull can be used as a simple counter measure to the confusion which could be caused by the stunts. To counter the games without using the zone blocking schemes, the guard may simply step to read the linebacker as the tackle latches on to the defender, no matter which direction he stunts. If the 4 technique tackle stunts inside, the guard reads the linebacker scraping over the top and pulls around the horn to junction him. If the 4 technique tackle stunts outside, the offensive tackle pins him, and the guard reads the linebacker filling inside the tackle's stunt. When the guard reads the linebacker hanging inside to fill the "B" gap, he simply drives off his outside foot and blocks the linebacker with a proper run-blocking demeanor.

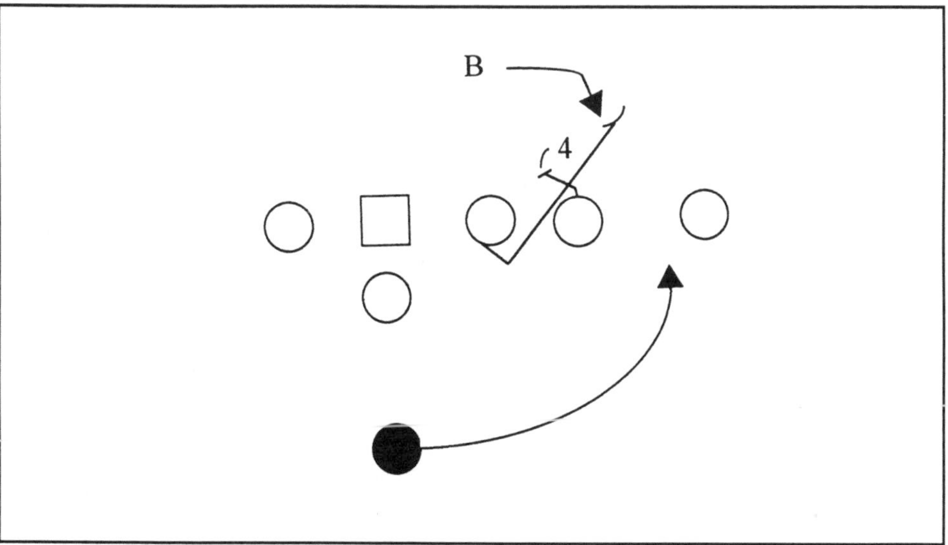

Diagram 6-19b: The guard can use the horn block to pull around the "horn" and to seal the scraping linebacker against a defensive tackle who is stunting inside.

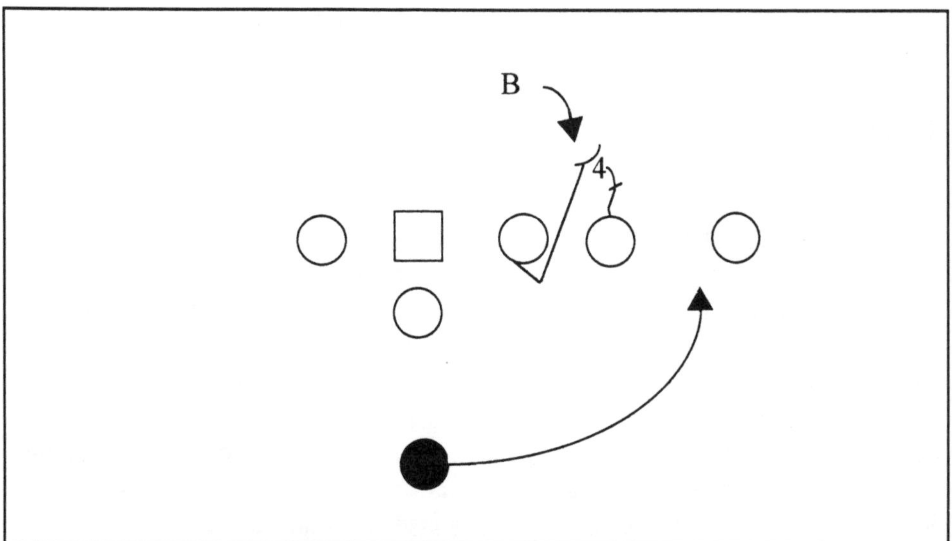

Diagram 6-19c: The guard can use the horn block to read the linebacker plugging the "B" gap when the defensive tackle stunts outside.

QUICK SCREEN PULL

The quick screen pull is executed by the playside tackle. Sometimes called a "running pull," the quick screen pull is used to kick-out a cornerback who is attempting to cover the wide receiver. The quick screen, also known as the slip screen, involves the wide receiver driving off the line for two steps and then planting his feet to circle around behind the line of scrimmage to catch the ball on the run. Since the pass is a screen, the other offensive linemen are also using a screen blocking technique against the other defenders. However, the playside tackle's block is the key block that springs the wide receiver on the play. While his teammates fan out to block their assigned defenders, the offensive tackle sprints to a point approximately two yards in front of the line of scrimmage. The tackle can visualize this pull as a type of extended fan block. He should pull neither too flat nor too sharply upfield. He must make contact with the cornerback with a tight fit. Ironically, while his block is a key block, it isn't the tackle's responsibility to make him get into position to contact the cornerback. It is the wide receiver's responsibility to bring the cornerback to the offensive tackle. The offensive tackle needs only to get his body under control just as he comes to within four yards of the receiver. Because the pass is a screen pass, the tackle does not need to be concerned with being downfield illegally or being flagged for interference. The tackle may legally block the cornerback past the line of scrimmage as the ball is thrown and he may legally block the cornerback while the ball is in the air.

The other four offensive linemen basically perform a type of fan pull toward their assigned defenders as the ball is released. Some coaches run this play as a double screen with both tackles pulling to the widest cornerback. Other coaches run this play in the nature of a kick-off return blocking scheme—giving the interior linemen a numbered defender to block outward in the same manner as a kick-off return blocker.

REVERSE SPIN PULL

An extremely deceptive pulling technique for the reverse, the reverse spin pull resembles more of a ballet move than a block. The reverse spin pull is normally run by one or both of the guards. It seems to be most effective when the guards fake a block to one direction and then reverse spin to the opposite direction as shown in Diagram 6-21. The reverse spin pull calls for the guard to fake a zone block for three steps to the side of the initial fake. If running the reverse to the left, the guard will fake his zone block to the right for three steps. He will then plant on his right foot and cross over with his left foot. He should zone block hard on an overly flat angle when he zones to the right. This action allows him to turn his shoulders nearly perpendicular to the line of scrimmage as he faces the right sideline. By overemphasizing the set to reach and turning his shoulders, the guard can quickly cross over with the left foot (or bucket step with the right foot) to spin around and begin pulling in the opposite direction.

Ideally, the lead guard of the reverse will pull around the end and log any defender who redirects his pursuit as he recognizes the reverse. The backside guard will pull around the wall block and hammer block the cornerback who—by the time play develops—should be coming off his man or should be out of his zone to provide late run support. The reverse spin pull can be a game-breaking technique when used with a timely reverse off of a common sweep series.

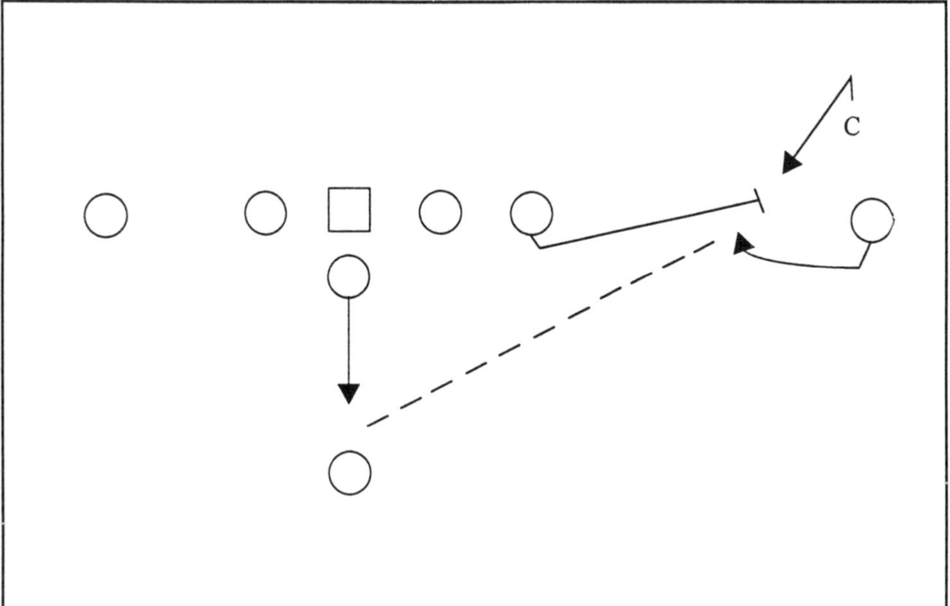

Diagram 6-20: The quick screen pull.

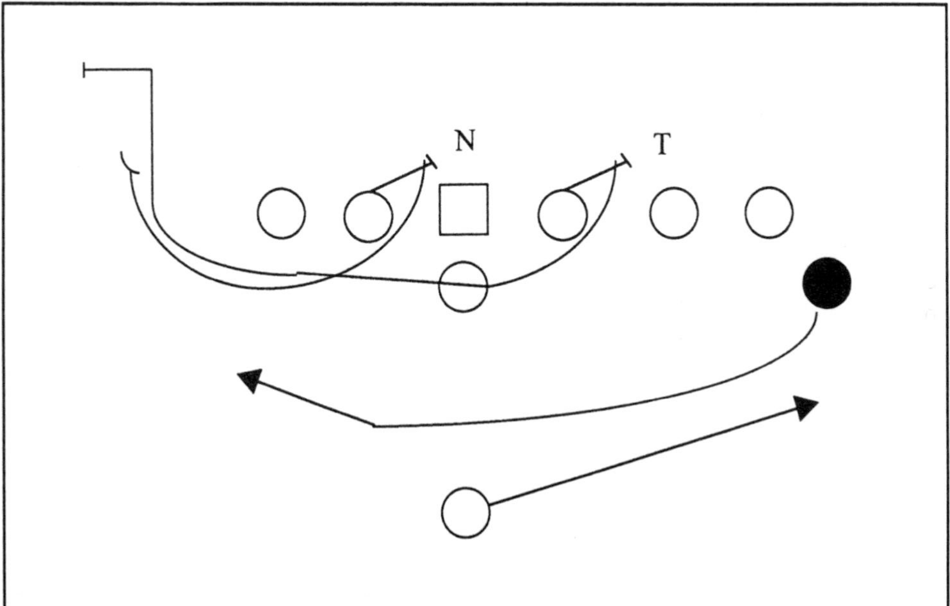

Diagram 6-21: The reverse spin pull.

CHAPTER 7

Run-Blocking Drills

DRILL #1: EVERY DAY DOT DRILLS (EDDD'S) FOR RUN BLOCKING

Objective: To develop an offensive linemen's ability to master the first three steps of the various run blocks.

Equipment Needed: Cones or bags.

Procedure: The five interior linemen form lines within a marked ten-yard area according to their position. On the coach's command, five players execute one repetition of the specified run-blocking technique for ten yards. The techniques that the players execute include:

- The demeanor walk.
- The set to drive with the right foot.
- The set to drive with the left foot.
- The set to reach with the outside foot.
- The down block.
- The trap pull.
- The sweep pull.
- The cut off.

Coaching Points:

- During the early stages of the season, the coach should focus on the execution of the first step of the blocking sequence.
- As the players begin to demonstrate mastery of the first step, the coach should shift his attention to developing the correct technique of the second and third steps.

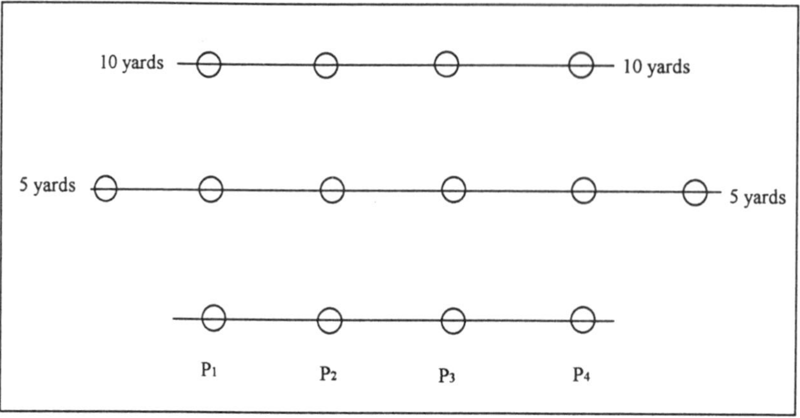

Diagram 7-1a: Dots (or cones) within a 10-yard grid for the EDDD's run-blocking drills.

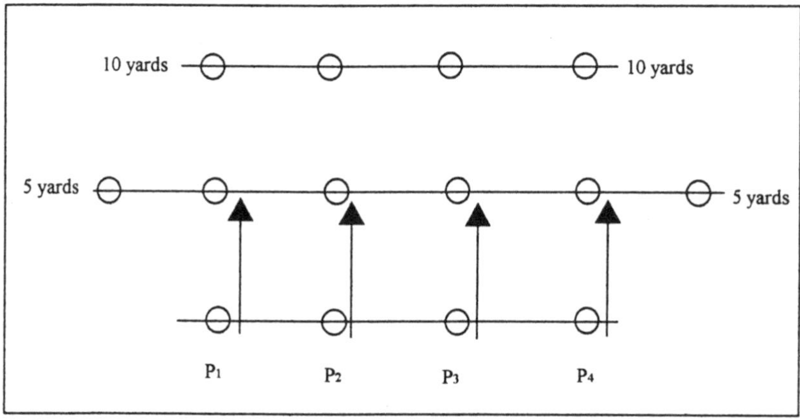

Diagram 7-1b: Players walk straight ahead with a good run-blocking demeanor during the demeanor walk EDDD drill.

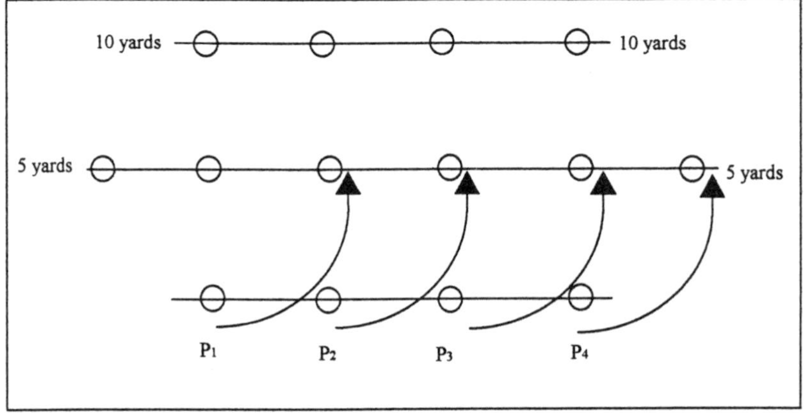

Diagram 7-1c: Players set to reach to the right with a good run-blocking demeanor during the set to reach EDDD drill.

DRILL #2: TWO-MAN SLED FIT

Objective: To help an offensive lineman develop a feel for the proper fit into the defender.

Equipment Needed: Two-man sled.

Procedure: Two linemen position themselves in a three-point stance to block the two-man sled. On the coach's command, the players fire out on the pad and make contact. The linemen should exhibit the proper run-blocking demeanor as they fit with the sled's pads. The proper fit position involves the blocker keeping his knees and ankles bent. He should keep his back flat as he strikes the pad with his hands, thereby creating the triangle. The three points of the triangle consist of his hands and his head, as his thumbs strike the pad in an up position. The blocker's facemask should be positioned between both of his hands. The head should be slightly higher than the plane on which his hands are placed. The player freezes in the fit position as the coach checks the technique of the fit.

Coaching Points:

- The players should fit with a right foot set to drive and a left foot set to drive.
- The player's elbows should be held close to his body.
- His face should make minimal contact with the pad; his hands should punch the pad away from his face.
- The player should take two steps before striking the pad—the set-to-drive and the attack step.

Diagram 7-2.

DRILL #3: TWO-MAN SLED FIT AND DRIVE

Objective: To help an offensive linemen develop a feel for the proper run-blocking demeanor.

Equipment Needed: Two-man sled.

Procedure: Two linemen position themselves in a fit position with the respective pad. The players should exhibit the proper run-blocking demeanor as they fit with the sled's pads. The proper fit position involves the linemen keeping his knees and ankles bent. He should keep his back flat as he strikes the pad with his hands, thereby creating the triangle. The three points of the triangle consist of his hands and his head, as his thumbs strike the pad in an up position. The blocker's facemask should be positioned between both of his hands. On the fit, the lineman's head should be slightly higher than the plane on which his hands are placed. Each player extends his arms as he punches through the pad of the sled. After the players have driven the sled for several feet, the coach blows the whistle, and the players stop driving the sled and return to the fit position.

Coaching Points:

- The players should fit with a right foot set to drive and a left foot set to drive.
- The player's elbows should be held close to his body.
- The player's should make minimal contact with the pad; his hands should punch the pad away from his face.
- The player should take two steps before striking the pad—the set-to-drive and the attack step.

Diagram 7-3.

DRILL #4: TWO-MAN SLED PUT IT TOGETHER DRILL

Objective: To help offensive linemen develop a feel for the proper fit and run-blocking demeanor when blocking the defender.

Equipment Needed: Two-man sled.

Procedure: Two linemen position themselves in a three-point stance to block the two-man sled. On the coach's command, the players fire out on the pad and drive the sled. The players should exhibit the proper run-blocking demeanor as they fit with the sled's pads. The proper fit position involves the player keeping his knees and ankles bent. He should keep his back flat as he strikes the pad with his hands, thereby creating the triangle. The three points of the triangle consist of his hands and his head, as his thumbs strike the pad in an up position. The blocker's facemask should be positioned between both of his hands. His head should be slightly higher than the plane on which his hands are placed. The players drive their hands through the pad and extend their arms as they drive the sled. The coach blows the whistle, and the players stop and return to the fit position.

Coaching Points:

- The player's elbows should be held close to his body.
- The player's face should make minimal contact with the pad; his hands should punch the pad away from his face.
- The player should take two steps before striking the pad—the set-to-drive and the attack step.
- The upper screws of the player's facemask should be positioned below the top of the sled pads.
- This drill can be done with the players blocking from three positions: directly in front of the pad; offset to the inside of the pad; and offset to the outside of the pad.

Diagram 7-4.

DRILL #5: LINE SURGE DRILL

Objective: To develop the offensive unit's explosiveness off the ball and anaerobically condition the blockers' legs.

Equipment Needed: Five-man sled.

Procedure: The offensive line aligns in a three-point stance to block the five-man sled. On the coach's command, the players fire out on the pad and drive the sled. The players should exhibit the proper run-blocking demeanor as they fit with the sled's pads. The proper fit position involves each linemen keeping his knees and ankles bent. He should keep his back flat as he strikes the pad with his hands creating the triangle. The triangle consists of his hands and head, as his thumbs strike the pad with the thumbs up. The blocker's facemask should be positioned between both hands. The head should be slightly higher than the plane on which his hands are placed. The players drive their hands through the pad and extend their arms as they drive the sled. The coach blows the whistle to stop the players.

Coaching Points:

- The player's elbows should be held close to his body.
- The athlete's face should make minimal contact with the pad; his hands should punch the pad away from his face.
- The player should take two steps before striking the pad—the set-to-drive and the attack step.
- This drill can be performed with the players blocking from three positions: directly in front of the pad; offset to the inside of the pad; and offset to the outside of the pad.
- This drill is an excellent drill to hone the player's ability to respond to audibles.
- The offensive line may be directed to come out of a four-point goal line stance to sharpen their goal-line surge technique.

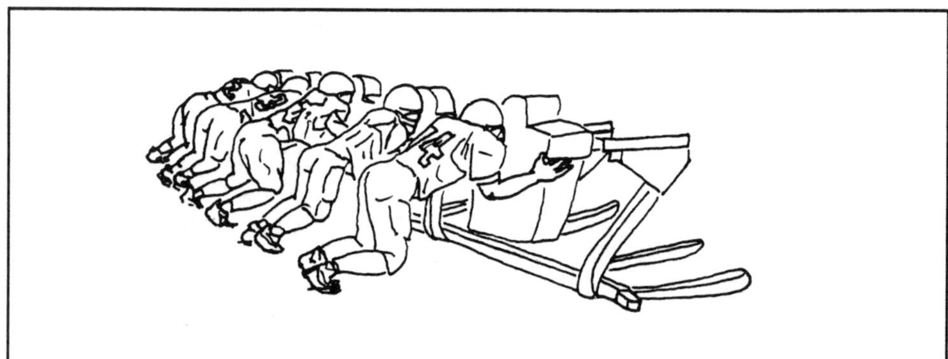

Diagram 7-5.

DRILL #6: THREE-ON-THREE DRILL

Objective: To develop the offensive lineman's ability to get off on the ball, knock the defender backward according to the three-inch rule, and finish the block.

Equipment Needed: Four cones to designate the corners of a ten-yard square.

Procedure: The drill is structured so that the blockers work across the field between two ten-yard designations. The ball is placed in the middle of the ten-yard segment—on a line marking the five-yard designation. The cones are placed on the four corners of the ten-yard area. Three running backs are aligned in a T set and a quarterback is positioned behind the offensive line. Three defensive linemen or linebackers align in head-up alignments on the blockers. The offensive linemen and the backs are told where the ball will hit and which back will carry the ball. On the snap of the ball, the offensive linemen execute a drive block on the head-up defender, as the quarterback hands the ball off to one of the running backs. As the one back gets the ball, the other two backs run laterally to fake. The blockers sustain contact until a coach blows the whistle.

Coaching Points:

- The coach should make sure that the blockers fit into the defenders and that they maintain the techniques of a proper run-blocking demeanor.
- The offensive line may be directed to come out of a four-point goal line stance to sharpen their goal line surge technique.
- The players should be rotated out of the drill either after three snaps or after the ball carrier breaks the plane of the ten-yard "end zone" line.

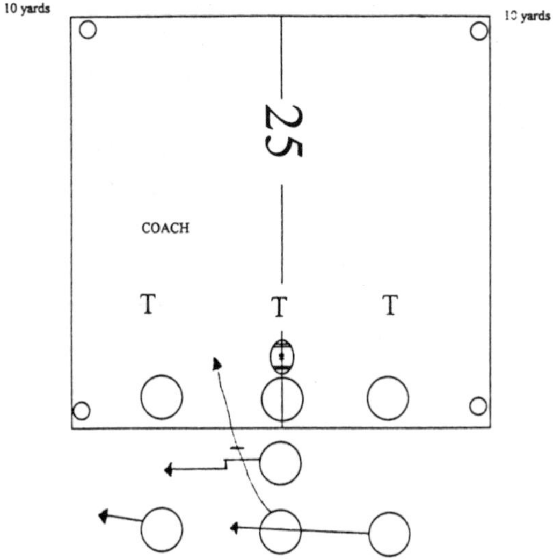

Diagram 7-6: Three-on-three drill.

DRILL #7: SEMINOLE DRILL

Objective: To develop the offensive lineman's ability to get off on the ball, knock the defender backward according to the three-inch rule, and finish the block.

Equipment Needed: One 8" x 2" x 12" blocking board.

Procedure: Two players straddle a blocking board near the midpoint of the board and face each other. The players take their stance approximately a football's length apart. The coach initiates the contest with a verbal or whistle command. On the starting command from the coach, both players attempt to drive the other off the end of the board. The coach blows the whistle to signal the end of the contest either when one blocker knocks the other off the end of the board or when one blocker breaks his straddle of the board by stepping one foot over the board.

Coaching Points:

- If feasible, I recommend matching an offensive lineman against a defensive lineman in the drill. If not, two offensive linemen could be matched against each other.
- The players should attempt to keep their feet on either side of the board (i.e., straddling the board).

Diagram 7-7.

DRILL #8: GROUP RUN DRILL

Objective: To develop the offensive line's timing of the running game at full speed versus a scout team defense.

Equipment Needed: A football.

Procedure: The drill is usually structured according to a script and typically involves part of the defense (i.e., no secondary) and only part of the offense (i.e., no wide receivers). A defensive scout coach shows the defense an alignment card or calls a known front. Two offensive huddles form in front of the defense. A play is communicated to the quarterback of the lead huddle. The quarterback calls the play and the snap count, and the offensive line sprints to the line of scrimmage. The play is executed, the whistle is sounded, and the players jog back to the huddle. The coaches should provide feedback to the players (i.e., do their coaching) as the players return to the huddle. Once the first group returns to the huddle, the coaches switch their attention to the second huddle as the play is communicated to the quarterback. The sequence repeats for the second group.

Coaching Points:

- The coaches should not stop the players to talk to them between the huddle break and the snap of the ball.
- The coaches should move about quickly, running along with the players and giving them feedback as they return to the huddle.
- A play should be repeated after the next huddle break if the play's execution was flawed.
- This drill is an excellent drill in which to include the weekly check-offs for the team's audible system.
- The script should be structured so that the defensive unit keeps the same alignment for three to four repetitions before changing alignments.

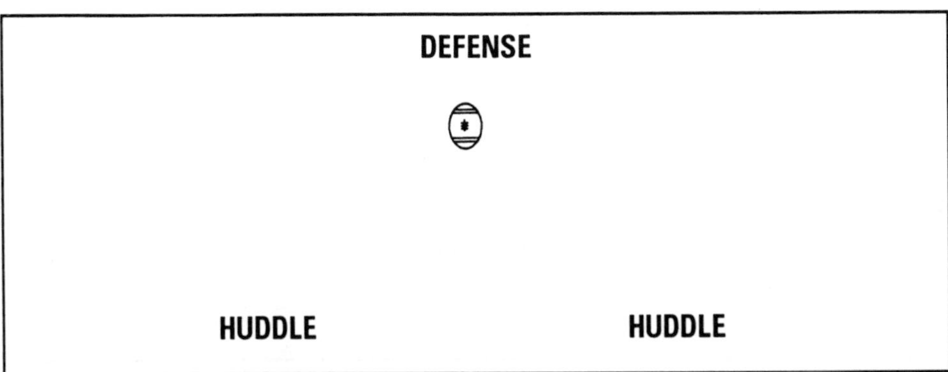

Diagram 7-8: Group run drill.

DRILL #9: TEAM RUN DRILL

Objective: To develop the offensive line's timing of the running game at full speed versus an 11-man scout team defense.

Equipment Needed: A football.

Procedure: Similar to Drill #8 (the group drill) this drill involves an entire offensive and an entire defensive team. The drill is usually structured according to a script. A defensive scout coach shows the defense an alignment card or calls a defensive front. A full offensive huddle forms in front of the defense. A play is communicated to the quarterback. The quarterback calls the play and the snap count, and the offensive line sprints to the line of scrimmage. The play is executed, the whistle is sounded, and the players jog back to the huddle. The coaches should do their coaching as the players return to the huddle. Once the group returns to the huddle, another play is immediately signaled to the quarterback. The sequence repeats until the drill is concluded.

Coaching Points:

- The game situation is scripted and explained to all of the participants.
- The ball is moved according to game situations.
- The play is directed as a simulated game.
- When the offense is playing live versus the number one defensive unit, the yard chains may be used instead of scripting down-and-distance.

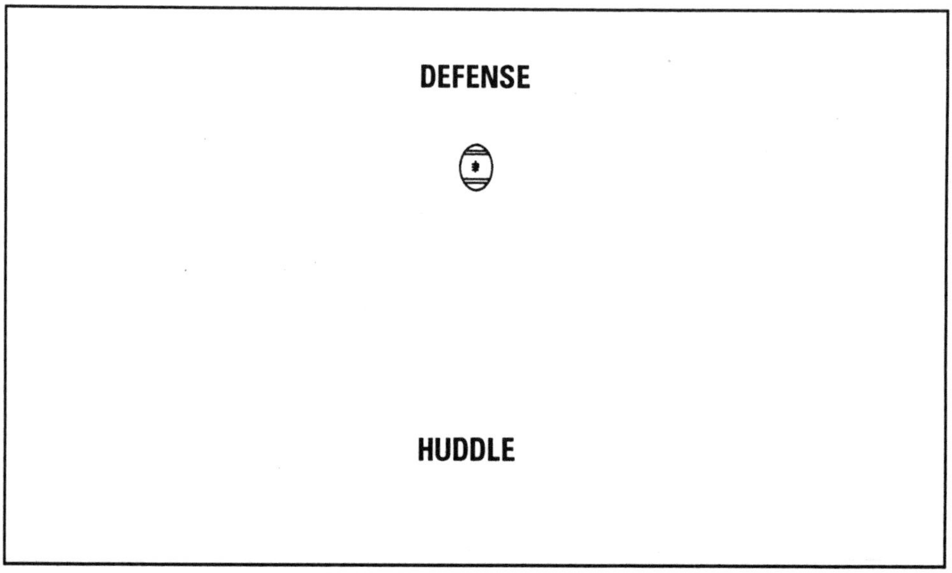

DEFENSE

HUDDLE

Diagram 7-9: Team run drill.

DRILL #10: SHOOT FIT TO DRIVE DRILL

Objective: To help the offensive lineman develop a feel for the proper fit of a drive block.

Equipment Needed: A shoot.

Procedure: A blocker stands assumes a three-point stance in the shoot (i.e., chute) and a defender stands immediately outside of the shoot. The blocker engages the defender with the proper fit of a run-blocking demeanor. The coach checks the coaching points of the fit and provides feedback to the blocker. Once the proper fit is established by the blocker and confirmed by the coach, the coach signals the blocker to drive block the defender from the fit position. When the coach blows the whistle, the blocker finishes the block by forcefully extending his arms and pushing the defender off the fit.

Coaching Points:

- The blocker should demonstrate a proper run-blocking demeanor as he uses small power steps to drive block the defender.
- The blocker should be positioned just under the far end of his shoot, with his head just outside of the shoot.

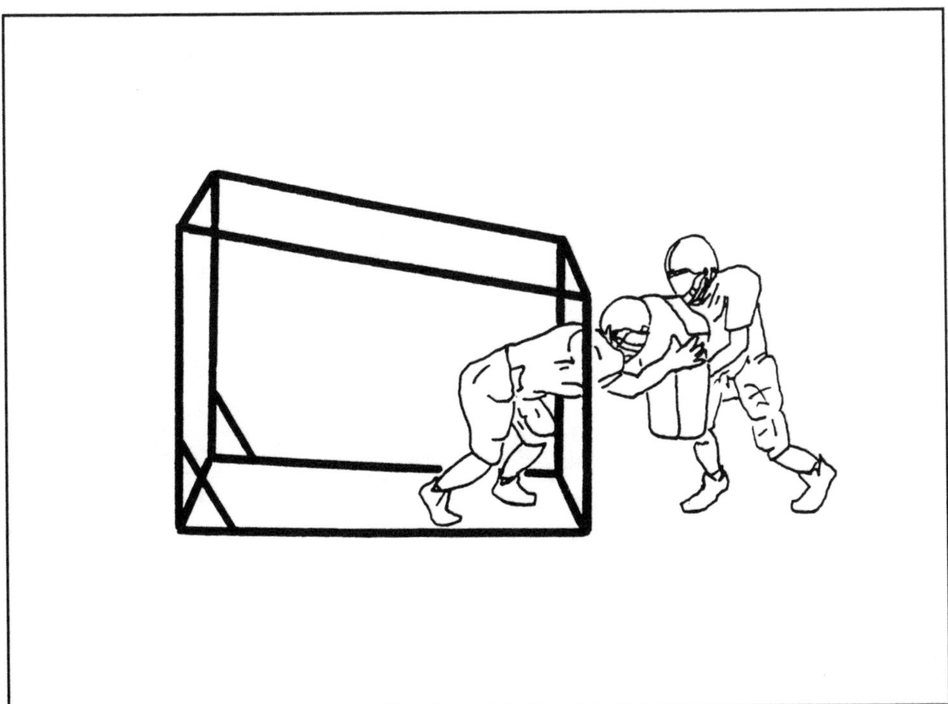

Diagram 7-10.

DRILL #11: DRIVE SETS

Objective: To practice firing off the ball in three of the eight possible directions with the proper set to drive.

Equipment Needed: Six cones.

Description: The linemen are stationed in two lines. The cones are positioned as shown, five yards from the starting point of the corresponding line. The drill is divided into three phases. The first phase is straight-ahead starts. Each lineman sets to drive with the outside foot, while pushing off the inside foot. The lineman sprints to cone number one and jogs around behind the cones to return to the line. The second phase is an angle step to the second cone, while the third phase is a trap pull step to the cone on the line of scrimmage. The linemen switch lines so that they practice setting to drive to the right and left, angle stepping to the right and left, and pulling to the right and left.

Coaching Points:

- The athlete should be reminded to place his weight on his inside foot.
- The athlete should be encouraged to throw his hands forward in a simulated punch as he pushes off the push foot.
- The coach checks for mastery of the set to drive techniques by observing the length of the first step. He should set to drive with a four- to five-inch stride.
- The athlete's stride should be a firm plant, not a heel-strike.

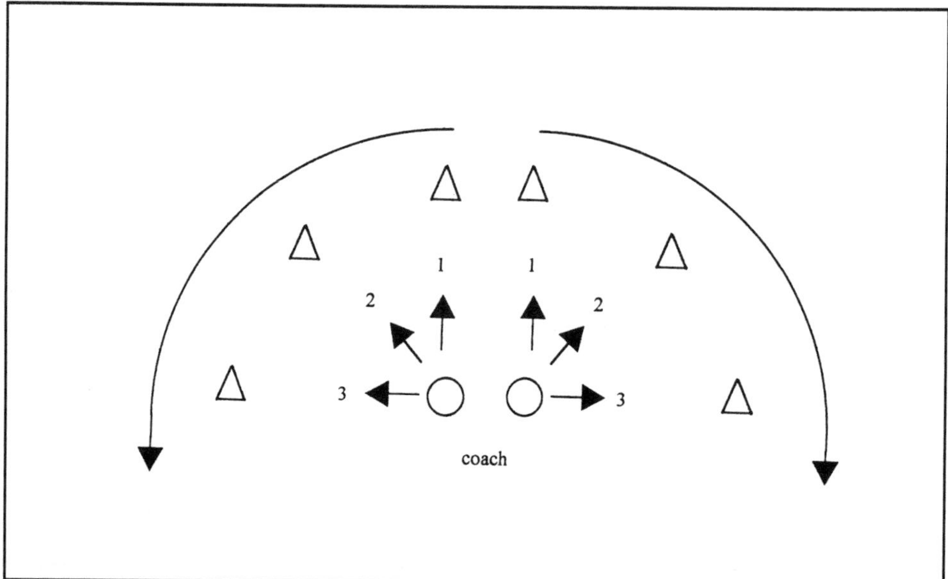

Diagram 7-11: Starts.

DRILL #12: OFF THE BALL DRILL

Objective: To practice the punch and lift of the drive block.

Equipment Needed: Two large blocking dummies.

Description: Two lines are formed. Each player area blocks the dummy, with his face in the middle of the dummy. The player throws his hands on the snap and punches and lifts the dummy, as his feet churn and his hips sink. The players alternate using a right and left set to drive against various defensive alignment shades.

Coaching Points:

- The blocker should drive the dummy with a lifting motion and the punch of the hands prevents the face from making a forceful contact with the dummy.
- The coach should check the stride length of the first step in order to reinforce the set to drive technique.
- The players should block the dummy for an unspecified distance until the whistle is blown. The point to remember is that the players should not block for a designated distance (i.e., 10 yards, 5 yards, etc.).

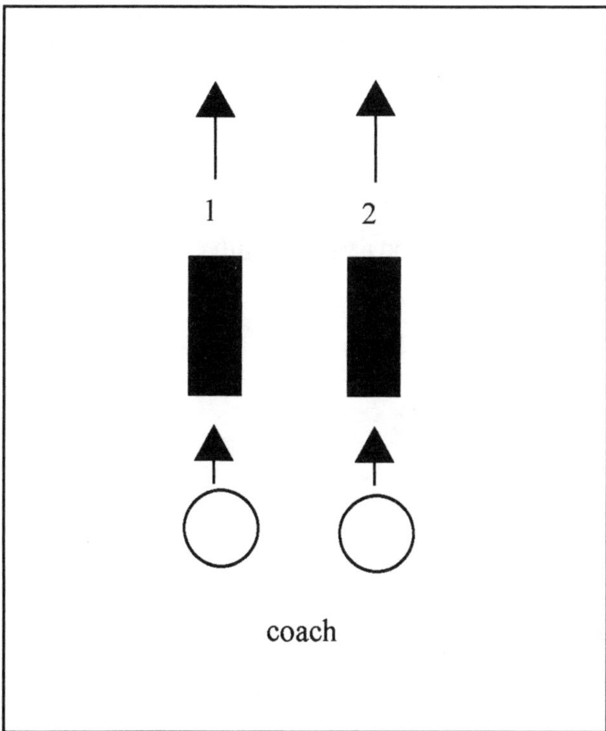

Diagram 7-12: Off the ball drill.

DRILL #13: DOUBLE TEAM COMBO DRILL

Objective: To refine the technique of the double team combination against two possible defensive reactions by a linebacker and a defensive lineman.

Equipment Needed: Two large blocking dummies.

Description: Two lines are formed. One line is designated as the post blocker line. The other line is designated as the seal blocker line. To simulate a defensive lineman, the dummy holder positions his dummy on the outside shade of the post blocker. To simulate a linebacker, the second dummy holder stands to the inside in a ready position. On the coach's command, the blockers drive the defensive lineman backward, while executing the proper technique of a double team/combo block. The linebacker attacks the line of scrimmage on one of two paths. The linebacker can scrape over the top as the defensive lineman attempts to slide inside, or the linebacker can force underneath the double team as the defensive linemen attempts to maintain outside leverage on the post blocker. Both blockers should drive the lineman until the linebacker shows his intentions. If the linebacker scrapes underneath, the double team turns into an inside-out combo with the inside linebacker on the linebacker. If the linebacker scrapes over the top of the double team, the double team turns into a post-seal combo with the outside blocker sealing the linebacker.

Coaching Points:

- The coach checks for the proper technique of the post blocker and the lead blocker.
- The lead blocker must get his hip to contact the hip of the post blocker.
- The dummy must be blocked on a vertical path.

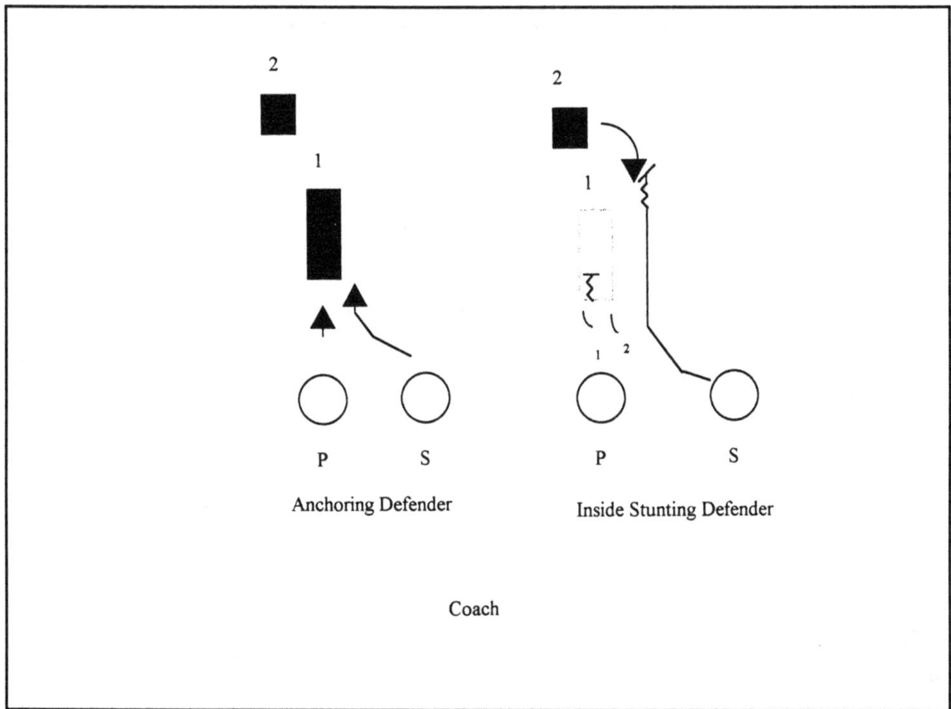

Diagram 7-13a: Double team combo drill.

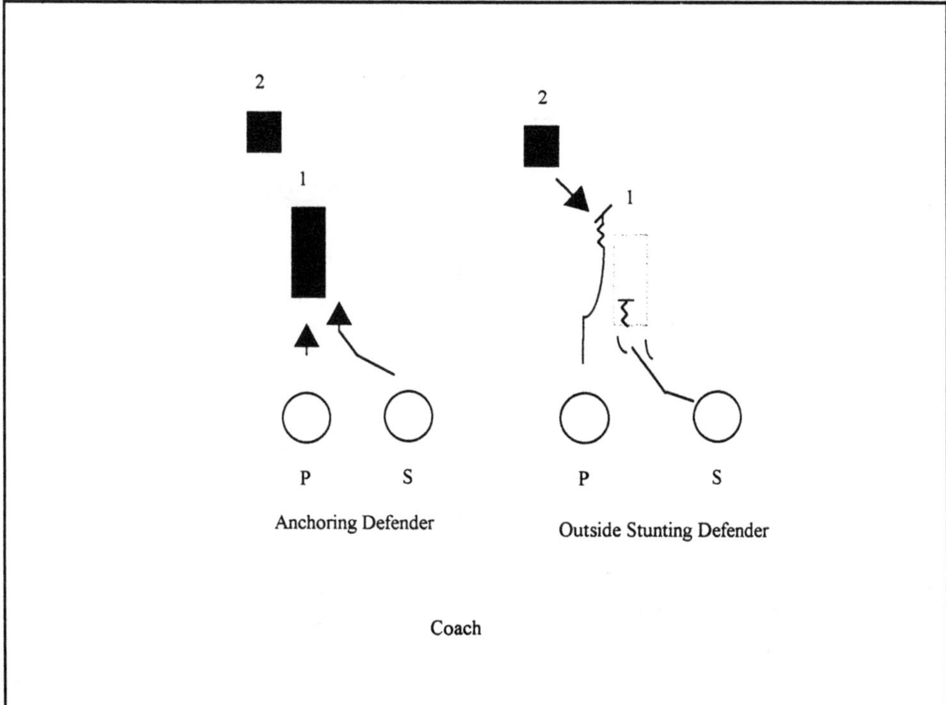

Diagram 7-13b: Double team combo drill.

DRILL #14: OUTSIDE ZONE DRILL

Objective: To teach the technique of the fire block.

Equipment Needed: One large blocking dummy and one hand-held small shield.

Description: The large blocking dummy is held on the inside shade of the outside blocker while the defender holding the hand-held shield simulates a linebacker. The outside blocker sets to reach with his outside foot and takes an upfield step at slightly less than 45 degrees. The outside blocker rips his inside arm to the pad and drives his inside shoulder through the outside 1/2 of the dummy. The outside blocker should knock the dummy inside to his teammate and continue to the second level to execute a shoulder block on the shield-holder. The inside (i.e., backside) blocker steps laterally with his outside foot opened slightly and pointing upfield. The backside blocker attempts to get his outside earhole to the near hip of the outside blocker. The backside blocker then continues on an arcing path upfield and places his head to the outside of the large dummy. The backside blocker should drive the large dummy on a vertical path as he swings his tail around to the outside.

Coaching Points:

- The coach checks for spacing between the blockers. No spacing should exist between the blockers as the trail blocker takes over the large dummy.
- A vertical push on the large dummy should be accomplished before the outside blocker moves to the next level.

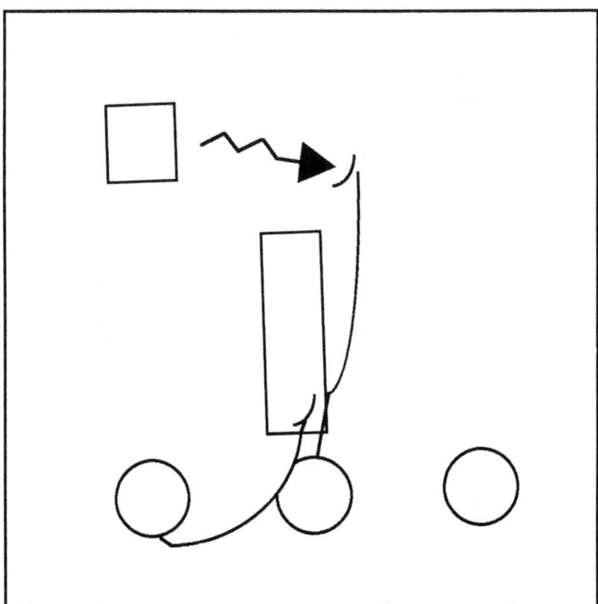

Diagram 7-14: The outside block.

DRILL #15: ANGLE BLOCK DRILL

Objective: To practice the two angle blocks—the down block and fan block—versus a gap charging defender.

Equipment Needed: Two large blocking dummies and a hand-held small shield.

Description: Two dummies are placed on the ground five to six feet apart. The hand shield holder aligns on the shade of the blocker. On a snap count, the defender charges across the line of scrimmage. The blocker angle blocks the shield holder, using the proper angle block technique. The coach may widen the shield holder once the blocker becomes skilled at the angle block. The drill may also be run live without the shield.

Coaching Points:

- The blocker must place his head across the defender at the appropriate landmark.
- The blocker must punch the offside arm to the armpit of the gap charging defender.
- The coach should make sure the blocker's head is up.

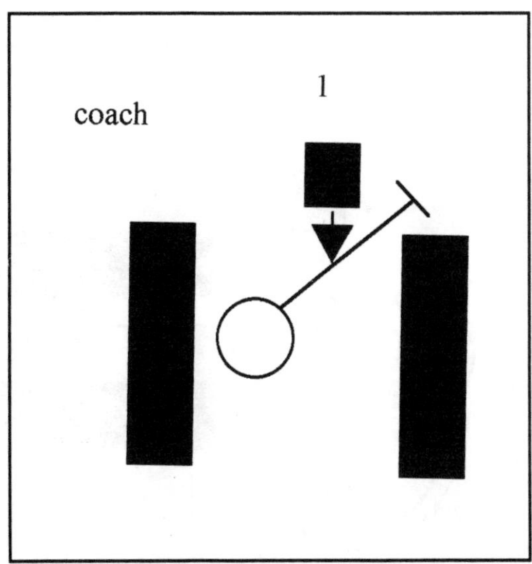

Diagram 7-15: Angle block drill.

DRILL #16: SWEEP PULL DRILL

Objective: To develop the hammer pull technique and the wall pull technique of the sweep pull.

Equipment Needed: Two large blocking dummies, two small hand shields, and five cones.

Description: Two lines of offensive guards are formed. The large dummies are lain on the ground as shown. One shield holder stands at position #1, while another shield holder stands at position #2. The lead guards pulls to a three-yard depth, gets his shoulders upfield, and hammer steps to drive through the large dummies on the ground. The hammer blocking guard will block the shield holder to the outside. The backside guard pulls on the inside hip of the hammer guard and drives through shield #1. The backside guard uses his inside shoulder to deliver a blow on the shield as he continues downfield for 10 yards. The drill is flipped over so that the guards can work on the sweep pull techniques to the left.

Coaching Points:

- The coach checks to see if both guards enter the vertical alley with their shoulders square.
- The hammer pull and the wall pull are used on other plays (e.g., bootleg, reverse, waggle).

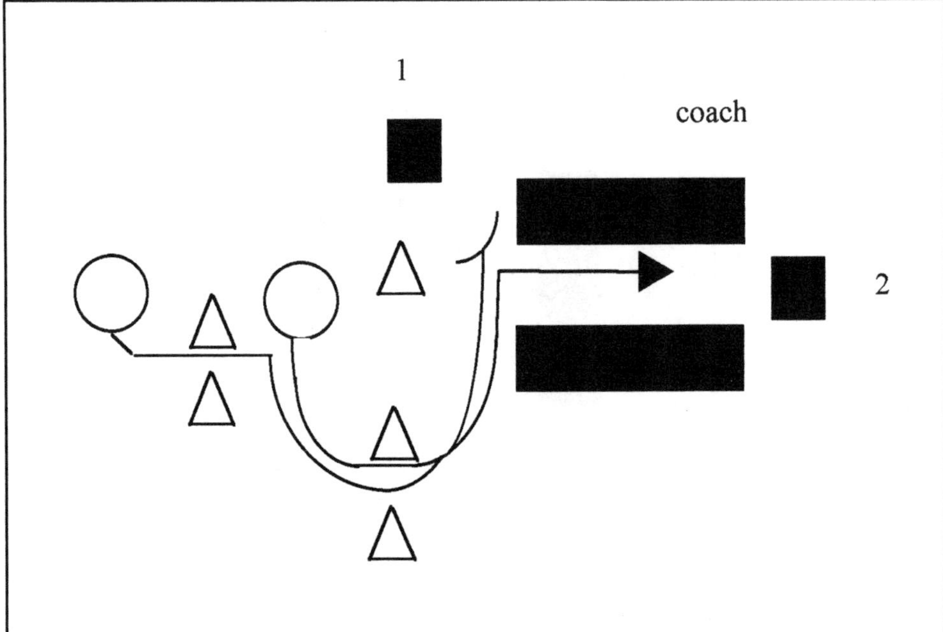

Diagram 7-16: Sweep pull drill.

DRILL #17: SHORT TRAP DRILL

Objective: To sharpen the timing of the center's back block and the guard's short trap technique.

Equipment Needed: A football and two large blocking dummies.

Description: During the drill, the center snaps the ball to the backup center and executes a back block (i.e., down block) against a large blocking dummy positioned headup on the guard. The guard handshake points and tracks to the target dummy positioned across the ball. The trapping guard uses a shoulder block to dig out the dummy, as the center blocks back for the guard. The trap dummy holder alternates between closing the gap and charging up field. The dummy holders should turn the dummies inward.

Coaching Points:

- The coach checks the center's footwork to see if he pushes off the opposite foot.
- The coach checks the pulling guard to make sure he is using the correct shoulder to hit the dummy.

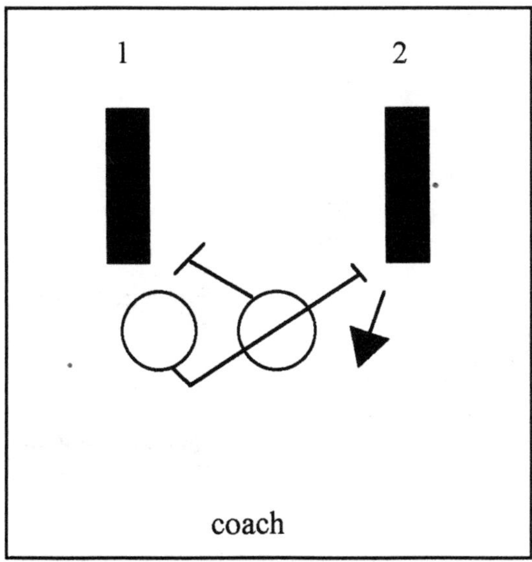

Diagram 7-17: Short trap drill.

DRILL #18: CUTOFF AND ALLEY BREAK DRILL

Objective: To perfect the cutoff block and practice the horizontal break to the alley.

Equipment Needed: One large blocking dummy, two small hand-shields, and four cones.

Description: The blocker dips under the large dummy, throwing his outside arm into the large dummy. The blocker continues on an arc inside of the shield-holder at four-yards depth. The blocker angles to the cone at a seven-yard depth and cuts across the field on a 90-degree angle. The blocker delivers a face-up blow to the second hand-shield. The second hand-shield simulates a linebacker, while the third hand-shield simulates a free safety attempting to fill the alley. The coach may alter the drill by having the second shield holder attack the alley from a free-safety position to simulate the free safety. In this case, the blocker must get his head across the front of the shield holder.

Coaching Points:

- The coach should emphasize to the blocker that he must throw an uppercut punch through the large dummy and the simulated linebacker.
- The coach should encourage the blocker to sprint full speed to the alley.

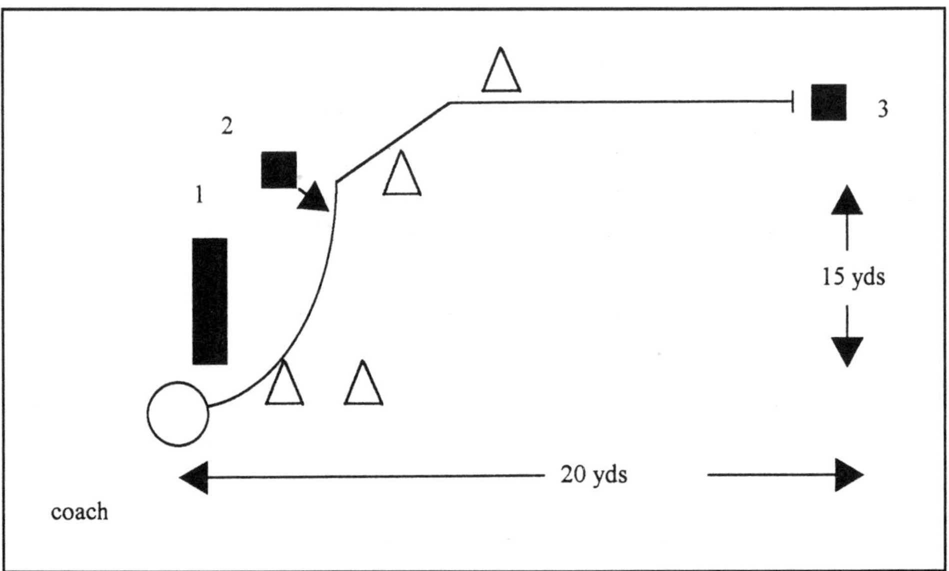

Diagram 7-18: Cutoff alley break drill.

DRILL #19: WAGGLE DRILL

Objective: To isolate the offensive guard's pulling and reading technique needed for the waggle.

Equipment Needed: Five cones and two small hand shields.

Description: The guards practice the appropriate technique for pulling on the waggle. The lead guard executes a log pull, while the backside guard executes a long sweep pull. The coach may evolve the basic drill to a read drill by having shield #1 charge upfield on a defensive stunt, thereby forcing the lead guard to kick the shield holder out. The backside guard must read the action of the lead guard. If the lead guard logs, the backside guard kicks out shield #2. If the lead guard kicks out, the backside guard can log at the edge. The coach may further increase the difficulty of the drill by directing the shield holders to run an X stunt, thereby forcing the lead guard to kick out as the backside guard log blocks.

Coaching Points:

- The coach should stand in front of the drill to check the guard's eyes.
- The coach should emphasize that the waggle will be likely be set up for a situation in which the lead blocker logs and the backside blocker kicks out.

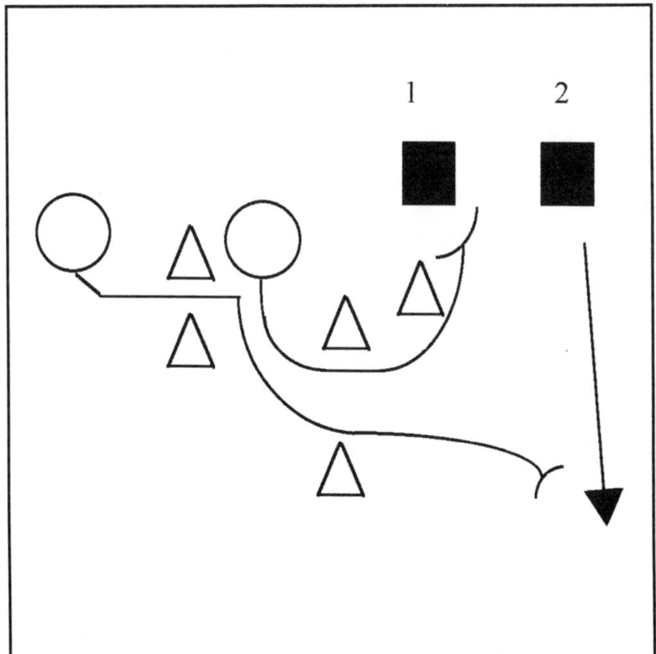

Diagram 7-19: Waggle drill.

CHAPTER 8

Pass Blocking

Effective pass protection begins with a complete knowledge of the fundamentals involved and a mastery of the various techniques attendant to sound pass protection blocking. As such, your offensive linemen must not only be well-trained in the various skills, they must also know when to apply a specific technique. A protection technique can be categorized as a dropback protection technique, a play pass technique, or a sprint out/dash pass technique. A list of the individual dropback pass protection techniques includes the following:

- Hard post
- Soft post
- Soft kick
- Jump 'em
- Kick slide

The offensive lineman's selection of a particular technique is directly related to the defensive alignment of his opponent. As with any football position, the proper technique begins with the proper stance. Normally, the ideal stance serves both the run-blocking and the pass-blocking technique. A balanced stance gives the offensive lineman the ability to move in eight different directions without tipping off his assignment to the defense. The eight directions of movement from the balanced stance are diagrammed in Diagram 8-1.

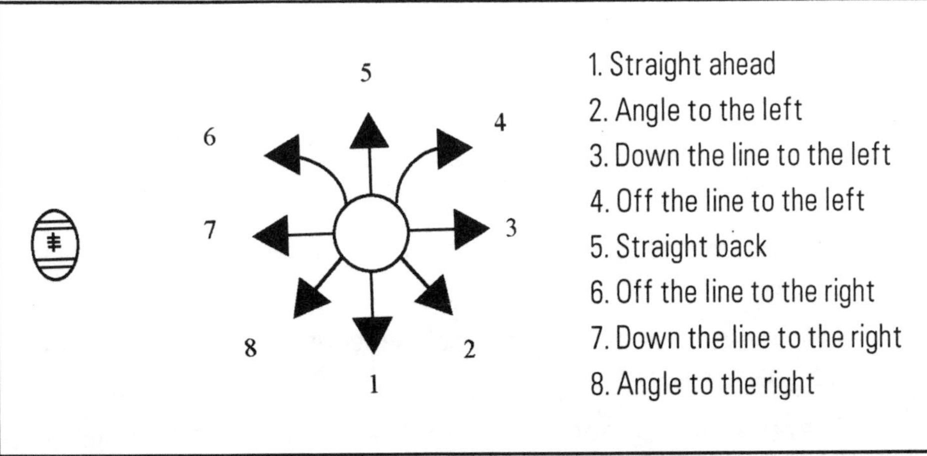

Diagram 8-1: The right directions in which the offensive lineman moves.

As was previously discussed in Chapter 3, the basic football stance that I prefer (and recommend) is a three-point balanced stance. A three-point stance gives the player an opportunity to maximize his leverage when performing all of the tasks of blocking. In Chapter 3, it was pointed out that the three-point stance is the best stance to initiate a proper run-blocking demeanor. We also teach our linemen to move comfortably into their pass protection set up from a three-point stance. The fundamental components of a three-point balanced stance should address the following coaching points:

- The base.
  - The feet should be positioned slightly wider than the width of the shoulders.
  - The feet should be placed close to a parallel position (i.e., not staggered).
  - The toes should be pointed forward.
  - The lineman's weight should be centered on the inside of the feet—especially on the inside foot.
- The power angle.
  - The ankles should be flexed.
  - The heels should be on the ground (never raised).
  - The knees should be ahead of the toes.
  - The hips should be flexed along with the knees bent and the ankles flexed.
- The hands.
  - The thumb of the down hand should be positioned inches forward of the shoulders.
  - The lineman's weight should be slightly forward on the fingertips of his down hand.
  - His off hand should be held open, with the thumb pointing forward and placed on the side of the knee.
  - Offensive linemen on the left side of the center use a left-handed stance (i.e., left hand down).
  - Offensive linemen on the right side of the center use a right-handed stance (i.e., the right hand down).
  - The center may use a one-handed (i.e., three-point) stance or he may use a two-handed (i.e., four-point) stance.

- The shoulders.
  - The shoulders should be square to the line of scrimmage.
  - The shoulders should be parallel to the ground.
- The head and eyes.
  - The head should be positioned so that the upper screws which connect the facemask to the headgear are facing forward.
  - The eyes should be focused straight ahead.
- The base.
  - The player's base should be centered in his hips and buttocks.
  - The player should be able to lift his down hand without affecting his balance.

As an offensive line coach, I also understand that situations arise during the game where everyone from the popcorn vendor to the opposition's defensive coordinator knows that we have to pass. When one of these situations is presented to us, we feel that a two-point stance is best for enhancing our set up move for pass protection—particularly dropback pass protection. A proper two-point stance exhibits the following features:

- The base.
  - The feet should be positioned slightly wider than the width of the shoulders.
  - The feet should be positioned in a slight stagger, with the outside foot slightly back.
  - The toes should be pointed forward.
  - The lineman's weight should be centered on the inside of his feet—particularly on his inside foot.
- The power angle.
  - The ankles should be flexed.
  - The heels should be on the ground (never raised).
  - The hips should flexed, along with the knees bent and the ankles flexed.
- The hands.
  - Both hands should be held open and with the thumb pointing forward and placed on top of the thigh.

- The center may use either a one-handed (i.e., three-point) stance or a two-handed (i.e., four-point) stance.

- The shoulders and back.
  - The shoulders should be square to the line of scrimmage.
  - The lower back should be arched, as the shoulders are pulled back and the back is held straight.

- The head and eyes.
  - The head should be positioned so that the upper screws which connect the facemask to the headgear are facing forward.
  - The chin should be tucked back, so that the head is level.
  - The eyes should be focused on the defender the lineman is blocking.
  - The player's eyes should sight his opponent through the bridge of the nose.

- The base.
  - The base should be centered in the hips and buttocks.
  - The player's weight should be on his inside foot—particularly when expecting to make a kick move.
  - The player's weight should be shifted to the inside of his inside foot.

SET UP

The stance is the first phase of any type of block. The second phase of the pass block is the set up. The set up is defined as the snap up or the kick out to the prescribed depth of the pass set. The key to executing the proper set up is the quickness in making the move. The set up has to be made as quickly as possible. The outcome of an entire pass protection scheme is usually determined by the speed in which each offensive lineman makes his first move in setting up for the block.

For the pass-blocking offensive lineman, the main purpose of the set up is to establish a cushion between himself and the pass rusher. The appropriate depth of the cushion—the proper amount of the separation—between the pass rusher and the pass protector is dependent upon the technique of the defender and the particular offensive line position. For example, an offensive tackle may kick-out to gain a separation of three to four feet against an angled defensive end aligned to his outside, while a center punches with his up hand on the snap to gain a maximum of 12 to 18 inches of separation against a nose tackle. Setting to gain depth is also necessary for an offensive lineman to be able to read the pass rush, whether the scheme is either a man protection or an area protection scheme.

An offensive lineman is required to master several types of pass sets. The one characteristic of every type of pass set is the inside-out relationship of the pass protector. An offensive lineman must set to protect the inside-out relationship to the pass protector. Simply setting to an inside-out relationship doesn't guarantee that the offensive lineman will effectively protect the quarterback. It does, however, put the offensive lineman in the most suitable position for accomplishing his objective. Chapter 4 details the coaching points of the proper run-blocking demeanor. Among the factors that relate to a blocker snapping up into a proper pass-blocking demeanor include the following coaching points:

- Keeping his shoulders square.
- Setting his base to a staggered relationship to the blocker's base—with the outside foot pointing to the crotch of the defender.
- Keeping most of his weight balanced with a slight emphasis on his inside foot.
- Keeping his butt low and his knees bent.
- Keeping his elbows inside his body's frame.
- Keeping his hands up with his thumbs pointing up.
- Keeping his chin tucked and his head back.
- Keeping his chest out.
- Keeping his feet slightly wider than shoulder-width apart.

On all pass set moves, the pass protector snaps up and gets his eyes on the target. I recommend that coaches teach their offensive linemen to target the breast plates of the defender. The pass protector should snap up and use the heels of his hands to punch the defender the chest. The blow should be made in an upward motion, as the blocker drives his hands up through the defender's breast plates in a low-to-high plane. The blocker's goal in punching the defender is to stop the defender's charge so that the defender has to restart and redirect his pass rush to another lane. The bag punch drill and the medicine ball drill are great drills for teaching the punch.

HARD POST

For an offensive guard who is facing an inside shaded defender, the desired pass set against an inside shaded defender is the hard post. The hard post is used against a 2i technique defender, a 1 technique defender, and an onset-offset nose tackle aligned to his side. The main feature of the hard post move is a sharp lateral jab step to the inside. The guard should push off his outside foot to throw his body inside to seal the "A" gap off from penetration. The primary objective of a hard post set is to get to an inside-out or a head-up leverage position on the defender. The blocker should push off his outside foot and plant his inside foot to point at the toes of the defender's inside foot. As the guard hard post sets inside he should punch the defender in the breast plates while keeping the proper pass-blocking demeanor. His outside foot should also slide inside so that the blocker doesn't overextend his base as he sets the hard post. It is important that both feet shuffle along the turf as the blocker shuffles inside. The guard should keep his feet in close contact to the turf as he sets inside. Both steps should be quick, hard, jab steps.

If the guard is uncovered and is helping the center according to the area rule against an offset/onset nose tackle aligned to his side, the guard should hard post but keep his outside arm free. He should use his inside arm to drive to the near breastplate of the nose tackle. Striking the nose tackle's breastplate stops his charge through the "A" gap and allows the center to punch and slide to a head-up position on the nose tackle. It is especially important that the guard punch upward into the nose tackle's breast plate when using only his inside arm. By striking the nose tackle in the chest with a low-to-high block, the guard forces the defender's shoulders upward and creates a better target surface for the center. Striking the nose tackle in the near breast plate also helps the guard to keep the guard's shoulders square. An area protection scheme requires that the guards keep their shoulders square when helping the center. Keeping their shoulders square is important for the guards if they are to pick up an inside twist game between the inside linebackers and the nose tackle.

A tackle or a tight end would also use a hard post move if their assignment is to block an inside shaded defender. The tackle must be particularly alert to the possibility of the guard "talking." If a dog blitz from a Eagle front shows inside the "A" gap, the guard will hard post to take the linebacker after making an "alert" call. The tackle should always keep his eyes inside when the guard is facing a 3 technique. If an inside backer shows in the near "A" gap, the guard will have to slide inside and take the backer. By keeping his eyes to the inside, the tackle can visually pickup this stunt at the last second without the guard having to make the call.

If the backer subsequently backs out on the snap, the guard will use the *"jump 'em"* technique to grab the 3 technique. The tackle can easily recognize the guard jumping the 3 technique and quickly kick-out to help on the edge with no harm done to the basic integrity of the protection scheme.

The center will hard post set when he is applying his *man blocking* rule against an even front. Against a front that is characterized by having a backside 1 technique or a stack alignment, the hard post technique by the center can secure backside "A" gap.

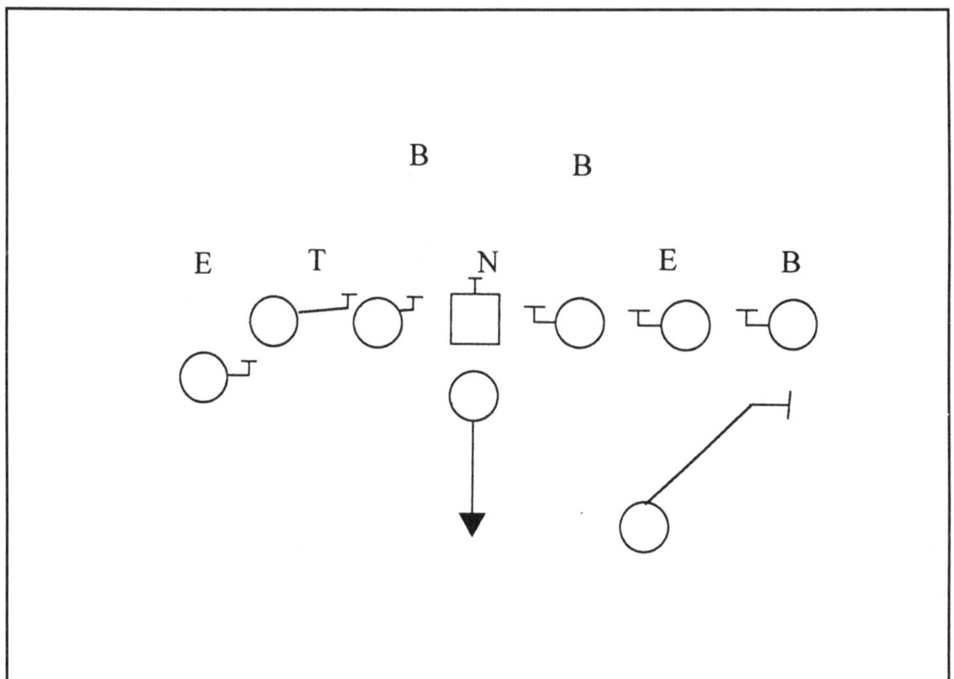

Diagram 8-2: An area protection.

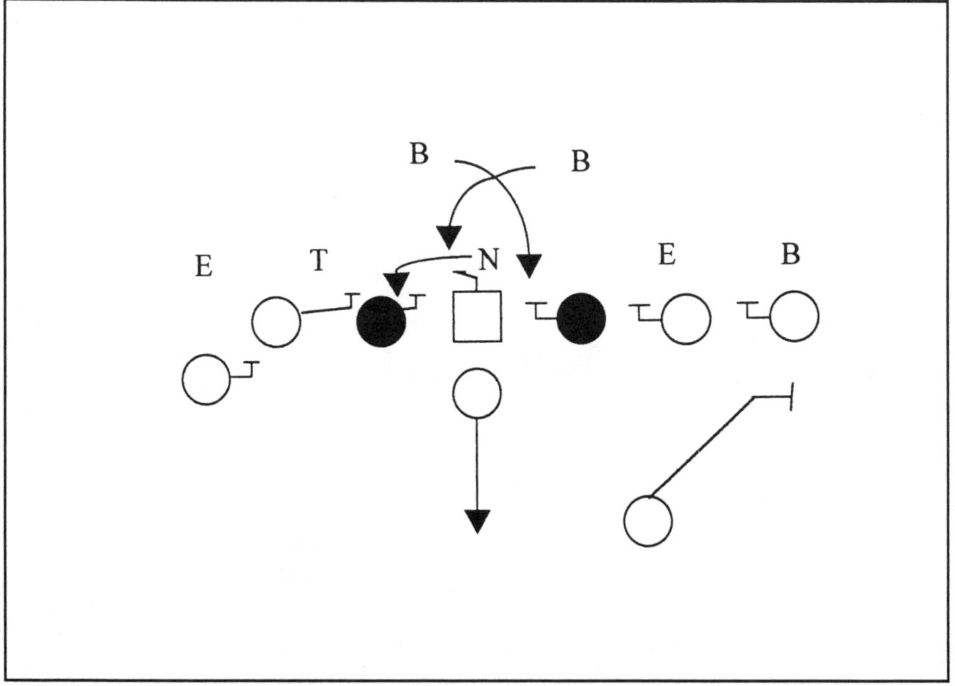

Diagram 8-3: The guards help the center in an area protection scheme versus a 30 front.

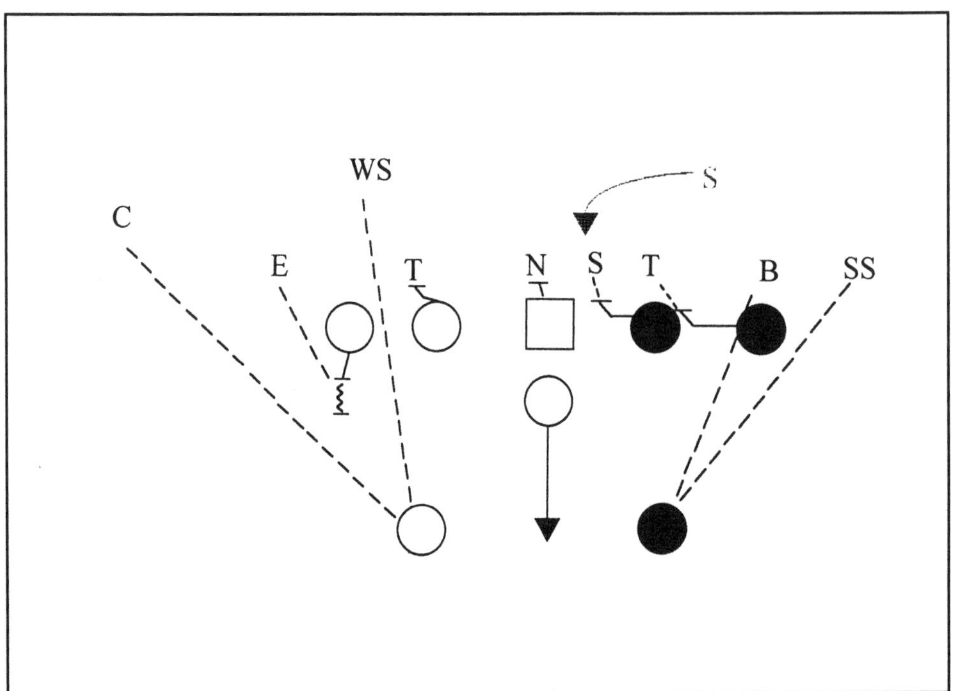

Diagram 8-4: The guard, the tackle and the running back recognize the Sam backer lining up in the "A" gap with a solid look and adjust.

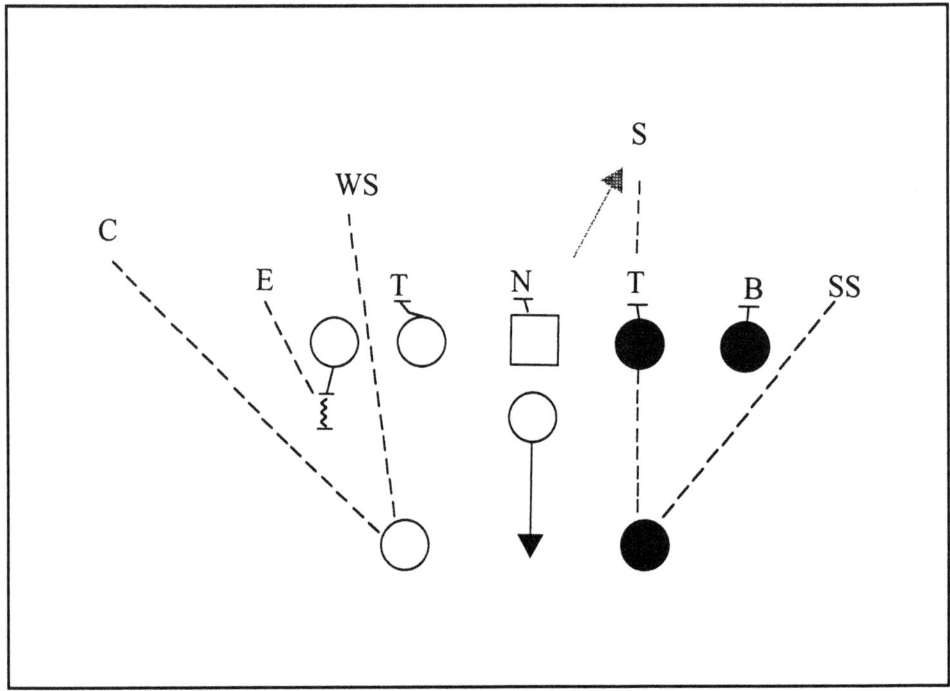

Diagram 8-5: The linebacker backs out and the guard, the tackle, and the running back adjust.

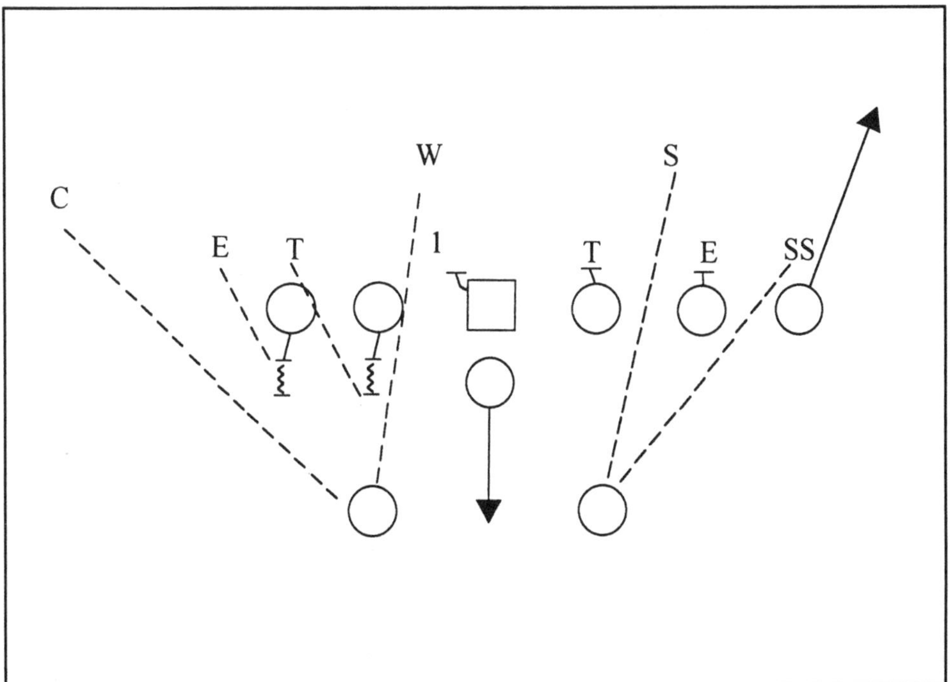

Diagram 8-6: The center hard posts the backside 1 technique.

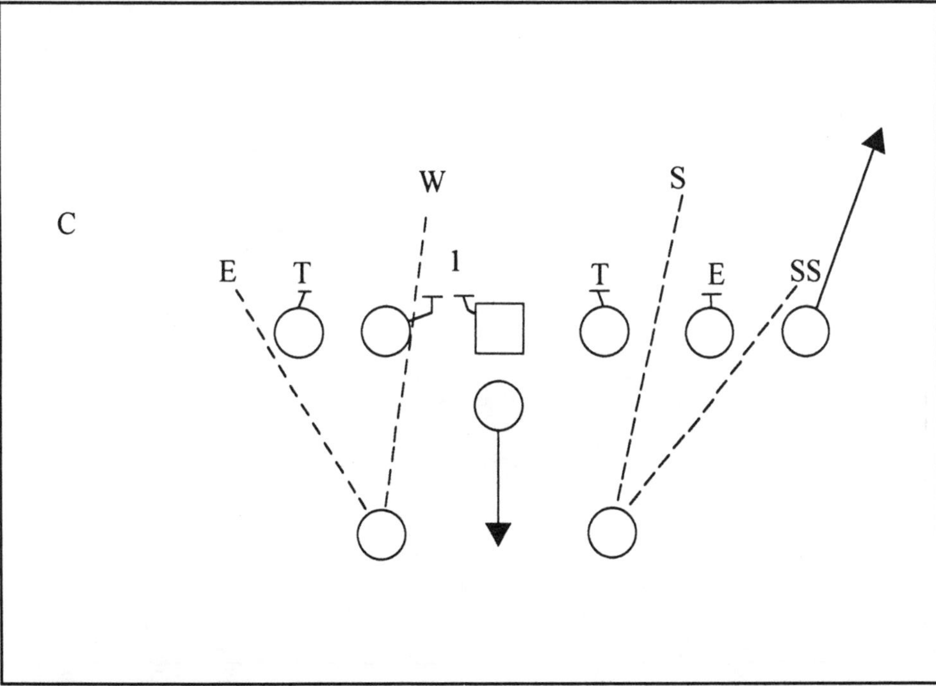

Diagram 8-7: The center hard posts the backside "A" gap and works with the guard to block the stack.

Against a front that is characterized by a middle linebacker, the center can hard post to the near lineman to help the guard. When the center hard posts to help the guard, he should keep his eyes on the middle linebacker. If the linebacker over the center delays and dogs straight ahead, the center will simply push off the hard post set and slide a half-step to pick up the dog stunt.

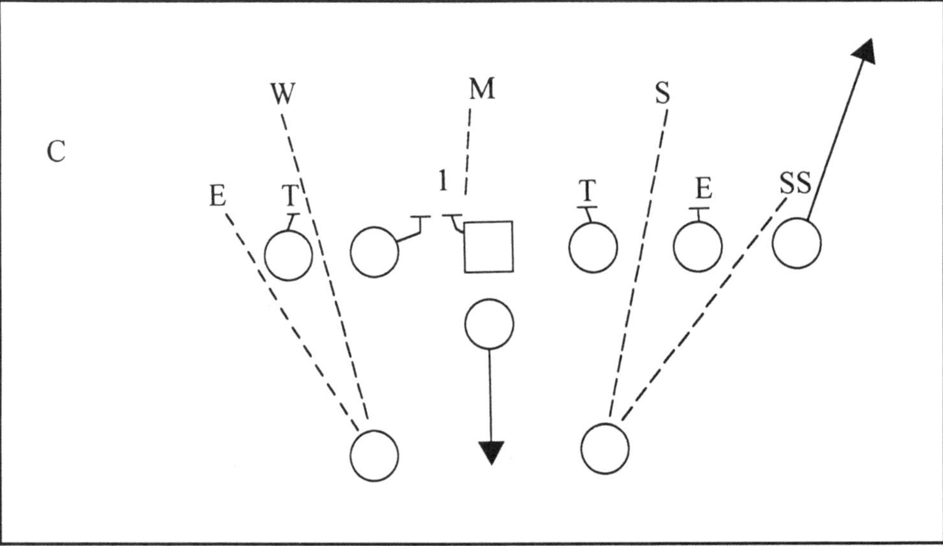

Diagram 8-8: The center hard posts the backside "A" gap but peeks at the middle linebacker.

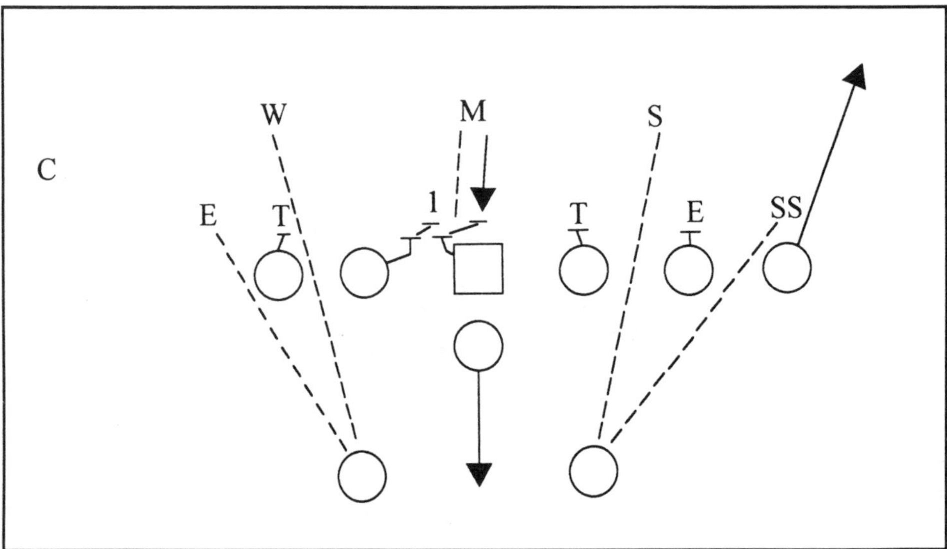

Diagram 8-9: The center hard posts the backside "A" gap and picks up the delayed dog by the middle linebacker.

If the middle linebacker loops around behind the near defensive lineman, the center and the guard can either switch assignments or remain locked in. If the lock-in scheme is used to pick up the twisting stunts, the center should remember to set slightly behind the guard's inside foot.

By setting behind the guard's near foot, the center can simply slide behind the guard to pick up a twisting dog stunt. When the offensive linemen slide with the twist stunts and remain locked in, the offensive lineman who is locked in on the linebacker should use the soft kick to set slightly off the line of scrimmage.

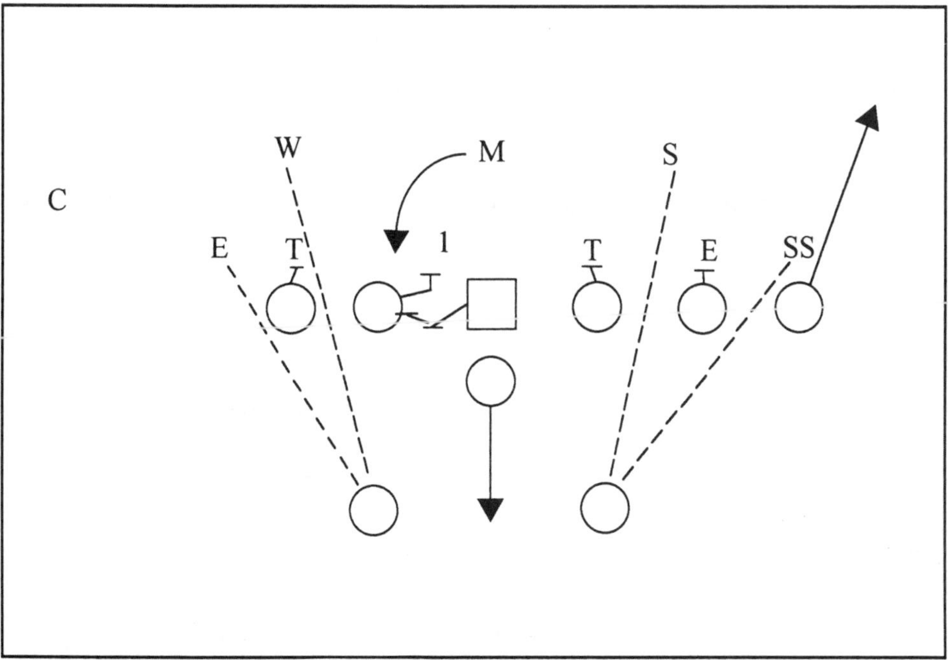

Diagram 8-10: The center soft kicks behind the guard when the scheme locks in the guard on the down defender.

If two offensive linemen are pass blocking according to an area protection scheme, they will switch assignments on the middle twist. In an area protection scheme, the center should use the hard post technique when helping the guard. The hard post of the center builds a shoulder-to-shoulder wall, as he and the guard set shoulder to shoulder. If the center sees the middle linebacker looping, he should yell "switch, switch," as he physically pushes the guard outward with his outside arm. Pushing the guard and yelling "switch" helps the guard recognize the stunt and cues him to push off the penetrating defensive lineman and pick up the middle linebacker dogging through the "B" gap.

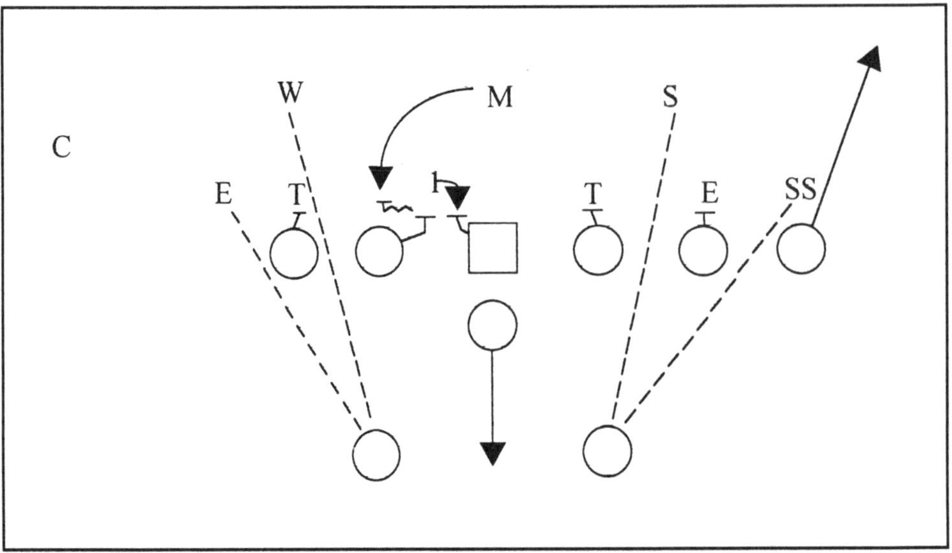

Diagram 8-11: In an area protection scheme, the center and the guard switch versus an inside twist.

SOFT POST

The second pass set is the soft post. The main move of the center versus a nose tackle—the soft post technique—requires the offensive lineman to simply jab step his inside foot without moving hard to the inside. An offensive lineman uses the soft post move when a defender is aligned head-up on him. When pass blocking a 2 technique, the guard will soft post by quickly picking up his inside foot.

Picking up the foot helps the guard to snap up and punch his hands to the 2 technique's breastplates. The soft-post technique also helps rein in the guard's natural tendency to attack the 2 technique. A pass protector should never move forward into a defender; he should only move side-to-side or back. Upon picking up his foot, the guard immediately puts down his foot. The soft-post inside step is made in the manner of a boot stomping on a scurrying insect. It is a quick, forceful step in one spot.

As with every pass set technique, the pass protector should establish an inside-out staggered relationship to the pass rusher. He should soft post with his foot slightly inside of the defender's inside foot and set to the proper pass-blocking demeanor. A defender using a head-up technique may have the option of rushing to either side. Therefore, the pass protector should be ready for a pass rushing move to either side.

The soft post is used by a center against a head-up nose tackle. The center should use a one-two punch combination as he soft posts with the foot corresponding to his up hand. A center using a four-point stance will deliver a one-two punch with his off-hand, followed by his ball-hand as he soft posts with the foot corresponding to his off-hand. Against a head-up nose tackle, a right-handed center should soft post with his left foot; a left-handed center should soft post with his right foot.

The center, the guards, the tackles, and the tight ends all use the soft post move when dropback pass protecting against a head up technique. The snap-up and punch to the breastplates are crucial points to getting into the proper pass-blocking demeanor when using a soft post move. It is also very important that the blocker keep his chin tucked, head back and back flat when making the soft post move.

SOFT KICK

The third pass set technique is the soft kick. The soft kick is used against a tight outside shaded technique, such as a regularly aligned 3 technique, 5 technique, or 9 technique. To soft kick, the blocker will push off his inside foot to take a short jab step with his outside foot. A coaching point that should be emphasized is: *An offensive guard doesn't jump outside when he soft kicks. He basically picks up his outside foot and returns it to nearly the same spot on the turf.*

For a guard, the soft kick is essentially the mirror technique of the soft post, except that the soft kick will results in a small degree of lateral movement as the kick foot slides approximately four inches outside. Unlike his soft post technique, the blocker will allow his back foot to slide with the kick foot. For example, when a guard soft posts against a 3 technique, his outside foot will kick and jab, while his inside foot will slide to reestablish the good base for a proper pass-blocking demeanor. If his inside foot doesn't slide with his kick foot, the blocker's base will get too wide, causing him to lose his power leverage.

Punching the outside hand is an important coaching point involving the proper execution of the soft post. The heel of the outside hand should be driven through the outside breastplate of the outside shade. Punching the hand to the defender's near breastplate gives the pass rusher free leverage with the outside half of his body, since no resistance is applied. He can easily escape around the short edge of the pass set, if the blocker doesn't reach to punch through his outside breast plate. By punching through the outside breastplate, the blocker actually pulls the inside half of his body outside and squares up on the defender. A lazy inside foot and a dead inside arm are common flaws of the undisciplined lineman's soft kick technique. Teaching the "outside-hand-to-the-breastplate" coaching point forestalls the problem of a pass rusher getting off against the short edge.

While an offensive guard doesn't move much laterally on the soft kick, the offensive tackle does soft kick outside to gain more leverage on an outside shade. Since the tackle is further from the ball, he soft kicks one step off the ball as he widens by approximately two feet. The offensive tackle should soft kick with a proper pass-blocking demeanor—slightly inside-out of the defender. After kicking to set in the proper demeanor, the tackle should initially keep his shoulders square. His outside foot should be slightly staggered behind the inside. His hips may be opened slightly to facilitate a quick pivot to the outside should the defender attempt a quick speed rush around the edge. If the pass rusher attempts to speed rush, the offensive tackle may quickly punch and open his stance to wall the pass rusher from the pocket.

JUMP 'EM TECHNIQUE

The fourth pass set technique is the jump 'em set. The jump 'em technique is a change-up technique for the soft kick set. Most often used as a quick pass protection, dash protection, or play pass protection, the jump 'em technique is a quick jump to the outside into the proper pass-blocking demeanor. On the snap of the ball, the blocker using the jump 'em technique literally jumps out to the side—landing in the proper pass-blocking demeanor to the defender. Not only does the jump 'em technique blocker hop into the proper demeanor, he simultaneously punches both hands into the breastplates of the defender. From that position, the blocker works to maintain a snug inside-out relationship, while stalemating the pass rusher.

KICK SLIDE

The kick slide is the fifth pass set technique. The kick slide is used by an offensive tackle when he is presented with a wide pass rusher who is pointing in to the backfield. The kick slide gives an offensive tackle added depth on the pass set. To kick slide, the tackle pushes hard off his inside foot—an easy task since most of the weight of the two-point stance should be on the lineman's inside foot. The hard push off the inside foot gets the tackle moving backward and outward to intercept the angle of the wide pass rusher. Even though the kick sliding tackle is moving outside on the snap, he doesn't turn his shoulders. Although his path is diagonal, his shoulders and hips remain facing forward.

Once an offensive tackle kick slides, he can then shuffle backward to intercept the path of pass rusher. The kick slide puts the offensive tackle into a position that may appear to make him vulnerable to an underneath move, but this vulnerability is deceiving. Most offensive tackles would be happy to see a wide rusher attempt to cross his face and slip under the pass set. If an offensive tackle keeps his shoulders square, a defender cannot beat him to the inside. Once the inside pass rusher closes, the offensive tackle can punch the defender, knock him off balance, and pin him down inside.

If the pass rusher doesn't take the bait inside, he must attempt to get around the long corner. When an offensive tackle kick slides, the pass rusher must go deeper upfield before he can attempt to make a move on the blocker. Because of the kick slide, the pass rusher has to take two extra steps to speed rush around the edge.

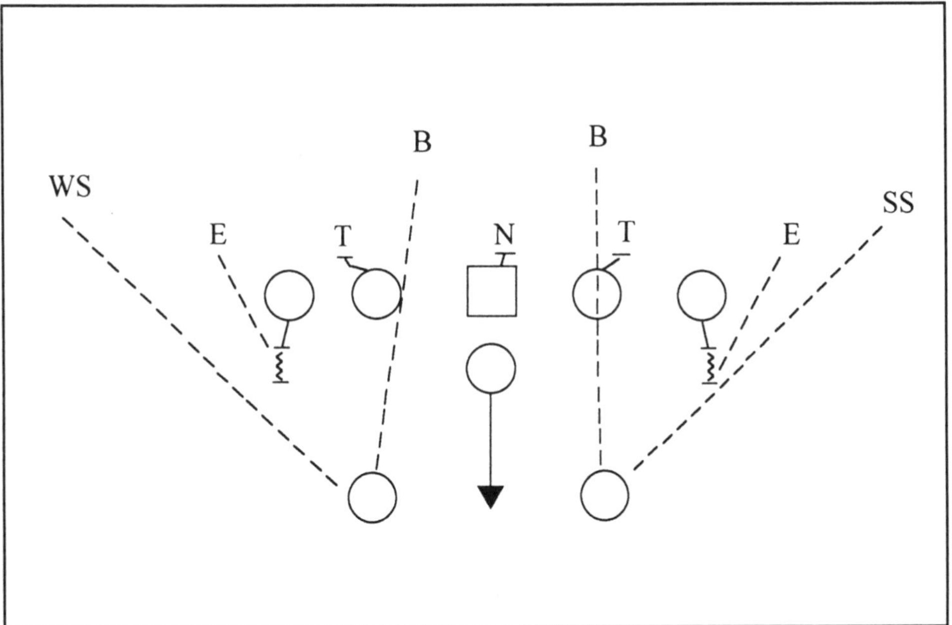

Diagram 8-12: Both tackles are shown using a kick slide to create the long corner.

The kick slide is a technique sometimes used by offensive guards in drop back passing schemes which call for a fan pass protection. In such a scheme, the guard will have to kick slide versus a 50 front structure.

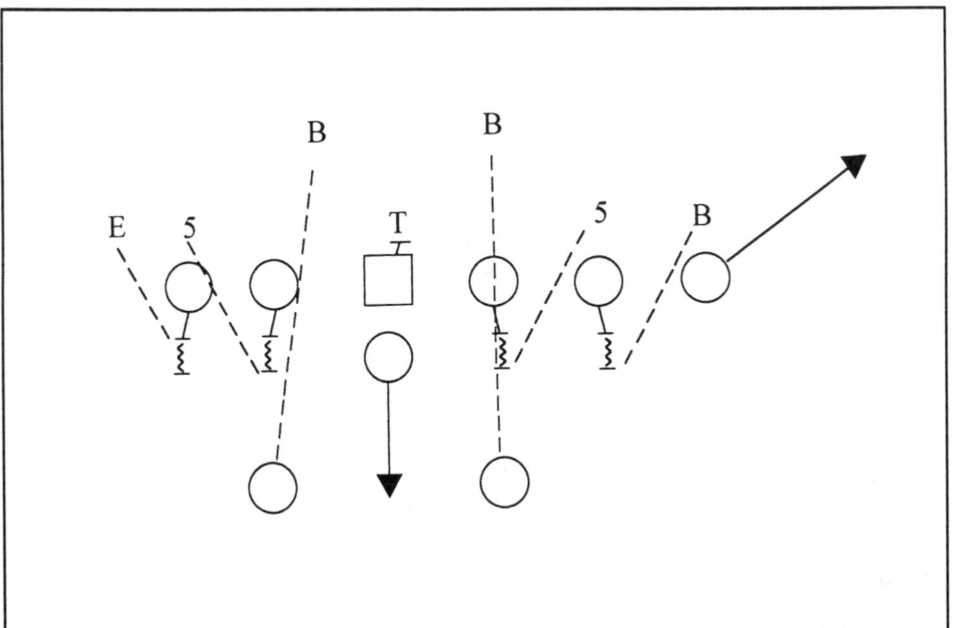

Diagram 8-13: The guards kick slide against the 5 technique in a fan pass protection.

Normally, a kick slider will punch first with his outside arm. As when punching from a soft kick technique, an offensive tackle should make sure that he punches his outside hand to the outside breastplate of the defender. Failing to punch the outside hand to the outside breastplate of the defender will give the pass rusher free leverage with the outside half of his body and make the corner short.

DOUBLE READ

The double read is a play pass protection technique. Although I am not an advocate of the double read protection (I only employ it in a no-back formation), I have included it in this chapter for those coaches who want to use it. Since the play pass is off of a run fake, the backside protection is sometimes outnumbered—and almost always outflanked.

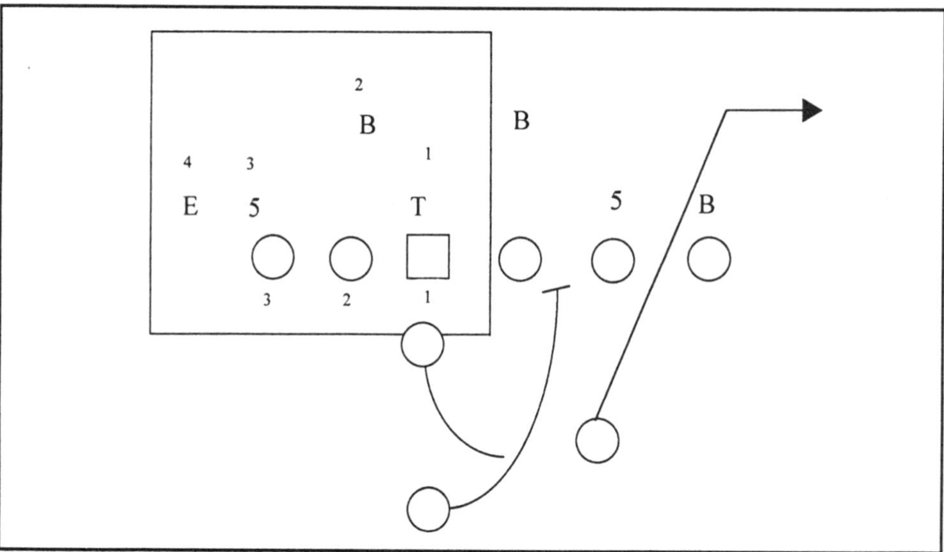

Diagram 8-14: On a play pass, the backside protection is outnumbered; if the linebacker and the defensive end both rush, a team could have protection problems.

A team can support the backside protection and balance the protection through one of two measures. One way to reinforce the backside protection is to send a running back to the backside. This approach is solid in theory and practice, but it has its drawbacks. The first disadvantage is the protection's demand for a two-back or a three-back scheme. With a one-back scheme, you clearly don't have another running back to fill the role of a blocker. The second flaw of sending an extra back to the backside to support the protection is the almost certainly distinguishable difference between the running play and the pass protection for the play pass based off of the same running play. Diagram 8-15 and 8-16 illustrate these differences.

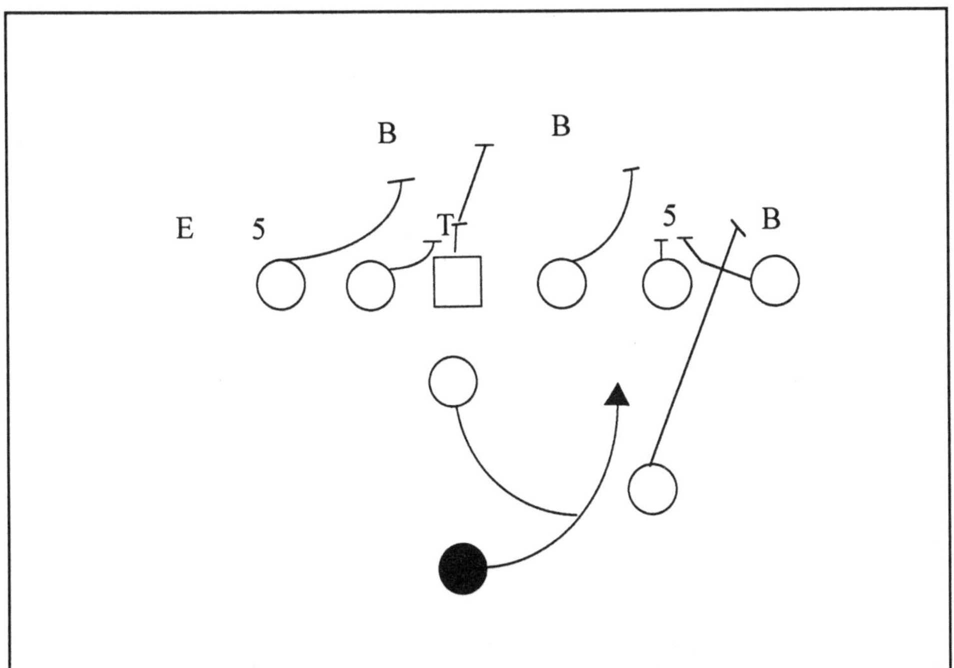

Diagram 8-15: On a running play, a team can be successful despite being outnumbered on the backside.

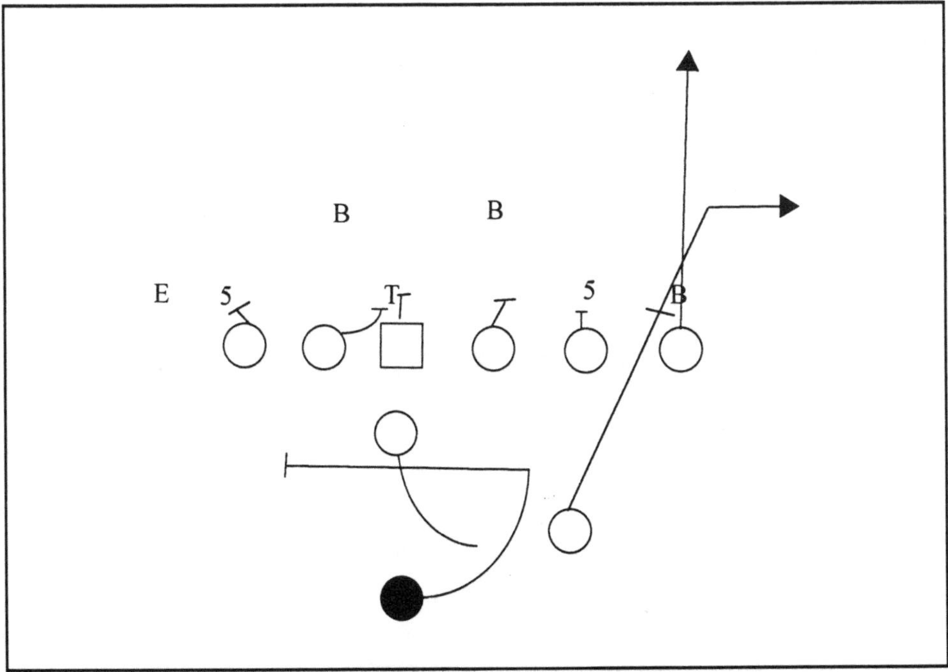

Diagram 8-16: A play pass off of the play shown in Diagram 8-18; tailback goes backside for protection.

Another way to reinforce the backside protection of the play pass is through the offensive line scheme. While this approach doesn't provide the safety afforded by an extra man, it does give a team a way of having a solid protection if only three defenders blitz from the backside of an odd front (four from an even front). The plan involves the uncovered lineman double reading. A double read is a technique carried out by a lineman who is facing a linebacker over him. In the first phase of the double read, the double-reading lineman hard posts inside with his shoulders square. As he hard posts, the lineman peeks at the feet of the near linebacker. (The lineman wants to make it appear to the linebacker as if he is zone blocking playside.)

If the linebacker blitzes in the immediate area, the double-reading lineman disengages from the hard-post move and sets his demeanor to block the linebacker. If the linebacker's movement shows that he is not blitzing in the immediate area, the blocker then pushes hard off his inside foot as he shoves the near defender with his inside arm in a punching manner. Pushing off the near defender assists the blocker who is engaged with that defender and helps to propel the blocker back off the hard post. The key coaching point is to emphasize the outside pivot of the double reading lineman. As he pushes off with his inside hand, the lineman must pivot on his inside foot and open to the backside. He should pivot in a way to allow him to move in a perpendicular path off the line of scrimmage (i.e., straight back). Any slight angling of the lineman's path backward off of the pivot could result in the blocker being beaten by the outside linebacker blitzing from the edge.

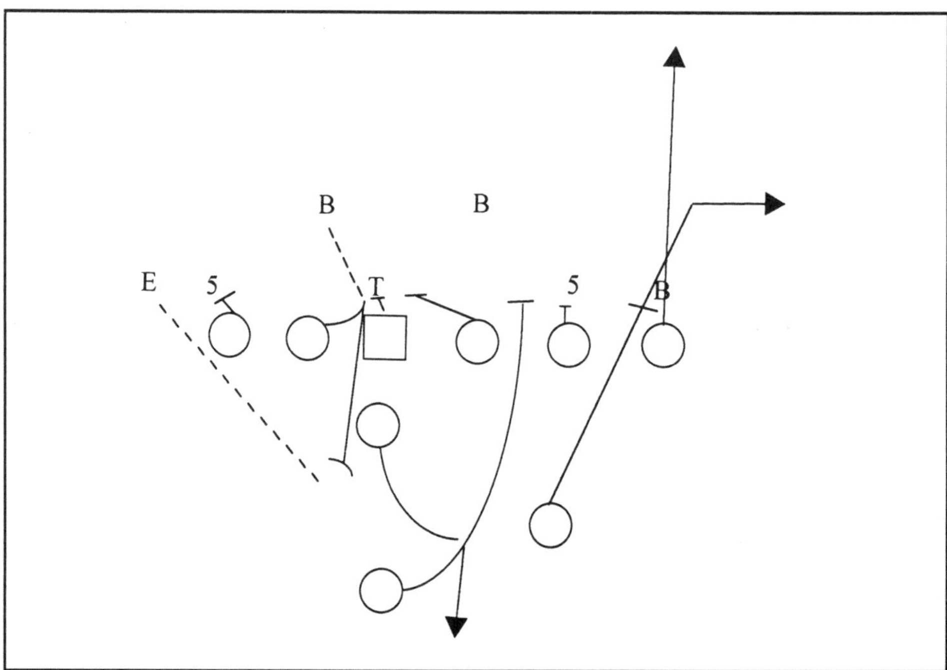

Diagram 8-17: A play pass with the backside guard double reading allows the running backs to fake the run and block playside.

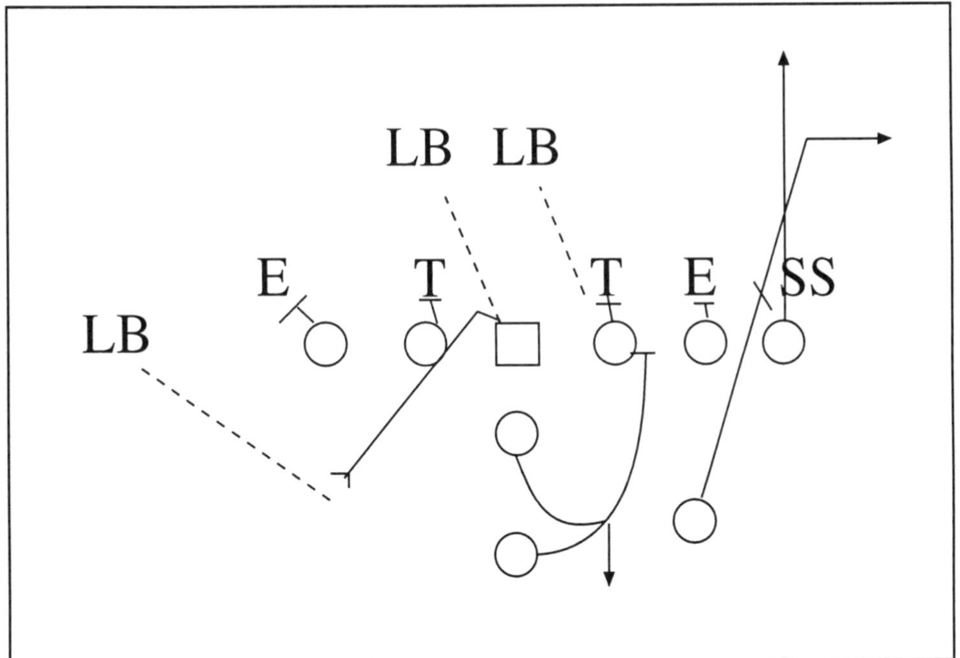

Diagram 8-18: A play pass with backside uncovered double reading allows the backs to fake the run and block playside.

If no outside linebacker shows, the double reading lineman can set up approximately three to four yards deep and get his head on a swivel to protect the quarterback on the backside.

Against some fronts such as the 4-3 structure, it is quite possible to have two offensive linemen double reading—the center and the backside tackle. Although I have never seen or used the double read scheme in my career, the only way to defeat a properly executed double read scheme is by blitzing both the inside and outside linebacker on flow away. Since the situation being described involves a run fake away from the backers, it is an unusual situation when both linebackers blitz the backside. While it is common for an outside linebacker to blitz a play pass action away from him, it requires the combination of a great defensive call and a poorly timed play pass call to result in both linebackers coming. Because of the relatively unlikely occurrence that a full backside blitz will be called against play pass action, the double read protection scheme can prove to be a highly effective way of providing near maximum protection with the full benefit of the play fake. The double read technique of backside play pass protection can also make the play pass a safer call from the one-back attack.

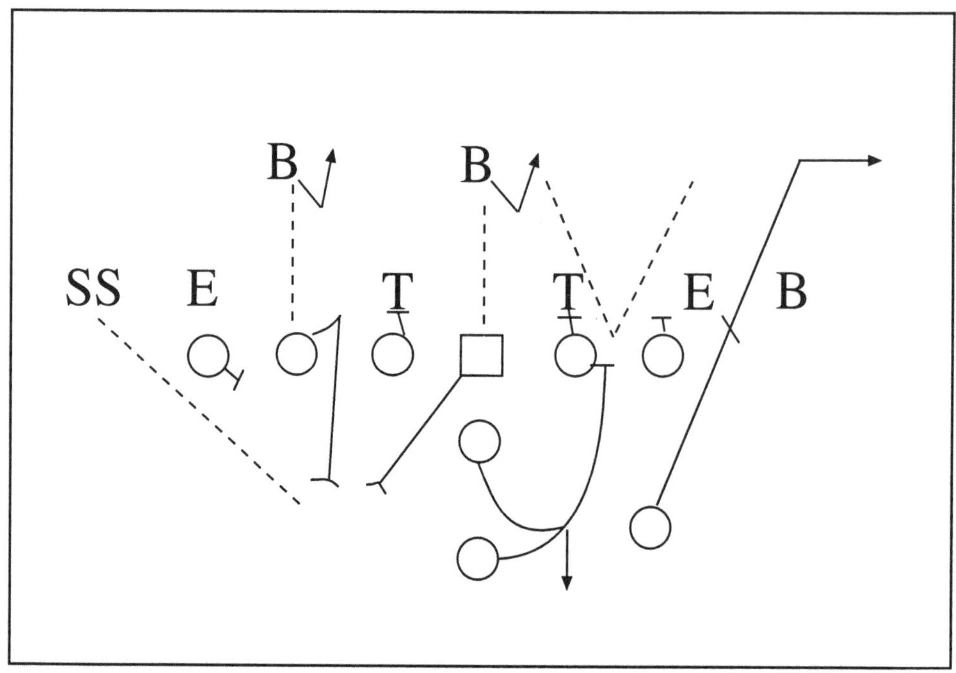

Diagram 8-19: A play pass with the backside uncovered linemen double reading versus a 4-3 front can result in both the center and the tackle double reading to the tight end side.

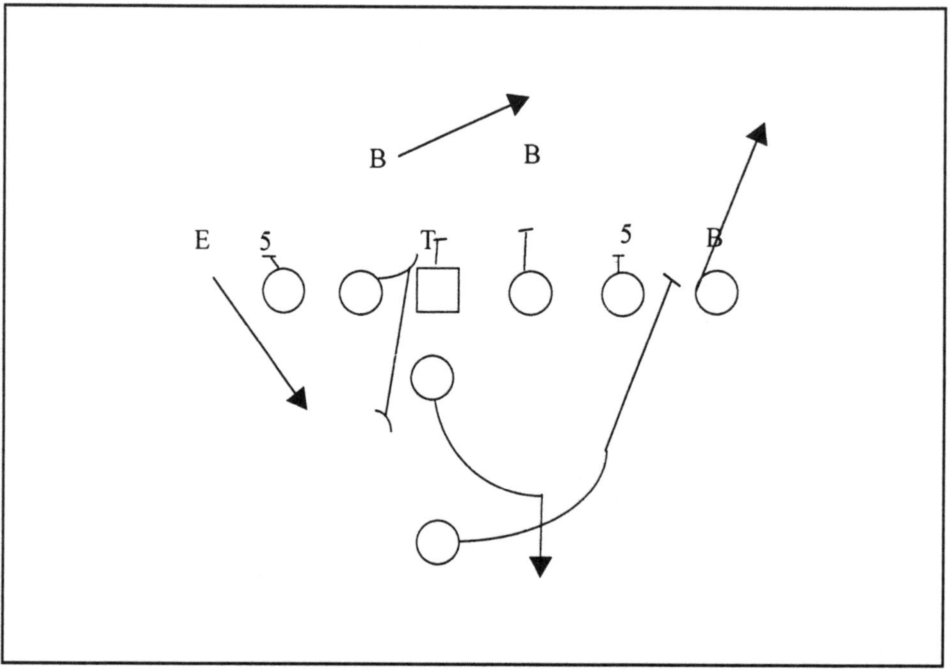

Diagram 8-20: A double read by the guard gives a solid quality to the backside protection of the one-back set play pass.

THE STACK TECHNIQUE

A proper stack blocking technique requires each defender to punch hard to the near breastplate of the defender. When using a stack technique, the blockers will punch to their shared gap. The blockers punch with their gapside arm, while making a hard lateral step with their gapside foot. They should avoid getting their leverage arm tied up with the defender. Both blockers should keep their head on either side of the defender and should avoid getting caught up with the defender.

When blocking a stack, the inside blocker must keep his inside arm free as he punches the defender with his outside hand. The outside stack blocker must keep his outside arm free as he punches the defender with his inside hand. Both stack blockers should visualize blocking one-half of the defender's body. They should also understand that if the defender drives toward a particular blocker, that blocker will assume full responsibility of the defender and engage him with both arms in a good passing-blocking demeanor. The blocker who is "freed" by the down defender's movement should assist his teammate by forcefully shoving the defender toward his offensive teammate. He should, however, take care to keep his shoulders square as he shoves the defender. The free blocker must be alert for a twist stunt from another defensive lineman or linebacker.

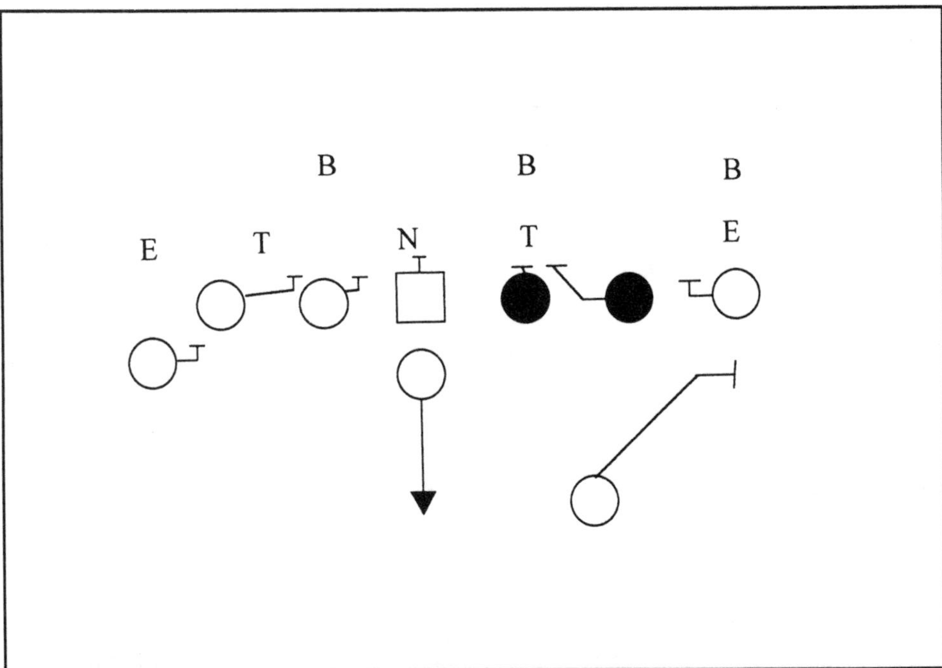

Diagram 8-21: The stack technique by the right guard and the right tackle.

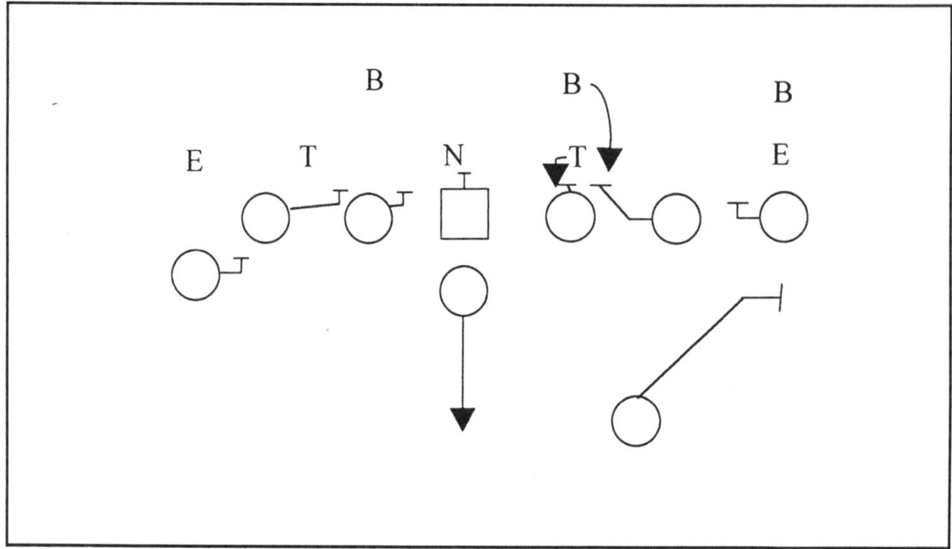

Diagram 8-22: A stack technique against a stunt.

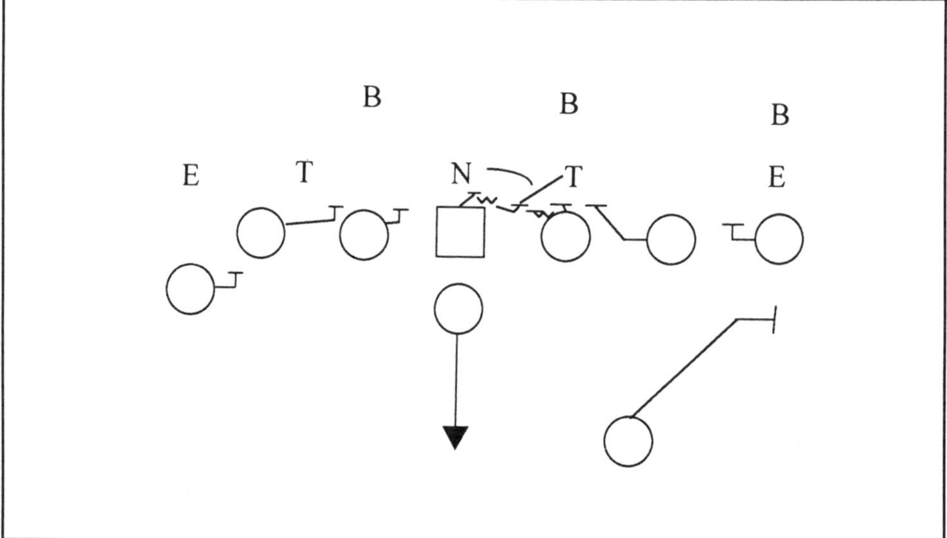

Diagram 8-23: A stack technique versus a nose and a tackle twist.

ONE'S INSIDE (THE TRIANGLE)

If a linebacker aligns between the 3 technique and the nose tackle, a triangle is formed. Diagram 8-24 shows the described alignment to the weakside. When a triangle is formed to the weakside as shown in Diagram 8-24, the guard must alert the offensive tackle that a nose tackle is present and that a triangle exists. In other words, the guard always assumes that the tackle cannot see the nose tackle.

The mere presence of a nose tackle can be a problem for the tackle's recognition of the front. The presence of a nose tackle and a man on the guard give rise to the possibility of a triangle over the "A" gap. If such a triangle exists, the guard alerts the tackle by saying "One's inside." Whenever the guard tells the tackle that number 1 is inside, the tackle must use the jump 'em technique to block the 3 technique on the guard. In fact, until the linebacker flattens the triangle (i.e., walks up on the line to blitz), the guard and the tackle will block the 3 technique with a stack blocking technique. If a linebacker shows a blitz in the "A" gap, the guard can yell " backer" to the tackle. Whenever the guard makes an alert call to the tackle, the tackle knows that he must take the man on the guard. The alert negates the stack technique of blocking by the offensive guard and tackle. When an alert call is made, the tackle blocks the down defender with the jump 'em technique and receives no assistance from the guard.

Note: If a defensive lineman is particularly physical, the tackle may opt to use a down block technique against the defender and cave him down when the guard makes an alert call.

The offensive linemen—particularly the guards—must learn to quickly recognize triangles inside the tackle box. Whenever a triangle exists inside the tackle, the guard should automatically make a "one's inside" call to the tackle . Even if the scheme doesn't require the alert, the guard should make a habit of calling out the fact that one's inside. Against a triangle, all of the linemen's eyes should be up. Not only are the guard and the tackle affected, the near back must focus his scan to the outside hip of the tackle if a triangle blitz shows.

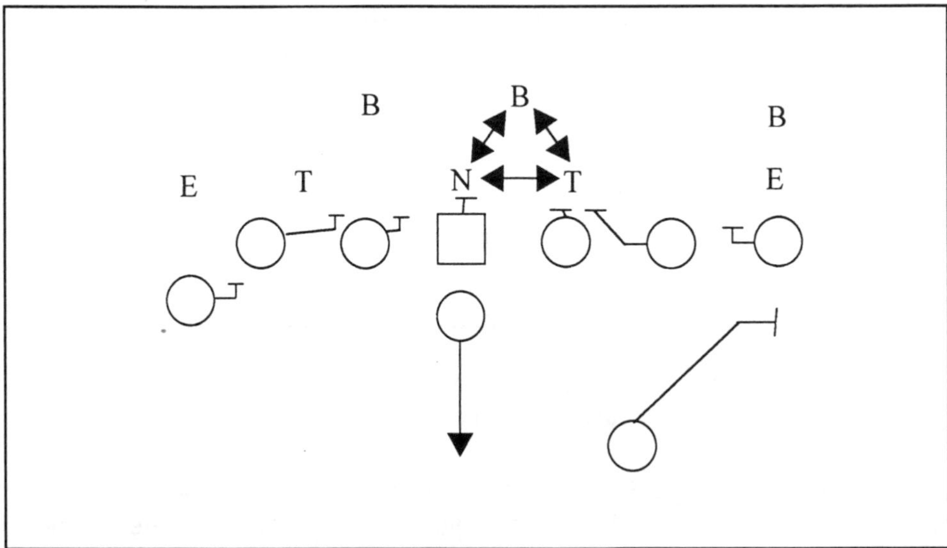

Diagram 8-24: A triangle between the guard and the center.

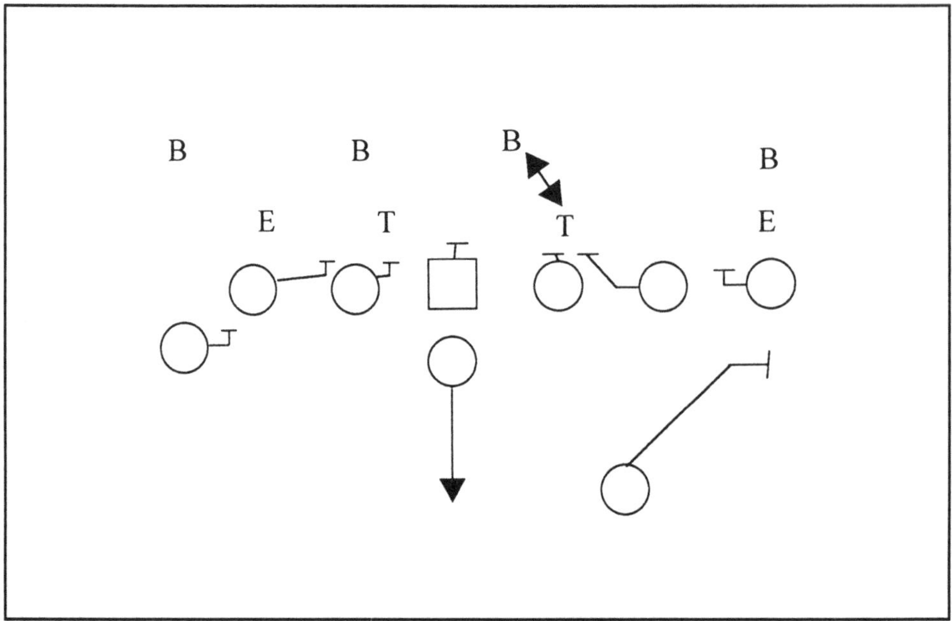

Diagram 8-25: No triangle between the guard and the center.

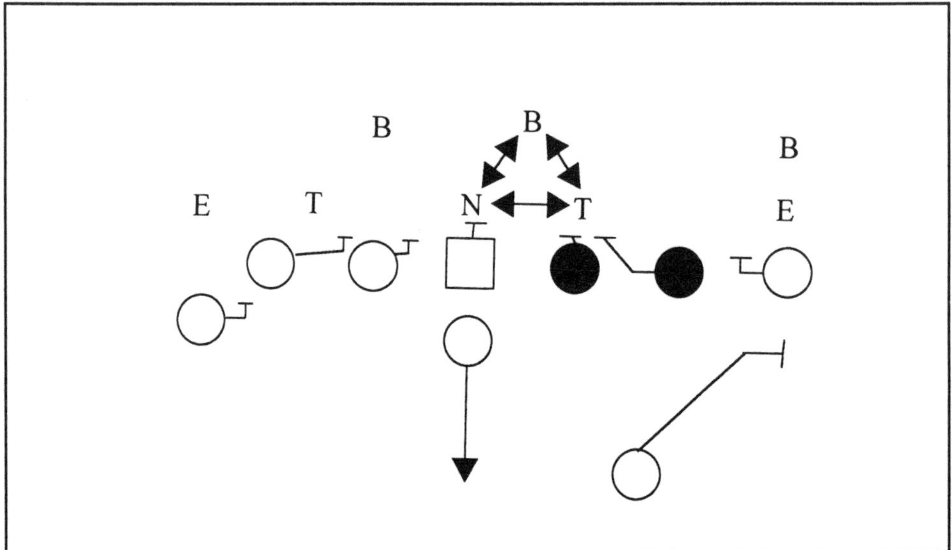

Diagram 8-26: The guard and the tackle should use the stack technique when facing a triangle between the guard and the center.

The presence of a triangle is a critical consideration whenever the protection is a man pass-blocking scheme. Missing a triangle call can result in a big defensive play and a quarterback sack. Consistently picking up the triangular blitz can be equally disheartening for the opponent and will certainly result in big plays offensively. The last scenario of the triangle and "one's inside" call is related to the backer attempting to slip outside through the "B" gap. The 3 technique will drive across the face of the guard as the backer loops through the "B" gap. If the guard and tackle use a good stack blocking technique, the guard will keep his shoulder's square and pick up the down defender while the tackle meets the backer in the "B" gap.

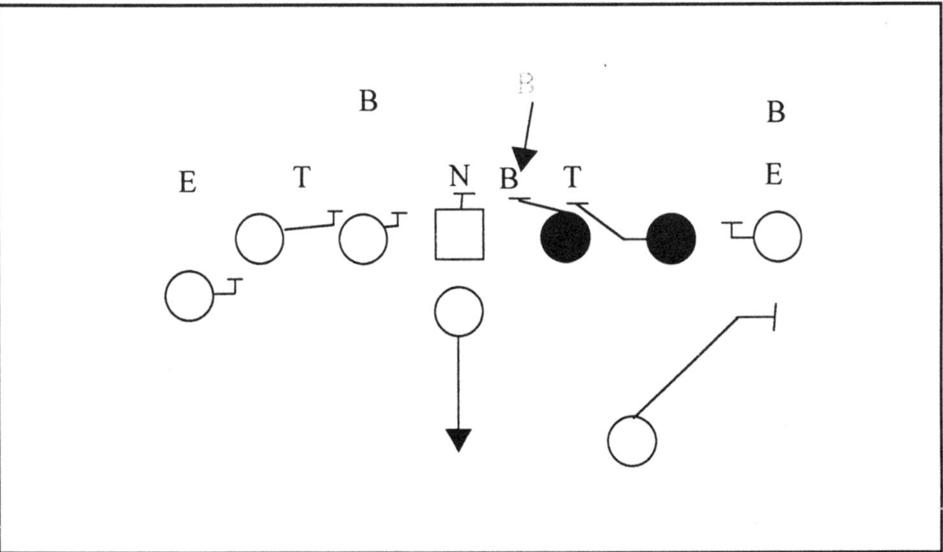

Diagram 8-27: The guard makes an alert call when the backer flattens the triangle as shown in the "A" gap.

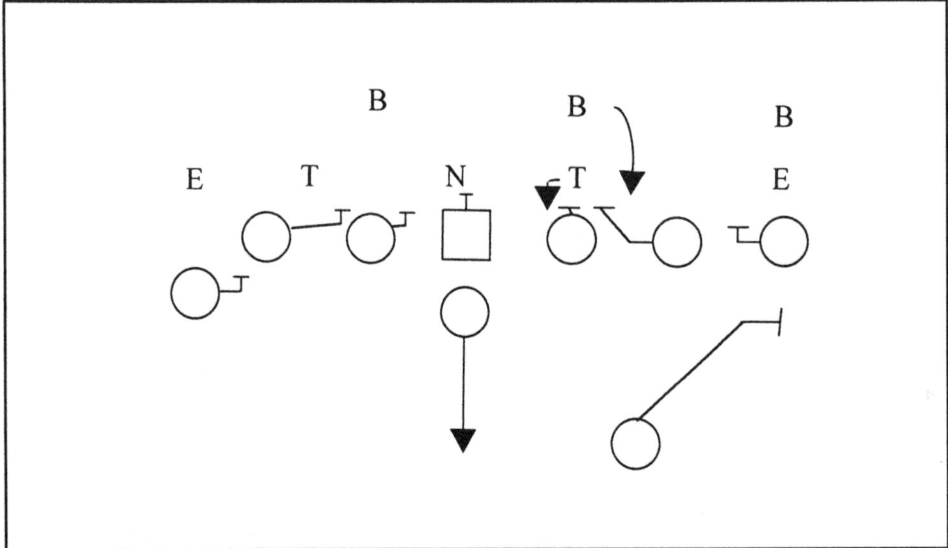

Diagram 8-28: The stack technique versus a backer and a 3-technique twist with the backer going through the "B" gap.

CHAPTER 9

Pass-Blocking Drills

DRILL #1: EVERY DAY DOT DRILLS (EDDD'S) FOR PASS PROTECTION

Objective: To develop an offensive lineman's sense of balance and sharpen his footwork in executing various pass protection techniques.

Equipment Needed: Cones.

Procedure: The five interior linemen form lines within a marked ten-yard area according to their position. On the coach's command, the five players execute one repetition of the specified technique for ten yards. The pass protection techniques that the players should execute include:

- Pass sets.
  - The hard post technique.
  - The soft post technique.
  - The soft kick technique.
  - The hard kick technique.
  - The jump 'em technique.
- Shuffle movement.
  - The right-foot post technique. The players keep their hands behind their back and move laterally with their right foot forward.
  - The left-foot post technique. The players keep their hands behind their back and move laterally with their left foot forward.
- Front, then back balance movement.
  - Without hands. Paired with a defender, the blocker keep his hands behind his back as the defender grabs the jersey of the blocker and jerks the blocker forward and backward. The blocker has to maintain his balance first with his right foot forward, and then switch to move with his left foot forward on the next repetition.
  - With hands. Paired with a defender, the blocker uses his hands to punch and counter the defender as the defender grabs the jersey of the blocker and jerks the blocker forward and backward. The blocker has to maintain his balance with his right foot forward, and then switch to move with his left foot forward on the next repetition.

- Lateral balance movement.
  - Without hands. Paired with a defender, the blocker keep his hands behind his back as the defender grabs the jersey of the blocker and jerks the blocker side to side. The blocker has to maintain his balance with his right foot forward, and then switch to move with his left foot forward on the next repetition.
  - With hands. Paired with a defender, the blocker uses his hands to punch and counter the defender as the defender grabs the jersey of the blocker and jerks the blocker side to side. The blocker has to maintain his balance with his right foot forward, and then switch to move with his left foot forward on the next repetition.
- Spinner
  - Lock out. The players use their hands to punch and control the defender while moving laterally with their right foot forward. The defender makes alternating spin moves, as the blocker switches feet on each repetition.

Coaching Points:

- The first man in each line should step out and turn to face his line to execute the offensive technique.
- The second man in each line should be a defensive player.
- The players should switch roles at the ten-yard mark and perform the techniques until they reach the starting point.
- Each player should perform one repetition of each specified technique.

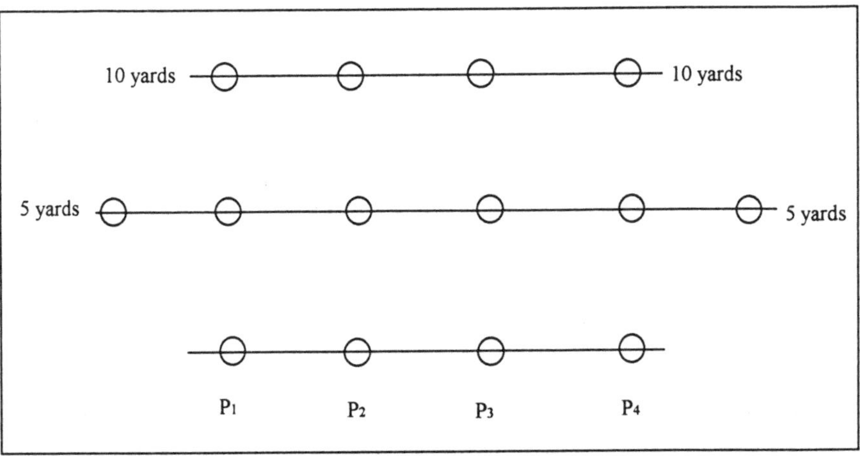

Diagram 9-1: Dots (or cones) within a 10-yard grid for the EDDD's pass-blocking drills.

DRILL #2: MIRROR DODGE DRILL

Objective: To develop an offensive player's ability to move laterally and to maintain proper leverage on the defender.

Equipment Needed: Two cones.

Procedure: Two cones are placed approximately four yards apart on a line. Two players positioned themselves as shown in Diagram 9-2. One lineman plays the role of a pass protector, while the other lineman assumes the role of a pass rusher. The pass protector places himself in a proper pass protection demeanor. The pass rusher works from cone to cone in an attempt to beat the pass protector to either side. The pass protector works to keep his body in front of the pass rusher as the pass rusher moves from side to side.

Coaching Points:

- The pass protector should get repetitions from both a two-point and a three-point stance.
- To emphasize footwork, the pass protector should be required to participate in the drill with his hands held behind his back.
- The coach should emphasize to the players that this drill is a non-contact drill. The players should keep a cushion between them as they compete in the drill.

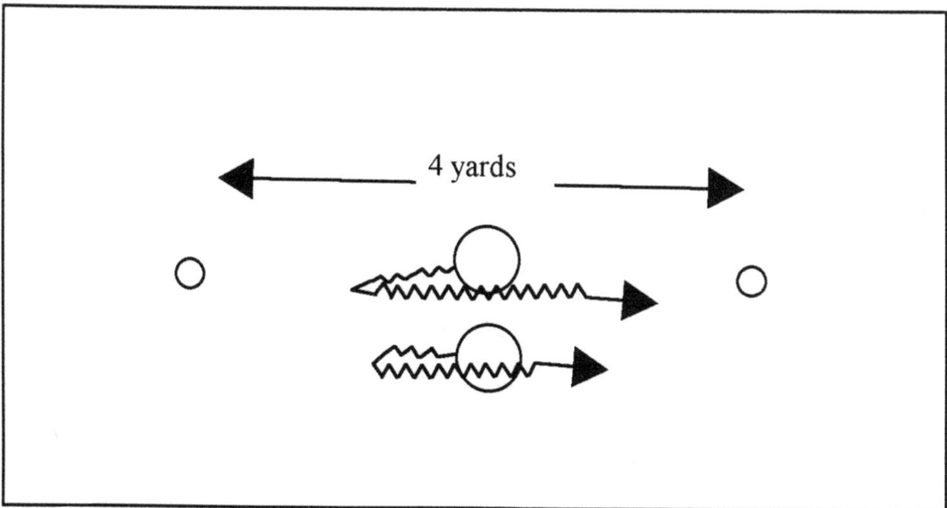

Diagram 9-2: Mirror drill.

DRILL #3: PUNCH THE LINE (SET TO INSIDE RUSH)

Objective: To develop the offensive lineman's punching ability when pass protecting versus an inside rush.

Equipment Needed: Five-man sled.

Procedure: The players form a single line at the left end of the sled. One at a time, the players slide across the face of the sled. Each player shuffles down the sled and strikes each pad with his hands. A shuffling player should keep his right foot forward as he shuffles down the line. The player strikes each pad with his thumbs pointing up. His head should be back and his elbows should be held close to his sides. His feet should maintain a solid base under his body. The player may step into the pad with his forward foot to increase the force of the punch to the pad. After each player has completed one repetition to the right, they reverse directions, while employing the same technique. When moving to the left, the player keeps his left foot forward.

Coaching Points:

- The coach should remind the players that they are practicing the set-to-inside rush technique.
- The coach should check to make sure that the players are using the proper pass-blocking demeanor.
- The coach should structure the drill so that adequate spacing between the players is maintained.
- In place of a five-man or seven-man sled, the drill may be run with five players holding shields.
- The player should punch the pads with great intensity, lifting the sled if possible.

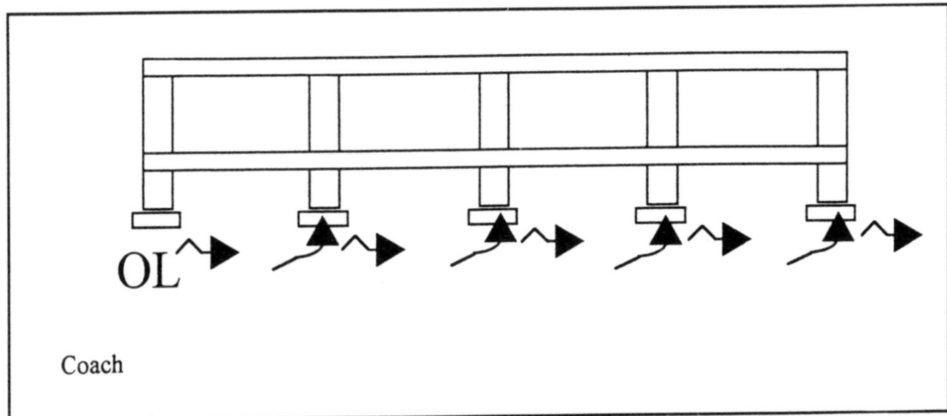

Diagram 9-3: Punch the line (set to inside rush).

DRILL #4: PUNCH THE LINE (SET TO OUTSIDE RUSH)

Objective: To develop the player's punching ability when pass protecting versus the outside rush.

Equipment Needed: Five-man sled

Procedure: The players form a single line at the left end of the sled. One at a time, the players slide across the face of the sled. Each player shuffles down the sled and strikes each pad with his hands. A shuffling player should keep his left foot forward as he shuffles down the line. The player strikes each pad with his thumbs pointing up. His head should be back and his elbows should be held close to his body. His feet should maintain a solid base under his body. The player may step into the pad with his forward foot to increase the force of the punch to the pad. After each player has completed one repetition to the right, they reverse directions while employing the same technique. When moving to the left, the player keeps his right foot forward.

Coaching Points:

- The coach should remind the players that they are practicing the set-to-outside rush technique.
- The coach should check to make sure that the players are using the proper pass-blocking demeanor.
- The coach should structure the drill so that adequate spacing between the players is maintained.
- In lieu of a five-man or seven-man sled, the drill may be run with five players holding shields.
- The player should punch the pads with great intensity, lifting the sled if possible.

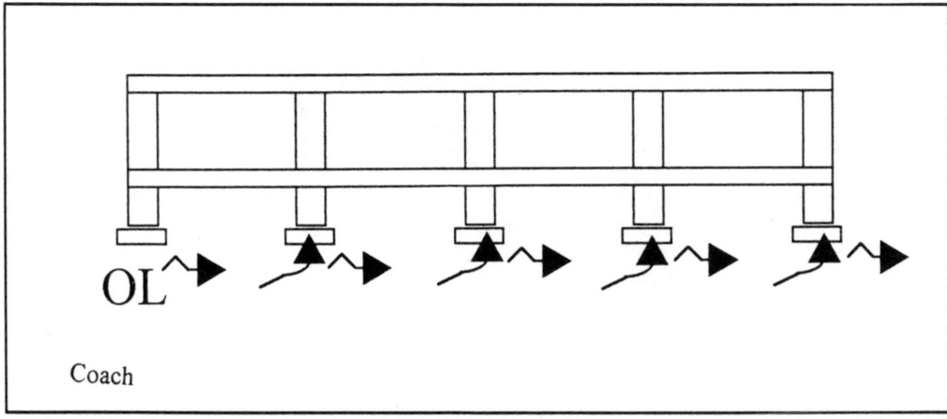

Diagram 9-4: Punch the line (set to outside rush).

DRILL #5: SNAP UPS

Objective: To increase an offensive lineman's speed in getting out of his stance and into the proper pass-blocking demeanor.

Equipment Needed: None.

Procedure: Two players face each other. One player is the pass protector; the other player is the defender. The pass protector assumes a three-point stance. The defensive player stands in front of the pass protector and holds his hands over the head of the pass protector. On the coach's command, the pass protector snaps his head up and sets in the proper pass demeanor. The defensive player's objective is to provide resistance to the pass protector. The pass protector should snap his head and chest upward through the hands of the defensive player.

Coaching Points:

- The defensive player should not interfere with the snap-up to such a point that the integrity of the drill is lost.
- This drill is a good time to work on the team's check-off audible system.
- This drill may be done against a simulated defensive lineman. The pass protector's objective in this case would be to set and punch the hypothetical defender before the defender can grab the pass protector.

Diagram 9-5.

DRILL #6: PASS SETS

Objective: To sharpen an offensive lineman's pass setting ability against the three basic shades of a defensive lineman: inside; head up; and outside.

Equipment Needed: None.

Procedure: This drill may be structured as a group drill (e.g., 5-on-5, 3-on-3, etc.) or a 1-on-1 drill. In the 1-on-1 procedure, two players position themselves across the line of scrimmage from each other. The player acting as a defensive player aligns in the specified shade. On the coach's command, the offensive player executes the appropriate pass set. The offensive lineman should use the hard post set technique against an inside shade alignment. Against the head up alignment, the offensive player should use the soft post. Against the outside alignment, the offensive player should use the soft kick. After the offensive player has performed the three specified techniques, the two players switch roles.

Coaching Points:

- The coach should emphasize to the offensive lineman the points of correct footwork and body position in his set.
- The pass protector may use either a two-point or a three-point stance.
- The pass protector should set himself to gain an inside-out relationship on the defender.
- The pass protector's inside foot should be positioned slightly inside of the defender.
- The center should use the hard post technique against shaded alignments. He should use the soft post technique against a head up nose tackle.

Diagram 9-6.

DRILL #7: 1-ON-1 PASS PROTECTION

Objective: To develop an offensive lineman's pass protection skills against a live pass rusher.

Equipment Needed: A pop-up bag.

Procedure: The offensive line unit is aligned along a scrimmage line. A defensive lineman aligns over each offensive lineman, and the pop-up bag is placed seven yards behind the center. On the coach's command, the center snaps or moves the ball, the designated pass protector pass sets to punch the defender. The defender uses one of his pass rushing techniques in an attempt to get to the pop-up bag. After the first man in line (i.e., the offensive tackle) completes his repetition, the offensive line coach signals the next lineman (i.e., the guard) to get ready for his opportunity. The drill then progresses down the line of scrimmage.

Coaching Points:

- The center should have someone to whom he can snap the ball on his repetition.
- The pop-up bag can be moved to different depths to practice the various protection schemes.
- The pass protector should block until the whistle is blown.

Diagram 9-7.

DRILL #8: MULTIPLE MAN

Objective: To develop an offensive linemen's ability to work together and to pick up the two-man defensive pass rushing games.

Equipment Needed: A pop-up bag.

Procedure: A pop-up bag is placed approximately seven yards deep to simulate a quarterback setting to pass. The offensive linemen are grouped in different combinations (e.g., tackle-tight end, tackle-guard, guard-center-guard). The offensive line coach selects a combination to execute the block and positions two defenders over the selected alignment combination. One coach stands behind the offensive linemen and signals the desired defensive twist stunt. Another coach stands behind the defensive linemen and signals the snap count. On the snap, the defenders execute their stunt and the offensive linemen work together according to their protection rules. The offensive linemen block until the whistle is blown.

Coaching Points:

- The coach should make sure that each blocking combination encounters each of the basic defensive pass rush games.
- The coach should check to ensure that each player is demonstrating the proper blocking demeanor and techniques.

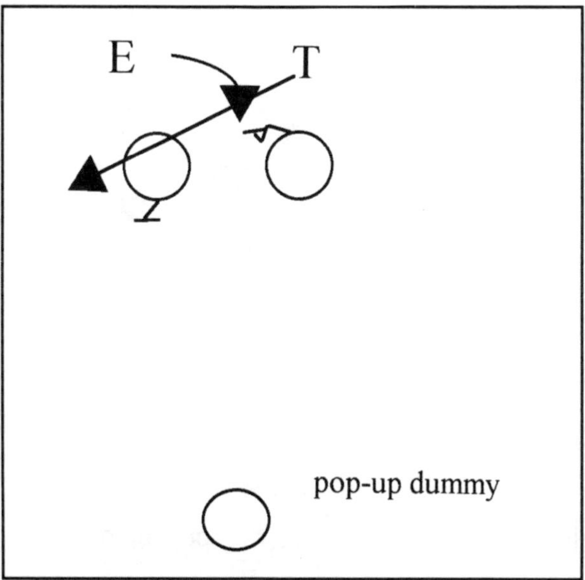

Diagram 9-8: Multiple-man games.

DRILL #9: COMBINATION-MAN GAMES

Objective: To develop offensive linemen's ability to work together and pick up the three-and four-man defensive pass rushing games.

Equipment Needed: A pop-up bag.

Procedure: A pop-up bag is placed approximately seven yards deep to simulate a quarterback setting to pass. The offensive linemen are aligned in different combinations (e.g., left side, right side, whole line, etc.). The offensive line coach selects a combination to execute the block and positions three or four defenders over the selected alignment combination. One coach stands behind the offensive linemen and signals the desired defensive game. Another coach stands behind the defensive linemen and signals the snap count. On the snap, the defenders execute their stunt, and the offensive linemen work together according to their protection rules. The offensive linemen block until the whistle is blown.

Coaching Points:

- The coach should make sure that each blocking combination encounters each of the basic defensive pass rush games.
- The coach should check to ensure that each player is demonstrating the proper blocking demeanor and techniques.

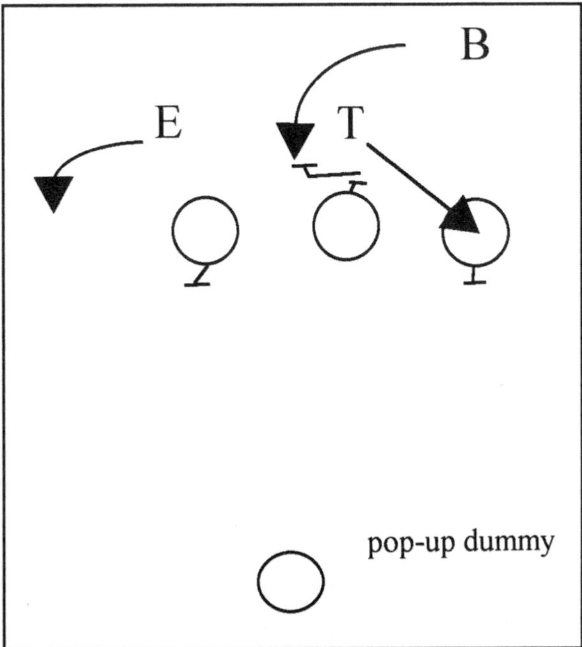

Diagram 9-9: Combination-man games.

DRILL #10: MEDICINE BALL SET

Objective: To develop an offensive lineman's ability to punch the pass rusher.

Equipment Needed: A medicine ball.

Procedure: Two offensive linemen stand approximately seven feet apart. Both linemen assume a proper pass-blocking demeanor. While chopping their feet in place, the linemen pass the medicine ball back and forth between them. The offensive lineman receiving the pass punches the ball back to the passer's chest. The punch pass is made from the chest, as the offensive linemen continually move their feet.

Coaching Points:

- The linemen should pass the ball as if they are playing the children's game of "hot potato."
- The linemen should keep a proper pass-blocking demeanor during the drill.
- This drill is an excellent pre-practice, warm-up drill.

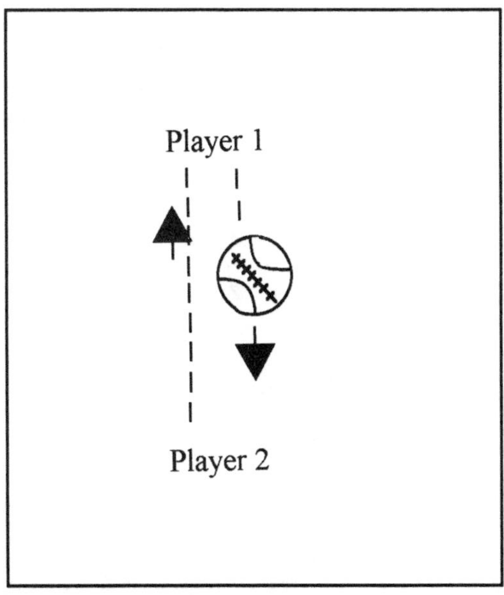

Diagram 9-10: The medicine ball.

DRILL #11: SOFTBALL SHUFFLE DRILL

Objective: To develop an offensive lineman's hip flexibility and footwork.

Equipment Needed: A softball.

Procedure: Two cones are positioned approximately 12 feet apart. Standing next to one of the cones, one lineman assumes a proper pass-blocking demeanor. The other lineman rolls the softball to a point near the other cone, as the offensive lineman stays low and shuffles to tap the ball back to his teammate. The lineman continues to shuffle back and forth between the cones, as his teammate alternately rolls the ball to each cone. The players switch roles after approximately 20 seconds.

Coaching Points:

- The shuffling lineman should keep his shoulders low as he shuffles from side to side.
- The shuffling lineman should bend at the knees and keep his back slightly arched in a proper pass-blocking demeanor.
- This drill is an excellent pre-practice, warm-up drill.

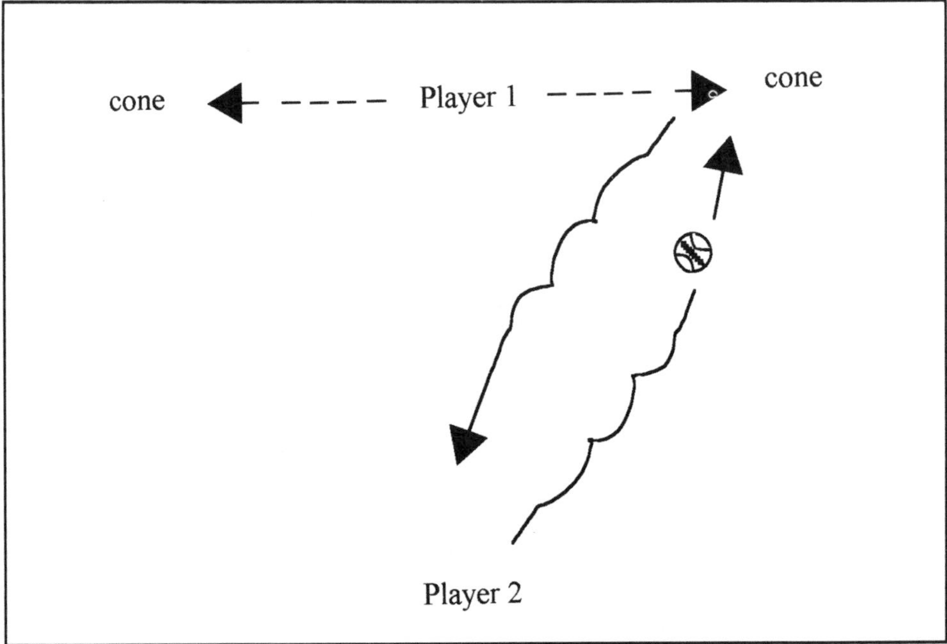

Diagram 9-11: The softball shuffle.

DRILL #12: LEVERAGE DRILL

Objective: To develop an offensive lineman's ability to regain leverage and to execute proper hand positioning against a defender who uses his hands.

Equipment Needed: None.

Procedure: Two players assume the proper pass-blocking demeanor approximately two feet apart. One player acts as an offensive lineman, while the other serves as a defender. The offensive lineman establishes the proper hand positioning to the pass rusher's chest and drives the defender for a couple of steps. After a few steps backward, the defender fights to gain proper hand positioning against his teammate. The defender then becomes the blocker, as he establishes proper hand positioning with the proper pass-blocking demeanor. The drill continues until each player has had several opportunities at fighting to regain the proper hand positioning.

Coaching Points:

- Both linemen should keep their shoulders low and their backs flat.
- This drill is an excellent pre-practice, warm-up drill.

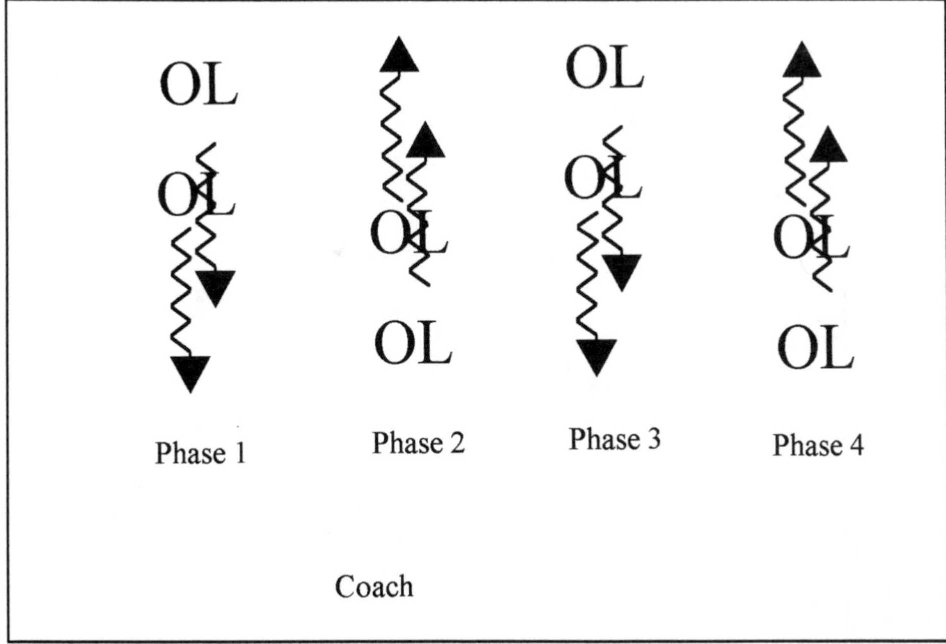

Diagram 9-12: Leverage drill.

DRILL #13: BAG PUNCH DRILL

Objective: To develop an offensive lineman's ability to punch with a low-to-high thrust through a defender.

Equipment Needed: A hanging bag.

Procedure: Two offensive linemen stand on opposite sides of a hanging bag. One player functions as a "feeder" to a pass blocker. The pass blocker rapidly punches the bag with an upward thrust as the feeder stabilizes the bag, while helping return the bag to the blocker. The feeder makes sure that the bag "yo-yo's" during the drill, forcefully pushes the bag into the pass blocker's body.

Coaching Points:

- The pass blocker should keep a proper pass-blocking demeanor during the drill.
- The pass blocker should keep his feet moving as he punches the bag.
- The pass blocker should punch the bag with the heels of his hand while keeping his thumbs up.

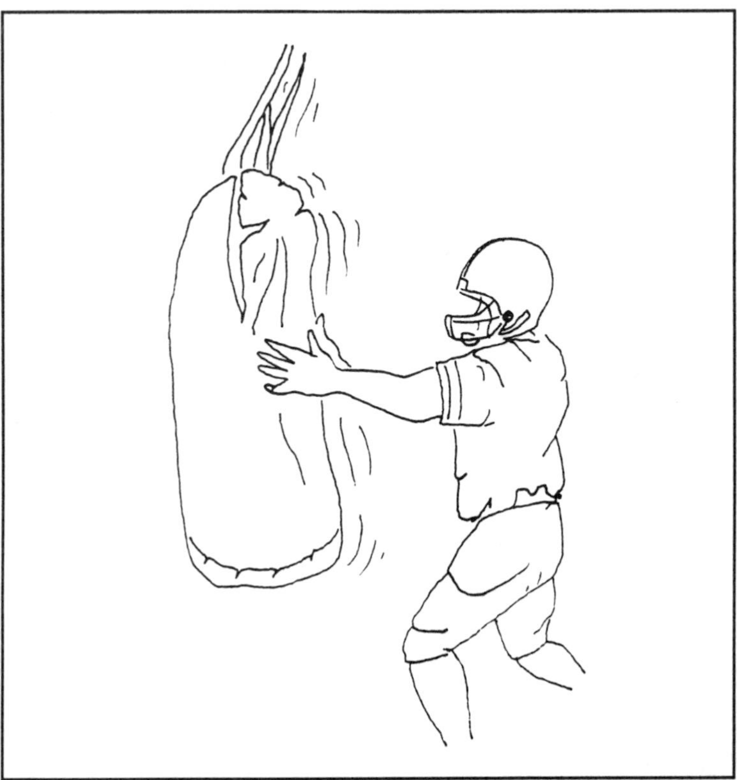

Diagram 9-13.

CHAPTER 10

Goal Line Blocking

Once an offensive unit penetrates its opponent's ten yard line—especially inside the five yard line, it may be faced with a defensive scheme characterized by an interior line charge and aggressive play from the secondary. The closer the ball gets to a defensive unit's goal line, the more aggressive the defensive play, particularly from the secondary personnel. With less area to cover, the secondary will be able to play underneath the receiver (i.e., between the receiver and the quarterback). Most defensive secondary personnel know that the end line of the end zone functions as an extra defender.

Defensive goal line fronts normally use an "eleven man" in-the-box scheme. Four of the more popular goal line fronts are the 6-5 goal line front, the 7-1 front, the 5-3 front and the gap-8 front. These pressure fronts are normally used when the ball penetrates the defender's five-yard line. Another common characteristic of the inside-the-five, situational goal line defense is a man-to-man scheme coverage scheme.

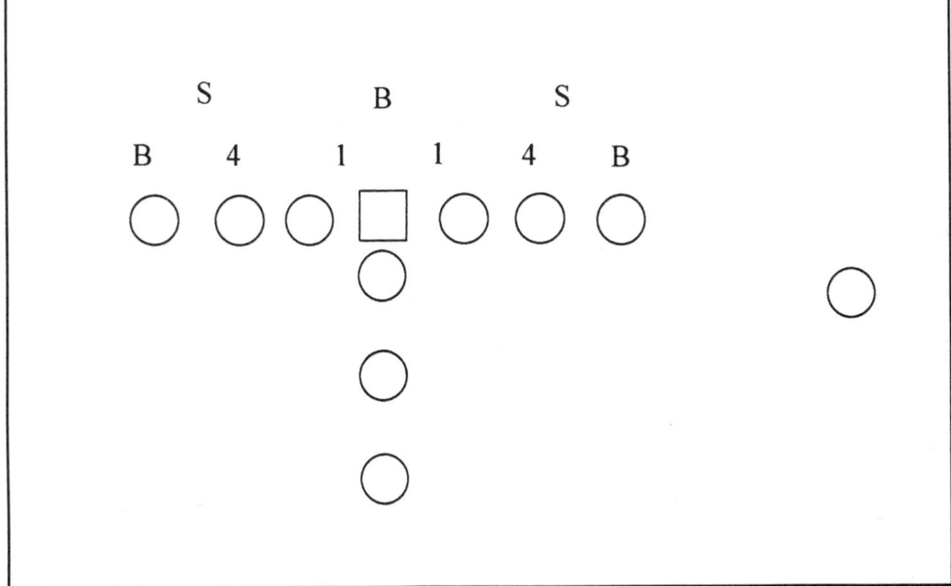

Diagram 10-1: 65. (The 62 alignment is a very popular defensive scheme that becomes the 65 when the secondary moves up.)

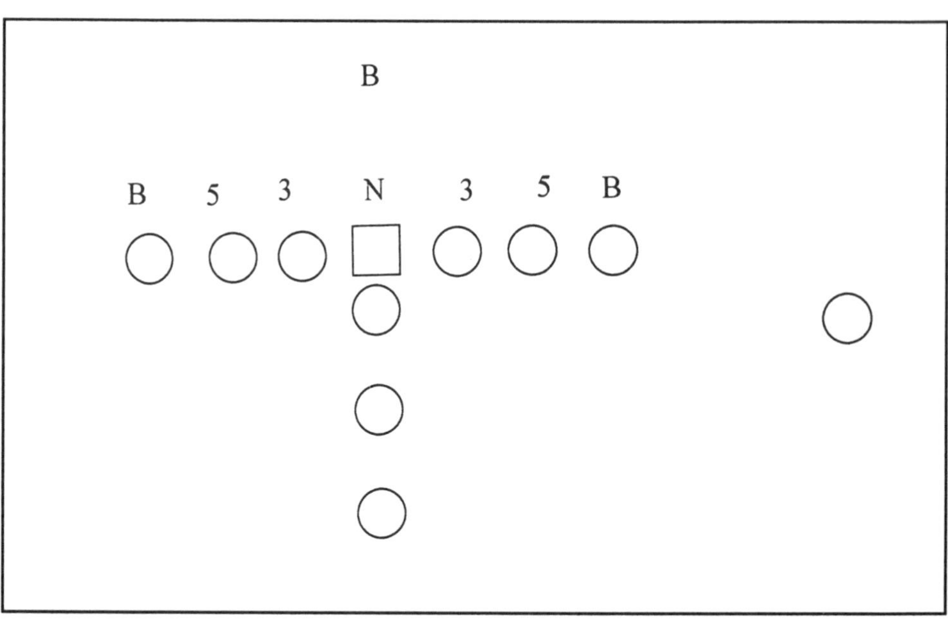

Diagram 10-2: 7-1. (The 7-1 is a variation of the old Chicago Bear's 46 defensive alignment.)

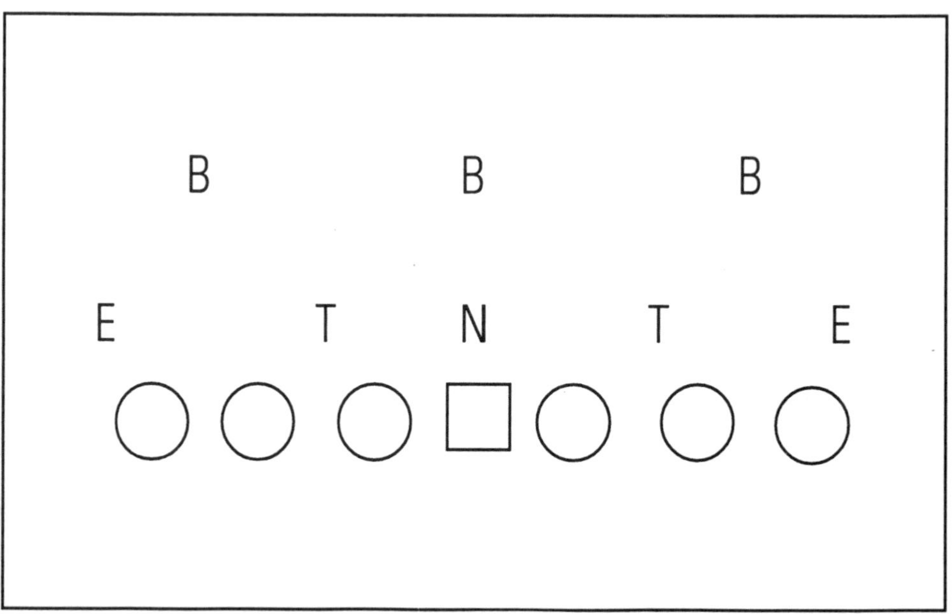

Diagram 10-3: 5-3. (This defensive alignment is seldom used if a high likelihood of a quarterback sneak exists.)

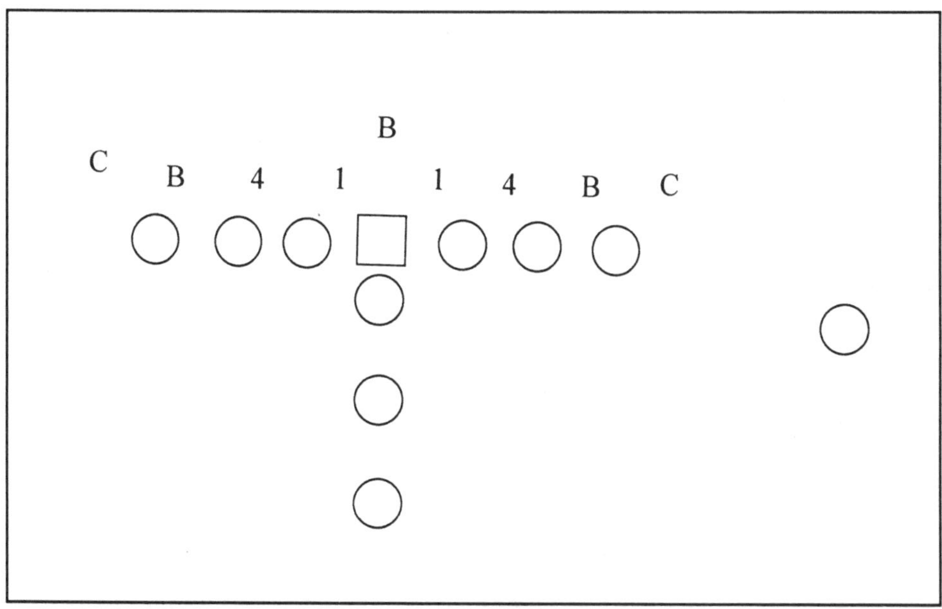

Diagram 10-4: Gap 8. (In goal line situations, two defensive linemen (B's) are normally substituted from one linebacker and one defensive back.)

Goal line blocking presents a unique problem for an offensive line in that the defensive line will concentrate on penetrating into the backfield. Defensive line defenders on the goal line will normally get in a "nose to the turf" stance with their elbows bent. They will typically key the ball and charge through their assigned gap on the snap of the football. Perimeter defenders (i.e., strong safeties and cornerbacks) will contain by charging up the field.

To block goal line defenders, offensive linemen should utilize their own goal line stance. When facing a definite goal line charge by the defensive front, offensive linemen should use a four-point stance. A good four-point offensive goal line stance is a characterized by the following components:

- Weight forward.
- Hands slightly forward of the shoulders.
- Elbows bent.
- Feet balanced under the hips.
- Heels slightly off the turf.
- Head up and neck bowed.

Against a penetrating style of defense, the landmarks of the various blocks are slightly exaggerated. The set to drive landmark is approximately four inches below the normal blocking plane. The set to reach landmark is extended to the far elbow of the defender. When setting to reach, the blocker should attempt to get his facemask through the far elbow of the defender. The blocker can exaggerate his set to reach step because the nature of the goal line defense is a penetrating nature.

Penetrating defensive linemen will not attempt to fight across the face of angle blockers. Therefore, under normal circumstances against a goal line front, offensive linemen should not worry about the defender playing underneath the exaggerated set to reach.

Because a full line slant can open up running lanes between the ends, few defensive coaches run a full line slant from a goal line look. While some defensive coaches slant their front on the goal line, in reality, the probability of a full goal line front slant is decreased as the ball moves closer to the goal line. If the scouting report shows a probability of a full line slant, the offensive linemen should be taught not to extend to the set to reach landmark. Against a slanting front, the offensive line should keep a normal set to reach landmark and should aim to the opposite breastplate of the defender.

If the blocker does get to the far elbow on the set to reach, he is in a position to "get around" on the defender and to work his shoulders upfield in a cutoff technique. When reaching a penetrating defender, it is important for the blocker to get his backside shoulder across the defender's face and to work his frontside shoulder upfield. Getting the shoulders square and scrambling into a vertical blocking position are key factors in the success of a cutoff or a reach block against a penetrating defender.

Generally, two-man combination blocks do not work well against a goal line penetrating defense. With the defense working to stay low and to get penetration into the backfield, combination blocks become relatively difficult to execute. The hip-to-hip seal that is crucial to the success of a two-man zone block is hard to maintain against a penetrating defender. Likewise, fold blocks are not normally effective strategies against a penetrating front.

A few combinations are effective against the various goal line fronts. One of these combinations is an over scheme. An over scheme enables the center to reach a charging 1 technique as the guard drives through the outside shoulder of the 1 technique, to seal the middle linebacker. Diagram 10-5 shows an over scheme against a 6-5 goal line front. Despite the fact that a 6-5 goal line front is designed to free the middle linebacker, an over scheme can account for the 6-5 middle linebacker.

Another effective blocking scheme on the goal line is gap blocking. Onside gap blocking can seal the defensive penetration and isolate the end defender for a kick-out block by a blocking back or the backside guard. The gap scheme calls for the playside offensive linemen to use a down blocking technique, while the center blocks the playside "A" gap. Diagram 10-6 shows an onside gap blocking scheme versus the gap 8 goal line front. A gap scheme is a good scheme to use when running off tackle or outside the end.

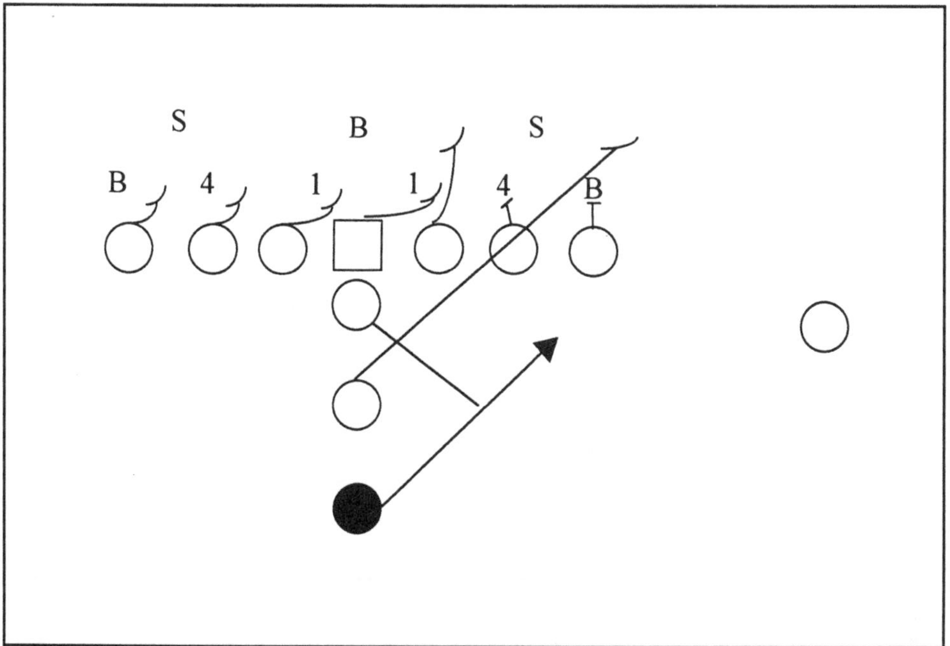

Diagram 10-5: The over scheme by the playside guard and enter versus the 65 goal line defense.

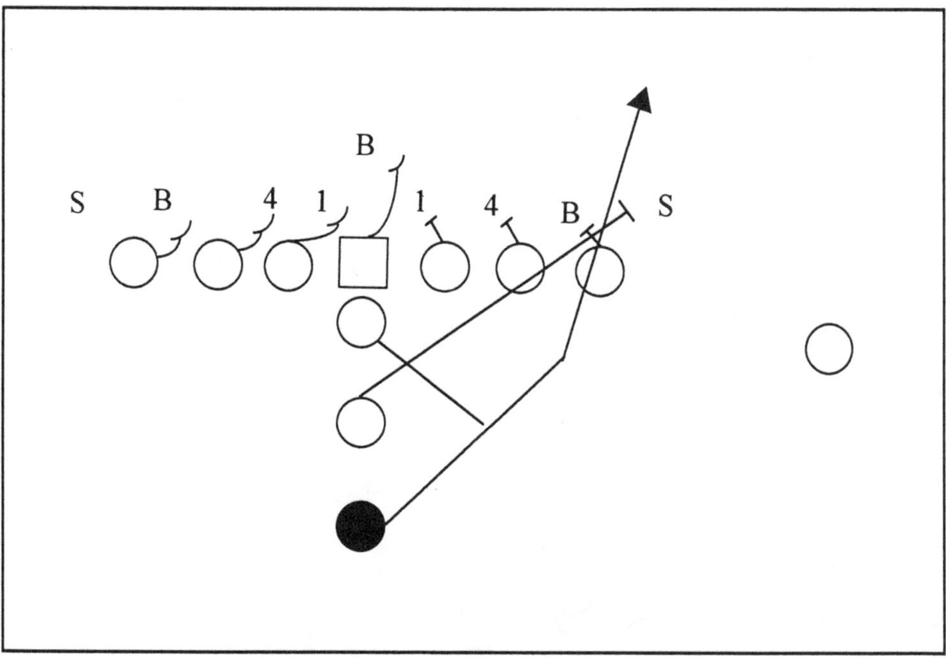

Diagram 10-6: A gap scheme by the playside versus a gap 8 goal line defense.

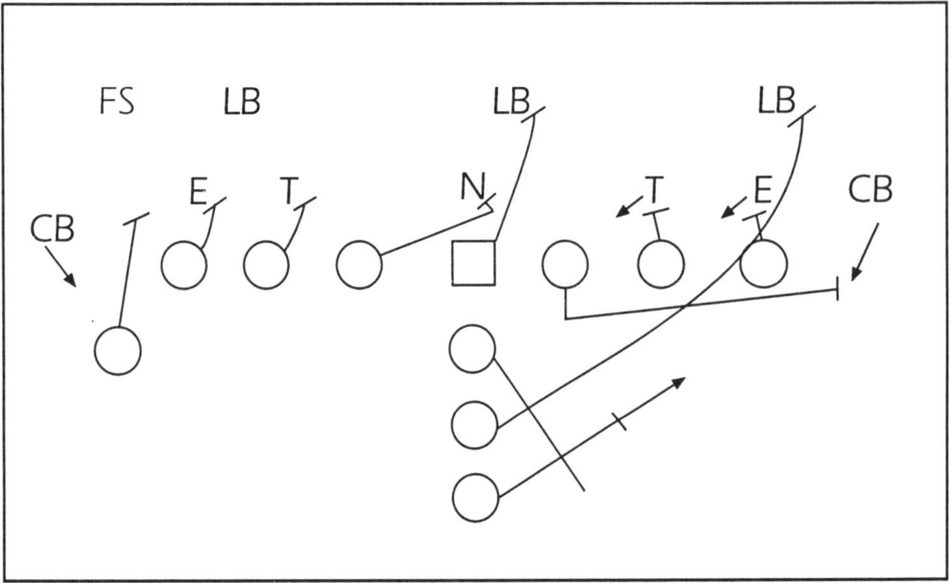

Diagram 10-7: A strongside G scheme versus a 53 double crash defensive front. (All factors considered, I have found this goal line play to be very effective.)

A wedge blocking scheme is another effective goal line blocking scheme versus both the 6-5 front and the gap 8 front. A wedge blocking scheme calls for the playside blockers to fire off the ball shoulder-to-shoulder and to get a vertical push against the defenders positioned inside the playside tight end.

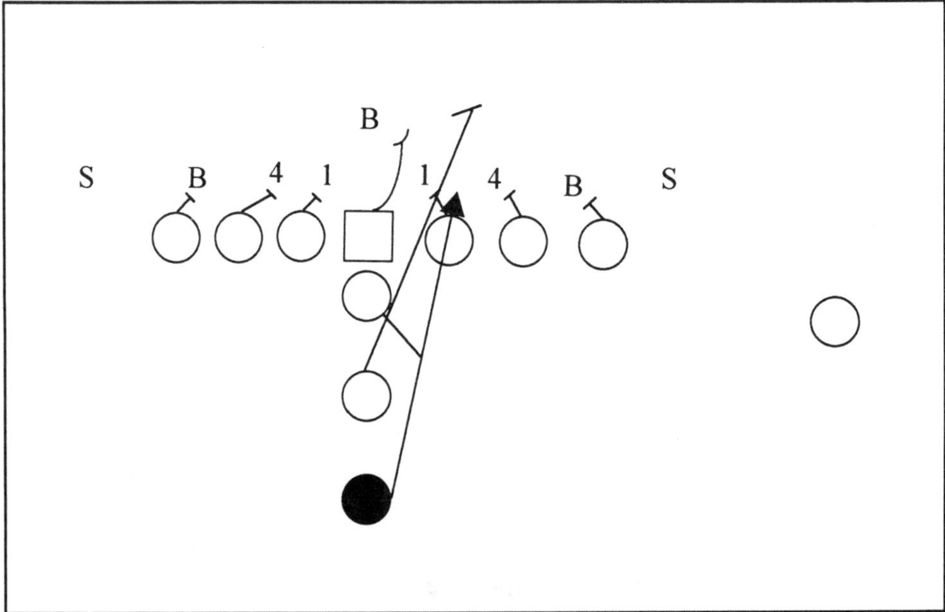

Diagram 10-8: A wedge scheme versus a gap 8 goal line defense.

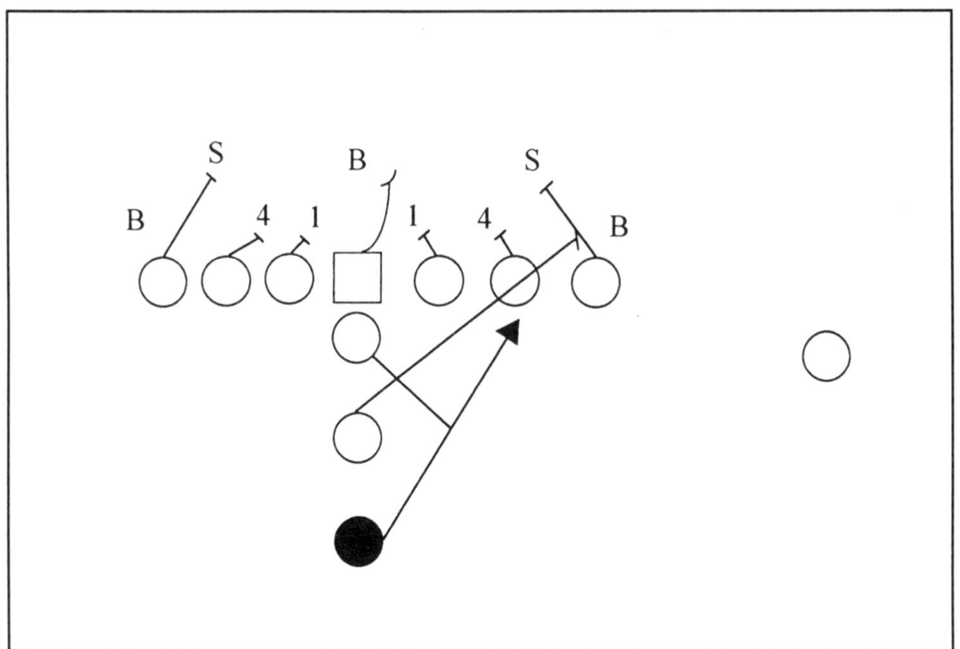

Diagram 10-9: A wedge scheme versus a 6-5 goal line defense.

One of the more neglected areas of offensive preparation is the goal line offense package. When it is adequately addressed, the goal line attack is often practiced as an incidental part of the practice moments before a break, or just before the end of practice. Many offensive coordinators tend to direct the focus of the goal line period to the big picture. In the process, they don't allow enough time for individualized practice of goal line blocking techniques. It is important that you not only take the time to walk through the goal line blocking assignments, but concentrate your teaching efforts and plan a concise goal line package which provides you an opportunity to attack either defensive flank and exploit any defensive conflict.

Adequate preparation of the goal line phase can mean the difference between a championship and a back-in-the-pack finish. An old football saying warns that it is the little things that can mean the difference between winning and losing. If little things can mean the difference between winning and losing, then consider the possible effects of neglecting the big things—such as goal line offense preparation.

CHAPTER 11

Offensive Linemen in the Kicking Game

An offensive lineman's responsibility in the kicking game is a relatively straightforward role. On kicks for points—such as an extra point and a field goal, the offensive lineman's role is to stop inside penetration. On kick-off returns, the lineman's job is to sprint downfield and execute his blocking assignment, while staying under control and blocking above the waist.

KICK-OFF RETURN

Many coaches use offensive linemen in the kicking game during the kick-off return phase. While this approach is an accepted practice throughout most levels of play, some serious consideration should be given to the efficiency of the practice. Several flaws exist in the philosophy of using the offensive linemen as the front line on the kick-off return team. Among the points that can be advanced against using this fairly common front line makeup are the following:

- The kick off involves open field blocks.

  While some offensive guards are exceptional blockers when pulling out on the perimeter because they receive a great deal of practice at this technique a pertinent question arises: who is less suited for open-field blocking than an offensive lineman? The answer is fairly obvious—nobody. The open field block typically required on a kick-off return requires several factors, including speed, agility, and a familiarity with making contact with an opponent in an open-field setting. As such, linebackers, tight ends, and back-up running backs tend to be much more suited for being front-line blockers on a kick-off return. As a rule, because they tend to possess the traits that are conducive to effectively operating in an open-field situation, they tend to be better blockers than offensive linemen on kick-off returns.

- The front line should be always prepared to field a surprise onside kick.

  Offensive linemen—with the exception of the center—never touch the ball. To further negate their ability to handle the ball, the offensive linemen commonly wear padded gloves. At best, a coach can require his lineman to take off their gloves on a kick-off return, they normally have little or no time to retrieve their gloves and put them back on before play resumes. Besides, most offensive linemen tape on their gloves to keep them from slipping when their hands get sweaty. All factors considered, five offensive linemen stationed as the primary receivers of a surprise onside kick is not a "winning" strategy.

- Effective kick-off return schemes normally require the front line to sprint 20 yards to get into position to set up a return.

  As stated in Chapter 1, foot speed is not a prerequisite for playing the offensive line. All factors considered, however, the kick-off return needs a front line who can run. On the other hand, fewer positions on the football team attract players who are slower as a unit than the offensive line. As such, placing five offensive linemen up front on the kick-off return works against the success of any kick-off return scheme other than the wedge return up the middle.

- The kick off removes the opportunity for regrouping the offensive line.

  A lot can be accomplished by huddling your offensive line together as a unit and giving them last minute instructions—particularly after a sudden-change touchdown by the opponent off of an offensive turnover. The time involved in the kick-off return can be used to regroup the offensive linemen and help them regain their composure and focus.

  If the offensive linemen are part of the kick-off return, no opportunity exists to help them regain their poise. The lack of an opportunity to meet with the offensive line after a sudden-change touchdown by a team's opponent is a detriment to achieving a quick recovery of the team's level of offensive intensity.

On the other hand, if it is inevitable that a team has to use its offensive linemen as an integral part of its kick-off return team, the linemen should be instructed on the proper two-point stance of the front line player. A proper stance for a kick-off return front player should adhere to the following points:

- The head is up.

  A common flaw of the kick-off return stance is caused by an offensive lineman leaning forward at the hips in the ready position. The blocker should keep his head back so that his facemask is tucked behind the front of the chest. If a lineman is leaning forward with his facemask in front of his shoulders and chest, he will have to pop his head back to elevate his chest if has to catch the ball. A surprise kick can strike an ill-prepared blocker in the face and shoulder pads. The blocker should not have the top of his pads as the forward portion of his body. He should squat with his torso erect.

- The knees and the elbows are bent.

  A lineman keeping his torso erect and his shoulders up will result in his chest being out. The blocker should then bend at the knees—not the hips—to lower his buttocks to the ground. Furthermore, he should bend his elbows so that his hands are in front of his body.

- The hands are held palm up.

  The universal ready position of any athletic stance involves rolling the thumbs out. This action forces the palm forward toward the kick-off team. By rolling the thumbs out with the elbows bent, the palms are then positioned facing up. This method gives the lineman the best position for basket-catching or trapping a bouncing ball against his body. He should not attempt to catch the ball with his fingers pointing to the sky and his palms facing the kicker. Rather, the offensive lineman should try to trap the ball against his body in a grasping manner, with his hands trapping the ball against his chest. If he misses the ball while attempting to trap it against his body, he has the added aid of being able to use his forearms to help trap the ball against his body. Plus, by using his arms in a clutching manner, he prevents the ball from ricocheting off his chest back toward the kicking team. If he holds his fingers skyward and his palms forward, the natural tendency is to bat the ball back toward the kicking team—should he mishandle the kick.

- The feet are under his armpits.

  An offensive lineman should keep a narrow stance when setting up as a front line blocker of the kick-off return. The second most common error involving an offensive lineman's kick-off return stance occurs when he widens his feet to lower his center of gravity. (The first most common error is the lineman leaning forward.) An offensive lineman who is unduly fatigued or an undisciplined offensive lineman will widen his stance instead of bending his knees as he should. The point to remember is that if a lineman sets his feet too wide, he limits his ability to quickly move to either side.

  He should keep his feet under him so that he can quickly move from side to side. While an offensive lineman shouldn't move to catch an onside kick (he should only field the balls kicked within approximately two feet of his position), an offensive lineman should be ready to step to one side and squarely field the ball. He should never reach for the ball, rather he should catch the ball squarely against his chest.

- The body is turned at a slight angle to the ball.

  The offensive lineman should not face the ball with his shoulders square. He should open his shoulders slightly and cock his stance to the inside.

Among the general rules that an offensive lineman should observe when he is fielding the ball are the following:

- Never move more than two steps to catch a ball kicked to either side.
- Never reach to catch a ball kicked just over your head.
- Never try to catch the ball and run with it.
- After recovering the ball, fall on one side and tuck your knees to your chest while cradling the ball to your stomach.
- Physically cover up your teammate when he receives the ball.
- Dodge a ball kicked directly at you. Allow a power kick or a line drive kick to go through to the back receivers.

The alignment of the front five on the kick-off team may vary from team to team. Normally, a kick-off return team aligns approximately 12 yards off the ball. The center should set the front alignment at the 47-yard line on a regular kick off. While he may alternate aligning to the right or left of the ball, the center should never align directly in front of the ball. The guards should also align on the 47-yard line, at a position approximately three yards outside of the NCAA regulation hashmarks. The tackles should align at the 48-yard line on the numbers. If the ball is kicked from a hashmark, the front line should slide their alignment approximately two yards toward the ball.

The various return schemes require the offensive line to master different techniques. A list of the possible return schemes includes the following:

- Middle return.
- Right sideline return.
- Left sideline return.
- Double sideline return.
- Wall return right.
- Wall return left.
- Double wall return.
- Reverse returns.

FIELD GOAL—EXTRA POINT

As with all scrimmage plays, the most important offensive line position is the center. Often, a team will replace its regular center on the field goal—extra point kick with a specialized player. Teams that adhere to this philosophy (i.e., use a specialty snapper) should make sure he begins snapping on the sideline whenever the ball is in a position from which a field goal or an extra point is possible. Likewise, if the clock is running down and the team is working to get a last second field goal opportunity, its deep snapper should be warming up on the sideline.

An important factor attendant to the deep snapper's effectiveness is the time it takes for the ball to get to the holder. Not only should the ball arrive on target to the holder's hands, the ball must be sharply snapped on a straight line to the holder. Ideally, the time from the center to the holder should be fast enough to allow the kick to be away in under 1.3 seconds. This factor means that the ball should be in flight for approximately 0.5 seconds.

A center snap on the field goal and the extra point is one of the toughest jobs in football. Most football teams have an individual who is a natural at deep snapping. If a team doesn't have such an individual, the player assuming the deep snapper's position can develop his skills provided he has sufficient confidence. A deep snapper who is attempting to refine his skills needs a relatively high degree of self-confidence because of the stress involved in snapping the ball in pressure situations. He also needs the self-assurance to maintain a positive outlook when learning to deep snap. Learning to deep snap involves extra time after practice. A prospective deep snapper has to be mentally tough enough to put aside any frustration that may arise if he incurs a streak of poor snaps and technique breakdowns. He also needs to be extremely coachable—an individual who is unaffected by stressful situations.

The snap begins with the center's grip on the football. The deep snap begins with the center gripping the ball with his four fingers on the laces. The ball should be positioned with the laces facing the ground. The center rolls his wrist under the ball, cocking his wrist with the ball's forward nose slightly raised so that he can firmly grasp the laces with his fingers. If the center were to stand up after gripping the ball, he should be holding the ball above his head with his wrist cocked in the throwing position. In other words, the center holds the ball exactly as a quarterback holds the ball when he is in the throwing motion. When gripping the ball neither the center nor the quarterback can allow his wrist to "break" and hyperextend.

A long snap is, figuratively, a pass thrown between the legs. If the center stands up from his snapping position as described in the preceding paragraph, he should be able to throw a spiral without adjusting his grip. The ball should be positioned under the center's helmet as he addresses the ball. The center's off hand (his left hand for a right-handed center) should be lightly placed on the top of the ball. The fingers of his off hand should be pointing toward the nose of the ball, as his off-hand rests on top of the ball. His strong hand snaps the ball without any assistance from his off hand. His off hand is merely a guidance mechanism to help the center deliver the snap.

The proper snap mechanics involve the strong hand releasing the ball at exactly the right moment. The center's forearms should contact the inside of his thighs as he releases the ball. Both hands should be facing upward as the ball is released. The common errors of a right-handed snapper and their respective causes are detailed in Chart 11-1.

Chart 11-1: A list of the common snap flaws of a right-handed center and their causes.

PROBLEM	CAUSE	SOLUTION
Ball sails over holder's head.	Releasing ball too late.	Release the ball sooner.
Ball hitting too low.	Releasing ball too early.	Release the ball later.
Ball skirts left of holder.	The guide hand is too weak.	Put more pressure on ball with guide hand.
Ball skirts right of holder.	The guide hand is too strong.	Put less pressure on the ball with guide hand.
Snap is affected by contact.	The center is picking up ball to snap.	Better practice habits; not hitching the ball.

The center should be given the opportunity to make the long snap at will. A ready sound can be used to alert the team that the holder is ready and that the snap is soon to follow. Most coaches advise the center to avoid locking himself into a rhythm. However, it is solely up to the center as to when he feels comfortable to snap the football. A coach should be careful about over coaching the center long snap. The long snap is much like a refined golf swing. Too much trivial input from too many sources can disrupt what is already nearly perfect.

In a long-snap situation, the remaining offensive linemen have a responsibility to block high with their shoulders square. Because the long snap is made on a silent count, they should look in at the ball as the center addresses the football. While many coaches position the guards and the tackles in two-point stances with their weight on their heels, I prefer (and recommend) that all of the offensive linemen in a long-snap situation (except the center) assume a three-point stance. I believe that such a stance enables a lineman to punch upward through the defender as he attempts to rush through the line. The guards and the tackles align three inches from their adjacent teammate. Their inside foot is back in a slight stagger. Among the coaching points for offensive linemen who are blocking on either a field goal or an extra point kick are the following:

- Never move the outside foot.
- Block an area, not a man.
- Think inside.
- Keep the shoulders parallel to the line of scrimmage; never turn the body.
- Get "big."
- Use your hands. Punch one hand in the inside gap, and one hand in the outside gap.
- Drop step the inside foot behind the outside leg of the teammate.
- Don't lunge; explode from low to high through the defender just prior to his contact.
- Cover the field goal kick (keep in mind that it is a live scrimmage kick).
- Listen for the thud of the kick.
  - The lack of a thud sound of the ball being kicked, the sound of a double thud of the ball being kicked and blocked, or a fire call alerts the lineman to a fumbled snap, a blocked kick, or some other mishap.
  - Don't go downfield unless the ball is kicked past the line of scrimmage. Never go downfield on a fire call. A fire call is a run/pass play after a fumbled snap.

The field goal and the extra point formation is a static formation throughout all levels of play. The test of time has proven one basic formation to be the most effective structure for providing protection of the kicker. Diagram 11-1 shows the basic balanced formation that is used for field goals and extra points. Diagram 11-2 illustrates an unbalanced set which is used when the ball is placed on the hashmark. An unbalanced protection provides added protection to the wide side of the field, thereby allowing the ball to be centered between the flanks in a location more toward the center of the field.

THE PUNT

Various punt formations and punt blocking schemes exist. For obvious reasons, football programs that have a large roster normally don't use offensive linemen in the punt-protection phase. A punt team that is ineffective at fanning out and covering the field is a sure way to lose the kicking phase of the game. Since the game consists of only three phases—offense, defense, and kicking, surrendering an automatic 33% of the game is not conducive to winning. Coaches should consider the fact that a tie in the two other phases of the game coupled with a loss of the kicking phase generally will result in the loss of the game.

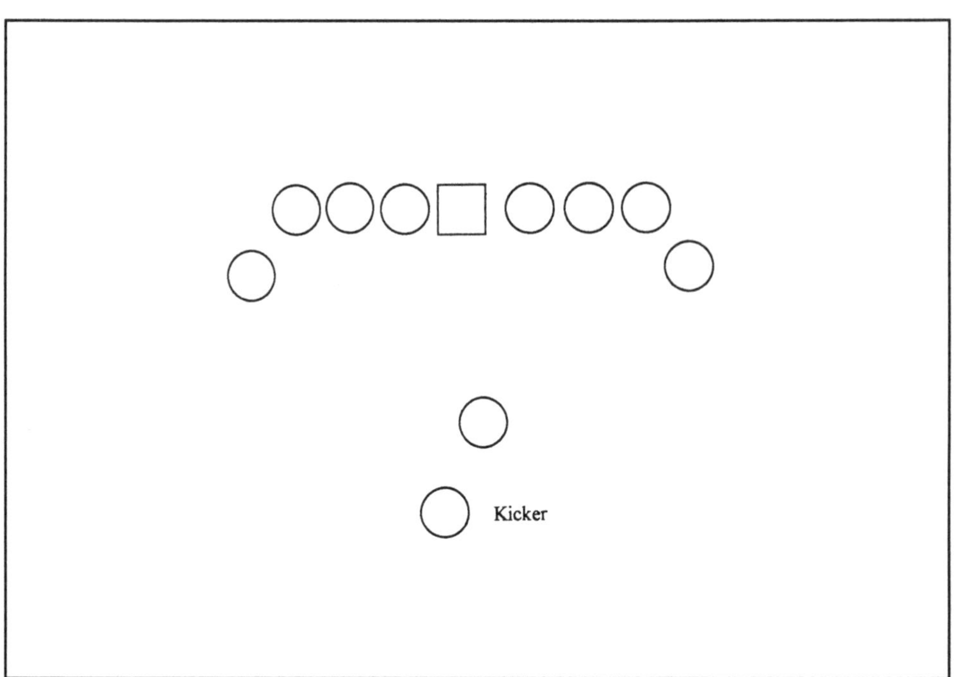

Diagram 11-1: The field goal/extra point set.

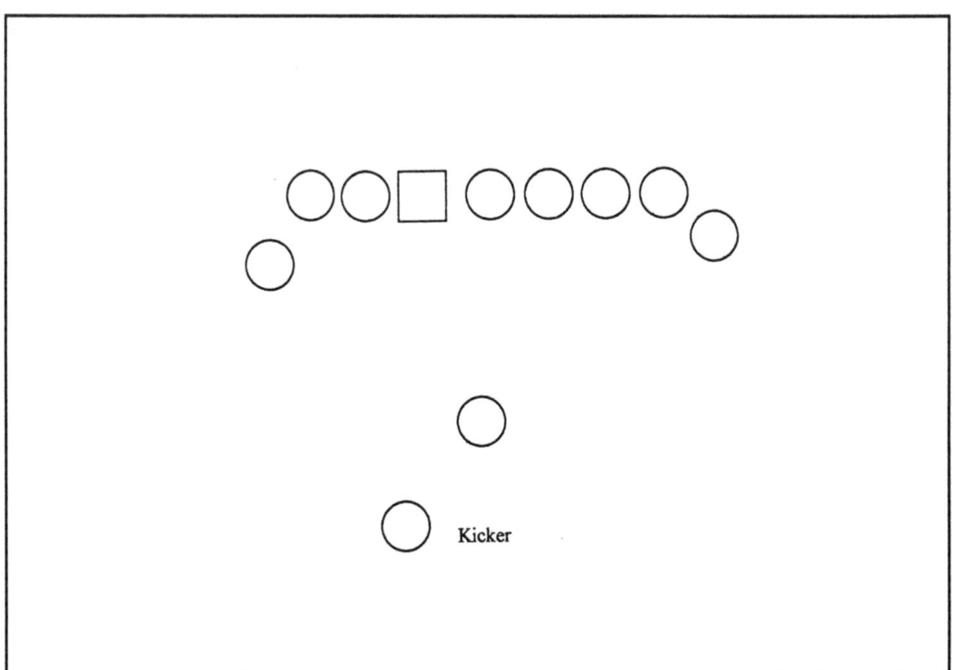

Diagram 11-2: The overload field goal/extra point set.

Clearly, most specialized offensive linemen are not well suited for covering kicks. All factors considered, in the punting game, a blocker who can't cover is a blocker that shouldn't be involved in the punt game. However, most coaches appreciate the situation of the small school coach who doesn't have two platoons of offense, defense and a special unit for each kicking phase. As such for those individuals who coach a team that has a relatively small number of players, no such substitution option exists. In these situations, everyone on the team plays every position—including the punt game.

Unlike the field goal and extra point formation, the punt game has sometimes become an "exotic tinker toy" for many coaches. As a result, a variety of punt formations exist along with various philosophies—philosophies that tend to mimic the offensive philosophy of the head coach. Punt formations can range from the wide open spread set, to the tight set double wing, to the wide split elephant set. Punt formations can involve motion and shifts. A few coaches align their quarterback as a personal protector so that they automatically fake when facing a certain defensive alignment or adjustment against a shift or motion. Diagrams 11-3 through 11-8 illustrate some of the various formations that are commonly used in punting situations.

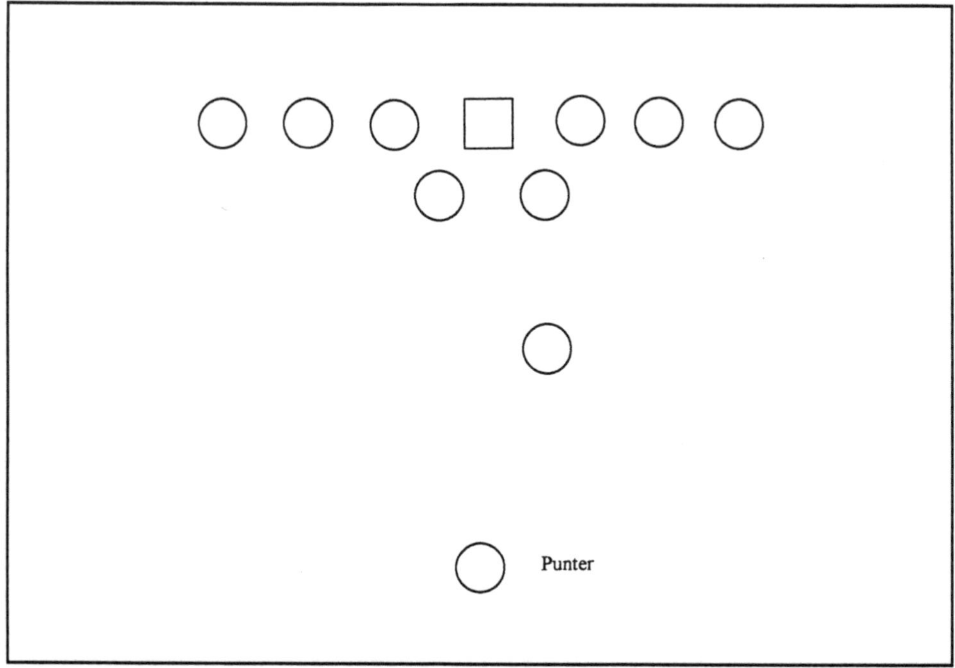

Diagram 11-3: The basic spread punt formation for a right-footed punter.

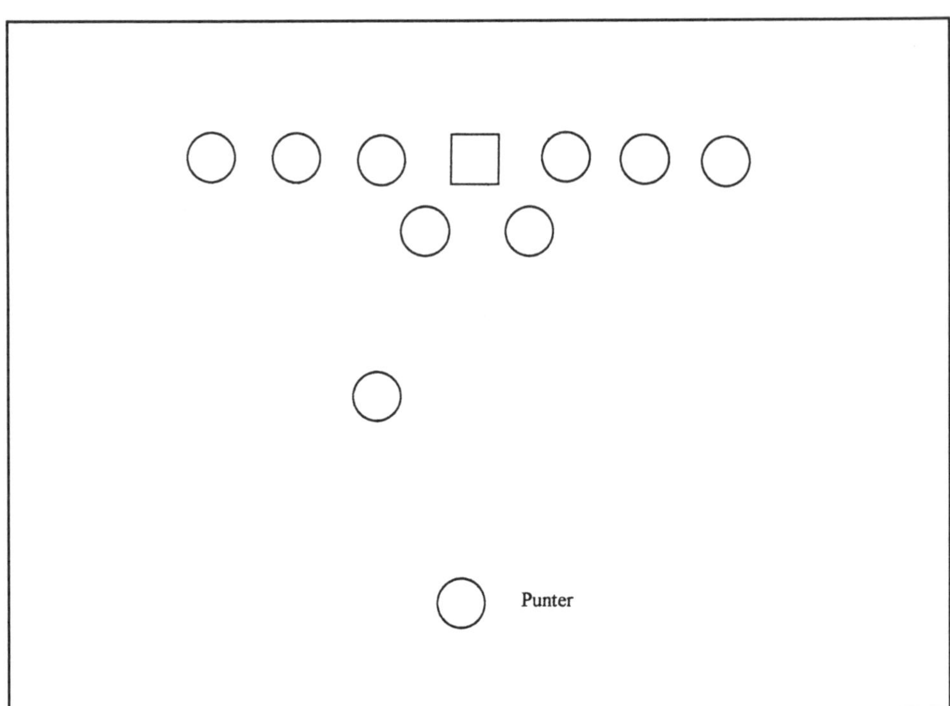

Diagram 11-4: The basic spread punt formation for a left-footed punter.

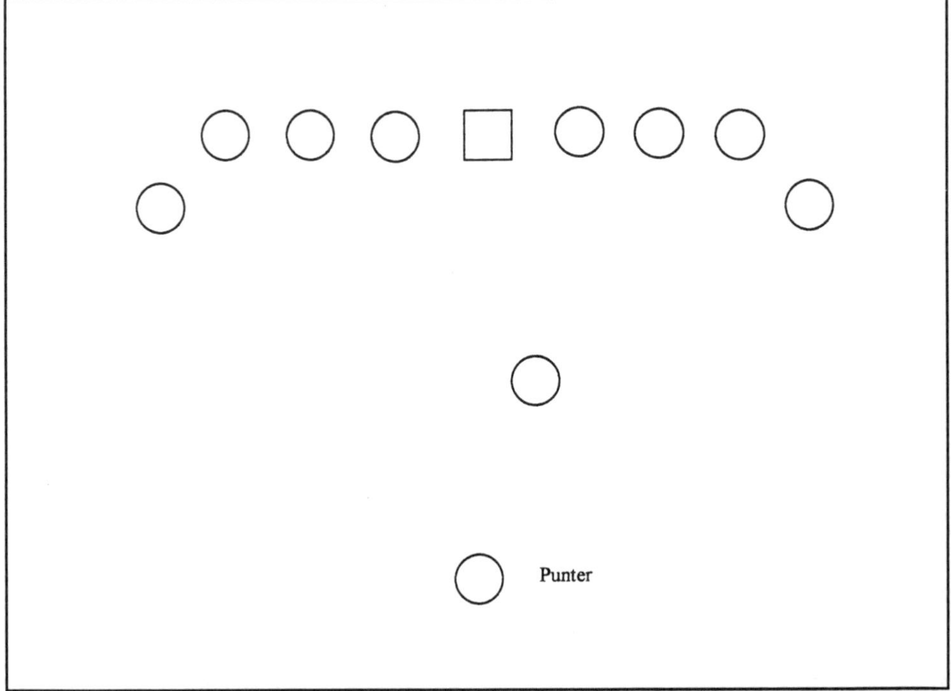

Diagram 11-5: The double wing punt formation for a right-footed punter.

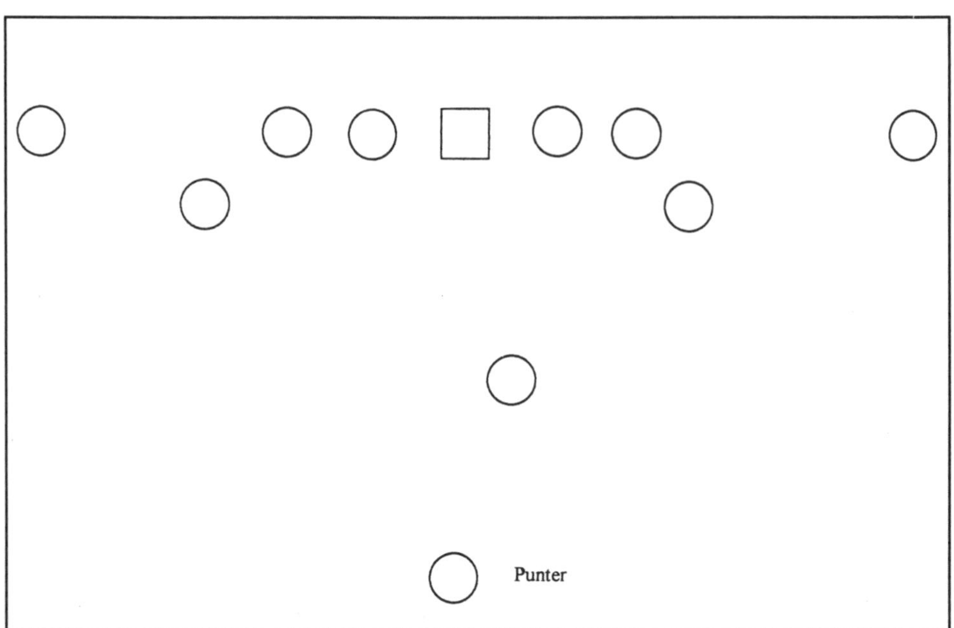

Diagram 11-6: The double wing punt formation with spread ends.

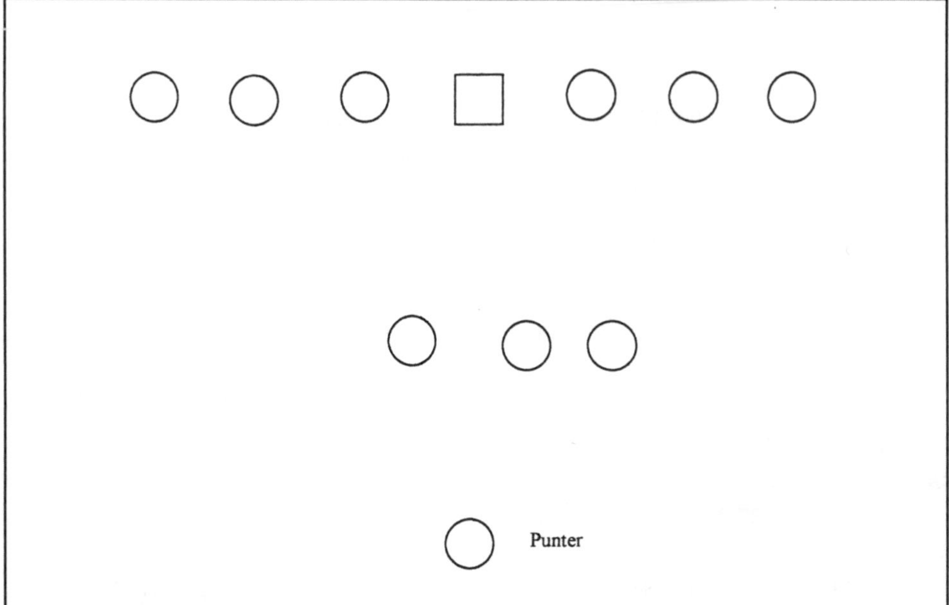

Diagram 11-7: The elephant punt formation.

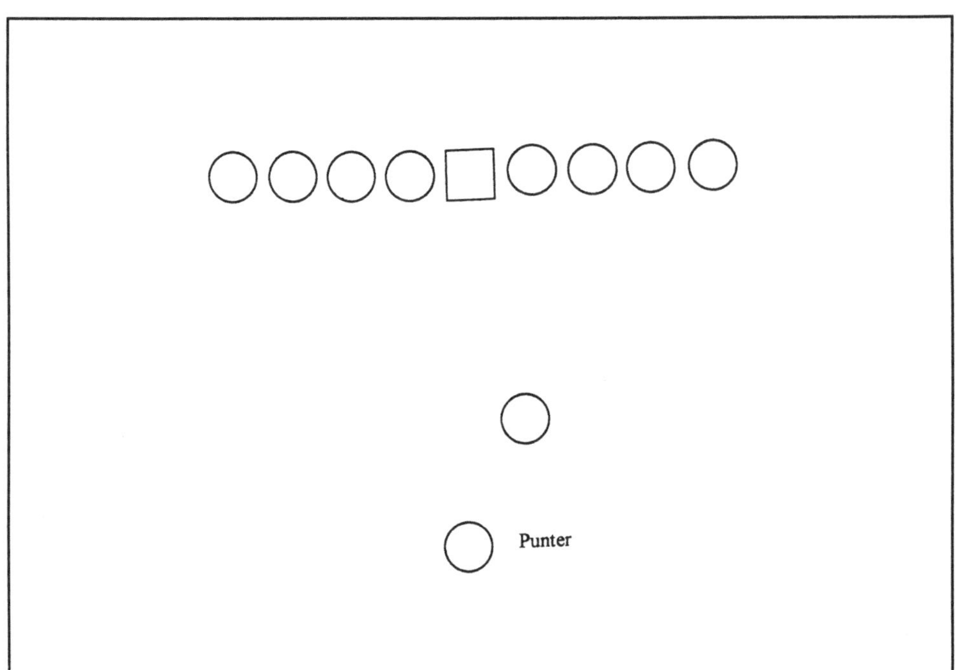

Diagram 11-8: The tight punt formation.

The width of the offensive line splits is a critical coaching point with regard to the punt formation. Most punt formations use a center-guard split of a minimum of three feet. The most common punt formation, the basic spread punt formation shown in Diagram 11-3 and 11-4, uses a center-guard split of three feet along with subsequent guard-tackle and tackle-end splits of two feet. The elephant formation uses an even wider center-guard split of three feet. The tight punt formation, a formation normally used when the punter is standing in the end zone, uses splits of slightly over one foot to prevent inside penetration by the defense.

Most defenders who block punts and who originate from an area outside of the offensive tackle get to the punter as a result of inadequate line splits. Blocked punts that are a result of defenders coming from an area between the offensive tackles are caused by a breakdown of protection techniques. Tightening the splits to correct a protection problem between the tackles normally results in a short edge and the increased possibility of a blocked punt from the corner. When attempting to diagnose a protection problem between the tackles, a coach should look first at his personnel or their technique. When attempting to remedy a protection problem occurring outside the tackles, the first factor that should be looked at is the line splits.

The depth of the punter is the second critical factor in the punt protection scheme. Specialty-team gurus at all competitive levels tend to have varying opinions on the proper depth of the punter. The standard depth of a punter in the basic spread formation is 15 yards. Some teams use a tighter formation and position the punter at 12 to 13 yards. A few teams even punt the ball from eight to ten yards behind the center.

The depth of the punter's alignment is occasionally related to the punter's leg strength and skill. A young athlete at the lower level can safely punt the ball from eight yards deep if he one-steps (i.e., punts the ball after taking only one step). If a team has a punter who normally punts the ball at least 20 yards from the line of scrimmage and has a deep snapper who can get the ball back to the punter, the punter can be positioned anywhere from 12 to 15 yards deep.

For a punter aligned at a depth of 15 yards, the center should deliver the ball to the punter in 0.8 seconds. The kick should be away in 2.1 seconds. Therefore, your offensive linemen must protect for at least two seconds for the punter before fanning out to cover the punt. The extra 0.1 second is of no consequence, since no football player will likely cover 15 yards in a tenth of a second! The snapping technique for a punt is identical to the snapping technique of the deep snap on the field goal and extra point. More information on the deep-snap technique is provided in the section in this chapter on the field goal and extra point.

The blocking technique of the offensive linemen who are positioned on the line of scrimmage in the spread punt formation is a head-up-to-outside blocking technique. The blockers use a two-point stance. They should keep their weight on their heels and look straight ahead, while keeping the ball in their peripheral vision. Similar to a snap for a field goal or an extra point, the snap for a punt is made at the center's discretion—no cadence is called. When the ball is snapped, the blockers push off their inside foot and drive through the defenders positioned immediately to their outside. The blockers extend their arms to punch and stun the defender, as the linemen step laterally to the outside. The blockers should attempt to keep their inside foot planted if a defender is aligned in a head up position in front of them. If a defender is aligned outside of the blocker in the gap, the blocker must drive through the rusher and protect the outside gap. If two defenders are in the gap, the blocker is responsible for blocking both of the defenders. The key to blocking an outside defender on the punt is to drive the inside fist and the forearm into the chest of the rusher.

Generally, a collision and a run through the defender's outside shoulder is adequate protection for the punter to be able to get the ball off. After protecting for the punt, the offensive linemen should continue to fan out approximately five yards apart as they cover the punt.

CHAPTER 12

Pass Protection Schemes

A scheme is a combination of blocks which serve as the protection mechanism of a play. A scheme can be either a running scheme or a passing scheme. Normally, the passing game is formulated around the basis of the protection scheme. As was discussed in Chapter 8, a protection scheme can be a play pass scheme in which a run is faked, but a pass is executed. A draw blocking scheme is a scheme in which a pass is faked, but a run is executed. Other types of pass protections include the dash protection scheme, the sprint out pass protection scheme, and the dropback pass protection scheme.

DROPBACK PASS PROTECTION SCHEMES

An appropriate dropback pass protection scheme is related to two factors: the depth of the quarterback drop and the objective of the passing series. A dropback passing series may be a three-step series, a five-step series, or a seven-step series. The protection for a three-step series is normally an area protection in which the offensive linemen aggressively block their men. The protection for a five-step series can be an area protection, a fan-fan protection, a fan-man protection, a man-fan protection. The seven-step series protection varies little from the five-man scheme. The only difference between a five-man and a seven-man protection is the added time needed for the protection of the quarterback. On the seven-step protection, the depth of the quarterback drop and the subsequent deeper pass routes of the receivers require the blockers to hold their blocks for a longer time.

AREA PASS PROTECTION SCHEME

An area protection assigns specific gaps to the offensive linemen. The most common area protection scheme calls for the offensive linemen to block the gap to their inside. In this type of area protection scheme, the center has no responsibility against an even front, other than to assist the guards in anchoring the "A" gaps. Against an odd front, or the 7-1 front, the center soft posts the nose tackle and anchors the middle. Diagrams 12-1 through 12-4 show this particular area protection scheme against four of the basic defensive fronts.

An area pass protection scheme can be structured as a pure gap protection scheme as previously described, or it can be structured according to the man-blocking rule. When used as an gap protection, the area scheme is best suited for the quick passing game (i.e., one-step and three-step drops).

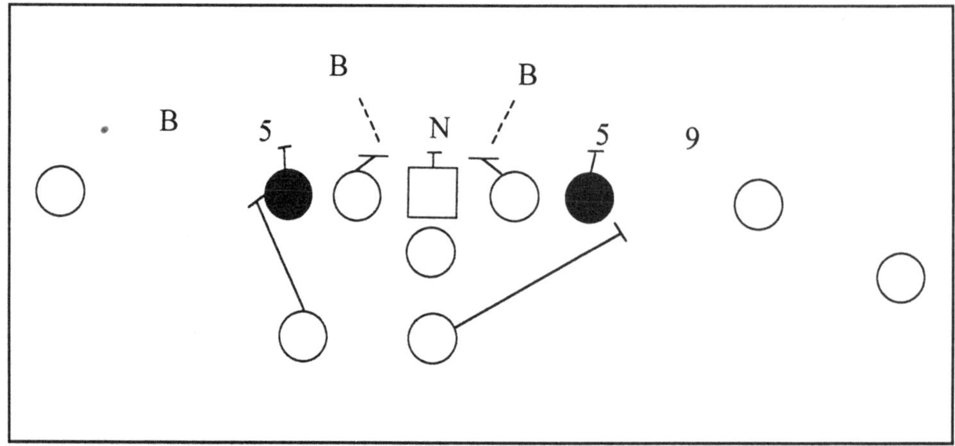

Diagram 12-1: An area pass protection scheme versus the 30 front. The tackles have no defender inside their gap; they, however, have a man on them. In such a case, the tackles apply their "don't block grass" rule and block the 5 techniques while keeping their shoulders square.

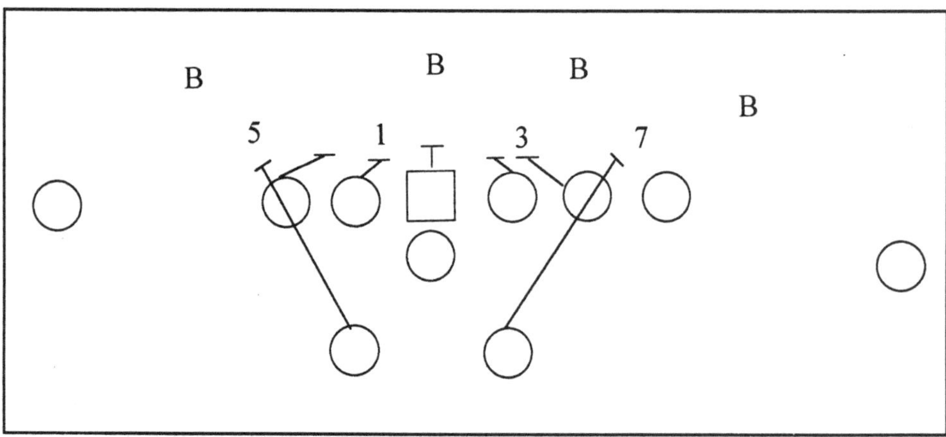

Diagram 12-2: A gap protection scheme versus a 4-3 front.

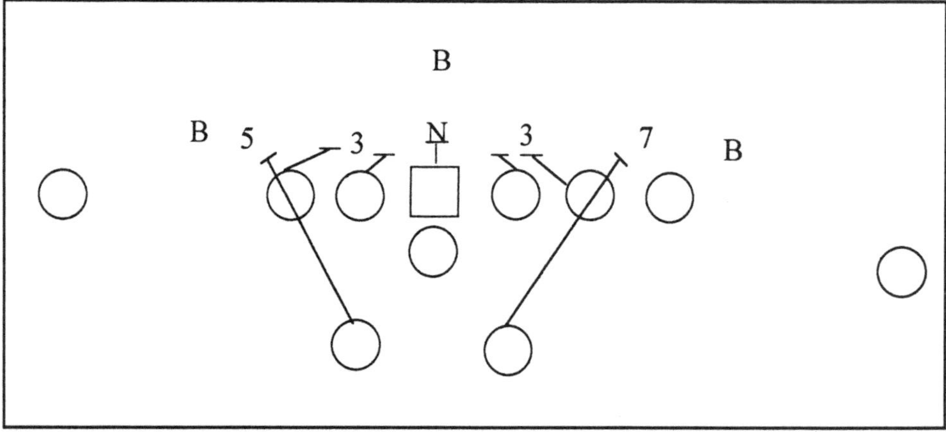

Diagram 12-3: A gap pass protection scheme versus a 7-1 front.

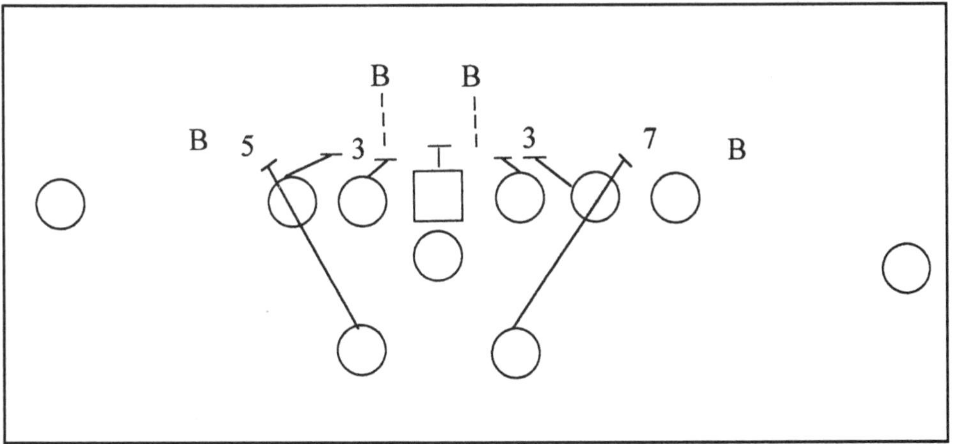

Diagram 12-4: A gap protection scheme versus a 4-4 front.

MAN PASS PROTECTION RULES

A man-blocking rule is a protection principle in which each offensive lineman is assigned a particular defensive man to block. Man-protection assignments number each defender, whereas gap protection assignments account for the gaps without regard to the location or action of the front defenders. As a pass protection scheme, the man scheme is best suited for the intermediate (i.e., five-step) passing game.

The man-protection scheme is built around the recognition and numbering of defensive fronts. Different defenders are numbered (usually from the inside-out), and the offensive linemen block the numbered defenders. The numbering of the defenders is dependent upon the declared strength of the offensive formation. In other words, even though the ball moves straight behind the center, the defense is counted as if the ball were moving to a specific side of the formation. Normally, the strength of the formation is toward the tight end, if a tight end is present in the formation. In all cases, the terminology of the passing game will dictate a strong and weak side of the formation, regardless of whether the formation is a balanced formation or an unbalanced formation.

When both sides of the line use the man-rule protection, the name of the protection is called the man-man protection. The first "man" refers to the strongside of the line (i.e., the guard and tackle aligned to the formation's strength). The second "man" refers to the weakside of the line. The center (the center is always a weakside protector), the guard, and the tackle to the weakside will apply the man rule. Therefore, man-man protection states that each side of the line will protect according to the man-protection rule.

Chart 12-1: Man blocking rules.

POSITION	MAN RULE	COACHING POINTS
Strongside Tackle	Number 2	Shoulders square, ready for alert
Strongside Guard	Number 1	Shoulders square, look for triangle
Center	Number 0	Shoulders square, alert for triangle
Weakside Guard	Number 1	Shoulders square, look for triangle
Weakside Tackle	Number 2	Shoulders square, ready for alert

Among the basic numbering rules for identifying defenders within a defensive front are the following:

- A head up nose tackle is always assigned the number "0" (see Diagram 12-5).
- A defender identified as a 0 technique nose tackle—either onset or offset—is assigned the number "0" (see Diagram 12-6).
- An even front middle linebacker aligned over the center is assigned the number "0" (see Diagram 12-7).
- In an even defense, the first defender aligned toward the formation's strength is assigned the number "1" (see Diagram 12-8).
- The first defender of an even front aligned opposite the formation's strength is assigned the number "1" (see Diagram 12-9).
- Stacked defenders are numbered according to which gap they attack on the snap. The defender who attacks the inside gap is assigned the lower number (see Diagram 12-10).

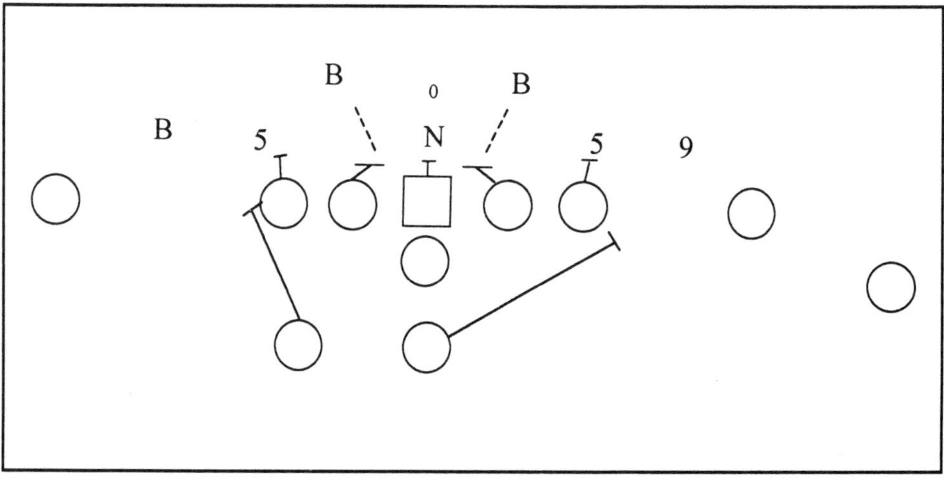

Diagram 12-5: A head up nose tackle is always assigned the number "0."

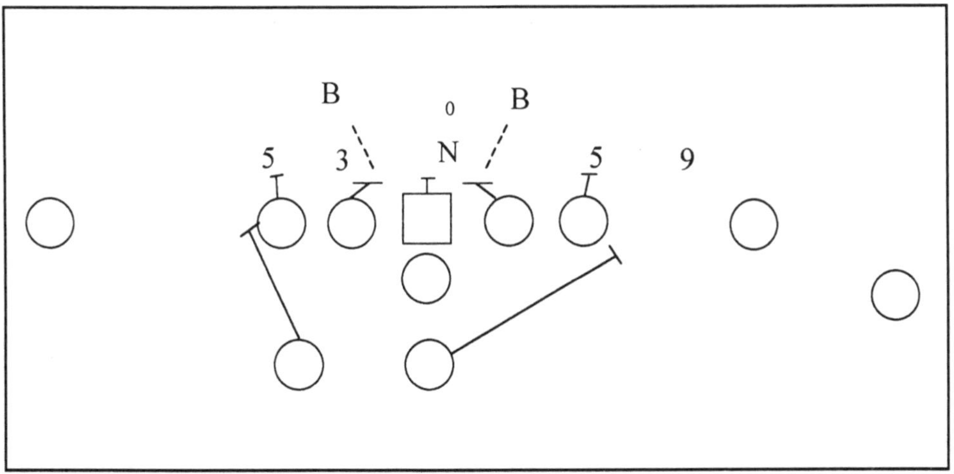

Diagram 12-6: An onset nose tackle is always assigned the number "0."

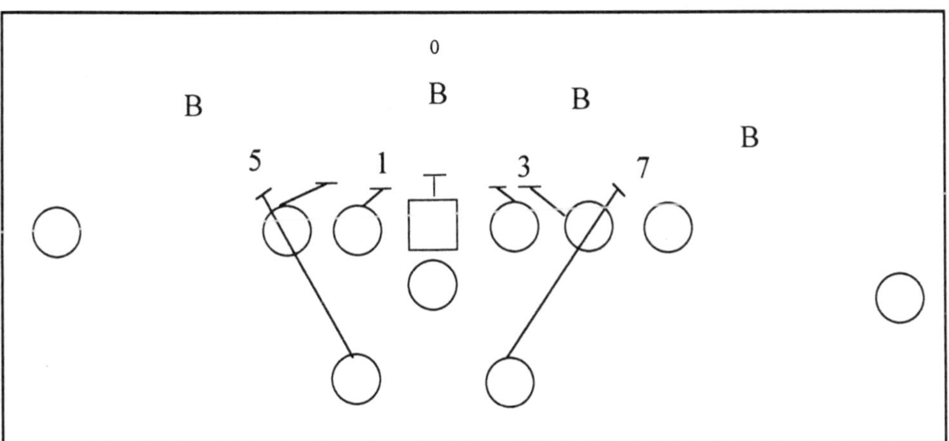

Diagram 12-7: An even-front middle linebacker is assigned the number "0."

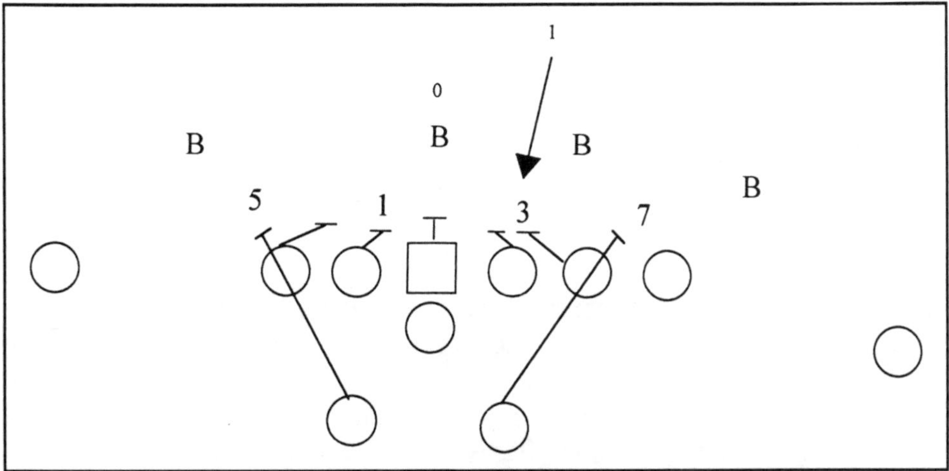

Diagram 12-8: In an even front, the first defender to the formation's strength is assigned the number "1."

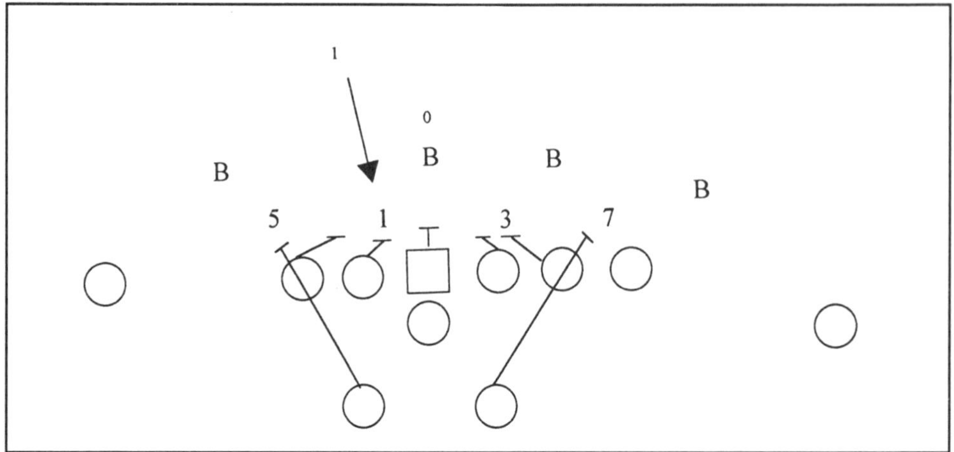

Diagram 12-9: In an even front, the first defender opposite the formation's strength is assigned the number "1."

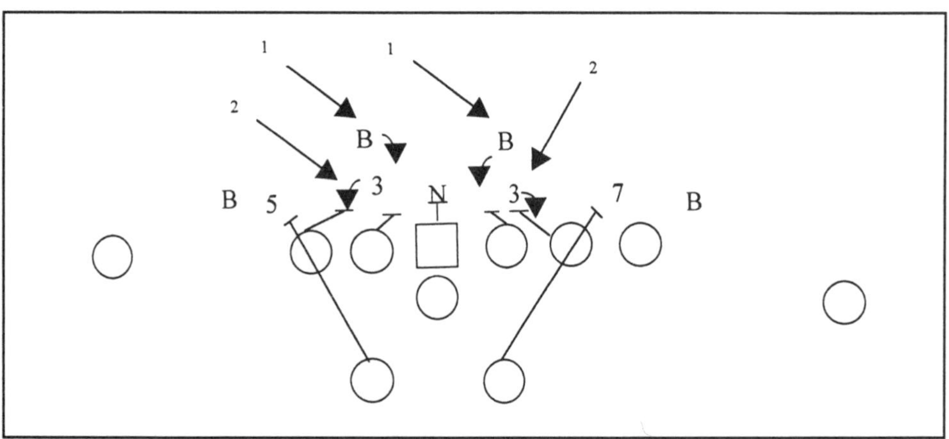

Diagram 12-10: Stacked defenders are numbered according to the gap they attack on the snap.

Numbering the defensive fronts requires communication among the offensive linemen. The dynamics of the numbering system are connected to the presence—or absence—of a nose tackle. The question of whether a front is an even or an odd front figures strongly in the area protection count of the defenders. Offensively, the center always has "0." The guards each have the respective number "1" to their side. The tackles have number "2."

An important coaching point that should be emphasized is: because the first man of an even front to the weakside is "0," the second man to the weakside of the center is actually "1," and the third man is actually "2." This type of numbering system works best when the offensive line flip-flops so that the weakside personnel are familiar with the numbering system. One way for a team's offensive linemen to grasp the concept is by understanding that in any man blocking system the center has a man—and the center's man is always number "0." Since the center always blocks weakside in man protection, the first defender counting weakside from the center out is numbered "0." In an odd structure, no such contradiction exists. The nose man is always "0," and the first man to either side of the center is counted as "1" if there is no stack over the nose.

Diagrams 12-15 and 12-16 demonstrate the critical link of the front structure to the numbering system. Diagram 12-15 shows a standard even front. The offensive formation is strong to the right. (For the sake of simplicity, all of the offensive formations discussed in this chapter are strong right.) Because the formation is strong right, the first man to the left of the center is counted as "0." The next defender is counted as "1," and the third defender is counted as "2." Also, because the formation is strong right, the first man from the center counting outward is "1." The next man to the right is counted as "2" and the third man is counted as "3."

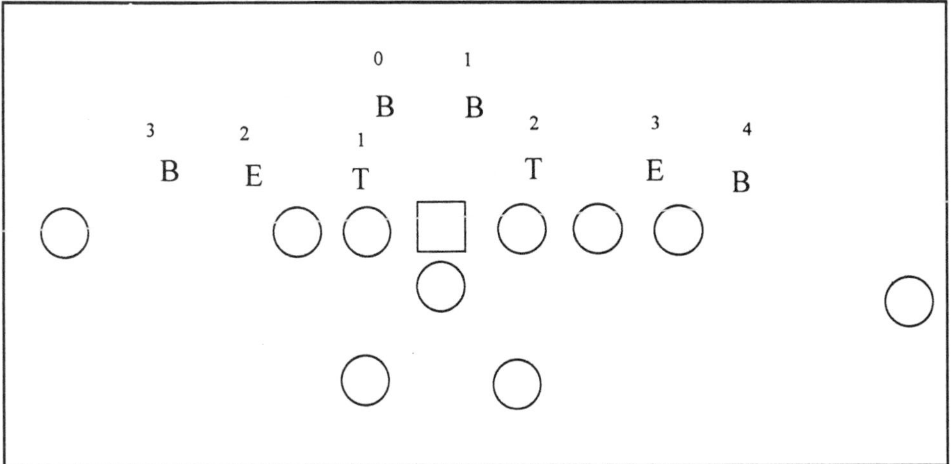

Diagram 12-11: In the split front, the weakside linebacker is number "0."

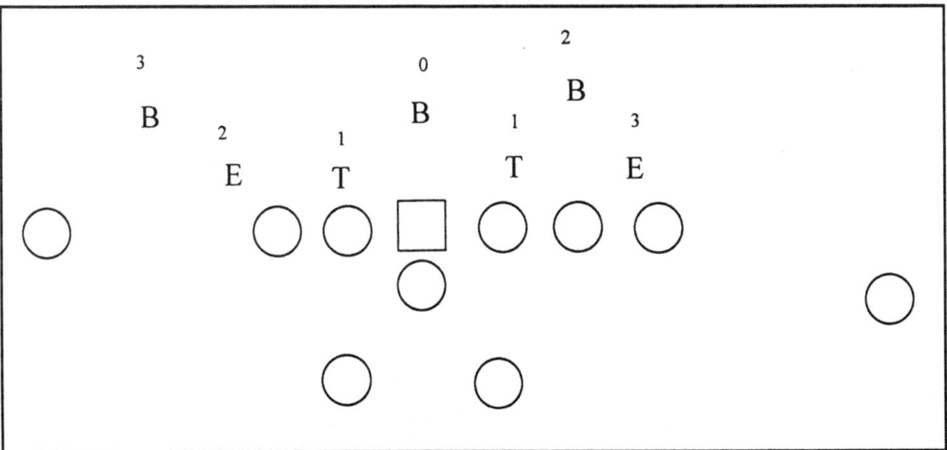

Diagram 12-12: In a 4-3 front, the middle linebacker is number "0."

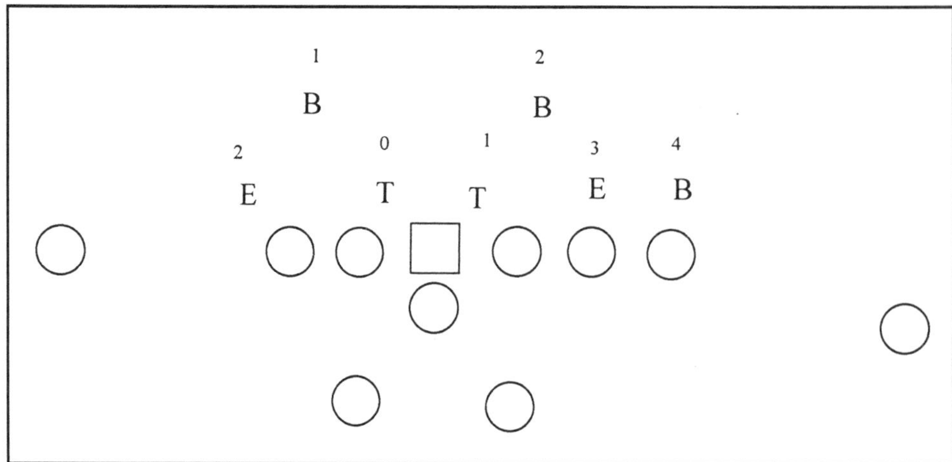

Diagram 12-13: In a 6-2 front, the weakside 1 technique is number "0."

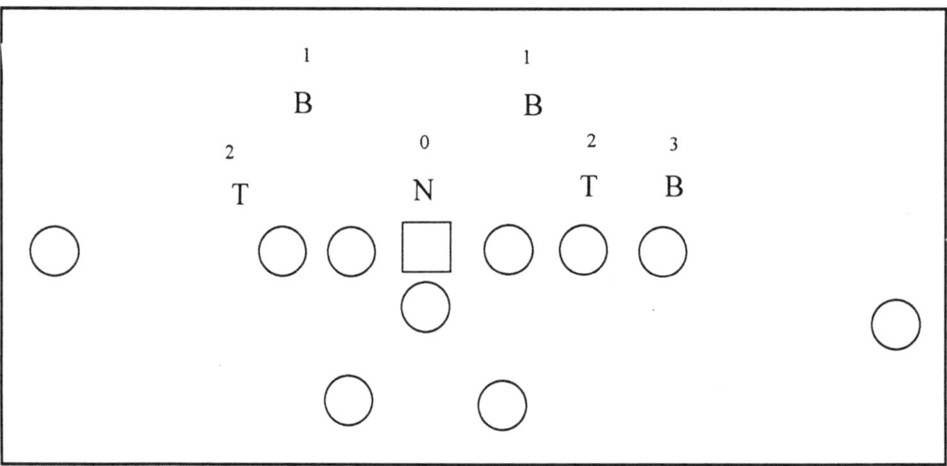

Diagram 12-14: In a 30 front, the nose tackle is number "0," while the backers are both counted as number "1."

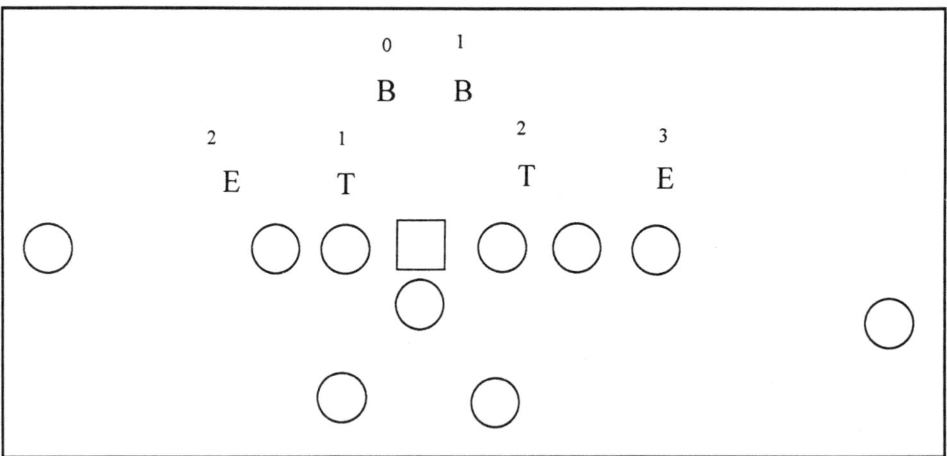

Diagram 12-15: A standard 4-4 look.

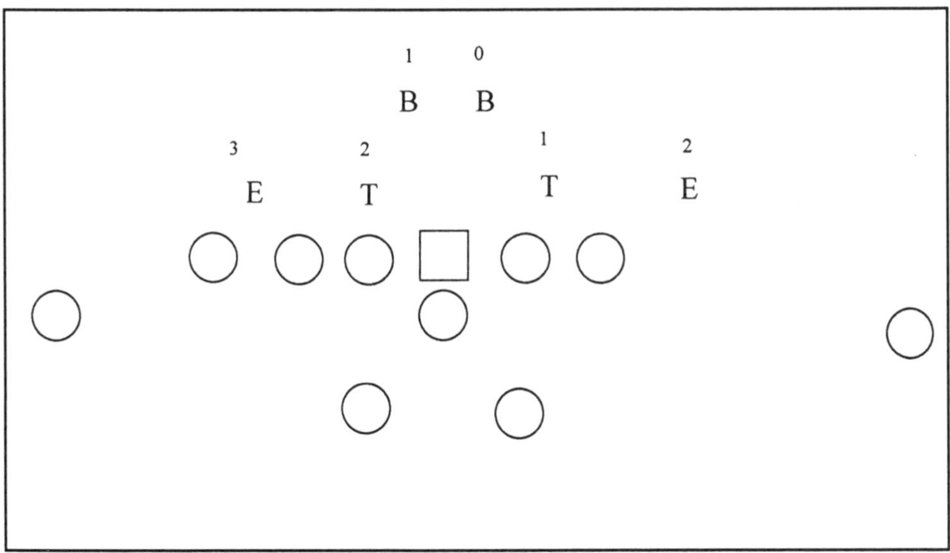

Diagram 12-16: A standard 4-4 look against a strong left formation.

FAN PASS PROTECTION SCHEME

Fan protection is also called big-on-big protection. In a fan pass protection scheme, the linemen block the defensive linemen and leave the linebackers to the running backs. The center will block the nose tackle of an odd front. Against an even front, the center will check the first linebacker to the weakside. If the weakside backer doesn't show, the center will work back to the weakside in a double-read scanning technique.

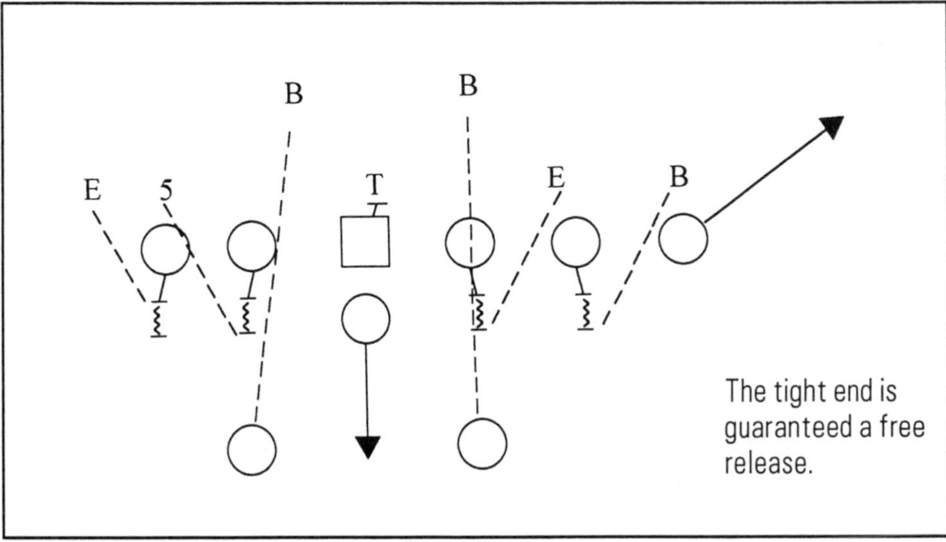

Diagram 12-17: Fan-fan protection against a 30 front.

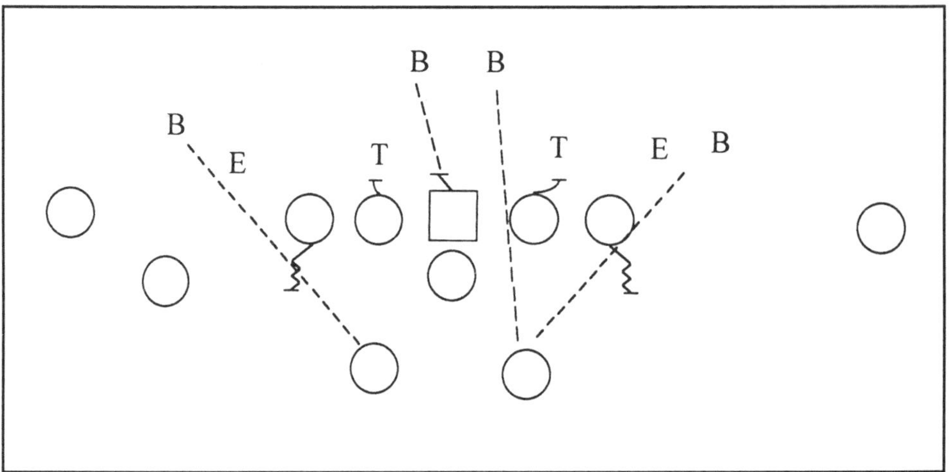

Diagram 12-18: Fan protection against a 4-4 look.

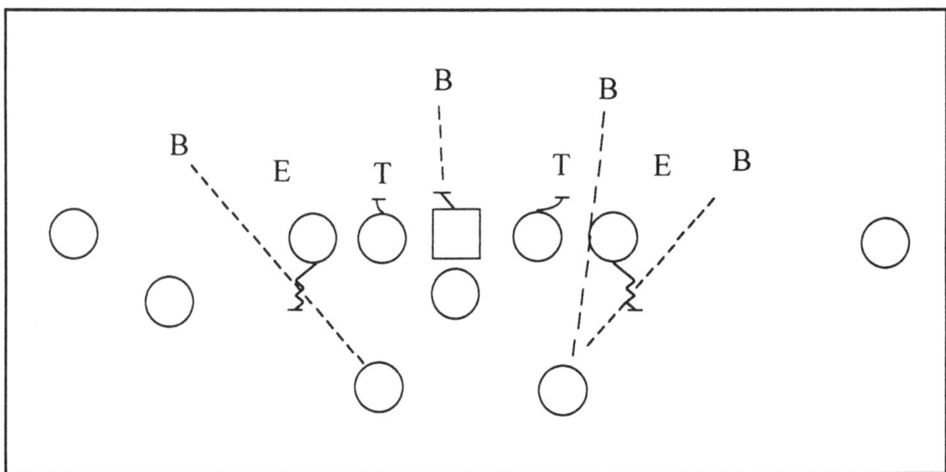

Diagram 12-19: Fan protection against a 4-3 front.

When fan blocking the front, the offensive lineman counts from inside out. The guard will block the first lineman, while the tackle will block the second lineman. If a defensive front is overshifted (i.e., overloaded) to one side, an overload call may be necessary to account for all of the rushers. Diagram 12-20 shows both an overload scheme and the protection adjustment to account for the four rushers.

Fan protection requires the running backs to scan from the inside out. If an inside linebacker blitzes from his linebacker depth, the running back can pick him up. If the linebacker aligns on the line of scrimmage to blitz, the running back alerts to the possibility of the rush and slides outside to pick up the third defensive lineman rushing from the outside.

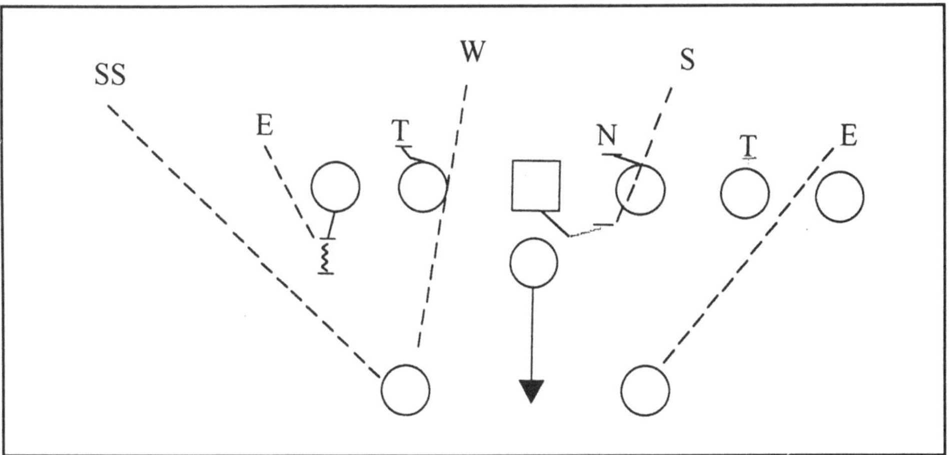

Diagram 12-20: Fan protection versus an overload front.

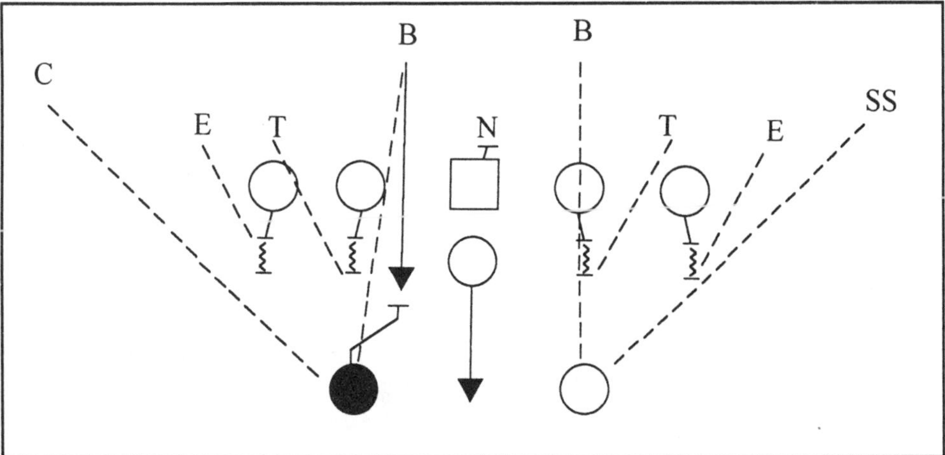

Diagram 12-21: In fan protection, the running back picks up the linebacker if he blitzes from off the line of scrimmage.

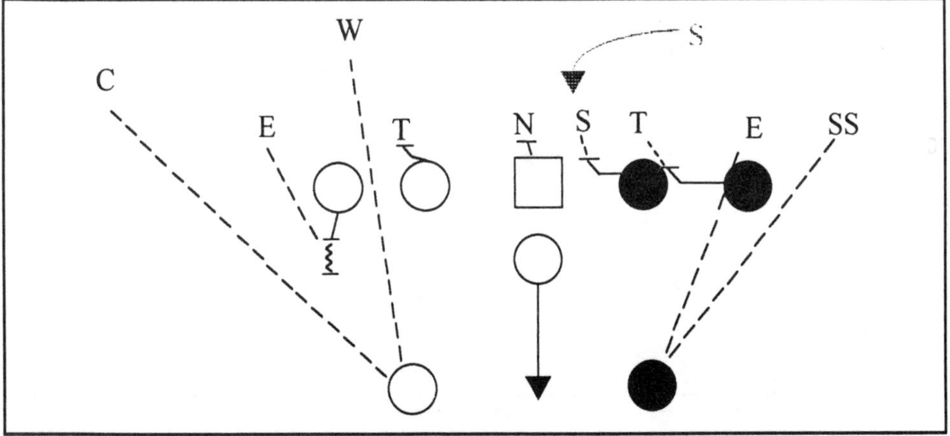

Diagram 12-22: Linebacker blitzes from a position on the line of scrimmage against a fan protection.

In the fan protection, the offensive lineman always picks up the most dangerous threat inside. Should the nose tackle align in an onset position on the center, the center must take the nose man, unless the center makes an overshift call. The overshift call tells the guard to take the shifted nose, while the tackle blocks the man on him (the defensive tackle). As shown in Diagram 12-20, the running back will block the defensive end as the center soft kicks behind the onside guard.

A fan protection scheme can be combined with a man protection scheme. Diagrams 12-23 and 12-24 show a fan protection scheme combined with a man protection scheme.

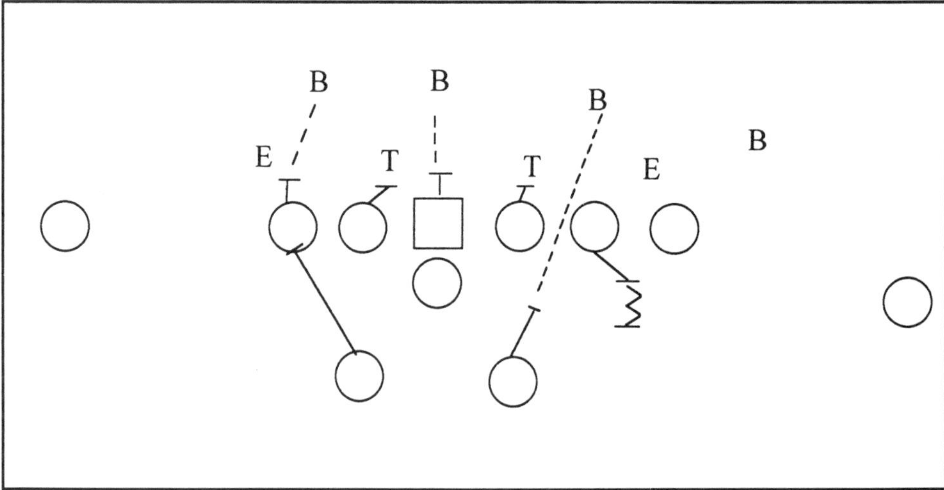

Diagram 12-23: Fan-man protection versus a 4-3 front.

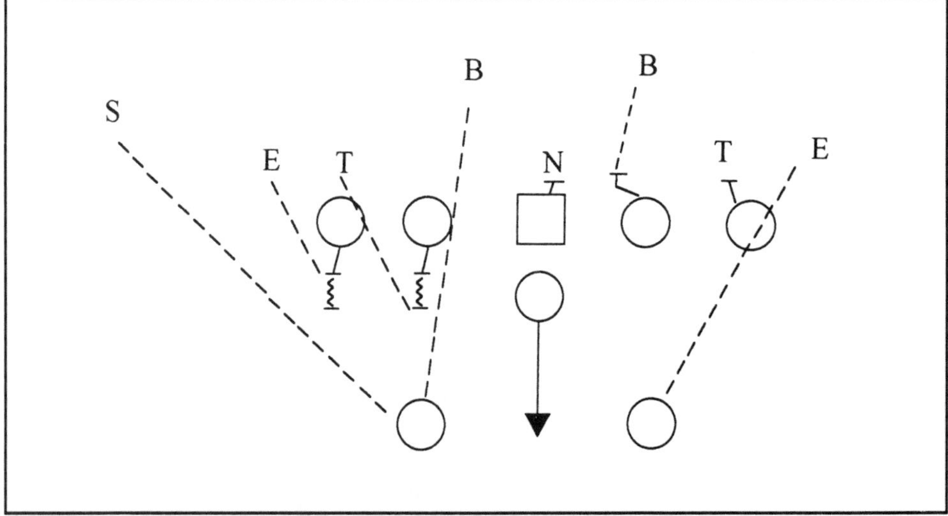

Diagram 12-24: Man-fan protection versus a 30 front.

DASH PASS PROTECTION SCHEME

The dash pass protection adhere is an alternative to the dropback scheme. On the dash pass protection scheme, the quarterback sprints outside the tackle box with a guard leading interference. The dash pass protection scheme helps get the quarterback outside—away from the pass rush while giving the offensive linemen an opportunity to execute the easier down block against a down defender to the inside. Successful dash blocking requires that the blocker not block grass when he blocks inside. The "don't block grass" rule states that a blocker shouldn't leave a defender on him unblocked if the inside gap is unoccupied, even though the blocker's rule is a down block. In other words, an offensive lineman should observe his down-block rule if a defender is aligned in the gap. But if no defender is aligned in the inside gap, the blocker should block the man on him regardless of the down-blocking rule requiring him to block inside. The critical point that should be emphasized is that an offensive lineman should never block grass.

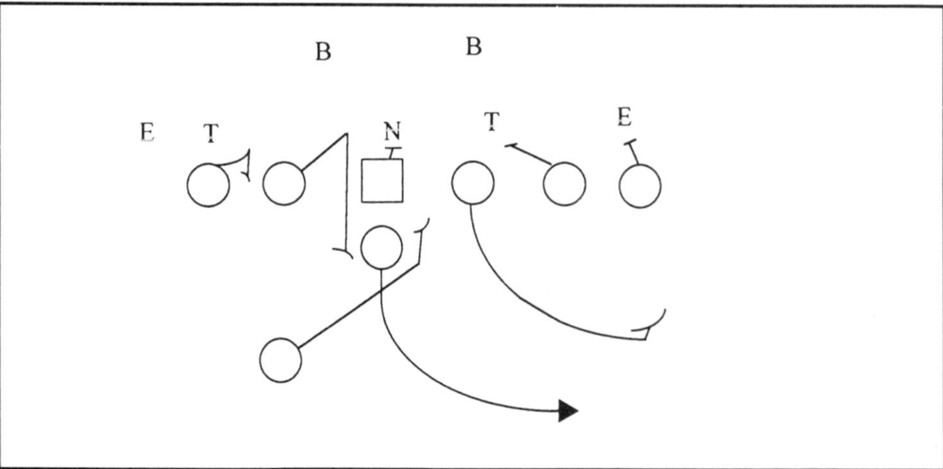

Diagram 12-25: Dash pass protection.

TURNBACK PASS PROTECTION SCHEME

Turnback pass protection allows the offensive lineman to angle block to protect a gap rather than block a specific defender. On turnback protection, the quarterback sprints out to one side of the ball. The offensive linemen simply turn inside and block any defender who attempts to penetrate the nearest backside gap. The offensive linemen don't react to defensive stunts. Instead, they build a wall that cannot be pierced by a defender's penetration. The defenders must go around the wall or attempt to work down the line across the face of the wall—either defensive action will allow the quarterback to get the pass off without pressure from his blindside.

To turnback block, the offensive lineman punches with his playside arm and pivots on his playside foot. He dropsteps with his backside foot and turns his shoulders perpendicular to the line of scrimmage. The turnback blocker then uses both hands to punch and drive any defender who attempts to penetrate the inside gap. The turnback pass protection scheme is an area protection scheme.

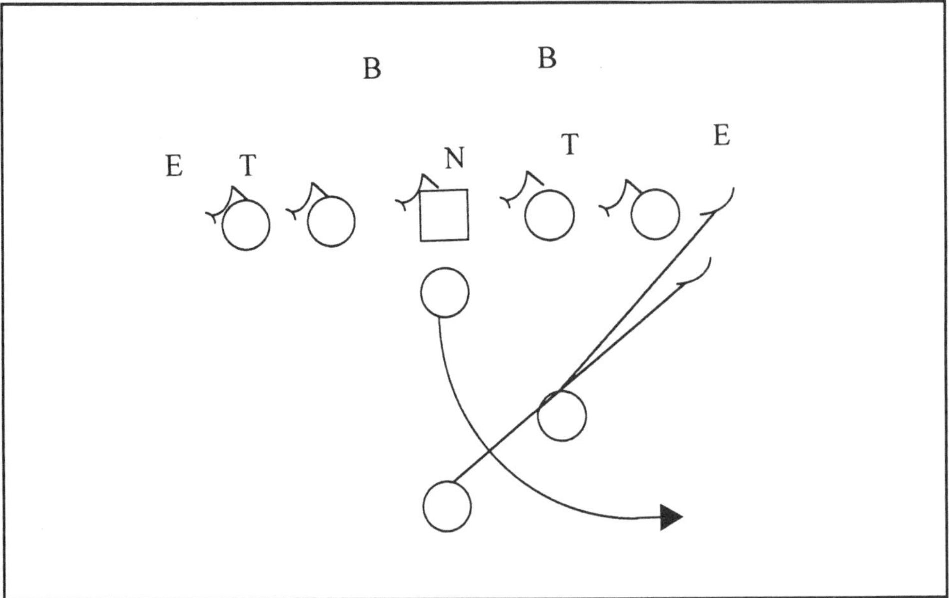

Diagram 12-26: Turnback pass protection.

SPRINT OUT PASS PROTECTION SCHEME

Sprint out protection involves a set to reach by the playside linemen. The playside linemen set to reach, while the backside linemen soft post and then pivot as a double reader on the backside. The blocking rules of playside sprint-out protection are normally the man protection rules with reach technique. The backside rules of the sprint out protection is an area protection scheme.

UNCOVERED DOWN PASS PROTECTION SCHEME

The uncovered down pass protection is a scheme used with play passing. A play pass fakes a run. It makes use of the double-read technique on the backside, as offensive linemen who have no immediate threat coming through their gap peel back to pick up an outside blitzer. The uncovered down pass protection scheme is primarily an area protection used with a two-back attack. The structure of the uncovered down protection requires that the first uncovered lineman to the side of the fake block inside using a down block technique. As the first covered lineman blocks the man on him, each succeeding lineman counting from the covered lineman to the backside then blocks the backside gap using a modified turnback technique. The appeal of the uncovered down pass protection scheme is the simplicity of the scheme. Because the uncovered down protection is an area protection, it requires no counting or recognition of fronts. Many coaches favor area protection schemes, such as the uncovered down pass protection scheme because such scheme is always simpler to execute than man protection schemes.

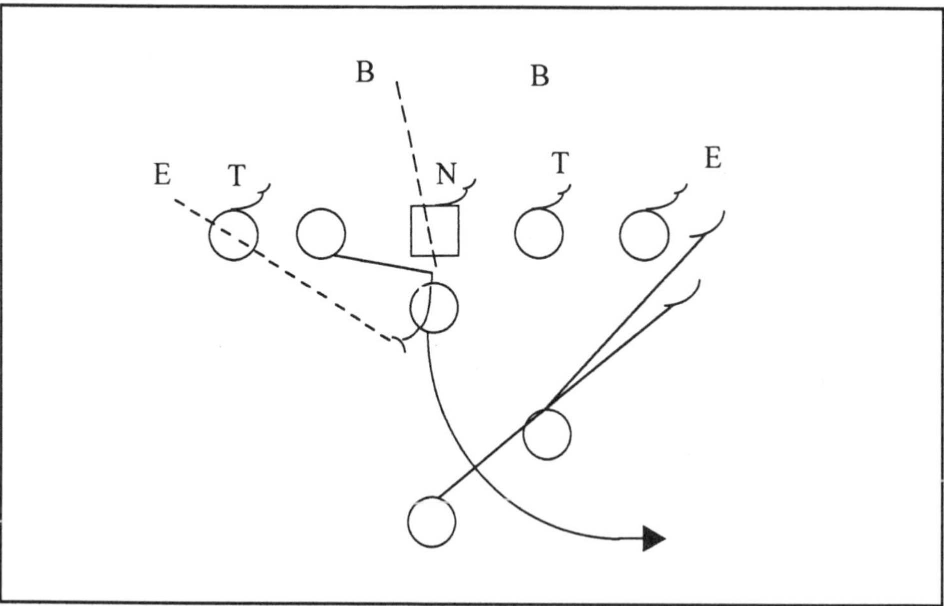

Diagram 12-27: Sprint out pass protection.

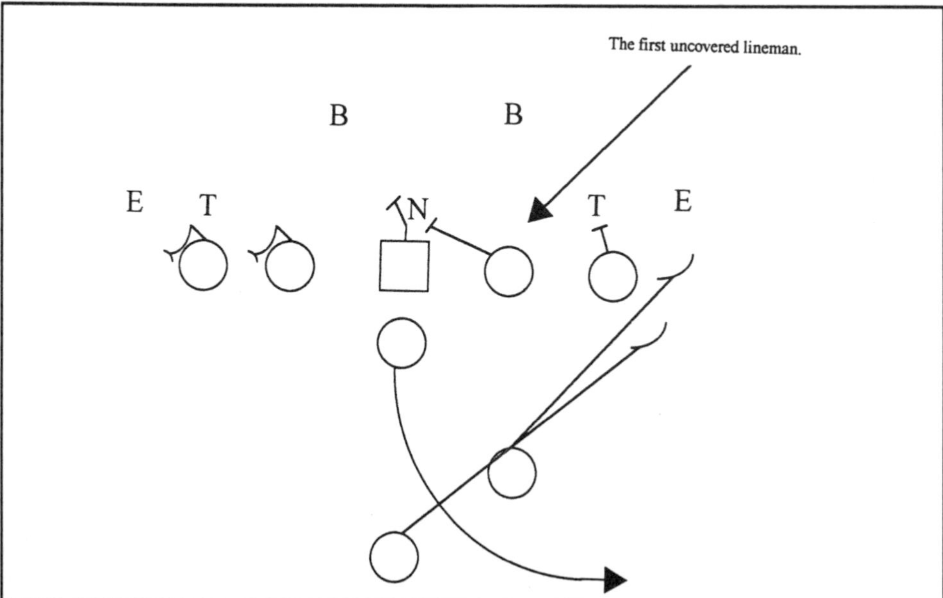

Diagram 12-28: Uncovered down pass protection.

DRAW BLOCKING

A draw can be run off of any pass action, but is most commonly run off of dropback action. Draws often are best with a fold block on the backside. On a draw, the offensive linemen will set to pass protect and engage the defender. An offensive lineman will then pass block the rushing offensive lineman, pushing him out of the running lane. Against a linebacker, the offensive lineman will set to pass protect as if he were area blocking. Once the linebacker opens his stance to drop into the pass coverage, the offensive lineman should attack the linebacker. If the linebacker recognizes the draw and moves toward the line of scrimmage to make the tackle, the offensive lineman should attack the linebacker with a proper run-blocking demeanor.

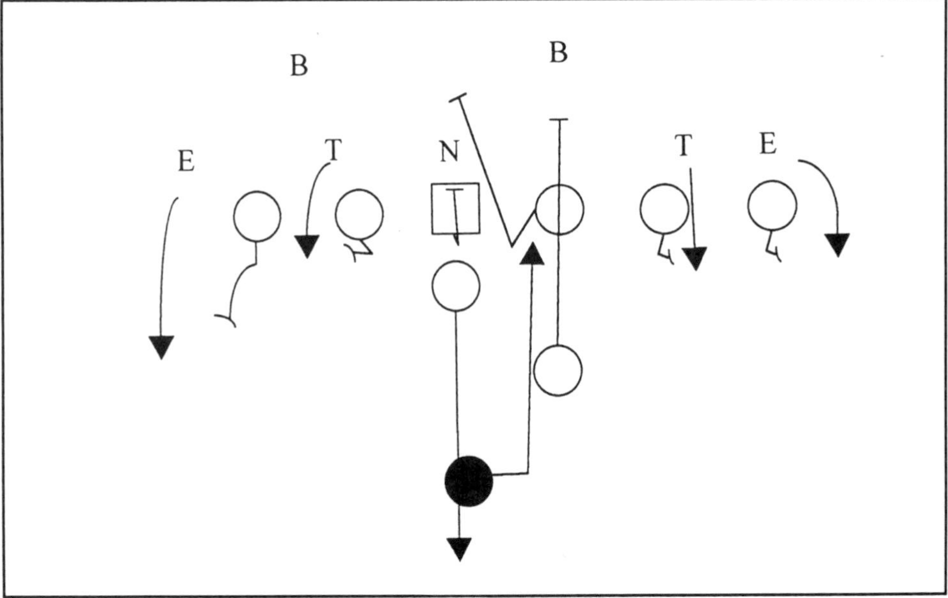

Diagram 12-29: Blocking for a draw.

CHAPTER 13

Run-Blocking Schemes

As a rule, most running attacks are identified as much through the principal blocking scheme involved in the offense as it is with any other factor. For example, the running scheme involved in the offense as it is with any other factor. For example, the running phase of the Wing-T attack is characterized by the predominance of angle-blocking (gap) schemes. In turn, one of the definitive traits of the I-back attack is its use of matchup man-to-man blocking employing a wheel-and-turn technique. Furthermore, depending on the principle style of option used, an option attack is normally based either on a veer-blocking scheme or a zone-blocking scheme. A one-back running game, on the other hand, is normally based around a zone-blocking scheme.

The point to remember is that different offensive running attacks tend to employ the various run-blocking schemes to one degree or another and in one assorted combination or another. In order to gain a better understanding of the more popular run-blocking schemes, this chapter provides a brief overview of six run-blocking schemes: trap-blocking scheme; gap-blocking scheme; man-blocking scheme; veer-blocking scheme; outside zone-blocking scheme; and inside zone-blocking scheme.

TRAP-BLOCKING SCHEMES

The trap-blocking scheme is employed in every offensive attack at every competitive level of football. The term "trap" is derived from the scheme's original designation—"mouse trap." One of the oldest blocking schemes in football, a trap scheme is designed to isolate a defender on the playside. The isolated defender is normally influenced (i.e., baited) upfield, as a backside offensive lineman kicks him out. A trap scheme is drawn up to take advantage of defensive front-line penetration. A trap can be an excellent play when it is run in certain down-and-distance situations (e.g., first-and-ten; second-and-long; second-and-medium; etc.). Diagram 13-1 provides an illustration of and a descriptive overview of one of the more popular trap plays.

GAP-BLOCKING SCHEMES

A gap-blocking scheme usually involves a double-team block between the center/guard, the guard/tackle, or the tackle/tight end combinations on the playside. In these gap responsibility schemes, the playside guard is responsible for the "A" gap; the playside tackle has the "B" gap; and the tight end is accountable for the "C"

Diagram 13-1: 20/21 Trap—either a one-back or a two-back play.

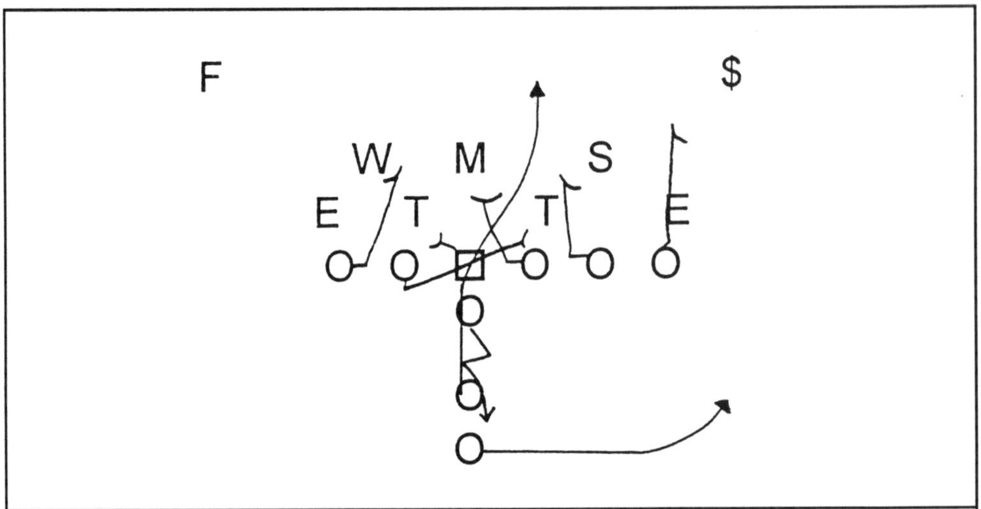

QB	Reverse pivot to 6:00; hand the ball to the back with depth; fake trap pass.
TB	Fake toss.
FB	Heels at $4\frac{1}{2}$; aimpoint opposite the cheek of the center; follow guard.
R	

FRONTS	4-3	20	40	EW	30	DE
Y	Set to drive through 9 tech to safety	Arc release vs. 7 tech to safety	Arc release vs 7 tech to safety	Set to drive thru 9 tech to safety	Set to drive thru 9 tech to safety	"Check" out
ST	"Tab"	"Tab"	Chip end to Sam	Cut off	"Matt"	"Check" out
SG	"Mike" call rip or o-lay	"Matt" call use rip or o-lay "Tom" call-influence	"Mike" call "Rip" or o-lay	"Trap"	"Dbl" to backer	"Check" out
C	"Back"	"Back"	"Back"	"Back"	"Dbl" to backer	"Check" out
WG	"Trap" possible GOB	"Trap"	"Trap" possible GOB	"Matt" call "Rip" or "o-lay"	"Trap"	"Check" out
WT	"T.A.B."	"Tom" call tab block "Matt" call chip end to levels	Chip end to Will	"Tab"	Cut off	"Check" out
Z						

FORMATIONS	Pro, Twins, Slot
MOTIONS	Zip, Zap

Diagram 13-1: 20/21 Trap (continued).

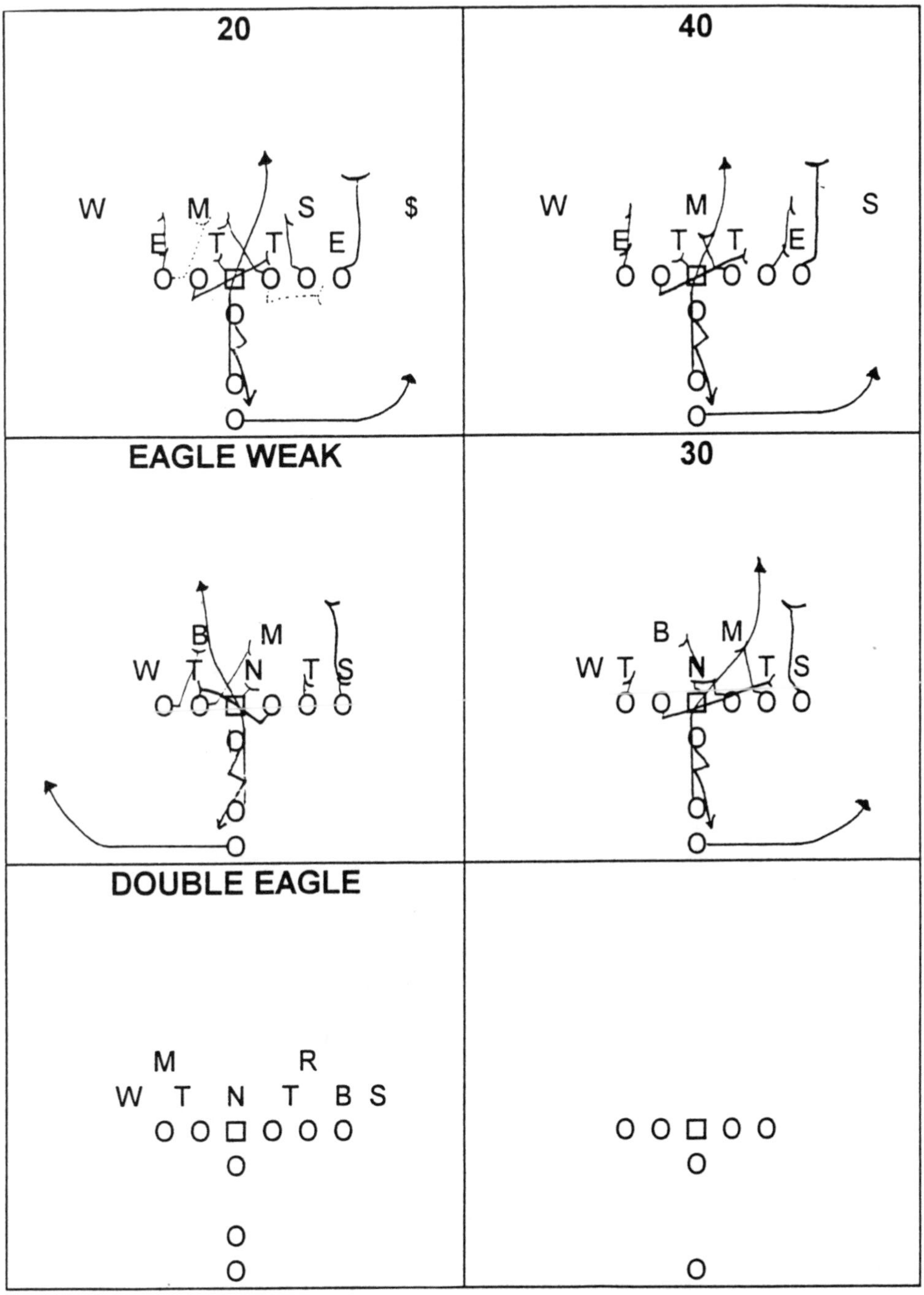

20	40
W M S $ E T T E	W M S E T T E
EAGLE WEAK	**30**
B M W T N T S	B M W T N T S
DOUBLE EAGLE	
M R W T N T B S	

Diagram 13-2: 36/37 Counter Trey—either a one-back or a two-back play.

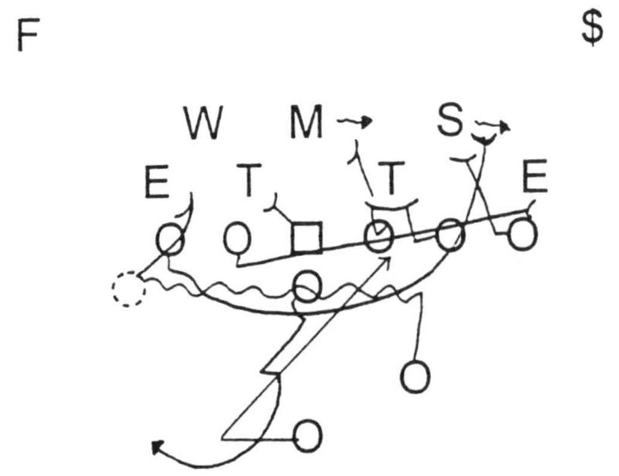

QB	Reverse pivot to 6:00; take the ball under control back to TB; get out of the TB's path; fake boot.
TB	Lead—crossover—plant; press the inside hip of the tackle; read the 1st covered lineman.
FB	Peel block the off tackle.
R	Peel technique.

FRONTS	4-3	20	40	EW	30	DE
Y	Block down Sam to Mike protect C gap	Block down on 7 tech	Block down on 7 tech	Block down (trey call) protect C gap	Block down trey call	Block down on bear defender
ST	"Deuce" get movement to Will protect B gap	"Deuce" get movement to Will protect B gap	"Deuce" get movement to Will protect B gap	"Trey" get movement to backside backer protect B gap	"Trey" get movement to backside backer protect B gap	"Back-back"
SG	"Deuce" get movement to Will protect A gap	"Deuce" get movement to Will protect A gap	"Deuce" get movement to Will protect A gap	Down block on nose protect A gap	Down block on nose protect A gap	"Back-back"
C	"Back"	"Back"	"Back"	Back to 3 tech come flat	"Blunt" nose then back block	"Back-back"
WG	Pull and kick out end	Pull and kick out end man on LOS	Pull and kick out end man on LOS	Pull and kick out end man on LOS	Pull and kick out end man on LOS	Pull and kick out end man on LOS
WT	Counter pull turn up first opportunity past the dbl tm	Counter pull turn up first opportunity past the dbl tm	Counter pull turn up first opportunity past the dbl tm	Counter pull turn up first opportunity past the dbl tm	Counter pull turn up first opportunity past the dbl tm	Counter pull turn up first opportunity past the dbl tm
Z						

FORMATIONS	Pro, Twins, Slot, Down
MOTIONS	Rap/Route

Diagram 13-2: 36/37 Counter Trey (continued).

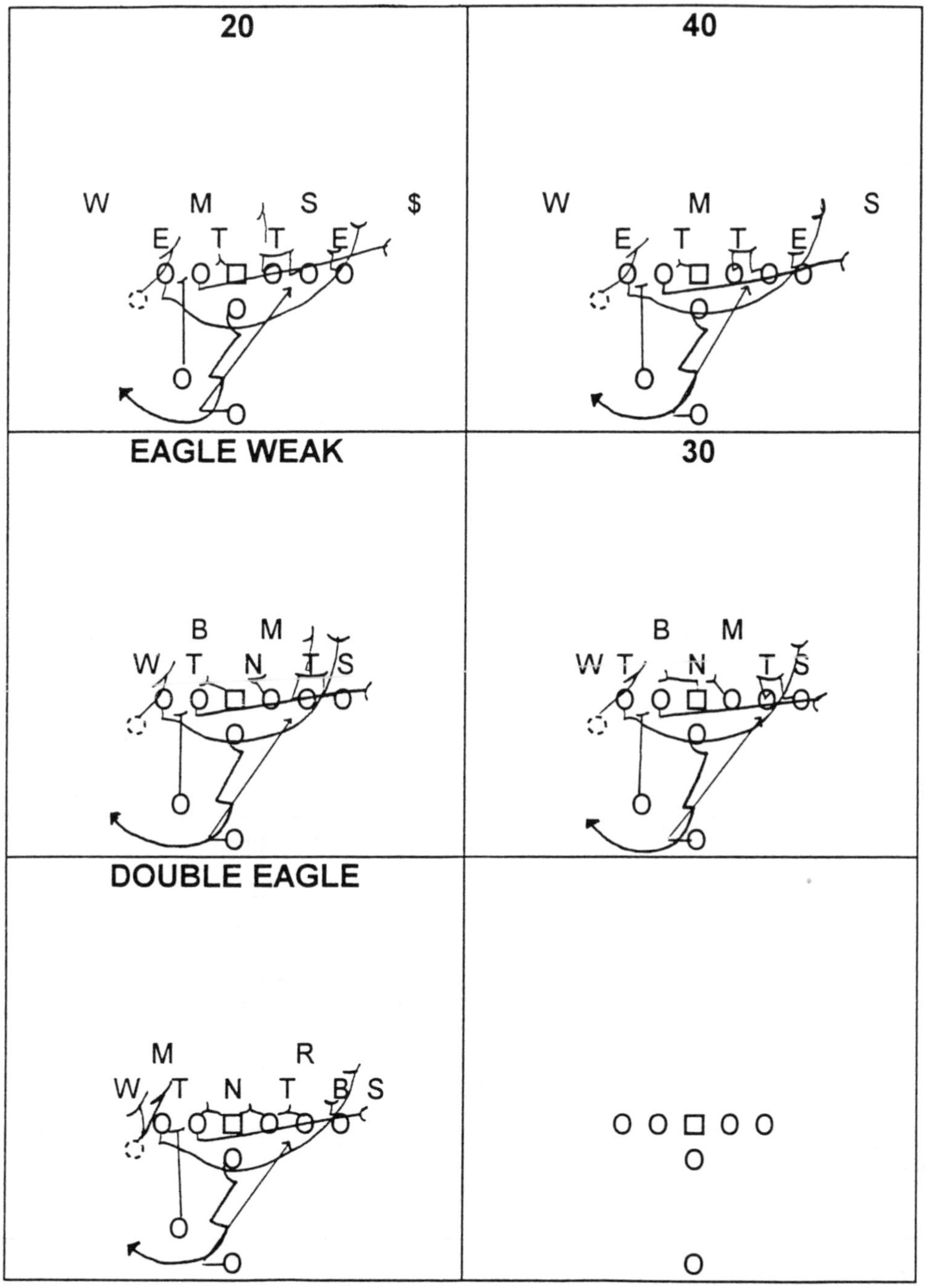

20	40
W M S $ E T T E	W M S E T T E
EAGLE WEAK B M W T N T S	**30** B M W T N T S
DOUBLE EAGLE M R W T N T B S	

Diagram 13-3: 44/45 Power—a one-back or two-back play.

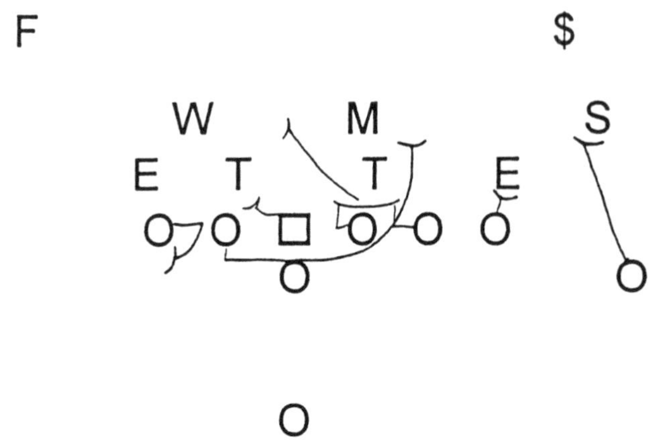

QB	Reverse pivot to 6:00; give to TB; sprint to the corner.
TB	Drop step; aimpoint is the outside hip of the guard; hug Dbl TM.

FRONTS	4-3	20	40	EW	30	DE
Y	Set to drive	Set to drive	Set to drive	Won't	Run	Block down on bear defender
ST	Deuce to Mike backer	Deuce to Mike backer	Deuce to Mike backer	Won't	Run	Deuce to Mike backer
SG	Deuce to Mike backer	Deuce to Mike backer	Deuce to Mike backer	Won't	Run	Deuce to Mike backer
C	"Back"	"Back"	"Back"	Won't	Run	Set to dive
WG	Pull and turn up right past dbl tm	Pull and turn up right past dbl tm	Pull and turn up right past dbl tm	Won't	Run	Pull
WT	Seal inside gap and hinge	Seal inside gap and hinge	Seal inside gap and hinge	Won't	Run	Seal inside gap and hinge
U						
H	Block force	Block force	Block force	Block force	Block force	Block force

FORMATIONS	Trey
MOTIONS	

Diagram 13-3: 44/45 Power (continued).

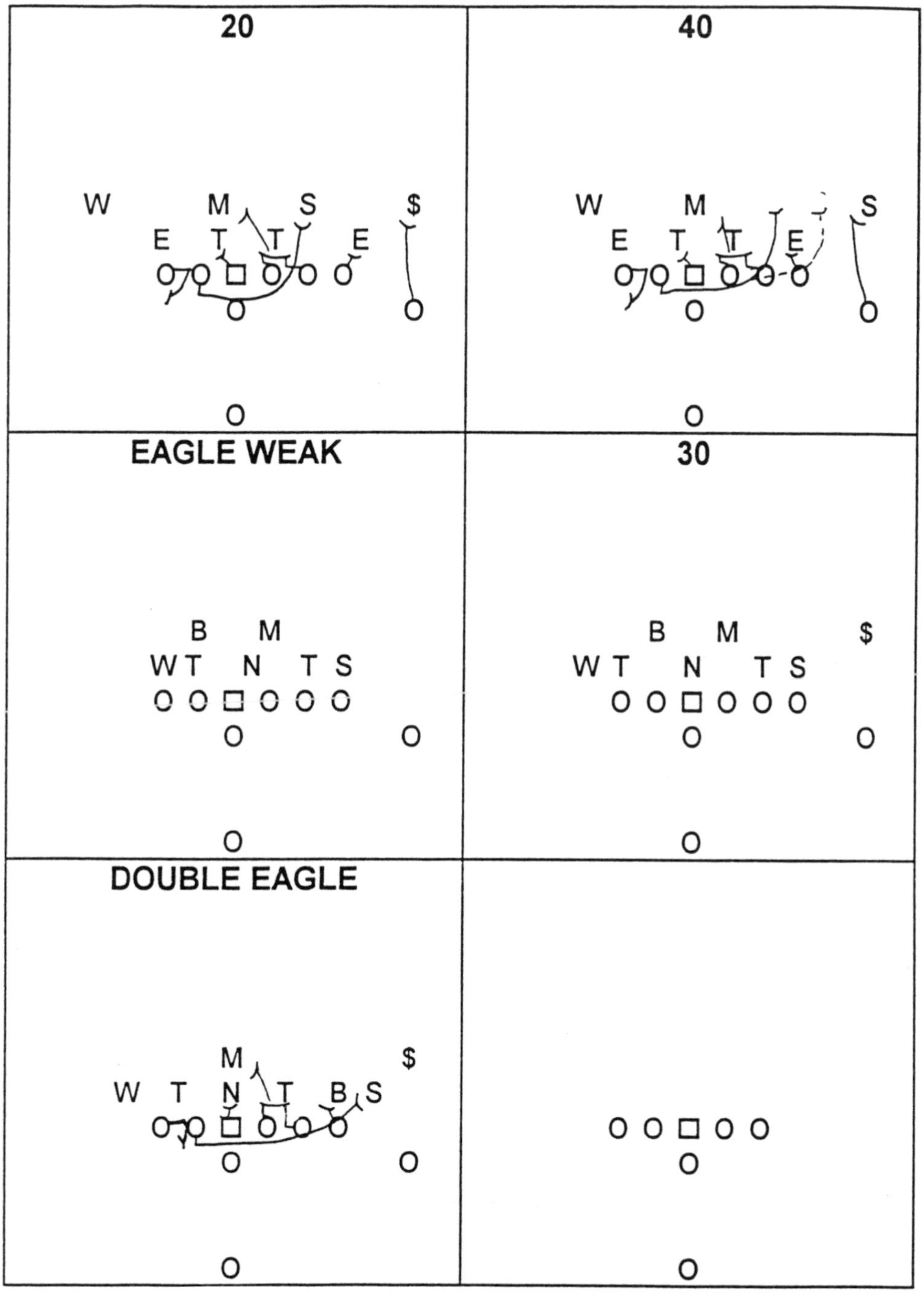

20

W M S $
E T T E

40

W M S
E T T E

EAGLE WEAK

B M
W T N T S

30

B M $
W T N T S

DOUBLE EAGLE

M $
W T N T B S

Diagram 13-4: 38/39 Stretch—a one-back or a two-back play.

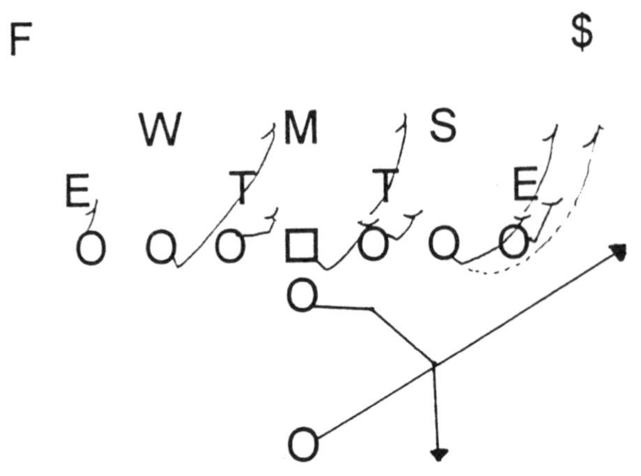

QB	Open to 3:30; take next two steps down LOS; reach for exchange w/TB; fake 434 PAP.
TB	Lead step; the aimpoint is 2 yds outside the TE; read block of the TE to force.

FRONTS	4-3	20	40	EW	30	DE
Y	Set to reach (Tex call)	Set to reach zone through playside l'ber (Tex call)	Set to reach (Tex call)	Set to reach	Set to reach (Tex call)	"Tag"
ST	Set to reach possible Tex	Set to reach or Tex	Set to reach or Tex	Set to reach possible "tag" possible "tree"	Set to reach possible "tag" possible "tree"	"Tag"
SG C	Set to reach	Set to reach	Set to reach	Set to reach possible "tag" possible "tree"	Set to reach possible "tag" possible "tree"	"Tag"
	Set to reach look for "3" to spark	Set to reach look for "3" to spark	Set to reach look for "3" to spark	Set to reach	Set to reach avoid contact	Rip thru to backer
WG	Swipe	Swipe	Swipe	Set to reach avoid contact w/dt	Scoop nose	Swipe nose
WT	Levels	Levels	Levels	Swipe	Levels	Swipe dt
U	Levels cut off	Levels cut off	Levels cut off	Levels cut off	Levels cut off	Cut off bear defender
H						

FORMATIONS Doubles, Trey

MOTIONS

Diagram 13-4: 38/39 Stretch (continued).

20	40
EAGLE WEAK	30
DOUBLE EAGLE	

Diagram 13-5: 48/49 Toss (force)—a two-back play.

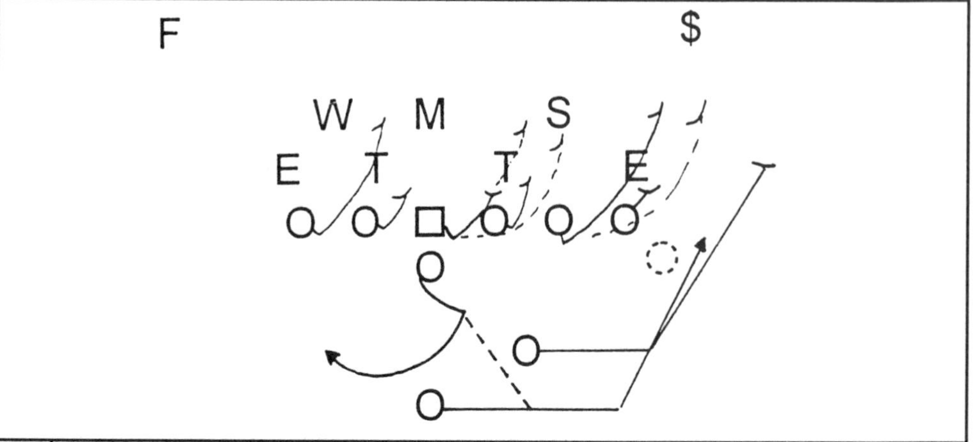

QB	Reverse pivot to 4:00 and pitch to TB; end-over-end pitch to the numbers; fake naked.
TB	Toss steps, read TE's block to force.
FB	Arc block to force.
R	Block force vs. 7-tech, combo through a 9-tech.

FRONTS	4-3	20	40	EW	30	DE
Y	Set to reach (Tex call)	Set to reach combo 7 tech to playside l'ber (Tex call)	Set to reach (Tex call)	Set to reach	Set to reach	"Tag"
ST	Set to reach possible Tex	Set to reach or Tex	Set to reach or Tex	Set to reach possible "tag" possible "tree"	Set to reach possible "tag" possible "tree"	"Tag"
SG	Set to reach	Set to reach	Set to reach	Set to reach possible "tag" possible "tree"	Set to reach possible "tag" possible "tree"	"Tag"
C	Set to reach look for "3" to spark	Set to reach look for "3" to spark	Set to reach look for "3" to spark	Set to reach	Set to reach avoid contact	Rip thru to backer
WG	Swipe	Swipe	Swipe	Set to reach avoid contact w/dt	Scoop nose	Swipe nose
WT	Levels	Levels	Levels	Swipe	Levels	Swipe dt
Z						

FORMATIONS Pro, Twins, Up

MOTIONS Rap/Route, Zip

Diagram 13-5: 48/49 Toss (continued).

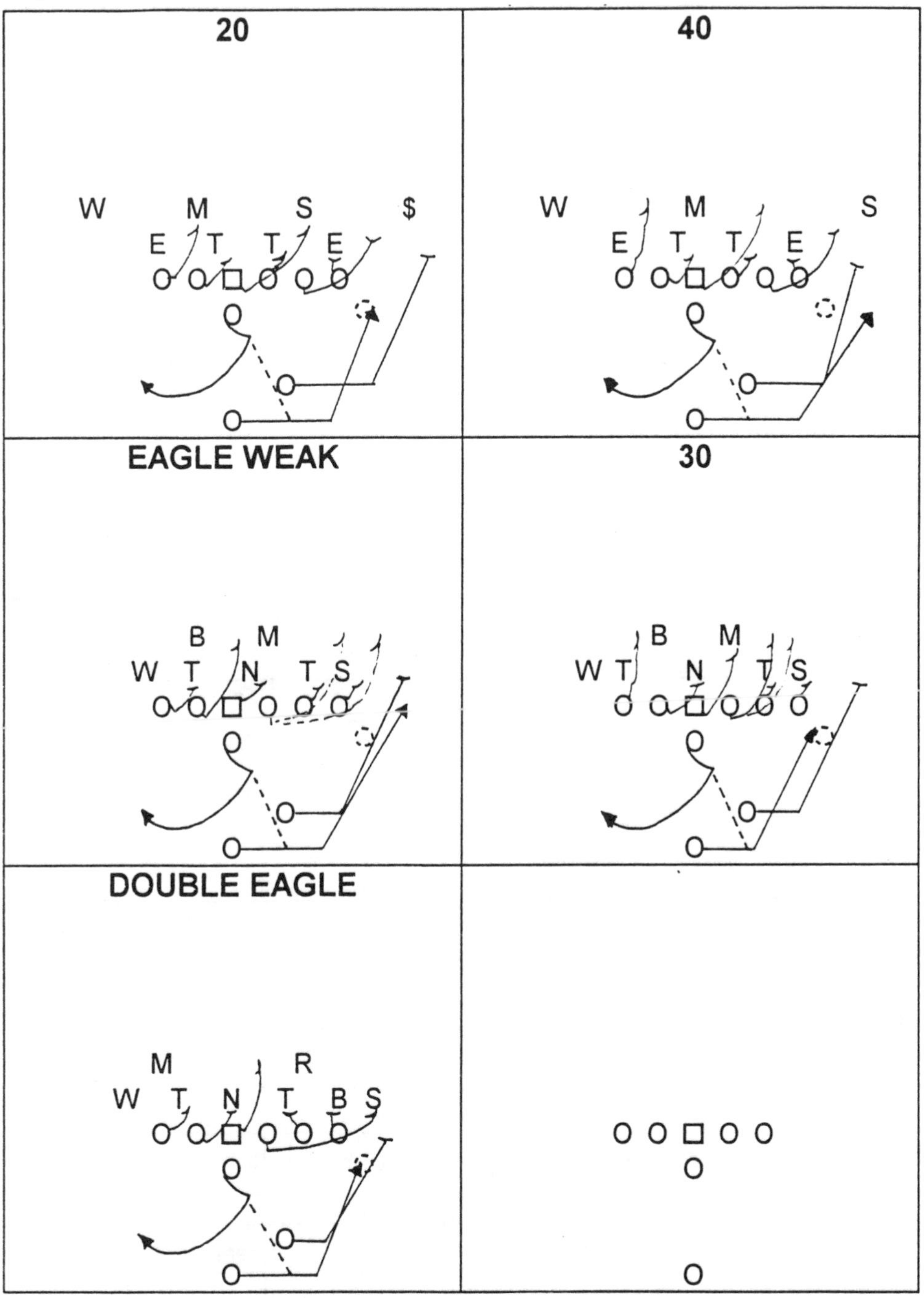

20

W M S $
E T T E

40

W M S
E T T E

EAGLE WEAK

B M
W T N T S

30

B M
W T N T S

DOUBLE EAGLE

M R
W T N T B S

Diagram 13-6: 34/35 Slant (to a 1 technique)—a one-back play.

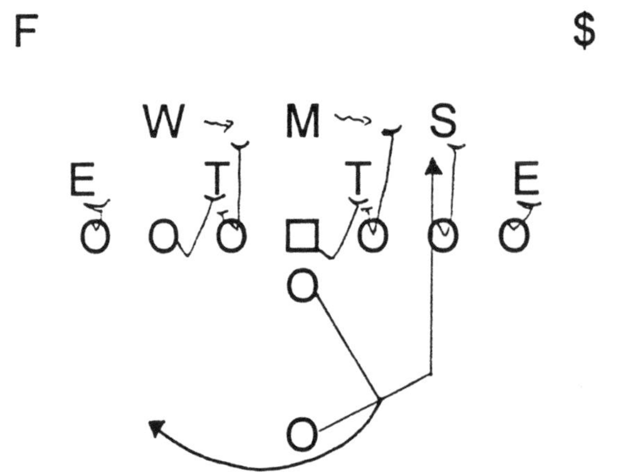

QB	Open to 4:30 gaining depth; give the ball to the TB w/depth; get out of his way; fake naked.
TB	Lead-crossover-plant; press inside hip of the tackle; read the 1st covered lineman.

FRONTS	4-3	20	40	EW	30	DE
Y	Set to drive	Fan	Fan	Set to drive	Set to drive	Tag
ST	Set to drive	Set to drive	Set to drive	Set to drive	Set to drive	Tag
SG	Set to drive flipper and hang to backer	Set to drive flipper and hang to backer	Set to drive flipper and hang to backer	Set to drive	Set to drive	Tag
C	Set to drive stop penetration	Set to drive stop penetration	Set to drive stop penetration	Set to drive	Set to drive	Scoop w/wg
WG	Set to drive flipper and hang to backer	Set to drive flipper and hang to backer	Set to drive flipper and hang to backer	Set to drive flipper and hang to backer	Set to drive	Scoop w/ center
WT	Set to drive	Set to drive	Set to drive	Set to drive	Set to drive	Swipe 3 tech
U	Set to drive	Set to drive	Set to drive	Set to drive	Set to drive	Cut off bear
H						

FORMATIONS Doubles, Ringo, Trey

MOTIONS

Diagram 13-6: 34/35 Slant (continued).

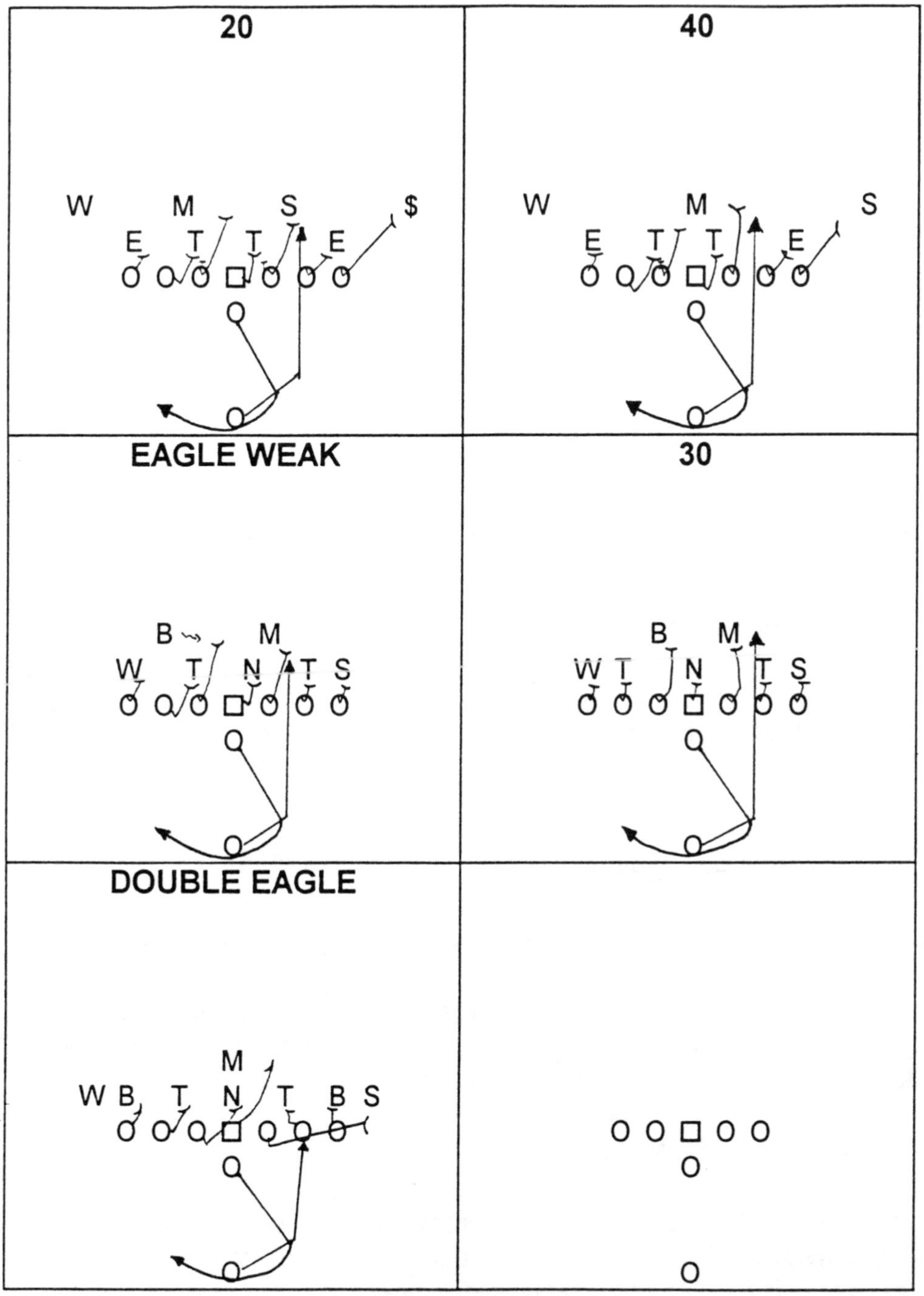

20

40

EAGLE WEAK

30

DOUBLE EAGLE

gap. The center has a back block versus an even front. The backside guard pulls to the point of attack, while backside tackle either pulls on some plays, such as a counter trey (see Diagram 13-2 for an overview of the assignment on a counter trey play) or uses a hinge technique on power plays (see Diagram 13-3 for an illustration of a game-tested power play).

MAN-BLOCKING SCHEMES

Man-on-man blocking is the base blocking scheme employed in offensive football. Man-on-man blocking is normally used in every offensive attack at every competitive level of the game. While man blocking is a sound scheme against balanced defensive fronts, it is easily outnumbered at the point of attack against over-shifted and shade-stack defensive alignments.

VEER-BLOCKING SCHEMES

The veer-blocking scheme was originally developed for the triple-option, Houston veer offense. As such, veer blocking is one of the fundamental backbone elements of the triple option concept. Veer blocking is based on isolating a specific defensive lineman as the "read" for the quarterback. On a play that utilizes veer blocking, the quarterback reads the reaction of the designated lineman and then makes a decision whether to give the ball and proceed to his third option (i.e., pitching the ball to a dive back or pull the ball and proceed to his third option (i.e., pitching the ball to the trail back). The veer-blocking scheme is used in veer-type offensive attacks (e.g., the flexbone, the wishbone, etc.)

OUTSIDE ZONE-BLOCKING SCHEMES

On outside zone-blocking schemes, the offensive linemen attempt to gain horizontal leverage on the defenders. On plays involving outside zone blocking, the offensive linemen set to reach. Everyone on the offensive line is responsible for his playside gap. Outside zone-blocking schemes are utilized in stretch plays (see Diagram 13-4), toss plays (see Diagram 13-5) and some option plays.

INSIDE ZONE-BLOCKING SCHEMES

On inside zone-blocking schemes, the offensive linemen work horizontally through their playside gap. On plays involving inside zone blocking, the offensive linemen set to drive. Inside zone blocking is designated to provide upfield push on the plays involving inside zone-blocking schemes. Among the plays that employ inside zone schemes are slant (see Diagram 13-6), roll, fullback cut, and any inside play that is drawing to get the linebackers to flow and is designed to give the running backs an opportunity to press the line of scrimmage and cut back.

CHAPTER 14

Adopting an Alignment Philosophy

Offensive coaches have a choice between two basic philosophies of formation strength alignment: the same-side philosophy of alignment and the flip-flopping philosophy alignment. Which choice the coach decides to adopt can be dependent upon one or more of the following factors:

- Coaching background. Coaches tend to coach in the system that is most familiar to them. As such, a preferred alignment philosophy tends to be rooted in the past experiences of the coach.

- Offensive philosophy. The offensive philosophy of the coach is a significant factor in considering the choice of which formation philosophy to adopt. For example, coaches who utilize the dropback passing attack usually favor the same-side philosophy.

- Personnel. One of the primary concerns of a coach is the degree of balance that exists in the talent level of his offensive line personnel. If his personnel is well-balanced along the line of scrimmage in talent and strength, the same-side philosophy is normally the favored alignment choice for that particular coach. The skills and competency levels of his running backs and their ability to deal with a flip-flopping system is also a consideration.

- Level of play. Each philosophy of the formation strength alignment has both good and bad features with regard to the complexity of assignments and the execution of the player's individual techniques. As a rule, the higher the level of play, the less need for flip-flopping of the formation strength.

- The base set. The base backfield set of the offensive attack lends itself to a particular formation alignment philosophy. For example, split-back alignments are more compatible with flip-flopping than single back and I-back alignments.

FLIP-FLOPPING VERSUS SINGLE-SIDE

In a flip-flop system, the twin positions flip sides according to a formation strength call. One side of the offensive line is designated the "strongside." When flip-flopping the line according to the strength of the offensive formation; the strongside guard, the strongside tackle, and the tight end will always align to the offensive strength. The remaining guard, tackle, and end are usually identified as the quick side, or the weakside, and will always align opposite the offensive strength. Other names for the quick side include the slot side and the split side.

The term flip-flop comes from the concept that a particular athlete who is playing guard will play on both sides of the center. If he is a strongside guard, he may align on the right side of the huddle as shown in Diagram 14-1. If the call is a Pro Right, the offensive strength will be to the right. When the offensive strength is to the right, the strongside guard (and his strongside teammates) align on the right side of the ball. If the call is a Pro Left, the offensive strength will be to the left. When the offensive strength is to the left, the strong guard (and his strongside teammates) align on the left side of the ball. Moving from one side of the ball to another based on the called offensive formation strength is called "flip-flopping."

When an offensive lineman plays exclusively on one side of the ball, the practice is said to be a same-side philosophy. The same-side philosophy is an easy concept to grasp. Each lineman simply plays on either the right or the left side of the ball on every snap, regardless of the formation called.

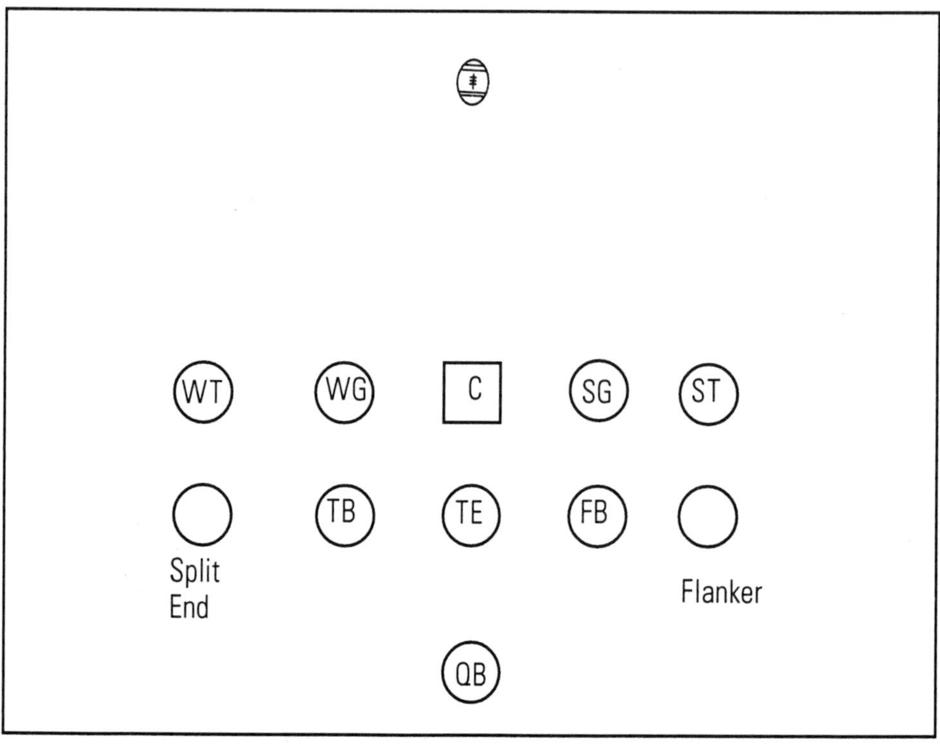

Diagram 14-1: A sample offensive huddle formation.

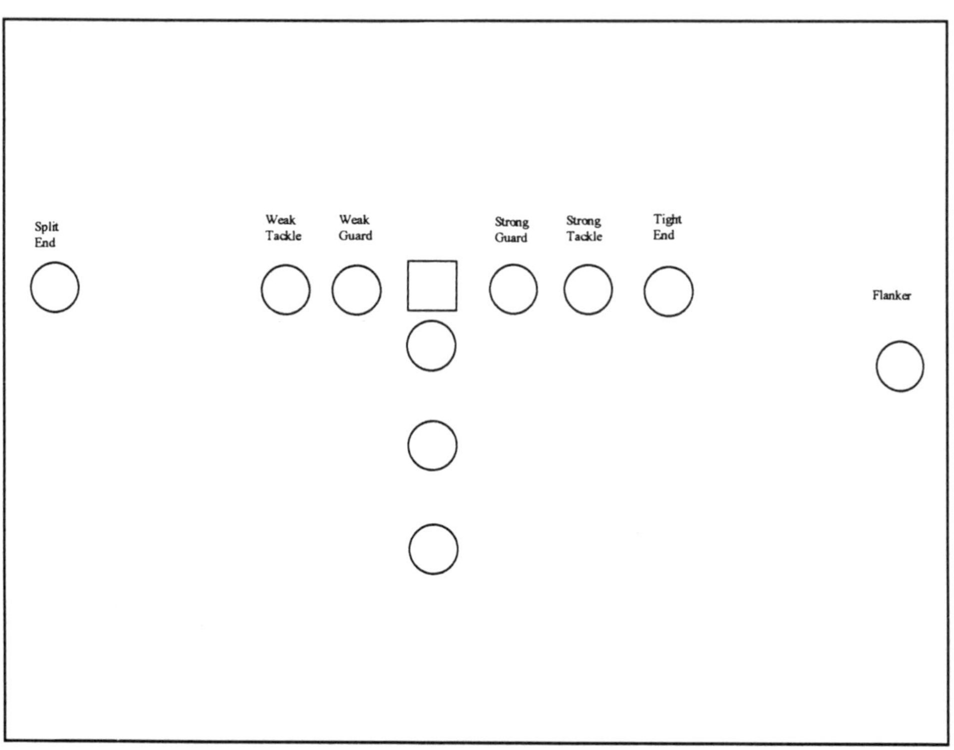

Diagram 14-2: A pro-right formation with a flip-flop system.

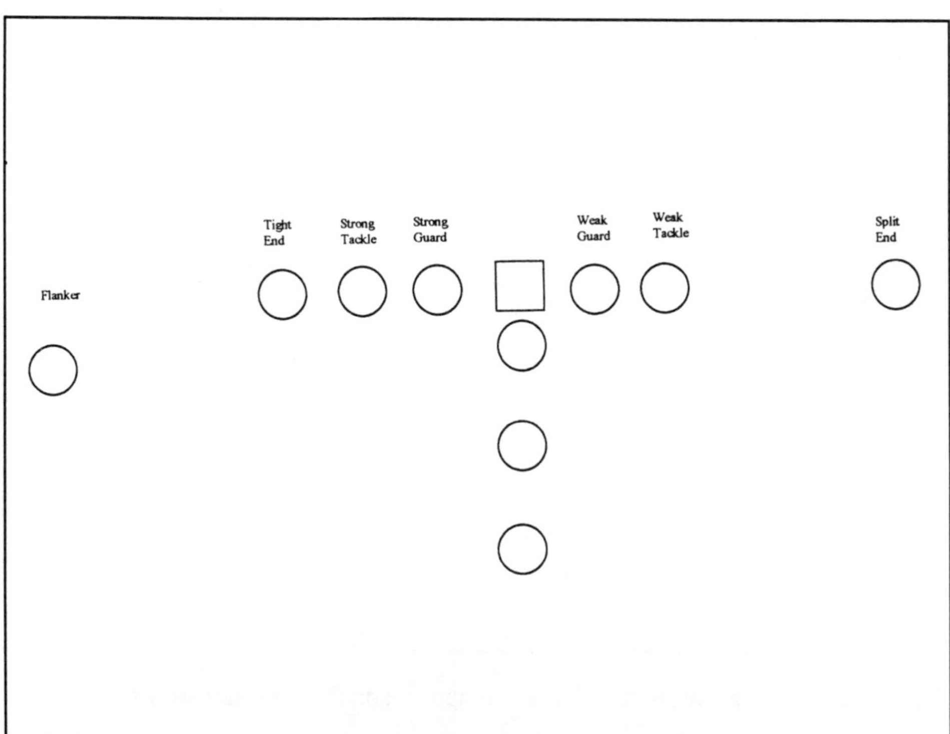

Diagram 14-3: A pro-left formation with a flip-flop system.

A somewhat confusing concept to those offensive line coaches who have been born and bred into the same-side philosophy, the flip-flop practice does have one major advantage over the same-side philosophy—it reduces the number of defense fronts a player sees in the course of the game. For example, if a defensive scheme utilizes an unbalanced front such as a 30 Eagle Strong, the defensive front has a definite strongside and a weakside structure. To the offensive lineman on the weakside of the offensive formation, the front has a characteristic appearance that is different from the appearance presented to the strongside offensive lineman. This scenario is shown in Diagram 14-4.

The flip-flop system guarantees that the offensive linemen will see the same "look" every time they face an over-shifted front such as the 30 Eagle Strong. Since the defense will always have a tailored "strongside" and "weakside," flip-flopping allows the strong guard and the strong tackle to work only against the strongside of the defense. Likewise, the weakside guard and the weakside tackle have to work only against the weakside of the defense. Despite the fact that defensive fronts declare the strength from one side of the ball to another on the basis of matching up to the strength of the offensive formation, the flip-flopping offensive line sees only one alignment structure.

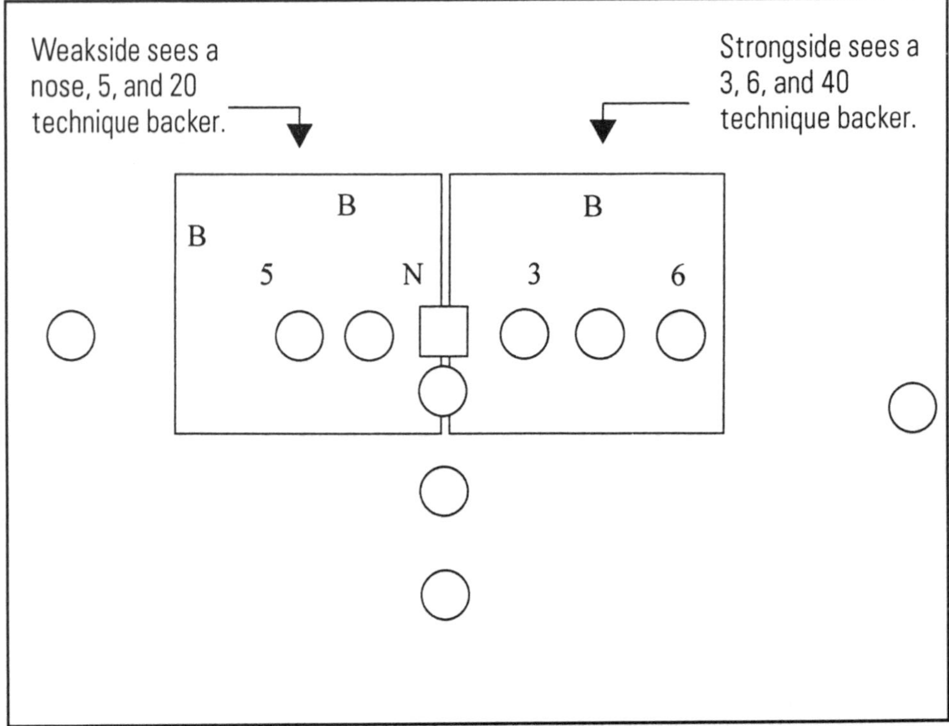

Diagram 14-4: The affect of a 30 Eagle Strong front on the structure of the formation.

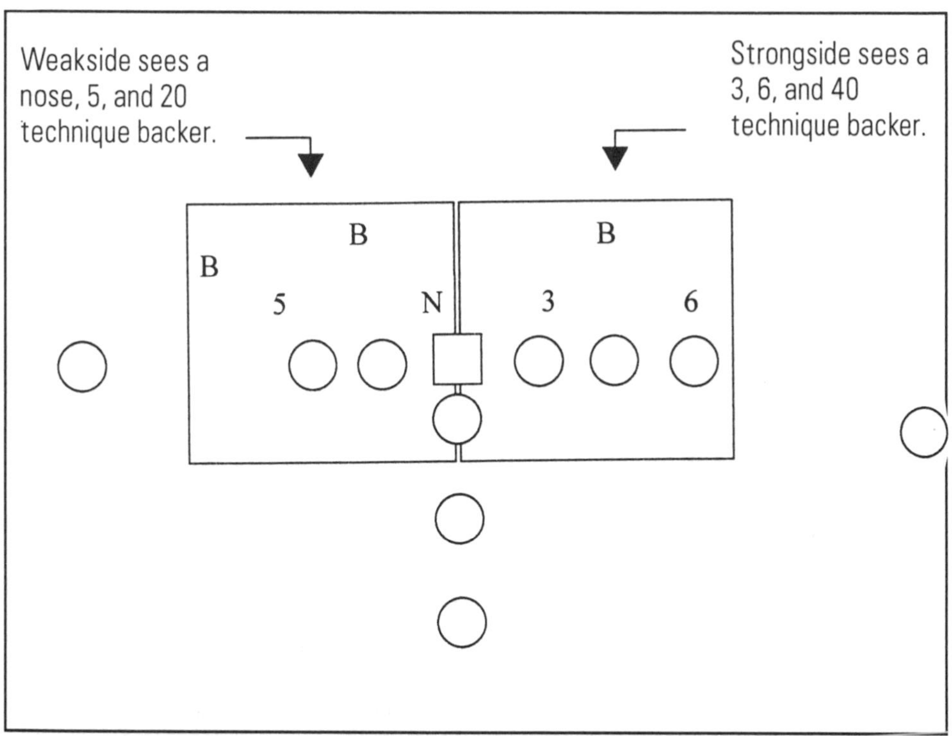

Diagram 14-5: 30 Eagle Strong declaration to the left versus pro right.

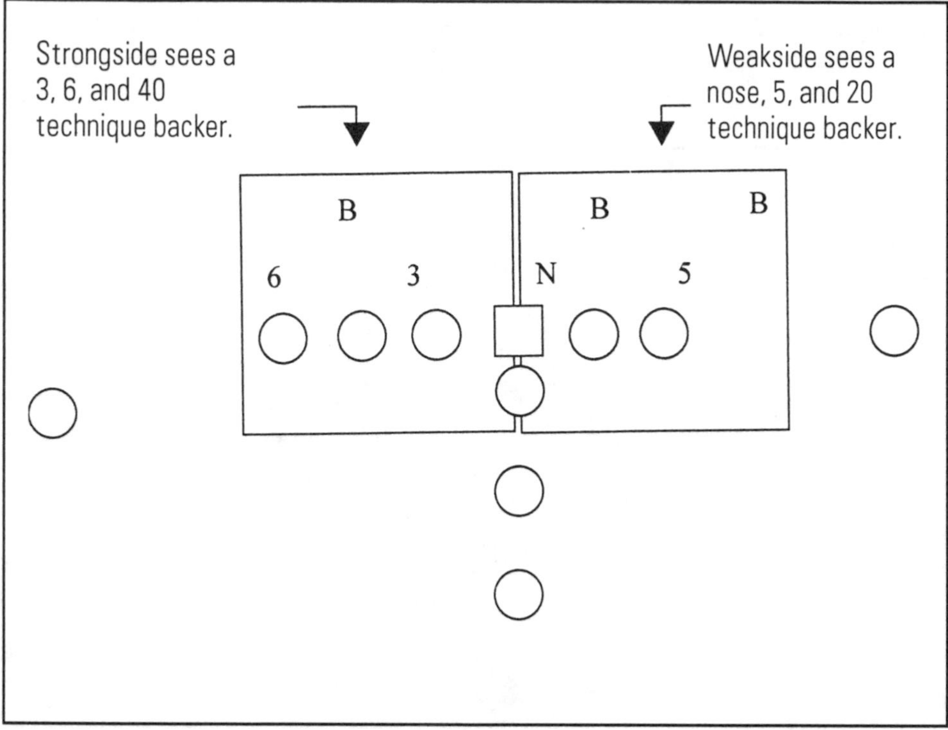

Diagram 14-6: 30 Eagle Strong declaration to the right versus pro left.

Given the dynamics of the same-side philosophy, it can be seen that a team is faced with added preparation against a defense that uses an over-shifted front. As pointed out previously, an over-shifted front will present a specific strongside look and a specific weakside look. The defense will also declare its strength to either the right and left side, depending on the offensive formation strength. In essence, the defensive structure flip-flops on every snap, even though the defensive personnel may not physically flip-flop. Since all defensive structures flip-flop on the snap, the same-side offensive system could force the offensive linemen to block two different looks on any given play. Having to block two different looks against one defense doubles the preparation time a team needs for a single offensive play. For example, when a team employs the same-side philosophy and is running an iso play versus an over-shifted defense, it is to practice running the same play against both the weakside look and the strongside look unless it plans on keeping its offensive strength consistent every time it runs the iso. Diagrams 14-7 and 14-8 illustrate this particular negative feature of the same-side philosophy (i.e., how practice time is doubled for only one play in the same-side system).

Flip-flopping the line also allows a team to be more creative in its approach to pass protection without adding an undue degree of complexity to the system that might otherwise confound the athlete. Pass blocking schemes can be designed that require the execution of two types of protection—one on the weakside and another on the strongside. If the offensive line is flip-flopping, they need only to learn the type of protection which corresponds to their side. If the offensive line is playing in the same-side scheme, they would have to recognize—according to the formation call—when they are supposed to use the weakside scheme and when they are

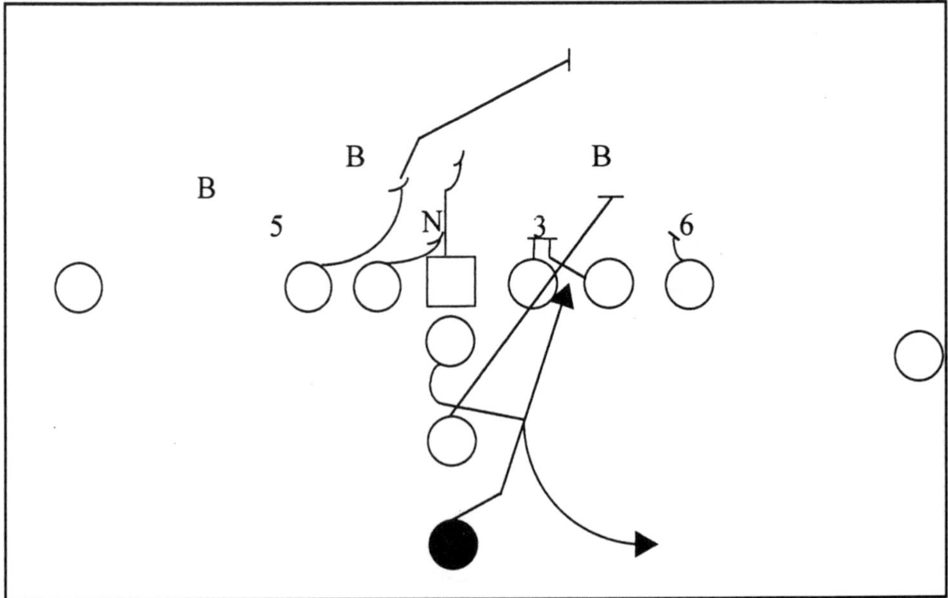

Diagram 14-7: A pro-right—iso play to the right—versus a 30 Eagle Strong front.

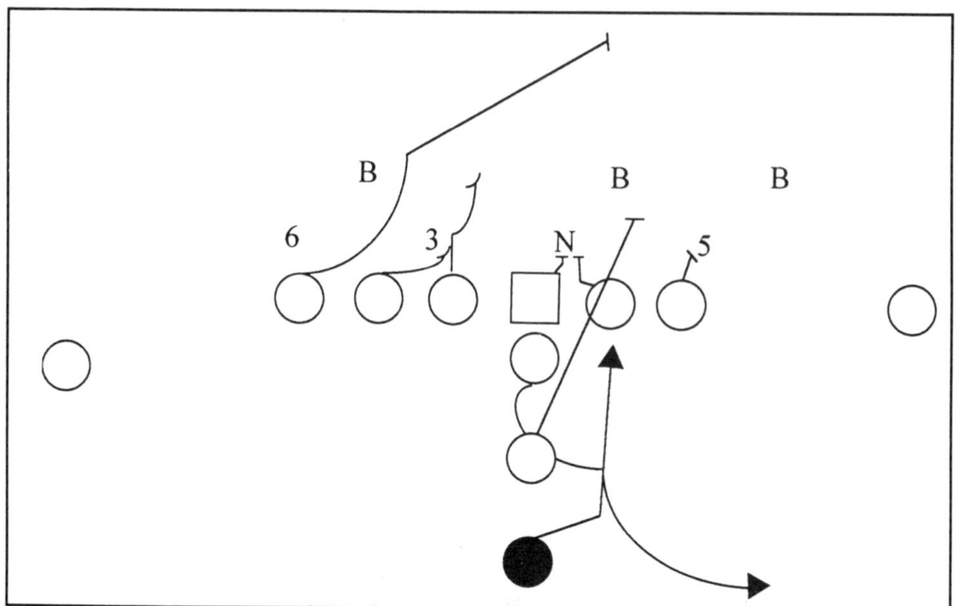

Diagram 14-8: A pro-left—iso play to the right—versus a 30 Eagle Strong front.

supposed to use the strongside scheme. Being able to tailor a team's protection scheme according to strong side and weak side protection rules provides a team with an opportunity to simplify its passing game structure, yet be more creative in the options it may select to attack specific defensive weaknesses.

Proponents of the same-side philosophy point out that the most important point in coaching the offensive line is the attention given to the repetition of technique. With the same-side scheme, the blocking assignments may change according to the defensive declaration, but the blocking technique will remain the same. For example, when a right tackle in the sameside blocking scheme blocks down, he will always execute the following actions: push off his right foot, angle step inside with his left foot, aim for the left hip or shoulder of the defender, use his right hand to punch and gain leverage under the defender's left armpit, and use his right shoulder to block the defender. A flip-flopping offensive tackle has to be able to master those techniques with either foot, either hand and either shoulder. The technique teaching time for one type of block is consequently doubled for the flip-flopping lineman.

Sameside alignment practitioners also point out that the communication required to teach and learn sameside blocking techniques is simpler than the communication involved in the flip-flop system. Instead of a right offensive tackle having to distinguish when he should step "inside" or drive "outside," he can learn his techniques as "right" or "left" techniques—a more natural and familiar mental processing.

Despite the scheme friendliness of the blocking rules and the front recognition cues of the flip-flop system, the sameside scheme is normally the preferred system in the college and professional levels. Since the main advantage of the flip-flop system pertains to the offensive lineman applying his assignment rules, the flip-flop system tends to lose its appeal at a level of play above the high school level. As a rule, college athletes (while student-athletes) don't have to spend the entire day each day pursuing a regimented academic curriculum. Because of the larger blocks of time available for instruction for these higher level athletes and primarily because of the experience and relatively higher levels of intelligence of these individuals, the benefits of the sameside structural philosophy for these players tend to far outweigh those of the flip-flop alignment format.

In the professional football ranks, a great amount of emphasis is placed on the backside tackle position. The predominance of the dropback passing attack, the multiple reads of the quarterback, and the irreplaceable quality of an NFL starting quarterback collectively require that the quarterback be protected from blindside hits. Consequently, the most valuable player on most offensive lines in the NFL is usually the left tackle.

When you think about it, only a small group of linemen exist who can protect against the talents of the numerous Pro Bowl candidates playing defensive end. With roster restrictions and salary caps, an NFL team is lucky to find the one lineman who can guarantee the safety of the quarterback's blind side. When the professional team does get the guy who can do the job, they don't want him flipping away from his primary role as a blindside protector—just because the formation strength has changed. This reason alone is reason enough to support the sameside concept of offensive line alignment. Several factors can be advanced to support either philosophy of formation structure. Chart 14-1 provides an overview of such factors.

THE BOTTOM LINE

Regardless of the formation structure adopted, an offensive lineman is ready to play when he has developed an understanding of the five bottom line techniques. Readiness to play can be viewed as a rite of passage for an offensive lineman. All factors considered, once he has demonstrated his abilities in each of the five bottom-line categories, an offensive lineman completes his apprenticeship as a developing candidate within the offensive line. The five basic bottom-line techniques include:

- Playing with intensity and enthusiasm on every down.
- Mastery-level knowledge of his assignments.

- Controlling his body and maintaining his balance in the execution of his assignments.
- Demonstrating an ability to control and dominate the line of scrimmage.
- Finishing the block on every snap from scrimmage.

Chart 14-1: Flip-flop and sameside formation structures.

FLIP-FLOP	SAMESIDE
Defensive looks are limited.	Defensive looks are compounded.
Techniques are compounded.	Techniques are simplified.
Hole numbering flip-flops with the line.*	Hole numbering remains constant.
Blocking schemes are simplified.	Blocking schemes can be complex.
The system can be confusing for running backs.	The system is much simpler for running backs.
*Some teams keep their hole numbers the same, whether the team is in a right or left formation. As a result, the odd numbers are always "left," while the even numbers are always "right." When flip-flopping, the weakside tackle (i.e., open-end tackle) is always the same. A team can put its best pass blocker at weak tackle to face the defenses' best pass rushing end. Figuratively, the weak tackle is in "space" by himself without the help of the tight end, unlike the strong tackle.	

AUTHORS

Dave Christensen is the offensive coordinator and the offensive line coach at the University of Toledo. Since joining the Rockets staff in 1992, Christensen has molded the offensive line into a solid unit that has powered a run through UT's offensive record books. The Rockets set 23 new school records in 1997, and in the last 4 years, the UT line has been an integral part in breaking or tying UT records. During Christensen's tenure at Toledo, Christensen's linemen have won all-conference honors eight times. Six of his former players are current NFL players.

Christensen came to Toledo from Idaho State University where he coached the offensive line, tight ends, and running backs for two years. Prior to his stint at ISU, he served two years as an assistant coach under Don James at the University of Washington, where he played football from 1980-'82. Christensen's coaching resume also includes stops at Spokane Falls C.C. (1988), Eastern Washington (1986-'87), Western Washington (1983), and the interscholastic level (1984-'85). He and his wife, Susie, reside in Sylvania, Ohio with their three children—Katie, D.J., and Emily.

James A. Peterson, Ph.D., FACSM is a freelance author who writes books on a variety of coaching and sports medicine-related topics. A graduate of the University of California at Berkeley (B.S.) and the University of Illinois (M.S. and Ph.D.), he served on the faculty of the United States Military Academy at West Point from 1971-'80 and 1984-'90. From 1990-'95, he was the Director of Sports Medicine for StairMaster Sports/Medical Products, Inc in Kirkland, Washington. He has authored or co-authored 53 books and more than 200 published articles. Among the football books he has helped write are *Bill Walsh: Finding the Winning Edge* with Bill Walsh and Brian Billick and *Coaching Defensive Linemen* with John Levra. He and his wife, Susan, reside in Monterey, California.